Unsettled Solidarities

In the series
Critical Race, Indigeneity, and Relationality, edited by
Antonio T. Tiongson Jr., Danika Medak-Saltzman, and Iyko Day

Unsettled Solidarities

*Asian and Indigenous Cross-Representations
in the Américas*

QUYNH NHU LE

TEMPLE UNIVERSITY PRESS
Philadelphia • Rome • Tokyo

TEMPLE UNIVERSITY PRESS
Philadelphia, Pennsylvania 19122
tupress.temple.edu

Copyright © 2019 by Temple University—Of The Commonwealth System of Higher Education
All rights reserved
Published 2019

Library of Congress Cataloging-in-Publication Data

Names: Le, Quynh Nhu, 1980– author.
Title: Unsettled solidarities : Asian and indigenous cross-representations in the Américas / Quynh Nhu Le.
Description: Philadelphia : Temple University Press, 2019. | Series: Critical race, indigeneity, and relationality | Revision of author's thesis (doctoral)—University of California, Santa Barbara, 2013, titled Unsettling solidarities : Asian North American and indigenous literary contacts, post-1968. | Includes bibliographical references and index. |
Identifiers: LCCN 2018046414 (print) | LCCN 2019011024 (ebook) | ISBN 9781439916285 (E-book) | ISBN 9781439916261 (cloth) | ISBN 9781439916278 (paperback)
Subjects: LCSH: Race in literature. | Asians in literature. | Indigenous peoples in literature.
Classification: LCC PN56.R16 (ebook) | LCC PN56.R16 L4 2019 (print) | DDC 809/.933552—dc23
LC record available at https://lccn.loc.gov/2018046414

For Peach

Contents

Note on Terminology		ix
Acknowledgments		xi
	Introduction: Settler Racial Hegemonies: The Tense Crossings of Settlement, Empire, and Race	1
1	Historiographical Tensions: U.S. Asian American and Indigenous Crossings from Manifest Destiny to the Pacific Theater	25
2	Legal/Juridical Tensions: The Affective Temporalities of Canadian Redress and Reconciliation	59
3	Economic Tensions: Global Capital and *Mestizaje/Mestiçagem* Discourse in Latin América	95
4	Biopolitical Tensions: The Work of Shame and Anxiety in Native-Asian Mixed-Blood Narratives	127
	Coda	157
	Notes	167
	Bibliography	211
	Index	225

Note on Terminology

Given the cross-racial, critical Indigenous, and transnational scope, this book is fraught with terminology issues. Readers will note my use of the term "Américas" to identify the entirety of the American hemisphere. I include the accent mark to destabilize the linking of "America" with U.S.-centric logics and histories. Indeed, while the term "America/n" is often conflated with the United States, in the Latin American context it has long been a designation for all persons inhabiting the Américas. At the same time, I want to highlight (as scholars such as M. Bianet Castellanos, Lourdes Gutiérrez Nájera, and Arturo J. Aldama explain in relation to their own use of the term "Américas") that the use of the accent mark to identify the Américas, while strategic in its decentering move, continues to rely on settler colonial linguistics that problematically erase Indigenous peoples' designations of the geographic space and place that this project spans.[1]

Scholars have proffered terms such as "settler," "arrivant," and "alien" to delineate the variations of Asian immigrant/generational relationships to settler colonialism. Such terms may be more appropriate than "Asian American," which often centers U.S. settler national formation and minimizes different racial formations across the Américas. "Asian American" can also function as a kind of celebration of national assimilation, or resistant subjectivity, which can continue to elide the community's responsibility to ongoing Indigenous struggles for sovereignty and self-determination. In this book, I use the terms "hemispheric Asian American" and "Asian alien" to refer to the broader context of Asian racialized identities across the Américas. Instead of working to transport the histories of Asian American formations in the United States onto the diverse histories across other geographies in the Américas, my usage of "hemispheric Asian American" seeks to unmoor the term "American" from its position as designating solely people in the United States. When I refer to Asian racialized identities in specific settler national contexts, I employ terms such as "U.S. Asian American/U.S. Chinese American" (United States), "Asian Canadian/Japanese Canadian" (Canada), and "Asian Brazilian/Japanese Brazilian" (Brazil). These terms identify Asian immigrant and generational identities within their respective colonial borders. This usage, though problematic, is intended not as an affirmation or reification of settler national identity but to register the locational complicity and responsibility in settler processes.

Various terms have been applied to Indigenous peoples and their relationships to various settler states. In this book, I use specific names of tribes and Native nations when possible and applicable. I also use terms such as "hemispheric Indigenous," "Indigenous," "Native," and "Indian" interchangeably when referencing Indigenous relationships to broader settler national and global configurations. I apply specific terms to Native communities in specific settler national contexts. For example, I use the terms "Aboriginal" and "First Nations" in the Canadian context, and I use the terms "Native American" and "American Indian" in the U.S. context.

Acknowledgments

I am grateful for the guidance and care of many, without whom this book would not have been completed. First, I thank my parents: Gi Phong Le and Tinh Nguyen. Their struggles and triumphs throughout the years have inspired me to persevere. Their humor, care, and grounded perspectives provide me with a consistent anchor. Con cám ơn bố mẹ.

While the seeds for this book began earlier, at the University of Colorado, the form that it has taken on began at the University of California, Santa Barbara (UCSB). I thank my dissertation committee members for their support, mentorship, and guidance throughout the conception and completion of this book. Shirley Geok-lin Lim is an awe-inspiring example of energy, expertise, and dedication. I greatly appreciate the time she spent supporting me through each stage. Her writings have inspired the content of this project and have motivated me to become a resilient scholar, teacher, and writer. James Kyung-jin Lee asked important and difficult questions that helped me to articulate the urgency of the project. Carl Gutiérrez Jones provided crucial feedback and kind encouragement, from the formulation of the prospectus to the project's current manifestation. erin Khuê Ninh read through multiple drafts of chapters and writing samples and always provided the most incisive feedback.

Friends and colleagues at UCSB have consistently nourished me with food, conversation, and company. Mary Garcia has been a close friend and constant conversation partner for many years. Her patience and kindness have been crucial at key points in the writing process. Maricar Apuya, Sandibel Borges, Niccole Coggins, Gary Colmenor, Anne Cong-Huyen, Rosie

Kar, Joomi Kim, Karen Hanna, Douglas Hong, Cristina Serna, Kristie Soares, Tara Villalba, and Yan Zheng offered support and friendship throughout graduate school. Marysol Duran, Carlos Martinez, and Laila have been the best neighbors. Mimi Khuc offered much-needed support, urgency, and clarity to the project in its earliest conceptual stages. Her work continues to inspire me to think beyond the boundaries of academia.

The generosity that I have received since arriving at the University of South Florida (USF) has been vital. Ying Zhu has been a model writing partner. Her knowledge and boundless energy have spurred my work and work habits in crucial ways. Yao Chen, Mei-Hsuan Chiang, Jane Le Skaife, and Camilla Vasquez have provided steady friendship and guidance since my arrival at USF. I thank the USF Department of English faculty, staff, and students. Rita Ciresi, Nicole Discenza, Gurleen Grewal, Hunt Hawkins, Meredith Johnson, Nate Johnson, Ylce Irizarry, Gary Lemons, John Lennon, Susan Mooney, Laura Runge, Heather Sellers, Nancy Serrano, and Deedra Wollert, among many others, have all kindly shared their good energies, stories, and advice over coffee, tea, and meals. Gary Lemons and Cheryl Rodriguez generously invited me to write an essay for their collection. I am indebted especially to Gurleen Grewal and Ylce Irizarry. Their generosity of spirit, consistent support, and brilliant work have been invaluable. Crucial parts of this book were funded by the USF New Researcher Grant, USF Humanities Institute Summer Grant, USF Arts and Sciences Internal Award, USF Publication Council Award, and McKnight Junior Faculty Development Fellowship. I am grateful for the support.

Colleagues and mentors in the field have inspired my work in different but meaningful ways. Special thanks go to Keith Camacho, Santhosh Chandrashekar, Evyn Le Espiritu, Laura Fugikawa, Douglas Ishii, Beenash Jafri, Anne Jansen, Maria John, Long Le-Khac, Janey Lew, Marie Lo, Kit Meyers, Shaista Patel, Juliana Hu Pegues, Malissa Phung, Dean Saranillio, Stephen Sohn, Nishant Upadhyay, and Ma Vang. The Association for Asian American Studies Junior Faculty Retreat, Cornell University, and the University of Minnesota provided me with the opportunity to present early and later stages of the project. Many thanks go to those who provided commentary on the work in progress, including Derek Chang, Lisa Kahaleole Hall, Karen Ho, Viranjini P. Munasinghe, Crystal Parikh, Carol Edelman Warrior, Shelley Wong, and Xine Yao.

My editor, Sara Jo Cohen, provided good energy, prompt communication, and astute feedback through each stage of the revision process. I am grateful for her initial interest and sustained support of the project. The two anonymous readers for Temple University Press provided careful and critical feedback on the project. For this I am immensely grateful. Many thanks go to the *Critical Race, Indigeneity, and Relationality* series editors at Temple University Press: Antonio Tiongson Jr., Danika Medak-Saltzman, and Iyko Day. Tony and Danika provided much welcome advice on key elements of the publication process. My deepest gratitude goes to Iyko. She generously devoted her time and energy to provide a meticulous reading of the manuscript and key conceptual ideas. The book is stronger because of her efforts. A select portion of Chapter 2 appeared in Quynh Nhu Le, "States of Arrest: The Affective Temporalities Structuring Canada's Public Apologies," *Amerasia Journal* 42.1 (2016): 41–64. I thank Myla Vicenti Carpio and Karen Leong for the opportunity to be a part of their special issue, and *Amerasia Journal* for permission to republish. I also thank Kaili Chun and Hongtao Zhou, who generously agreed to include their beautiful work as the cover art for the book. I extend a thank-you to Simon Ortiz and the University of Arizona Press for providing permission to include a poem from *from Sand Creek* by Simon J. Ortiz. © 2000. The Arizona Board of Regents. Reprinted by permission of the University of Arizona Press.

I am fortunate for the support of my extended family: my grandparents, uncles, aunts, and cousins. The Campos and Kelly family welcomed me so affectionately into their lives. Nanny, Deb, and Bob have shared many warm dinners, conversations, card games, and hikes. Juan and Iris have provided kindness, good humor, and delicious recipes.

Chrissy Lau and Lily Wong have been dear friends and sisters in academia and life. I thank them for their patience and their responses to my calls and texts for help, no matter how minute. Their dedication to research, teaching, and justice have given me inspiration during the most trying moments of the revision process. They both motivate me to be a better scholar, professor, person.

My siblings continuously offer their love, support, and good humor. Bao, Vy Vy, Quynh Anh, and Nguyen have always been there when I needed them. I always look forward to our many long-distance phone calls, texts, and updates. Much love goes to Emily, Chris, Kevin, Jackie, Isla, Ivy, Claire, Lana, Charlotte, Norah, and Olivia. I am fortunate to be a part of such a loving, fun, funny, and fast-growing family.

And, finally, I am grateful to Juan (Peach) Campos. This book was deeply inspired by you and your commitment to communication, compassion, honesty, and justice. This book was also sustained by you. You have been there—each day—to encourage me, to challenge me, to motivate me. Thank you for the immeasurable richness that you have brought to my life. I look forward to our next chapter.

Unsettled Solidarities

Introduction

Settler Racial Hegemonies

THE TENSE CROSSINGS OF SETTLEMENT,
EMPIRE, AND RACE

In 1969
XXXX Coloradoans were killed in Vietnam

In 1978
XXXX Coloradoans were killed on the highways

In 1864
There were no Indians killed.

Remember My Lai[1]

In his 1981 poetry collection, *from Sand Creek,* Acoma Pueblo poet Simon Ortiz draws connections between the Sand Creek massacre of Cheyenne and Arapahoe people in their traditional homelands within the colonial borders of Colorado (1864) and the massacre of Vietnamese people over a hundred years later in My Lai, Vietnam (1968). Through this poetic alignment, Ortiz connects the brutal manifestations of U.S. settlement in the Américas to its imperial actions across the Pacific in Asia. In the chapter-opening quotation, the speaker highlights the elisions of these histories in popular memory, where the deaths of Vietnamese, Cheyenne, and Arapahoe peoples—most of whom were women and children—were erased by emphasis on U.S. deaths during the Vietnam War or, in the case of the 1864 Sand Creek massacre, wholly masked by lies. By emphasizing these erasures, the poem suggests that the production of settler and imperial violence hinges on a settler knowledge production that not only obscures these separate histories but also completely effaces their linkages.

In response to this doubled erasure, the speaker issues a seemingly simple imperative: "Remember My Lai." Given the thematic movement of the poem, the reference to My Lai suggests two meanings: (1) Ortiz's imperative suggests that to remember "My Lai" is also to remember "My Lie"—in other words, the lie that covers over the genocidal actions of the United States toward Indigenous peoples and on Indigenous lands. To fully acknowledge the event that is My Lai, the poem suggests, one must also work to comprehend the violence of Sand Creek and its cover-up. In this imperative call, Ortiz indicates the critical relationship among settler colonialism, imperialism, and the necessity to compare their racialized states of killing and forgetting. (2) Given that My Lai stands in for and effaces the conjuring of "My Lie," however, the poem conveys the dangers of comparison as an act of conflation. In this poetic doubling, where the remembrance of My Lai can also enact its own lie, the poet suggests that the memory of this historical event can, paradoxically, reproduce the erasures of violent U.S. settlements in the Américas through its attention to U.S. imperial encroachment in Asia. In addition, despite the 1980 Refugee Act, which allowed for the entry of 4,091 Southeast Asian refugees into Colorado, My Lai's overdetermination in the American imaginary about Vietnam can also overwrite the racialized experiences of Vietnamese refugees in the United States and their complicated incorporation into the ongoing violence of settlement.[2]

I begin with this discussion of Simon Ortiz's poem for two reasons. First, the poem speaks to my own position as a Vietnamese refugee who spent a number of my high school and college years in Denver and Boulder, Colorado, on traditional Cheyenne and Arapahoe lands.[3] In his poetry, Ortiz traces the violence of U.S. settler colonial and imperial technologies, as well as their racialized aftermaths, which led to my family's and my own displacement from Vietnam and our movements in settler colonial and Indigenous borders. Second, because of these contexts, the poem distills the potential of my own complex participation in these forms of remembering and forgetting through acts of comparison between racialized non-Indigenous and Indigenous communities. Such comparisons, in which I participate, can lead to the extension of settler imposition. That is, in the poem, Ortiz not only reveals how the disavowals of settler colonial and imperial violence determine which lives are considered deserving of remembrance; he also grapples with how efforts to resist these disavowals perpetuate the erasures of the intertwined yet separate productions of settler colonialism, imperialism, and racialization. This fraught relationship, between the political mobilization of racialized non-Indigenous and Indigenous communities, typifies a central conflict that undergirds settler colonialism and empire building in the histories of the Américas. It is this comparative constitution of settler colonialism in the Américas that this book seeks to illuminate.

In *Unsettled Solidarities,* I examine hemispheric Asian American and Indigenous encounters as they are represented in the contemporary literatures of these two communities. I trace the tensions arising out of these literary crossings as they emerge in different geopolitical sites, including the United States, Canada, Mexico, and Brazil.[4] I argue that these cross-community entanglements offer a condensed theoretical lens through which to trace the liberal logics and instabilities of settler colonialism in the Américas, and the complicated incorporation of Asian and Indigenous communities therein. As Lisa Lowe discusses, liberalism operates through the "economy of affirmation and forgetting," which privileges the liberal subject's movement toward abstractions of freedom while disavowing its reliance on global divisions produced out of colonialism, slavery, and racialized labor. For Lowe, while liberal narratives of freedom promise the emancipation of the human subject, they "innovate new means and forms of subjection, administration, and governance," which are in continual operation today.[5] Within these histories, Asian and Indigenous peoples have been asymmetrically (that is, differently) impacted by settler and imperial actions, such as land seizures, elimination, displacements, exclusions, and enclosures that seek to consolidate territories for the settler colonial state and the (white) liberal subject. In addition, the settler state has relied, unevenly, on Asian and Indigenous labor in the process of settler and imperial consolidation and violence—for example, in the case of Chinese immigrant men building the transcontinental railroad through Indigenous territories, or Native military service in the Pacific theater of war. While continually bound to the violent consolidation of the racialized settler state, these two communities have both been central—yet differently positioned—targets of liberal assimilation and inclusion projects, which have gained increasing fuel since the mid-twentieth century. From commemorations of national service that emphasize the triumph of the individual, to performances of civil progress through public apologies and reconciliation efforts for state crimes, to invocations of a future liberal multicultural paradise, the United States, Canada, Mexico, and Brazil have engaged political and cultural forces that work to neutralize impressions of the violent settler state.

The literary texts that I examine (all of which have emerged from the civil rights, cultural nationalist, and decolonization movements of the mid-twentieth century) engage the varying formations of antiracist and anticolonial political mobilization, conveying both the possibilities and the limits of these efforts as they are structured by or become incorporated within settler liberal narratives of freedom and progress. In particular, these texts' imaginations of Asian-Indigenous relationalities provide a window into how race-based and anticolonial social justice movements impact one another as they are unevenly incorporated within these liberal formations of settlement. This book centers these sites of convergence not only to trace the liberal logics from which different social justice movements interrelate but also to examine how these narratives work through these tensions to imagine different forms of connections and ethical relationships that are attentive to the asymmetries of violence and liberal beneficence produced by settler colonialism.

Throughout this book, I maintain that imaginations of Asian-Indigenous crossings illuminate and grapple with what I call "settler racial hegemonies." The term "settler racial hegemonies" names the uneven incorporation of Indigenous and non-Native racialized communities' social, cultural, and political articulations into the imperatives of the settler state, thus reinscribing the territorial claims and telos of the settler nation. The term "hegemony," famously popularized by Antonio Gramsci, has been used broadly to define state strategies to acquire the consent of the people.[6] In the Américas—especially given the asymmetrical process through which communities of difference have been made to encounter the settler, imperial, and racial logics of national formations—the protraction of settler power relies on the ways Asian and Indigenous formations of resistance are incorporated into the liberal values undergirding settler colonialism in the Américas.[7] While popular conceptions of hegemony often register consent as active or even passive participation, I am interested in the ways that consent within the context of settler colonialism can often manifest in the formation of liberatory *dissent*. That is, how consent to the settler state can be enacted through actions that are seen as a refusal of or counteraction against settler and racial power. This break down of the normative binary lens of "consent/dissent" is possible given the asymmetries of race and settlement that structure settler colonial states, where the liberatory demands (or resistance) of one racialized/colonized community can hinge on the very logics that dominate the other. The scenes of Asian and Indigenous relationships in the narratives that I examine—which range from elusive and spectral moments of encounters to more extended characterizations—all have in common their confrontation of settler racial hegemonies as a central crisis for social justice organizing and solidarity movements.[8]

This crisis in social justice organizing is especially relevant in our current moment, given the increasing attention to the incommensurabilities between race-based movements on the one hand and Indigenous struggles for sovereignty and self-determination on the other. Recent work in critical ethnic and

Indigenous studies, for example, has highlighted the tendencies to conflate discourses of settlement into theories of racialization and to obscure the land-based specificities of Indigenous struggles.[9] Contentions between hemispheric Asian American rights and Indigenous sovereignty movements have gained increasing critical focus, particularly in the context of Hawaiʻi and Canada.[10] The works that I examine engage the diverging and often colliding social justice imperatives, where hemispheric Asian Americanist calls for national inclusion into the settler state conflict with Indigenous struggles for territory, sovereignty, self-determination, and decolonization. At the same time, Indigenous assertions of autochthony can feed into settler constructions of national time that relegate Indigenous peoples to the past tense while racializing Asians as "alien" and thus outside of the machinations of the settler nation. Such nonalignments reveal the tensions embedded in the possibilities for solidarity across these two communities and illustrate the difficulties of meaningful mobilization for the mutual attunement to Indigenous struggles and racialized inequities.[11]

While the liberal logics of settler colonialism can be tracked through different geometries, the juxtaposition of hemispheric Asian American and Indigenous community articulations provides a theoretically heightened interpretation, given their often-opposing orientations within settler constructions of space, time, and tense. For example, such opposition is evident in the tropes of the Asian "perpetual foreigner" and the "vanishing Indian," tropes that operate through what Jodi Byrd has called a "meme" that resonates and creates meaning throughout the Américas.[12] As such, Asian alien and Indigenous crossings magnify the contours and grammatical structures of settler racial hegemonies. These crossings heighten, too, understandings of the affective relations that constitute the asymmetrical formations of power. I thus argue that, as a site for analytical inquiry, Asian-Indigenous crossings are key to revealing how settler racial hegemonies operate and congeal through what I term "settler racial tense." Specifically, the term "settler racial tense" refers to the ways that settler, alien, and Indigenous cultural and political articulations embody the *spatiotemporal logics* and *affective economies* of liberal ideologies. I highlight the multiple valences of tense (tense as a grammatical state and tense as an emotional state) as a metaphor for how settler colonialism functions, transforms, and finds meaning in the contemporary liberal moment.

Recent scholarship has engaged liberal extensions of settler colonial processes, from Byrd's "cacophony of empire" to Lowe's "intimacies of four continents," where liberal ideologies conjoin (and disremember) the interconnected processes of settlement, empire, and racialization. Both authors also implicate antiracist and anticolonial liberatory movements that participate in the critical affirmations of liberalism's central tenets, which in turn reproduce inequities across the chasm of race and settlement.[13] Adding to their scholarship—which focuses primarily on the legacies of British colonialism—*Unsettled Solidarities* highlights the liberal reproduction of racialized settlement in the United States, Canada, Mexico, and Brazil, expanding the scope of analysis to the hemisphere. Focusing on these four sites in the Américas, I trace the continuities of British, Spanish, and Portuguese colonialism. By centering Asian-Indigenous figurations across the hemisphere, I reveal how these distinct settler colonial legacies are continually sustained through the proprietary dimensions of liberal ideology that thrive on the asymmetrical incorporation and neutralization of Indigenous and Asian political movements.

Throughout this book, I examine works by Maxine Hong Kingston, Gerald Vizenor, Joy Kogawa, Marie Clements, Karen Tei Yamashita, Leslie Marmon Silko, Dorothy Christian, and Greg Sarris. Taken together, these texts reveal how Asian Americanist and Indigenous critical movements across the hemisphere—from the heroic/warrior traditions, to calls for reparations and redress, to transnational/cross-racial mobilization against global capital, as well as mixed-race narratives—are incorporated within or are structured by settler liberal ideologies that produce tensions across asymmetries of race and indigeneity. In so doing, these texts trace the liberal tenets undergirding settler colonialism—from individualism, state civility, multiculturalism/mixed-race futurity, to race as private property—and the ways they unevenly bring these community formations into collision. Ultimately, the texts provide opportunities to theorize strategies for solidarities that can attend to such tensions productively.

By tracing Asian and Indigenous crossings across different geopolitical sites in the Américas and examining what they reveal about liberal productions of settler racial hegemonies, *Unsettled Solidarities* offers three unique interventions within the fields of critical ethnic and Indigenous studies. First, this book constitutes the first monograph on Asian and Indigenous cross-representations in the Américas.[14] While other book-length studies have explored the embeddedness of the Asian figure within settler colonial logics, or the figure of the Indian structuring critical (race) theorizing, my comparative approach provides a more sustained reading of the mutual participation of these two communities within the long (liberal) histories of the Américas. Second, by examining Asian-Indigenous crossings from a hemispheric American perspective, this book provides critical insights into the overlap and divergence between British, Spanish, and Portuguese colonialisms in the Américas. A pairing of these two communities not only destabilizes some of the major operating paradigms of racial formations and settlement from the

United States (black-white binary), Canada (Aboriginal-white binary), Mexico (*mestizaje*–La Raza, or mixed Spanish–Native), and Brazil (*mestiçagem*, or mixed Portuguese-black-Native); it also links the productions of these two identities to the mutual constitution of racialization, settlement, and militarized imperialism across the Pacific.[15] Finally, by emphasizing the reproduction of settler racial hegemonies through the matter of tense (as spatiotemporal logic and affective formation), I offer a framework for considering the life of settler colonialism as an ongoing process that is continually negotiated by differently positioned communities. Centering settler racial hegemonies as produced through the matter of tense reveals the formations and the instabilities of the settler state and unsettles the logics of complicity and resistance that have often informed inquiries into power.

Critical Comparative Race and Indigenous Difference

Unsettled Solidarities draws from a genealogy of critical comparative work that registers both the distinctions and the entanglements of racialization, imperialism, and settlement as the formative conditions of settler states in the Américas. Although it is hemispheric in scope, this book is similar to the work of Byrd and Iyko Day in that it centers the logics of settler colonialism as they are constituted by the triangulation of settler, alien, and Native categorizations and articulations.[16] I engage a distinct split between white settler and racialized categorizations, while at the same time working to highlight the duress under which that split interacts and congeals through the settler colonial logics that work to disappear Native peoples.[17] This includes the different logics and dynamics through which settler states have enlisted Indigenous peoples into participation within settler colonial projects, for example, through military service in U.S. imperial wars that regenerate white settler access to economic dominance and territory. This emerges differently than but occurs adjacent to how racialized communities' affirmations of settlement can work to maintain the racialized and imperial logics of the settler state. The histories that produce these instances of complicity with settler state processes are complicated and differently enacted, which I work to highlight. Nevertheless, these complex relationships and interactions reveal the intricate overlapping and mutual impact of communities within what Byrd has aptly articulated as the "cacophony of empire."[18]

This emphasis on the asymmetries of race and colonialism emerges in opposition to previous (hegemonic) models of comparison, from Western epistemologies of comparison that posit the Western ideal against non-Western "deviants" to antiracist and anticolonial epistemologies of the long 1960s, such as Robert Blauner's conceptualization of an "internal colonial model," which registered communities of color as differentially yet commensurably oppressed. As Grace Kyungwon Hong and Roderick Ferguson have suggested, Western epistemological models of comparativity rest on the notion that bodies, identities, and nations are discrete entities. This spatial imaginary allows for the work of comparison to enact what Shu-mei Shih points out (via Frantz Fanon) is the doubled French and Creole sense of the word *comparaison,* simultaneously an act of delineation and of "contempt." Fanon's account makes clear that this invocation of *comparaison* by racialized and colonized subjects emerges out of and reproduces the dynamics of colonialism, imperialism, and racism.[19] It is this materialized facet of comparativity that propelled the mobilization of antiracism and anticolonialism during the long 1960s. Although such models of equivalencies directly repudiate dominant notions of *comparaison,* when they are taken as a "blueprint for coalition," as Hong and Ferguson suggest, they continue to presuppose the spatiality of dominant Western models of the self and other. These models, too, overlook "the ways in which these examples of racialized dispossession and abjection might depend, at different historical moments, on differentiated life chances and modes of incorporation for some racialized groups over and against others."[20]

Unsettled Solidarities also intervenes in critical tendencies toward racial triangulations, which often conflate or erase Indigenous communities in the processes of racialization. Recent emphasis on racial triangulation, laid out most explicitly by Claire Jean Kim, provides a model for moving away from white-nonwhite binaries and racial ahistoricities, two conditions that haunt previous "internal colonial" models of racial comparativity. In her theorization, Kim examines how popular U.S. discourses about various racial "others" have produced a "field of racial positions" imagined along two axes: superior-inferior and insider-foreigner. She argues that Asian Americans have been racially triangulated vis à vis African Americans in this field. In this triangulation, Asian Americans are valorized relative to black communities, yet ostracized from the U.S. body politic, thereby effectively keeping both groups under the control of Euro-American hegemony.[21] This racial theory disrupts tendencies to hierarchize racial injury while also bringing into clear focus the relational terms on which racial groups are defined. However, attempts to engage racial triangulation tend to place a third racialized group up against the operating logics of white-black dialectics, which reinscribes U.S.-based models of racial formations. In addition, as Shu-mei Shih highlights, triangulation continues to privilege some groups that are readily triangulated over others, leaving some, particularly Native American/Indigenous communities, undertheorized.[22]

In contrast to dominant models of racial comparison and triangulation, then, I locate my work among scholars in Native American/Indigenous studies, critical ethnic studies, and adjacent fields. Following these scholars, I center the qualitative differences between Indigenous and non-Native racialized communities' positionalities and untangle processes of colonization and racialization. By distinguishing colonization from racialization, I strive to foreground the territorial specificities of settlement and the continued dispossession of Indigenous lands and sovereignty that are often administered as a foregone conclusion in settler colonial and racial rights discourse, as scholars such as Byrd, J. Kēhaulani Kauanui, Jean M. O'Brien, Eve Tuck, K. Wayne Yang, and Mark Rifkin, among others, have argued.[23] The difference between Indigenous and non-Native racialized communities amounts to the different relationships that Indigenous peoples have with the settler state, where struggles for justice become inextricably linked to land, national sovereignty, self-determination, or, in the case of Indigenous communities in Mexico, autonomy. In concert with these scholars' works, this book also disinvests in the assumption that the call for equal rights can redress the effects of settler colonization.[24] The deep entrenchment of these assumptions, despite Indigenous studies scholars' and organizers' foundational calls to the contrary, can be traced back to the instantiation of what Rifkin terms "settler common sense." Rifkin uses the term to describe a common sense experienced by non-Natives that works to naturalize settler epistemologies and their concomitant material reach.[25] While asserting that settler colonialism is the foundational condition of dispossession in the critical inquiries of power in the Américas, I untangle and then retangle race as part and parcel of the affective economies that activate settlement. In other words, the formation of settler colonialism is separate from and yet formed by the racialization of Indigenous and Asian alien communities, a racialization that circles toward proprietary whiteness on Indigenous lands.[26]

Through this untangling and retangling of racialization and settler colonialism, *Unsettled Solidarities* addresses questions of how to register and theorize the role of non-Native racialized communities within the processes of settlement. Here disagreements about the usefulness of racial binaries or triangulations as theoretical lenses must, once again, be considered. In the context of Hawai'i, scholars such as Haunani-Kay Trask, Candace Fujikane, Jonathan Y. Okamura, J. Kēhaulani Kauanui, and Dean Saranillio have argued that the rubrics for articulating Asian American belonging as well as Asian American resistance to white domination within the context of Kānaka Maoli (Native Hawaiian) lands are often vested in settler state logics and apparatuses that erase Kānaka Maoli presence and sovereignty. As such, recognition of Asian settler collaboration within settler colonial apparatuses of power, or what Fujikane and Okamura term "Asian settler colonialism," provides a necessary starting point that ensures the continual centering rather than erasure of Indigenous concerns.[27] For Fujikane, considering the status and role of Asian settlers need not register intent but instead "the historical context of U.S. colonialism of which they unknowingly became a part."[28] Fujikane argues that this emphasis on Asian settler colonialism provides a more "complex analysis of colonial power" by highlighting "Asian settlers' maintenance of the colonial system from their differing locations within."[29]

In the process of centering Asian settler complicities, this book seeks to track these "differing locations" of Asians within different settler colonial contexts in the Américas.[30] As such, my work bridges, on the one hand, the theories that emphasize Asians as settlers within the Native-settler dyad and, on the other hand, those that highlight their asymmetrical position in relation to configurations of white settlement across different settler spaces. Of the latter, a number of scholars have theorized whether different triangulations and geometries may be more applicable in different settler colonial contexts. Byrd, for example, moves beyond the dyad of settler-Native to include a third term, "arrivant," that identifies communities and descendants of communities who arrive in the Américas not by choice but through the compulsory drive of settler capitalism and imperialism. Byrd charts the relationships of settler, arrivant, and Native through the analytic of "cacophony," derived from the Chickasaw/Choctaw concept of *haksuba*.[31] For Byrd:

> In geographical localities of the Américas, where histories of settlers and arrivants map themselves into and on top of indigenous peoples, understanding colonialism as a cacophony of contradictorily hegemonic and horizontal struggles offers an alternative way of formulating and addressing the dynamics that continue to affect peoples as they move and are made to move within empire.[32]

The analytic of cacophony thus decenters settler-colonized binaries, which place historically aggrieved communities on one side of the dyad in contemporary critiques of settler colonial assemblages. Framing her analysis in the North American context, Day expands Byrd's inclusion of arrivant in the Native-settler dialogic by positing the category of "alien" as an operative term that distinguishes enslaved persons and racialized migrants from settlers. For Day, the triangulation of Native, settler, and alien is dynamic, and they shift in relation to each other and to white settler investments in property and accumulation. These triangulated categories move the differentiated groups away from the language of choice toward recognition of the compulsory logics of white capitalism. Within Day's conceptualization of alien, then, the term "arrivant" operates as one key but nonexclusive category that differentiates itself from "settler."³³ Rather than occlude the role that alien presence has had in settler colonialism, Day acknowledges the "inconsistencies" where "the alien may not only be complicit with the settler colonial regime but may eventually inherit its sense of sovereign territorial rights, such as Asian settlers in Hawai'i."³⁴

In conversation with this long history of critical comparison and Indigenous difference, I offer the term "settler racial" as an imperfect but nevertheless malleable identifier with which to describe the relational formations of power and complicity that structure settler states. By using "settler racial" as a modifier for processes of power, I work to identify the distinct yet interconnected processes of settlement, imperialism, and racialization in the context of the Américas. As an adjective, "settler racial" modifies structures and logics of power, such as "hegemonies," to highlight the participation of white settler and racialized communities in settler colonial projects. The participation of these various groups, however, given racialized communities' uneven statuses as "alien," cannot be completely conflated—thus the grammatical precedence of "settler" prior to "racial." At the same time, the term "settler racial" also emphasizes the connection between the two terms, since racialized communities can and do reproduce and benefit from settler colonialism. In my use of "settler racial," I also want to highlight the complex position of Indigenous communities within the "cacophony of empire." That is, as communities also racialized within settler colonial processes, attention to Indigenous participation within settler racial hegemonies is central to this book.

My entanglement of "settler" and "racialized" subjectivities is intended to highlight, rather than obscure, the foundational processes of settler colonialism in the Américas and the collusion of racialized communities. While recognizing how "settler racial," a key descriptor in *Unsettled Solidarities,* may continue to occlude different relationships of power across and within identity categories, I deliberately invoke the gendered, class-based, and imperial implications that are attached to both the terms "settler" and "racial." In addition, through my analysis here and my use of the term "settler racial," I intend to center women of color feminist, queer of color, and Indigenous epistemologies of relationality (what Elizabeth Povinelli has termed "cosubstantiation" and Aileen Moreton-Robinson calls "intersubstantiation") that emphasize the porosity of embodiment beyond the privatized individual, toward relationalities to other human/nonhuman, animate/less-animate, and ancestral beings.³⁵ In the narratives that I examine, representations of Asian alien and Indigenous crossings highlight the complicated nexus of "settler racial" entanglements and, taken together, produce critical knowledge through which these two communities "move and are made to move" in the context of the settler colonial Américas.³⁶

Settler Racial Hegemonies as a Matter of Tense

Unsettled Solidarities centers on the argument that hemispheric Asian American and Indigenous literary cross-representations reveal what I term "settler racial hegemonies," or the liberal logics out of which settler, alien, and Indigenous communities come to participate in the reproduction of settlement and empire across the Américas.[37] The theoretical basis of this book is grounded in my argument that, given their often diametrically opposing positionalities in the settler imagination, hemispheric Asian American and Indigenous convergences provide a unique illumination of settler racial hegemonies, which are reproduced through what I call the matter of "settler racial tense."[38] I use the term "tense" as an apt metaphor for how Asian-Indigenous crossings highlight the spatiotemporal logics and affective formations propelling racialized settler processes.

The Space and Time of Settler Racial Tense

In its spatiotemporal aspect, settler racial tense indicates a settler grammar, which produces relationships of proximity across communities and events along the continuum of time and tense. Among its definitions in the *Oxford English Dictionary*, "tense" identifies "any one of the different forms or modification . . . in the conjugation of a verb which indicate the different times (past, present, or future) at which the action or state denoted by it is viewed as happening or existing." "Tense" also considers "the different nature of such action or state . . . as continuing (imperfect) or completed (perfect)." By this definition, we might best consider settler racial tense as an inherited settler colonial grammar that conjugates the cultures and actions of asymmetrically positioned communities into different tenses. As Povinelli writes regarding the logics of liberalism, "the actions of different cultures were assigned different tenses—not merely different times, as Johannes Fabian so nicely demonstrated, but different tenses."[39] For example, not only were Indigenous communities rendered outside of settler space and time but settler governance also often responded to Indigenous mobilization for justice by registering such demands into a future-oriented projection. Such a reorientation, from reparation for what has happened or is happening to its deferment into a future when such possibilities can be fully addressed, neutralizes decolonization efforts and creates ongoing effects of settlement. She maintains that liberalism wields the "tense of the other" as an available strategy through which demands for justice can be dissolved or resolved according to the directionality of the state.[40] This book adds to Povinelli's considerations of tense by highlighting how both Asian and Indigenous cultural and political articulations can unevenly inherit or become incorporated within settler colonial grammars (space, time, and tense) that interact with and promote the continuation of settler colonialism across the Américas.

Asian-Indigenous convergences offer key insights into this settler racial grammar, in part because these two groups have been spatially and temporally configured in diametrically opposing ways.[41] Although with variations, the image of the "alien" and "Native," central to the logics of national inclusion and exclusion that helped shape common concepts of the settler nation, has been asymmetrically transposed onto these two communities, and meaning is attributed to their images (and bodies) along a temporal rubric. The figure of the Asian has often been conceived as "alien" to the settler colonial body and described as "technologically advanced" along a temporal scale that slides toward the depiction of their unassimilable "old worldliness," depending on predominant economic needs and prevailing social sentiments.[42] Such depictions conjugate Asian aliens outside of, and yet central to the continual rewriting of, the "normative" time and space of settlement, placing them varyingly in the past perfect or conditional perfect future tense. Assertions of "native-ness" have marked the dialectics of settler colonialism and thereby Indigenous peoples in these colonized spaces. Indigenous studies scholars have argued that the contradiction between claims of white settler "nativeness" and the existence of communities "prior" to colonization has been negotiated through settler narratives that situate Indigenous peoples in the past tense, thereby allowing white settlers to maintain their own discursive constructions from inside the "sanctified" space of colonial rule. For Povinelli, this "governance of the prior" and concomitant logics of tense are the inherited grammar that fuels engagements with Indigenous presence within late liberal forms of governance. Indigenous peoples have also been configured, paradoxically, as alien to the continent, specifically through scientific proliferation of the Bering Strait theory, which has collapsed Indigenous peoples as Asian and has enabled conceptualization of Indigenous peoples as both outside the white telos of time and space and as historically alien to the continent. This alienation of the Indigenous from the continent reveals the malleability of settler logics to legitimize settler claims to land.[43] I expand Povinelli's theorization of social tense by elaborating on what I call settler racial tense, which identifies how the protection of normative settler time in the Américas depends on the attribution of different times and tenses to both the colonized and the non-Native racialized "other." The literary moments of Asian-Indigenous connection that register the temporality of these two communities' experiences reveal how liberal settler strategies toward the neutralization of demands for justice rely on the interconnected histories and malleable logics of settler racial time and tense.[44]

The meetings between the Asian and the Indigenous in the literary narratives that I examine also reveal the settler racial conjugations through which these two communities respond to settler colonial productions of time and tense and to each other. Here I use the term "conjugation" to identify how Asian and Indigenous communities have also placed themselves or other communities into a different tense in relationship to the settler nation. Although far from monolithic, hemispheric Asian American responses to narratives of the "perpetual foreigner" and "yellow peril," coupled with anti-immigration and anti-miscegenation laws, have long informed hemispheric Asian American identity formation and resistances. Such seemingly resistant articulations often include assertions of national belonging and an emphasis on the "modernity" of one's existence, thus taking as a given settler renderings of time. On a different trajectory, settler histories of broken treaties and land theft with Indigenous nations have been abetted by the narratives of the vanishing Indian.[45] This history has informed Indigenous calls for sovereignty based on claims to autochthony, a claim of "first-ness" that often speaks through logics of settler temporality but can elide what Rifkin terms "temporal sovereignty" and "temporal multiplicities."[46] For Rifkin, temporal sovereignty opens up access to temporal multiplicities, thereby providing space to articulate Indigenous presence and legitimacy without relying on settler rubrics of belonging. As sovereignty struggles in Hawai'i illuminate, the convergences of hemispheric Asian American and Indigenous communities lay bare these intersecting strategies as an ongoing present. They also reveal the often-colliding temporalities and spatialities through which justice is understood and demanded by the two communities.[47] These colliding spatial and temporal moorings depend crucially on the matter of tense, where, for example, critical expressions of Asian and/or Indigenous futurity can reverberate in ways that undergird the givenness of different aspects of settlement, empire, and racial inequities.

From varying thematic and political vantage points, the narratives that are the focus of this book register and respond to what Linda Tuhiwai Smith by way of Ashis Nandy has called the "'code' or 'grammar' [the deep structure] of imperialism" in the context of racialized settlement in late liberalism.[48] For Povinelli, late liberalism describes the forms of governmentality implemented as a response to, and the neutralization of, the demands made by social justice movements of the long 1960s. The critiques of colonial domination, dispossession, and racial paternalism by Native and non-Native communities of color were partially neutralized by what Wendy Brown terms the "culturalization of politics," whereby contradictions in the "frameworks of liberal justice" were registered, reinterpreted, and redistributed as a problem of "cultural" inclusion.⁴⁹ "Culture" was then defined and measured within the rubrics of social science as an artifact that could be recognized and dealt with, without rupturing the foundational frameworks of what Povinelli terms "the liberal diaspora." For Povinelli, neutralization is contingent on a grammar of social tense whereby different communities and events of social harm are temporally situated, grammatically marked, and refigured into "problems of threshold, scale, and performative realization." These performances by the state deflect questions of ethical action in the "durative present" into the "absolute difference between presence and absence or the critical difference between the future anterior and the past perfect."⁵⁰ Liberalism's reconfiguration of demands for social justice into different social tenses and the concomitant politics of recognition are one avenue through which the liberal diaspora maintains its hegemony.

In the texts that I examine, hemispheric Asian American and Indigenous articulations for social justice are unevenly structured by or become incorporated within settler liberal tenets of individualism, civil progress, liberal multiculturalism, and race as private property. These liberal tenets operate through what Lowe terms "the economy of affirmation and forgetting" and, the literary texts reveal, are structured through the malleable grammars of social tense. The scenes of Asian-Indigenous crossings convey the different ways that the two communities' social justice articulations can activate liberalism's codes and grammars of settler racial domination. Such scenes also reveal how these compromised articulations converge and impact one another. That is, given the "intimacies" embedded in the knowledge production of settlement, empire, and racialization, Asian and Indigenous political and cultural articulations "authorized by liberal political humanism" unevenly and often unwittingly reproduce the givenness of settlement, and/or the participation of imperial projects across the Pacific, and/or the obscuring of the fact that these processes are mutually constitutive phenomena.⁵¹ The interconnected yet often indeterminate clauses that grammatically structure my previous sentence point to the very process of settler liberal arrangements and consolidations of settler racial hegemonies. Through the critical juxtaposition of these two communities, this book seeks to convey the uneven spatiotemporal logics and ruptures of settler racial liberalism. It is precisely the extenuation or erasures of these connections that mark the seeming impossibility of attributing complicity or resistance to contemporary projects that fall under the categorization of liberation. These crossings thus open opportunities to conceive of the microdynamic orientations (of tense) that anchor ethical/political action, providing needed insights into how frameworks for solidarity can miss and meet each other in time, space, in the short and long term.

The Affective Production of Settler Racial Tense

Although I contend that the Asian-Indigenous meetings in the literary narratives that I examine provide a critical and malleable lens through which we can trace the grammatical reproductions of settler colonialism, these literary convergences also tell much-needed stories about the people bound within, mobilizing, and interrogating those very logics. While the scholarship in affect studies is marked by disagreements about the distinctions between affect and emotions, this study draws specifically from Sara Ahmed's conceptualization of affect as emotional forces that mobilize and congeal collectivities.[52] Ahmed writes: "Emotions are not simply something 'I' or 'we' have. Rather, it is through emotions, or how we respond to objects and others, that surfaces or boundaries are made." That is, emotions convey not some discrete internal architecture but "create the very effect of the surfaces and boundaries that allow us to distinguish an inside and an outside in the first place."[53] In my analysis, I consider Asian-Indigenous crossings as affective encounters that reveal emotions as forces that simultaneously index and drive the tense conditions of settler colonial domination in the Américas.[54]

Engaging affect as emotional forces, this book specifically argues that a settler racial grammar of tense is mediated and mobilized by what Raymond Williams calls "structures of feeling." According to Williams, structures of feeling indicate the "affective elements of consciousness and relationships: not feeling against thought, but thought as felt and feeling as thought: practical consciousness of a present kind, in a living and interrelating continuity."[55] My conceptualization of settler racial tense assumes that the grammar of social tense is formed through the affective economies of the settler state, the embodiment and instabilities of which are constituted by the state's reliance on the *tensions* across settler, alien, and Indigenous communities. Here I speak of "tense" or "tension" in its emotional and mechanistic sense, where the affective formations of settler racial relationalities work "to stretch tight" the spatiotemporal proximities that generate late liberal settler arrangements of relations and power.[56]

In the texts that I examine, Asian-Indigenous crossings reveal how settler racial hegemonies are produced and reproduced through the affective economies of hemispheric Asian American and Indigenous communities. At the same time, differentiating ideology from affect—that is, differentiating an idea from how the idea is actively lived—these texts also register settler racial hegemonies as constituted by Williams's notion of "dominant," "residual," and "emergent" formations and collectivities. For Williams, feelings are distinguished from ideology in that feelings capture "meanings and values as they are actively lived and felt."[57] Thus, while the texts of my study reveal the work of affect/emotions in the reproduction of settler racial hegemonies, this affective lens also provides a window into the instabilities, and the anxieties, of the settler racial state.[58] That is, in the imaginative encounters between hemispheric Asian American and Indigenous communities and their delineation of settler racial logics, there emerges an affective genealogy, which I argue evokes the "residual" and "emergent" ruptures constitutive of "dominant" formations.[59] This affective potentiality can be traced specifically through the critical emotions across collectivities represented in the narratives.

That is, these moments of literary crossings not only encapsulate settler racial hegemonies as structures of feeling; they embody affective excess that has the potential to undermine the coherence and reveal the instabilities and anxieties as *tensions* of the settler state. The conjuring and performance of such emotions exist as a potential that can both delineate or hail collectivities that can reconstitute the dynamics of settler racial power, while at the same time opening up orientations toward others that can leave a critical impression. Ahmed writes, "If bodies do not arrive in neutral, if we are always in some way or another moody, then what we will receive as an impression will depend on our affective situation. . . . It suggests that how we arrive, how we enter this room or that room, will affect what impressions we receive. After all, to receive is to act. To receive an impression is to make an impression."[60] As she suggests, the effect of being affected by another is contingent on the "angle of our arrival."[61] Hemispheric Asian American and Indigenous narrative encounters reveal how these two communities emerge out of different angles of arrivals (informed by the very context of their divergent emergences) and so leave different effects or impressions on one another. It is precisely in these moments of connection, as represented in the literary texts, that elided or new impressions can be illuminated or formed. I suggest that the literary encounters provide us with a window into unseen impressions that hint toward possibilities of the mutual attunement to decolonization. While the representations of such impressions may not fully form into a material realization (particularly within the narrative frame), they nevertheless possess a meaningful trace that can be drawn across an archive of literary crossings.

The narratives that I examine often track affective ruptures of settler racial hegemonies through the concomitant ruptures of literary form. Williams highlights art as a privileged medium that embodies given social forms, or what Povinelli terms "social projects."[62] Yet he also suggests that these cultural productions do not fully encapsulate a given social moment, and instead have their "specific kinds of sociality" that work to transform preexisting social structures.[63] That is, emergent structures of feeling are lived within the interstices of a particular form or aesthetic. Williams writes that "although they are emergent or pre-emergent, they do not have to await definition, classification, or rationalization before they exert palpable pressures and set effective limits on experience and on action."[64] Similarly, Lowe argues that "modern liberal humanism is a formalism that translates the world through an economy of affirmation and forgetting within a regime of desiring freedom."[65] While the texts of interest emulate common genres and forms within the archive of hemispheric Asian American and Indigenous literatures writ large, the narrative encounters between hemispheric Asian American and Indigenous peoples often rupture the perceived narrative logics, trajectories, and temporalities inhabited by these structures. These rupturing encounters lead to affective detours. For example, while ostensibly about the histories, lives, and trajectory of her Chinese male relatives in the United States, Maxine Hong Kingston's *China Men* incorporates key scenes of encounters between her relatives and Indigenous figures in Hawai'i and California.[66] In one scene, the narrator's great-grandfather encounters a ghostly Hawaiian woman while on his break from his job clearing the land. She invites him to enter the decimated village, but he is too spooked and leaves the area immediately. Moments like these not only break from the typical conventions of the historiographical form (through its break from realism in its incorporation of ghostly figures); they also take the reader out of the celebratory trajectory of the narrative (where the triumph of her great-grandfather's labor on Hawaiian land is curtailed by histories of violence on Kānaka Maoli peoples). These ghostly presences open up expressions of Indigenous affective formations that can work to impress upon or circumvent the affective formations of Asian American settler belonging through labor. I argue that such formal and aesthetic divergences provide a palpable register to track the instabilities inherent in settler racial hegemonies. These formal divergences, which take place within scenes of crossings, offer intensities that give an emotional pulse to the "pre-formation" of connections and solidarities among communities situated asymmetrically across settler racial hegemonies.[67]

Chapters (across the Hemispheric Américas)

Through examination of Asian-Indigenous crossings, I illuminate how settler racial hegemonies operate within distinct colonial borders and yet reveal the liberal logics that unify different forms of settlement that have taken place in the United States, Canada, Mexico, and Brazil. Through this hemispheric scope, *Unsettled Solidarities* adds to previous theorizing of settler colonialism by centering links between contemporary British, Spanish, and Portuguese settler colonies. Across the hemisphere, these colonies continue to be shaped by the liberal neutralization of political resistance through the production of asymmetries and tensions across race and indigeneity.[68]

The geographic scope of this book is informed by the critical knowledge that has emerged from the turn toward the hemisphere in both Indigenous and hemispheric Asian American studies. Within Indigenous studies and political movements, hemispheric connections help to highlight the specificities of settlement within local and national zones while also linking such formations to the larger legacies of settler colonial logics and technologies across the Américas.[69] Seeking out hemispheric connections and patterns helps to unmoor settler production of knowledge and recenter Indigenous epistemologies, geographies, and environmental philosophies. More specifically, by emphasizing hemispheric Indigenous epistemologies, we can rethink the definitions of settler colonialism that have previously been developed in regard to British colonialisms in the United States and Canada. Of course, looking at settler colonialism as a hemispheric American structure is complicated by the different modes of colonial techniques in Latin América, such as extractive colonialism and/or internal colonialism.[70] As scholars such as M. Bianet Castellanos and Shannon Speed have argued, the critical hesitance to identify Latin American nations as settler states derives in part from tendencies to demarcate differences in colonial regimes based on their modes of dispossession and extraction: that is, of land or labor. Castellanos argues of this binary approach to defining forms of colonial dispossession:

> Efforts to distinguish regimes of colonialism in the Américas by their method of dispossession, as rooted in either land or labor expropriation, end up reproducing binaries (land/labor, settler/native, Latinx/Latin American) that mask articulations spanning imperial and colonial regimes. The emphasis on binaries risks reproducing a monolithic, self-contained theory of settler colonialism lacking historical and relational specificity, the very project initially challenged by Patrick Wolfe.[71]

In addition, since Latin American countries are vulnerable to U.S. neocolonialism, attention to these countries' continued settler colonial operations is frequently undercut.[72] Rather than classifying Mexico or Brazil as being an example of one or the other form of colonial strategy, in this book I read settler colonialism as operative yet differently produced across the colonial boundaries of the hemisphere.[73]

A hemispheric approach to Asian American studies also moves away from the centrality of the nation in the consideration of Asian immigration and racialization. In doing so, it opens possibilities to examine "Asian Americans" beyond the geopolitical boundaries of the United States and/or Canada and to emphasize how racialization within these boundaries is informed by the shifting dynamics across national entities north and south within the hemisphere and east and west across the Pacific.[74] A hemispheric Asian American perspective also provides much-needed insights into how settler processes of racial formations typically not connected to Asian racialization (for example, *mestizaje*) are as much informed by Asian racialization within imperial discourses as by the defining settler logics that are often attributed to its formation (Indigenous/Spanish formations).[75] In addition, a turn toward examining Asian positionalities in settler processes helps to illuminate the critical differences and yet the continuities of Asian racialization and complicity under settler liberalism across the Américas. Sau-ling Wong has expressed concern that a transnational approach to Asian American studies may deflect attention from U.S. processes of power but, as I demonstrate, *Unsettled Solidarities*' hemispheric approach provides insights into the racialized coloniality of the United States while re-energizing Asian Americanist imperatives for cross-racial and cross-national solidarities.[76]

Through critical attention to Asian and Indigenous connections in different colonial geographies in the Américas, this book conveys the differences and yet the unifying logics of settler colonial governmentality in the United States, Canada, Mexico, and Brazil. Settler colonial processes across these states thrive through the asymmetrical racialization and dispossession of alien and Indigenous communities. As such, while Asian racialization and Indigenous dispossession in Latin American countries such as Mexico and Brazil are different than they are in Canada and the United States, these countries nevertheless operate via similar logics insofar as the racial formations that underwrite them (*mestizaje* and *mestiçagem*, respectively) are dependent on the dispossession of Indigenous lands and autonomy as well as the racialized imperial logics attached to the Asian alien body. These forms of settler power persist and are enlivened through the settler state's reliance on the tense interactions across alien and Indigenous communities. *Unsettled Solidarities* specifically focuses on how the settler state operates through the liberal neutralization of critical resistance movements across Asian alien and Indigenous communities as they impact one another.

Each chapter provides comparative readings of texts by two major authors, connected by the similar geographic and thematic scope of their narratives. Within these chapters, I examine the uneasy incorporation of Asian and Indigenous formations of resistance into settler state apparatuses (from [1] historiography in the United States to [2] legal/juridical maneuverings in Canada, [3] economic processes in Brazil and Mexico, and [4] biopolitical discourses in the United States and Canada), which work to make coherent the liberal narratives of the settler state. Specifically, the chapters reveal how liberatory movements from alternative historical narratives to redress and reconciliation efforts, transnational/cross-racial anticapitalist critique, and mixed-race discourse undergird or become incorporated within liberal ideologies of individualism, civility, multiculturalism, and race as private property, respectively. Asian-Indigenous crossings represented in the texts convey the impact that these liberatory movements have on the reproduction of settler racial hegemonies and the maintenance of liberal ideologies, which rely on these uneven, and tense, interactions across racialized and Indigenous communities.

I do not sequence these chapters historically; that is, I do not organize representations of Asian-Indigenous crossings as they emerge in different time periods in the histories of the Américas. Rather, the chapters move thematically. To magnify how the project of settler liberalism is contingent on the tensions (in the doubled sense of tense as temporality and as emotional force/affect) across Asian and Indigenous communities, the chapters move from representations of more ephemeral/ghostly/evocative forms of crossings toward more material/literal/embodied crossings between Asian and Indigenous peoples. As the cross-representations featured in the chapters become more materialized, so too do the complex relationships between these two communities register as more palpably tense. This book considers the magnification of these tense crossings as a critical archive in which we can not only trace the different intensities through which settler racial hegemonies operate but also discuss the varying dimensions of cross-racial connections and dialogue that can spur possibilities for solidarities.

Chapter 1 examines how two alternative historical traditions—the U.S. Asian American Heroic Tradition and the Native American Warrior Tradition—constitute discursive extensions of the U.S. settler nation's reliance on Asian alien and Indigenous labor. While both traditions contest dominant narratives of U.S. history, from nineteenth-century westward expansion to World War II, they nevertheless invoke liberal tenets of masculine individualism, a central subject of the liberal settler nation's narration of freedom and progress. Through juxtaposition of these two historiographies, and readings of Maxine Hong Kingston's *China Men* and Gerald Vizenor's *Hiroshima Bugi: Atomu 57*, I illuminate how these two traditions invoke the racialized and colonized individual's affective relationship to such narratives of freedom and progress in ways that obscure the uneven settler and imperial violence on which this telos of the U.S. settler nation emerges. Closely reading Kingston's and Vizenor's destabilization of the historiographical genre, I also discuss the instabilities embedded within these two communities' participation in settler racial hegemonies. In their imaginations of ghostly crossings between Asian-

Indigenous peoples, Kingston and Vizenor conjure elided memories, alternative temporalities, and cross-community affective relationships repressed by the imperatives of both national and alternative historiographies. As such, Vizenor's and Kingston's texts gesture toward the always-incomplete project of memory making central to U.S. settler empire building.

Chapter 2 examines how redress and reconciliation movements by Nikkei and Aboriginal communities in Canada become incorporated into the settler nation's self-narrative of civility and progress. While emerging from a multitude of movements that sought varying forms of accountability for the damages produced by Nikkei internment and Indian residential schools, redress and reconciliation instead became registered within Canada's reconceptualization as a tolerant liberal multicultural state—one that has transgressed and yet reformed. Through comparison of Canada's 1988 and 2008 public apologies, and readings of Joy Kogawa's novel *Obasan* and Marie Clements's play *Burning Vision,* I examine how Canada's narrative of civil reformation relied on the redirecting of community grief and trauma toward settler national definitions of healing. The settler state works to define continued feelings of grief or anger as unhealthy emotions to be overcome, thereby mediating and foreclosing meaningful movements toward decolonization. Through imaginations of ephemeral crossings between Asian-Indigenous peoples, the novel and play evoke the expansiveness of settler-produced harm and grief and how such harm reverberates across Asian and Indigenous communities. Thus, while the grief and grievances of these two communities are often registered as separate, the texts illuminate affective links that move in excess of settler state narratives of emotional progress. Positing melancholic attachments to grief as emotional knowledge that productively tracks settler racial hegemonies, these texts suggest the potentiality of Asian-Indigenous affinities that reveal the connectedness between racialized harm and settler colonial imposition.

Where Chapters 1 and 2 center ghostly and ephemeral crossings to convey the often unseen tensions and yet potential relationalities across the liberatory movements of these two communities, Chapters 3 and 4 discuss more sustained representations of Asian-Indigenous characterizations and relationships. In addition, while Chapters 1 and 2 focus on settler racial hegemonic processes in the United States and Canada (thus centering British colonialism more so), Chapter 3 centers Mexico and Brazil and the liberal legacies of Spanish and Portuguese colonization. Chapter 4 returns to the United States and Canada and examines the incorporation of mixed-blood narratives in the context of liberal multiculturalism and color-blind discourse.

Chapter 3 examines how imaginations of transnational/cross-racial mobilization against global capital in Latin América can become incorporated within or structured by liberal ideologies that problematically center the mixed-race (*mestizo/mestiço*) subject as the primary figure of liberation. *Mestizaje/mestiçagem* (mixed-race) discourse has been crucial in propelling both revolutionary and neoliberal economic policies in Mexico and Brazil. Such ideology hails universal inclusion through racial mixture, with a privileging of Indigenous identity (*indigenismo*), and yet has unevenly incorporated and abjected Indigenous and Asian people under Iberian capitalist territorialization, privatization, and development. By comparing Karen Tei Yamashita's *Through the Arc of the Rain Forest* and Leslie Marmon Silko's *Almanac of the Dead,* I trace how differing imaginations of cross-community mobilization against global capital can discursively repeat the settler and racial legacies of *mestizaje/mestiçagem* discourse. These two texts narrate the impact of global capitalist economic policies and trade agreements that unevenly draw Asian and Indigenous communities into critical relationships in the United States, Mexico, and Brazil. The novels trace the transformations of hemispheric Asian American and Indigenous political mobilization in response to these economic changes, transformations that move from identity-based mobilization to transnational and cross-racial connectivity. I argue that representations of Asian-Indigenous intimacies within these scenes of political mobilization index the limits of transnational, cross-racial theories of economic resistance as they encounter the settler racial legacies of *mestizaje/mestiçagem* ideologies. At the same time, as self-reflexive and performative activist texts, both narratives also open up fraught but necessary lines of discussion about the pitfalls and future potential of different literary forms that can mobilize collectivities toward decolonizing futures.

Chapter 4 continues the discussion of mixed-race discourse by tracing its centrality in contemporary liberal ideology in Canada and the United States. Like *mestizaje/mestiçagem* discourse, mixed-race discourse in contemporary Canada and the United States can become incorporated within liberal multicultural projections that see racial blending as an already actuated road to postracial harmony. This liberal imagination and structure of feeling not only potentially obscures the histories and continuation of settler and racial imposition; it can also register race as a private domain and experience of the individual. While mixed-race discourse works to rupture the discrete categories of race and ethnicity, its incorporation within hegemonic liberal ideology can undergird the systemic dismantling of affirmative action, civil rights claims, and decolonial movements. Turning to readings of two Asian-Indigenous mixed-blood texts, I discuss how Dorothy Christian's essay "Articulating a Silence" and Greg Sarris's biography of Mabel McKay reveal rather than elide settler and racial histories and presences in Canada and the United States, respectively. Centering their emotions in regard to their mixed-blood identity, particularly feelings of shame and anxiety, the narrators of these two texts track the legacies of anti-miscegenation, adoption, and assimilation policies that bring Asian and Indigenous peoples into uncommon intimacy and direct tension. Furthermore, these narrators' feelings of shame and anxiety convey the continued impact of these biopolitical and sovereign strategies on the two communities and their progeny. Such feelings, the texts convey, have an impact on the potential relationships that these two communities can forge with each other amid the eliminatory logics of the (neo)liberal multicultural settler state. In highlighting their own vexed emotions as structures of feeling that convey and reproduce Asian-Indigenous tensions, the two texts posit an Asian-Indigenous mixed-blood epistemology that is distinguished from the privatizing of mixed-race emotions central in contemporary postracial settler discourse.

In thinking through Asian and Indigenous relationalities as they emerge across the Américas, my goal is to trace the liberal logics of settler colonialism that enjoin these two communities into active, passive, and resistive participation. At the same time, by examining the affective currents through which this participation manifests, I also hope to capture the contradictions and unfinished efforts that persist within the interstices of "settler racial hegemonies." While the narratives I examine all confront the difficulties of meaningful solidarities across the liberal logics of racial, imperial, and colonial formations, they nevertheless contain glimpses of emotional "excesses" that haunt the peripheries of settler racial hegemonies—nascent, yet-to-be-formed, structures of feeling. It is from this that I have drawn the title of this book. *Unsettled Solidarities* speaks to the inchoate refusals that persist in what might seem to be the most compromised aspects of cultural and political articulations within these two community formations. *Unsettled Solidarities* also gestures to the understanding that solidarities are indeed workings that move and are moved by the dynamic processes and assemblages that compose the thickness of their settler colonial worlds.

1

Historiographical Tensions

U.S. Asian American and Indigenous Crossings from Manifest Destiny to the Pacific Theater

On May 10, 1869, in Promontory Summit, Utah, photographer Andrew J. Russell captured images of the ceremony that formalized the completion of the transcontinental railroad. In the famous "Golden Spike Photograph," a large group of men, noticeably white, stand in front of and on top of two train cars that symbolically connected the Central Pacific Railroad with the Union Pacific Railroad. At the forefront of the picture are plants and bushes. At the center of the image are two men, Samuel S. Montague and Grenville M. Dodge, representatives of the railroad companies, shaking hands while gazing directly at the camera. The image looks simultaneously formal, serious, and celebratory, an effect that is enhanced by of the presence of bottles of alcohol being exchanged across the trains.

On February 23, 1945, in Iwo Jima, Japan, photographer Joe Rosenthal took his Pulitzer Prize–winning photograph of six U.S. marines raising the U.S. flag on top of Mount Suribachi. The photo is a play on visual contrasts. Taking up more than half the frame are white billowing clouds, which serve as a cleared background for the starker image of the soldiers at the forefront. The soldiers stand on uncultivated ground, which implies their position at the pinnacle of civilization. Since their faces are turned away from the camera, they are racially undemarcated, and the soldiers' separate bodies seem to merge into what looks almost like one multilimbed figure with a single goal—to proclaim the dominance of the United States.

These two photos, both immediately recognizable within the archive of U.S. national images, visually distill two major touchstones in the nation's consolidation as a settler colony and an imperial force: nineteenth-century westward expansion and mid-twentieth-century victory in the Pacific theater of war.[1] While linked to different stages of U.S. empire building, these moments cohere through their enactment of U.S. hegemony constituted by the logics of white supremacy, land seizures, racialized labor/service, and genocidal warfare. The completion of the transcontinental railroad, coupled with the 1862 Homestead Act, was of a piece with the acceleration of U.S. white settler movements westward, the violent seizing of Indigenous lands, and the logics of elimination that propelled the large-scale Indian wars of the nineteenth century. In like fashion, the overtaking of the island of Iwo Jima in the Pacific theater positioned the United States for victory against Japan during World War II, a victory that was punctuated by the United States' atomic bombings of Hiroshima and Nagasaki, its occupation of Japan in the postwar period, and its rising status as a major economic imperial power.

As visual commemorations of these two moments, these two photographs are also connected through the ways they distill the liberal logics of U.S. settlement and empire as constituted by what Lisa Lowe terms the "the economy of affirmation and forgetting." Within this economy, according to Lowe, "the state subsumes colonial violence within narratives of modern reason and progress [thus making illegible] the forcible encounters, removals, and entanglements omitted in liberal accounts of abolition, emancipation, and independence."[2] The photographs partake in this process through the positive depiction of heroism, strength, ingenuity, and camaraderie—of the potential that is seen as inherent in the liberal individual who is figured in default as white and male. The pictures suggest that it is through these triumphs of the individual human will that the nation-state can prevail against all that threatens its being and its progress: from the unforgiving wilderness to the threat of fascism. Even a brief critical examination of these nationally fetishized photos, however, reveals the disavowed entanglements between Asian and Indigenous peoples that structure the acceleration of U.S. settler and imperial power at these two crucial junctures. While the "Golden Spike Photograph" employs visual vocabularies central to the logics of settlement and Indigenous erasures (such as the containment of wilderness through industry), it completely erases the role of Chinese immigrant labor in the construction of the railroad. Similarly, while the Iwo Jima photograph presages U.S. imperial victory over Japan, the presence and yet symbolic absence of a Pima or Akimel O'otham man (Ira Hayes) as one of the flag bearers highlights the spectral role of Native servicemen in U.S. imperial projects.

U.S. Asian American and Native American/Indigenous studies scholars have long highlighted the erasures of Asian immigrant and Indigenous "service," respectively, within these two historical junctures. As such, much labor has been invested in rescuing these figures from the obscurity of history to highlight their heroism and struggles. Although they are critical of mainstream U.S. narratives distilled in the visual vocabulary, such alternative commemorations often continue to rely on the logics of masculine heroism, which not only feed into the narrative of the triumphant individual but also naturalize the violent settler and imperial logics of elimination on which this triumph rests. Thus, even within the liberatory or alternative historiographies invoked by both U.S. Asian American and Indigenous cultural productions, this "economy of affirmation and forgetting," so central to U.S. settler colonialism, maintains a meaningful afterlife.

In this chapter, I trace the settler racial logics of U.S. national formation by examining these two key contexts: mid-nineteenth-century westward expansion and World War II/occupation-era Japan. Although they are separated by different processes of land seizures and occupation (settler national seizing of Indigenous lands on the one hand, and militarized imperial expansion in Asia on the other), I argue that these historical moments cohere in their production of settler racial hegemonies, which unevenly draw U.S. Asian American and Indigenous communities into complicit participation. Specifically, through juxtaposition of Maxine Hong Kingston's *China Men* and Gerald Vizenor's *Hiroshima Bugi: Atomu 57,* I trace how the processes of settlement and empire at these major conjunctures are materially, logically, and affectively interlinked projects that enlist either Asian immigrant labor or Native military service in the processes of land seizures and genocidal warfare, both of which are critical to the sustenance of U.S. settler and imperial dominance and capitalist accumulation.[3] In addition, I analyze both texts as self-reflexive historiographies of these moments, and in doing so I illuminate the heteropatriarchal memorialization of heroism as a critical structure of feeling that propels these communities into sustained service to the United States, not only during the waging of wars but also, meaningfully, in their subsequent recollection.

This chapter is structured in three parts. First I examine two primary figures from the heroic and warrior traditions: the Chinese immigrant laborer and the Native American serviceman.[4] Both figures have occupied a problematic space within U.S. Asian American and Native American historiographies. I trace the critical dialogue that has surrounded these figures and emphasize how the various ways they have been memorialized have problematically upheld settler colonial logics. By centering the triumph of the individual as it is often connected to martial valor, these historiographies unevenly obscure the violence on and incorporation of Asian and Indigenous peoples in U.S. settler colonial and imperial processes. The complicated memorialization of these figures reveals the asymmetrical yet intersecting ways that U.S. Asian American and Indigenous historical narratives can become complicit in the liberal reproductions of U.S. settler colonialism and imperialism.

The later parts of the chapter analyze how Kingston's and Vizenor's texts address the logics and contradictions of U.S. settler racial hegemonies within the context of wars and their subsequent memorialization. In *China Men*, Kingston imagines her Chinese male relatives' labor in the clearing of lands and the building of economic and industrial infrastructure in nineteenth-century Hawai'i and the U.S. West. Vizenor's novel, on the other hand, sheds light on the histories of Native military service for the United States in the Pacific theater of war, as well as in the aftermath of the atomic bombings of Hiroshima and Nagasaki. In both narratives, ephemeral and ghostly moments of Asian/Asian American and Native American/Indigenous meetings and relationships arise in these contact zones of settler empire building. Such crossings convey the hidden yet affectively charged ways that one community's "service" to the United States can impact the other.

Kingston's narrative, for example, traces how the feelings, desires, and longings that inform her great-grandfather's and grandfather's arrivals in Hawai'i and the United States can mimic and supplement Euro-settler structures of feeling that propel the encroachment of Native American/Indigenous lands and peoples. Vizenor's work engages a corollary process, representing instances of Native military service for the United States during World War II and their ramifications for the U.S. occupation of Japan and Native American nations after World War II. Centering on the politics of memorialization in the postwar period, Vizenor's work traces how investments in narratives of Native masculine heroism, and their transformations into global productions of the cult of celebrity, can feed into U.S. and Japanese capitalist structures of feeling, which are in turn conditioned by the ongoing occupation of Japan and Native American nations by the United States.

Rather than rendering U.S. Asian American and Native American participation in these stages of U.S. history as a monolithic mimicry of settler and imperial imperatives, however, these two metahistoriographies also offer scenes where characters' triumphalist moments (of individual heroism, strength, ingenuity), either enacted or remembered, are haunted by contradictions. My analysis in this chapter examines such scenes as affective ruptures that conjure alternative temporalities and expansive geographical imaginaries repressed by the imperatives of both national and alternative historical narratives. These nascent structures of feeling that haunt the texts gesture to the always incomplete project of settler empire building and to the percolating, not-yet-manifest, feelings of an "otherwise" that can provide a groundwork for solidarities.

In examining U.S. Asian American and Native American relationality in the formation of U.S. settler colonialism and imperialism, this chapter expands on critical work about U.S. national power by paying particular attention to the mutual constitution of settler and cross-Pacific imperial technologies in the reproduction of U.S. settler colonial hegemony. This emphasis not only destabilizes the black-white, or white-nonwhite, racial binaries that infuse cultural discourses around U.S. national power but also highlights how settler colonialism is reproduced through the matter of settler racial tense, or the affective and temporal liberal logics long attached to Asian and Indigenous communities and bodies. While empire and settlement are often considered to have a different impact on Asian and Indigenous communities, my comparative approach highlights how these communities are unevenly but mutually brought into both projects. I examine, furthermore, the role of alternative historical narratives, which at first would seem to be resistant to U.S. hegemony, but nevertheless become folded into U.S. liberal logics that work to produce and yet obscure settler and imperial entanglements.

Historiography, as a crucial technology in the formation and maintenance of U.S. settler colonial power, has been unevenly employed by U.S. Asian American and Native American groups as a key strategy through which to contest settler conjugations that erase Asian and Indigenous labor in mainstream narratives. Throughout this chapter, I use the term "historiography" to identify bodies of writings on specific historical moments. Thus, I use "historiography" interchangeably with "historical narratives" and I use "counter-historiography" interchangeably with "counter-historical narratives." While I consider Kingston and Vizenor's texts to be creative forms of historical narratives, their destabilization of fact/fiction and their self-reflexive critique of historiography as being unequivocally mediated would also support the idea that their works are forms of historiographic metafiction.

In order to trace the liberal connections between alternative historical narratives and dominant historical narratives, I trace their converging spatial, temporal, and affective economies. Dominant U.S. historical narratives have proven central to not only the production of settler colonial constructions of space, time, and tense but also to how these spatiotemporal logics inform the making of intimate publics.[5] With respect to Benedict Anderson's formulation of newspapers as central to the production of a community imagining itself moving in simultaneity along homogenous empty time, U.S. historical narratives function to place an imagined community along a telos of progress that dynamically consolidates national attachments to its desired perpetuity.[6] When examining the comparative racial structuring of U.S. settler colonial formation, however, this production of sociality along a national telos relies on the (always uneven) exclusion and provisional inclusion of U.S. Asian American and Indigenous communities in such national narratives. The material contradictions of U.S. racial and settler colonial formations require, in the historiographical national consciousness, a processing of U.S. Asian American and Indigenous presences along this timeline. A tracking of U.S. Asian American and Native presences along this national timeline can reveal how the narrative telos of national progress is possible only through the rendering of these two communities along different times and tenses of the nation.

U.S. Asian American and Native American historiographies thus delineate spatiotemporalities differentiated from settler racial productions of space and time, or what Dipesh Chakrabarty terms "History 2."[7] While the scope of these counter-historiographies often work to contest the violently racialized and colonial timeline of settler national progress, they can also rely on settler logics that negatively impact differently positioned communities, given the asymmetries of settlement and racialization. U.S. Asian Americanist counter-historiographies can thus reiterate the givenness of the settler state and make invisible Indigenous dispossessions and environmental extraction. This elision can emerge in Native American/Indigenous rewritings of the past, where calls for recognition of Indigenous presence in war can unwittingly uphold settler nationalist rhetorics that emerge at the site of U.S. imperial projections.[8] This problematic facet of counternarration is particularly illuminative within the heroic tradition and the warrior tradition, two alternative historiographical discourses central to U.S. Asian American and Native American/Indigenous studies.

Heroic and Warrior Traditions

Within U.S. Asian American and Native American historiographies, the Asian American heroic tradition and the Native warrior tradition stand as seemingly equivalent sites for alternative traditions that counter the Eurohegemony of U.S. historiographies. The U.S. Asian American heroic tradition emerged amid the consolidation of U.S. Asian American movements and politics in the mid-twentieth century as a way to rememorialize and to renarrate the histories of Asian (particularly Chinese) immigrant labor to the United States and Hawai'i. This tradition has been expounded most vocally by playwright and critic Frank Chin in order to counteract perceptions of U.S. Asian American men as weak and effeminate, perceptions that have been entangled with histories of Chinese immigrant men taking on work that is perceived as traditionally within the woman's domain—such as laundry.[9] Working to counter these stereotypes, Chin has dedicated a number of critical and creative works to representing the Chinese immigrant/American man as a rugged, hypermasculine figure who is fully and ably participating in the economic and technological infrastructures of the United States. He links the value and valor of these men to their adherence to Chinese martial traditions that emphasize heroism through war and prowess.[10] While critiquing the hypermasculine aspects of Chin's recovery, Maxine Hong Kingston and other writers and cultural activists within U.S. Asian American studies have also highlighted the centrality of Chinese male workers in the building of the United States and worked to move these figures back into popular memory, from which collective memory such figures had heretofore been all but erased in the dominant historiographies of the time period.[11] Given this focus, and the controversy between Kingston and Chin, the Chinese laborer has become paradigmatic within discussions of the U.S. Asian American heroic tradition.

Scholar Julia H. Lee argues that there have been two prevalent discourses in regard to the historical recovery of Chinese labor on the sugar plantations in Kānaka Maoli lands (of what is now considered Hawaiʻi) and in the laying of the railroads of the U.S. West through Indigenous lands. The first discourse, most apparent in Kingston's work, has tended to reconjure these images in order to call for U.S. Asian American inclusion in the U.S. national polity given their backbreaking labor in laying the literal groundwork for U.S. westward expansion. The second, prominent in Chin's work, tends to punctuate the rigor of these workers as an antidote for the historical demasculinization of U.S. Asian American men.[12] This second discourse, which Viet Thanh Nguyen terms the "remasculinization of Chinese America," and King-Kok Cheung, Jinqi Ling, and other scholars term the "Asian American heroic tradition," may counter the dominant racist perceptions of U.S. Asian American men but do so primarily by upholding the gender binaries structuring the nation-state.[13] Ling argues that celebration of Chinese American participation in the construction of the United States via the building of the transcontinental railroad and the backbreaking labor in the Hawaiian cane fields "fundamentally revises the content of most institutionally sanctioned histories of the United States, even while it confirms the ruling assumptions of that history: rugged individualism, masculine valor, and social progress wrought through technological achievements."[14] Nguyen continues in this vein, analyzing how the railroad hero myth partakes in the formative U.S. mythology of masculinization through violence on the frontier. The performance of Asian American masculinity in the Asian American heroic tradition reinstates colonial rubrics defined by the United States even as it seeks to incorporate U.S. Asian American men on the privileged side of its logics.[15] In a related trajectory, Iyko Day reads this history in relation to settler colonial logics, tracing how the railroad workers provide a means through which to track the intersections of Asian labor and capital with the consolidation of settler colonial projects that hinge on the dispossession of Indigenous peoples and lands.[16] In regard to Asian labor in Hawai'i, scholars such as Haunani-Kay Trask, Candace Fujikane, and Jonathan Y. Okamura have argued that this emphasis on early Chinese labor, and its subsequent role in the plantation economy, feeds into the narratives of "local" identity. Trask writes: "Exploitative plantation conditions thus underpin a master narrative of hard work and the endlessly celebrated triumph over anti-Asian racism."[17] Fujikane and Okamura maintain that "ethnic histories written about Asians in Hawai'i demonstrate an investment in the ideal of American democracy that is ideologically at odds with indigenous critiques of U.S. colonialism."[18]

As each of these scholars suggest, while the historiographical celebration of the Chinese railroad worker may provide a necessary picture of the racialized dimensions of U.S. settlements westward, it has done so by affirming a compulsory U.S. American masculinity that implicitly upholds narratives of national progress calibrated by colonial capitalist sensibilities of space, time, and tense. In *Iron Cages,* Ronald Takaki traces how white settlers conceptualized the formation of national progress along the space of the frontier. Takaki pinpoints the comparative racial rhetoric through which dominant narratives of the period incorporated Chinese immigrants into this timeline of the nation: On the one hand, Chinese were rendered technologically advanced when their labor was necessary, on the other hand, Chinese were rendered unassimilable and backward when their labor was no longer needed. The crux of Takaki's argument is how these representations of the Chinese hinged on a racial calibration that triangulated Asian people with black and white people in the United States. Thus, the technological advancement of the Chinese, their incorporation into the forward movement of progress, was always already dependent on an opposing rendering of the black community. Following this logic of racial triangulation, the historiographical revival of U.S. Asian American (back-breaking) labor also already inflects the temporal framing of Indigenous nations. Often understated in Takaki's analyses is how the very space for the formation of national progress is produced through the clearing of Indigenous lands, lands on which these cross-racial dialogics continue to take place. Thus, the compulsory masculinity of the frontier, as attached to the Chinese railroad workers in alternative historiographies, also upholds the imperatives of settlement that render Indigenous peoples as obstacles to progress. Takaki cites former New York governor Horatio Seymour in his celebration of the railroad as violating Indigenous lands and thus the Indigenous community of human/nonhuman familial relationships:

Today we are dividing the lands of the native Indians into states, counties and townships. We are driving off their property the game *upon which they live,* by railroads. We tell them plainly, they must give up their homes and property, and live upon corners of territories because they are in the way of our civilization.[19]

Despite more recent discussions about the role of Chinese immigrant labor in the destruction and partitioning of Indigenous lands, the heroic tradition has largely celebrated the laborer's aid in the potential future of the settler nation and assumed that the conquering of Indigenous land had already been actuated, placing this part of history into the past perfect.

Like the U.S. Asian American heroic tradition, the Native American warrior tradition has occupied a contested space in Indigenous oppositional practices of memorialization. Like Chin's exaltation of the martial tradition in Chinese cultural forms and formations, the Native American warrior tradition often centers the physical strength and valor of Native warriors who have valiantly fought against U.S. colonial encroachment. Yet, as Kingston's gendered revision of the martial tradition in *The Woman Warrior* reveals, such emphasis on warriors within the community is not monolithic and unproblematized.[20] Most visible in the memorialization of figures such as Crazy Horse, the warrior tradition honors Native heroes who represent ongoing Native traditions, models of Native masculinity, and enduring resistance to colonial encroachment.[21] In literature, the memorialization of the warrior tradition produces consistent tropes that emphasize present and ongoing Indigenous resistance to colonial occupation. In addition to questions surrounding the elisions of gender and sexuality, writers such as Sherman Alexie (among many others) think through the efficacy and possibilities of the warrior tradition as a key modality of contemporary Indigenous resistance. In her reading of Alexie's *Fancydancing,* Becca Gercken argues that Alexie's warriors "at their best, invoke the traditions of Crazy Horse as an assertion of their own survival and Indian-ness. At their worst, the men invoke Crazy Horse to justify violence against themselves or others."[22] Vizenor's *Manifest Manners* also engages with the warrior tradition, delineating a chasm between the "kitschymen of the resistance enterprises" and the work of "postindian warriors of survivance."[23] Vizenor utilizes Matei Calinescu's definition of kitsch as an "aesthetic make-believe and self-deception [that is a] reaction against the 'terror' of change and the meaninglessness of chronological time flowing from an unreal past into an equally unreal future."[24] Attributing this notion of kitsch to figures who romanticize the image of the warrior, Vizenor writes that "the kitschymen soothe the nostalgia for manifest manners and the melancholy of dominance."[25] As such, Vizenor suggests that an embrace of the warrior tradition as a melancholic revival of a colonial and romanticized rendering of the past iterates rather than contests colonial simulations and colonial narratives of progress. Where the U.S. Asian American heroic tradition can potentially uphold narratives of American progress that render Native peoples in the past perfect, Vizenor suggests that the Native warrior tradition can reproduce this past perfect as a temporal loop within the affective formations of Indigenous communities. Fittingly, then, Vizenor's gesture toward an alternative memorialization of the Native warrior tradition speaks explicitly to its necessary relationship to Indigenous futurity.

The Native American warrior tradition is closely connected to the Native American veteran tradition of the twentieth century.[26] As Al Carroll notes, the warrior tradition comprises "cultural and spiritual practices" that were carried over into veteran traditions. Carroll argues that many Indigenous studies scholars have critiqued the veteran tradition as acceding to colonial logics and assimilationist imperatives of the United States. Rather than seeing the veteran tradition simply as upholding these imperatives, Carroll highlights how Native participation in war, and their subsequent veneration, is more explicitly tied to an investment in the futurity of Native nations. In addition, reading the Native veteran within the context of Native sovereignty ostensibly expands the meanings of the veteran beyond settler logics. That is, repudiating the notion that warrior traditions were simply romantic reenactments of the past, Carroll writes, "traditionally a warrior society carried out an amalgam of the roles of policing and supervising hunts and raids, teaching the young, caring for the elderly and helpless, punishing criminals, and carrying out a wide variety of rituals that varied greatly from tribe to tribe." He continues, "Veterans took the place of traditional tribal warriors" and adapted to the present needs and considerations of the community: "teaching, charitable, and ritual functions continued but with a modern element."[27] With this forward focus on Native national futurity, Carroll suggests two ways to "build better alternative traditions" that can ensure the endurance of Native communities.[28] The first promotes the recognition of other forms of heroism within Native societies, heroism that supports Native survivance. The second option, not mutually exclusive of the first, is to "syncretize warrior traditions with activism," whereby a nourishing of activism within and for Native communities produces materially constituted zones where combat may be necessary.[29] While taking seriously how the veteran tradition undergirds U.S. assimilationist, colonial, and imperial violence, he concludes by stating his desire to continue to support Native veterans: "What I certainly do not want to say is that Natives should honor veterans any less. As a veteran from a long line of veterans, I see that acts of honoring are the greater part of what enables veterans to bear their own pains more easily."[30]

These critiques of the heroic and warrior traditions express the deep anxieties about the function of alternative historiographies in the heteropatriarchal context of U.S. settler colonial and empire building. In addition to pointing out the ways that the celebration of these figures can undergird the racial, colonial, and imperial asymmetries of U.S. power, scholars have highlighted the ways such traditions can contribute to the affective attachment to the settler nation itself—an attachment that scholars have pointed out is conditioned by the foreclosure of Native futurity.[31] Yet, in pointing to the possibilities of healing that are present in honoring Native veterans, Carroll suggests that the emotional import in the warrior tradition is an active necessity for the survivance of Native nations, rather than an acceding to the terms of settlement. In fact, he argues that the memory and veneration of the warrior figure can rupture the very logics of U.S. imperialism and settlement. This rupture is made possible through the reinvestment of the Native warrior within traditional Native epistemologies. He writes:

> Contrary to what is portrayed in old Hollywood movies, generally Native spiritual beliefs teach that warfare is an unnatural or disruptive state, one that must be extensively ritually prepared for to survive with mind and body intact. Ceremonies before war protect and prepare the soldier. Ceremonies after the war honor his service and, like the songs, reintegrate him into the community and out of the unnatural state of war.[32]

Carroll's reflection suggests that the honoring of war veterans can disrupt rather than celebrate the commonsense settler notion of war itself; in addition, the veteran and his service, when rendered in traditional Native epistemologies, is seen as "unnatural" rather than natural to the order of Native community vitality.

Per my discussion here of the U.S. Asian American heroic tradition and the Native warrior tradition, the elision of gender and sexuality is part and parcel of the uneven and staggered consolidation of U.S. colonial and imperial projects. In short, the heroic tradition draws on affective attachments to the taking and processing of Indigenous lands in the consolidation of U.S. capital, while the veteran tradition often draws on patriotic sentiments toward imperial incursion across the Pacific to multiple Asian nations and settlement at home. As is evident from this overview, the stakes of historiography are high, and its spatial and temporal investments can inform possibilities for conjuring community alliances and coalitions that disrupt the entanglements of U.S. imperial and colonial logics. I now turn to two creative historiographies (or, texts of historiographic metafiction) that self-reflexively encounter the affective function of these hero/warrior traditions as part and parcel of U.S. settler racial hegemonies. As Linda Hutcheon argues, historiographic metafiction consists of texts "which are both intensely self-reflexive and yet paradoxically also lay claim to historical events and personages." She finds that the form's "theoretical self-awareness of history and fiction as human constructs (historiographic metafiction) is made the grounds for its rethinking and reworking of the forms and contents of the past."[33] In Kingston's and Vizenor's renarration of the past, this emphasis on history and fiction as constructs helps to demonstrate how the hero/warrior traditions participate in the heteropatriarchal consolidation of the state at the same time as the narratives "lay claim to" moments of ruptures that exist at the interstices of settler racial hegemonies.[34]

Maxine Hong Kingston's *China Men*

Written as a companion piece to *The Woman Warrior* (1976), Maxine Hong Kingston's *China Men* (1980) reimagines the lives of her Chinese male relatives through a self-reflexive historiography of their migrations to and labor for the United States and Hawaiʻi. While the former text centers on the impact of four "warrior women," the latter highlights the centrality of the male relatives in Maxine's, the narrator's, life. These two projects also diverge in their formal concerns: where *The Woman Warrior* sought to destabilize dominant understandings of autobiography/fiction, *China Men* critiqued the assumptions structuring the historiographical form. Organized into six substantial sections dedicated to major male figures in her life, and also interspersed with smaller pieces that engage mythic and legal/juridical details, Kingston's historiography immediately punctures perceived formal qualities of the genre. Rather than present these histories through an objective narration, Kingston's work frames the conjuring of this past as a constructed act of the imagination.[35] Thus, captured within the frame are instances that do not seem to have a place in legitimated historiographies: the indeterminacies of relations, leaps to conjecture, and ghostly presences (all of which also take on textual real estate in *The Woman Warrior*). In doing so, the narrative opens up questions about the workings and limits of historiography, and particularly its role in providing a usable past for the present. This generic destabilization coincides with the text's deep critique of the material and sociopolitical efficacy of the U.S. Asian American heroic tradition as an alternative historiographical enterprise.[36] While previous criticism on Kingston's *China Men* has tended to highlight feminist engagement with masculinist perspectives on history, I instead examine how the narrative grapples with the U.S. Asian

American heroic tradition's relationship to liberal settler narratives that continue to rely on the colonial erasure of Indigenous communities.[37]

In this section, I examine ephemeral moments of crossings between U.S. Asian American and Indigenous peoples as they are represented in Kingston's metahistorical narrative. I argue that such meetings dramatize the U.S. Asian American heroic tradition as a complicated cultural formation that, although critical of the United States, continues to invoke settler structures of feeling that erase the presence of Native peoples. In Kingston's narrative, depictions of Chinese immigrant laborers' struggles for survival and belonging often reiterate liberal settler narratives, emphasizing the triumph of the individual. Most frequently, this emphasis is achieved through the romanticization of the (racialized) settler subject as he integrates with Indigenous peoples ("going Native") and works to tame Indigenous lands. Kingston's heroic subject's triumph centers on liberal narratives of cross-racial belonging and solidarity among laborers, narratives that may differ from white settler imaginaries of "going Native" but nevertheless perpetuate the elision of Indigenous economies and struggles for sovereignty and self-determination. At the same time, Kingston's self-reflexive and creative rendering of the past, which emphasizes ghostly encounters, conveys also the laborers' intuitions of uneasiness and feelings of hauntings even in scenes of liberatory achievement. I argue that these destabilizing moments operate as emotional ruptures of settler common sense, revealing both the affective economies and the limits of settler racial hegemonies.

In a famous interview, Kingston argues that *China Men* is her way of "claiming America" for her Chinese forebears.[38] This claiming exacts not only a spatial but also a temporal belonging through the emphasis on Chinese immigrant labor. Such claiming is connected to white settler logics of space and time, which in turn hinges on the encroachment of Indigenous lands and the destabilization of Indigenous lives and livelihoods therein. As scholars such as Jace Weaver and Louis Owens illuminate, representations of Indigenous disappearance, distilled in the trope of the vanishing Indian, are inextricably linked to white settler claims over the land and to autochthony. Of this process, Owens writes that "the real Indians all disappeared long ago, the fantasy [of the dying Indian] insists. It is sad, but that is just one of the inevitabilities of history. Believing this, the conqueror is free to shed a crocodile tear for the people he has exterminated and romanticize them as an invaluable aspect of his—colonial—past."[39] As Owens's statement suggests, the affective energies emerging out of these projections of the Native provide the psychical space through which encroachment and possession can be legitimated. Guilt, sadness, mourning, and the shedding of "crocodile tears" about the dying Indian relegate the Native to the past, producing not only a virtualized and virtuous clearing of the land but also a cleansing of the emotional space from which a forging of a regenerated settler national spirit can be enacted. While Owens focuses primarily on how this central trope figures in the production of white settler identity and belonging, Kingston's imaginative historiography implicitly acknowledges and attempts to negotiate such problematic constructions of the "Native" in her narrative memorialization of her Chinese American forebears.

At first glance, in *China Men,* the assertion of belonging for Chinese laborers repeats a colonial claiming of space and time that depends on the disappearance of Indigenous peoples. Indeed, Indigenous figures appear mostly in narratives about the narrator Maxine's ancestors along the "frontier" and largely disappear from view in the stories set after the turn of the nineteenth century—the historic period that historian Frederick Jackson Turner suggests is the end of the frontier era.[40] In the scenes where Native figures do appear, they often emerge as remnants of a decimated community or as spectral presences. This is most explicit in "The Great Grandfather of the Sandalwood Mountains," a chapter about the experiences of the narrator's great-grandfathers, Bak Goong and Bak Sook Goong, laboring in the sugarcane fields of Hawai'i during the middle of the nineteenth century. Immediately after Bak Goong arrives from China, Kingston narrates his walk toward the cane fields, where he encounters a land full of lush fruits juxtaposed with a "hutment of grass shacks [where] they did not see brown people come and go," implying that the area had been abandoned.[41] Such absent presence continues on another day, when Bak Goong encounters an abandoned but haunted Native Hawaiian village while taking a walk on his day off from laboring in the sugarcane fields. There he sees the spectral appearance of a Native woman urging him to enter into the space. However, being spooked, Bak Goong abandons the village, never to look back. While the presence of Native peoples continues to haunt the space, Kingston's depiction of Bak Goong's first entry into Hawai'i suggests that the clearing of Native presence has largely already been enacted.

Where Indigenous figures do appear outside of the ghostly, they work to legitimize the Asian presence in Hawai'i. This insertion of the Native figure as a form of legitimization echoes another grand narrative of settlement, where desires to eradicate Indigenous presence coincide with desires to inhabit "Indianness." Owens describes this process as an "erotics of deadly desire" that is linked inextricably to the "perverse and almost grossly paradoxical yearning to be Indian, to inhabit not merely the continent but the original inhabitant as well. Ultimately, the dark heart of this desire is to kill and replace the Indian."⁴² In replacing the Indian, however, the settler does not become fully incorporated as an Indian but transforms the wilderness to his own ends, thus metamorphosing to a distinctly "American" character. Upon encountering the racist naming of one of the islands as "Chinaman's Hat," Maxine quickly asserts, "But Hawai'i people call us Paké, which is their way of pronouncing Bak-ah, Uncle. They even call Chinese women Paké."⁴³ Kingston here takes the term "Paké," a deeply localized racial slur usually meant for the Chinese, and usually implying that a person is cheap, and reformulates it, retranslating it, so as to align the Chinese with the Hawaiians as part of an extended family.

Besides presuming the Native Hawaiians' legitimation of the Chinese as "family," the narrative also imagines scenes of racial mixing that further dramatize the narrator's assertions of Asian belonging on the islands. Bak Sook Goong, the narrator's other great-grandfather, serves as the figure through which this process of U.S. Asian American belonging is discursively enacted. On his day off, Bak Sook Goong happens across a pool of bathing Native women who invite him to join them. In his amazement he exclaims that this is "just like the stories," and he proceeds to ask that they take him home and make him one of their family. This story goes on to conclude that Bak Sook Goong "became the godfather of many Hawaiian children. 'Paké godfather,' they called him."⁴⁴ In both her great-grandfathers' stories, the narrator includes Native people insofar as they can legitimate her forebears' settler presence, a move that has a long white settler colonial history. In Bak Sook Goong's narrative in particular, he comes out of the sexually suggestive scene as a godfather of subsequent Native children while still maintaining his own sense of identity as Chinese, not fully assimilating with the Native in the process and thus in a sense not vanishing into "Indianness." While this maintenance of his ethnic difference potentially disrupts his claiming of "Nativeness" through blood relations, it also potentially sets the stage for his being able to "replace the Indian."⁴⁵

The figure of the "Native" continues to propel the narrative's assertion of U.S. Asian American belonging in the chapter entitled "The Grandfather of the Sierra Nevada Mountains." This chapter gestures most explicitly to the U.S. Asian American heroic tradition in its focus on the narrator's grandfather Ah Goong's experience as a laborer for the transcontinental railroad in the late nineteenth century. In an intriguing scene during the historic strike of the Chinese railroad workers, Kingston narrates Ah Goong's illegal purchase of citizenship papers. This scene dramatizes the symbolic emergence of the Chinese American figure via citizenship, a citizenship that continues to hinge on the spectral figuration of the Indian. Kingston narrates:

> In a woods—he [Ah Goong] would be looking at a deer or a rabbit or an Injun watching him before he knew what he was seeing—a demon dressed in a white suit and tall hat beckoned him. They talked privately in the wilderness. The demon said, "I Citizenship Judge invite you to be a U.S. citizen. Only one bag of gold." He would accept this invitation. Also what advantages, he calculated shrewdly; if he were going to be jailed for this strike, an American would have a trial. He was already a part of this new country, but now he had it in writing.[46]

Here the Native, dubbed an "Injun," is again not physically present, now interchangeable with a deer and a rabbit, yet still serving as an important figure in the moment that marks Ah Goong's incorporation as a U.S. citizen.[47] Such a scene distinctly echoes moments of emergence of the American character as posited by Turner's frontier thesis. For Turner, the process of forging a distinctive (explicitly European) American character happens through the frontiersman's "taming" of the wilderness and of other successive frontiers. The taming that occurs creates not only the American character but also the changing infrastructures of the United States as the nation moves (violently) westward.[48] In Kingston's narrative, the fact that Ah Goong's attainment of citizenship happens in what Kingston terms "a woods," suggests through its spatial orientation Kingston's claiming of this distinctly frontier character for her Chinese American forebear.

This frontier character is strengthened by Kingston's multiple attempts to position the Chinese railroad laborers as "cowboys."[49] Through the voices of the workers as well as through the narration itself, Kingston writes that, like cowboys, her relatives are the "building ancestors of this place" by way of their often violent "marking [of] the land"— that is seen not only on the literal grounds of the Américas but also on the very bodies of the Chinese workers.[50] By positing violence as the means through which Chinese American belonging is forged, Kingston's narrative invokes the discourses, prevalent in the nineteenth century, that celebrate the connection between violent masculinity and the making of a distinct American national identity. According to Takaki, for example, Lieutenant Colonel George Armstrong Custer "personified [for settlers] the masculine advance guard of civilization."[51] For Custer, masculine regeneration, and the particularly American character, can be forged only through forceful experiences along the frontier. In a letter to his wife, Custer suggests that the men in their town "try their fortunes in the enterprising western country, where the virtues of real manhood come quickly to the surface."[52] Takaki continues: "There beyond the railroad and beyond the telegraph, Custer could still 'indulge in the wild Western life with all of its pleasures and excitements,' and recover the 'virtues of real manhood.'"[53] In particular, Custer takes this violent encroachment on Native land as the stage on which the necessary spectacle, ritual, and performance of masculinity is actuated.[54] For Turner, this forging of frontier masculinity requires a continual exercise of "pleasurable" violence—violence exacted on "wild" Indigenous lands—and thus a repetitive exercise contingent on the existence and yet necessary eradication of Indigenous peoples.[55]

Kingston's citizenship scene, when Ah Goong purportedly sees an Indian figure, symbolizes the continual settler reliance on the overtaking of Indigenous space and time. Ah Goong is unable to distinguish the Indian from an animal or, in fact, from any material figure whatsoever. As Kingston describes it: "In a woods—he [Ah Goong] would be looking at a deer or a rabbit or an Injun."[56] This inability to distinguish the Indian anywhere on the continuum of fact and fiction, or even that of person and animal, situates this figure in the space of mythic time. The narrative, too, punctuates this notion of mythic time by calling the space "a woods." The scene suggests that Ah Goong's spatial identification with citizenship along the frontier is immanently structured by the rendering of Indigenous peoples within a temporal loop that operates, as Jodi Byrd has argued, like a meme, through the physical forging of Indigenous lands.[57]

While perhaps it may be fitting to read this depiction purely as an iteration of white settler logics, the fact that the narrative is explicitly invested in "claiming America" for Maxine's Chinese forebears suggests the triangulated relations through which settler logics come into being. As Day and Byrd have argued, the relationship between settler, arrivant or alien, and Indigenous communities reveals the shifting racialization that makes possible the movements of capital within a settler colonial enterprise. The ways that Kingston's narrative relies on Indigenous figurations thus reveal the different roles the white settler and racialized communities play in working to reiterate settler logics.[58]

Returning to the chapter of *China Men* set in Hawai'i, notions of belonging are not solely imagined through the incorporation of the Chinese American figure into the extended Hawaiian family, as we see in Bak Sook Goong's narrative. Rather, Kingston more clearly portrays a notion of family and local incorporation in a scene of after-work communion—that is, through the breaking of bread among sugarcane laborers that includes but is not centered on Hawaiian people. The "eating system," established by the more senior workers, includes the ceremony where

> they passed around candy before dinner [and the] few Hawaiian workers passed around salt. Chinese take a bit of sugar to remind

them in times of bitter struggle the sweetness of life, and Hawaiians take a few grains of salt on the tongue because it tastes like the sea, like the earth, like human sweat and tears.⁵⁹

Although the passage does not explain the reason for there being such a "few" Hawaiian workers, the sharing of different cultural beliefs and practices creates a form of intimate community where "strangers ate *like family,* drank from the same soup tureen, ate from the same plates of accompaniments of rice."⁶⁰ Bak Goong's entry and assimilation into Native Hawaiian territory occur through a form of intimacy forged out of shared struggle, communion, and care constituted through the body. This scene, as with the earlier scene of Bak Sook Goong among the Native women, attempts to resist the implications and politics tied up in charges of cultural appropriation, racial mixing, and assertions of blood relationality.⁶¹

Although she disengages from the Euro-American myths of the vanishing Indian, the narrator's assertions of Chinese American belonging in this chapter—based on invocations of shared struggle among Native, Chinese, and other ethnic workers—presage the Asian settler and Kānaka Maoli collisions at play in Hawaiian politics today. In particular, the scene of communal eating invokes claims of the "local," which are so dynamically central in formulations of Asian immigrant identity on the islands, but which have overlooked the sovereignty struggles of Native Hawaiians. On identifying with notions of the "local," Fujikane warns "how easy and dangerous it is . . . for us to adopt egalitarian narratives of local 'solidarity' that hide systemic racism and our colonial status from view."⁶² This status is intimately connected to the spatiotemporal structuring of settlement. That is, the emphasis on shared struggle through the lens of labor positions Indigenous peoples within capitalist modes of production and naturalizes the capitalist domain over space and division of time. As such, while this scene of communion among the laborers diverges from earlier tropes of the vanishing Indian, it does so by reproducing the givenness of upholding Asian immigrant belonging through capitalist rubrics of settlement.⁶³ Indigenous peoples, who are necessary for the legitimation of belonging, are here recognized only insofar as they contribute to the reproduction of the labor of settlement. Other Indigenous approaches to the division of time and space are left unrepresented in this historiographical scene. This depiction of such naturalization opens up questions of what other forms of communion, of alliances, coalitions, and solidarities, might be imagined outside of the incorporation of Indigenous peoples within settler racial capitalist modes of production. That is, in its reworking of the U.S. Asian American heroic tradition, does the narrative suggest different ways of framing Asian immigrant labor and presence—

specifically, ways of framing it in relation to Indigenous economies and epistemologies—that can track the fissures of settler racial hegemonic productions of capitalist time and space?

Keeping my attention continually on the problematic representation of the vanishing Indian or settlers going Native, I now want to examine more closely the symbolic and emotional geographies that permeate Kingston's own rendering of this colonial trope. I argue that, through the self-reflexive and indeterminate way that Kingston narrates these scenes of Chinese American formation and belonging, the text exposes the symbolic and emotional geographies that signal ruptures within settler national logics. King-Kok Cheung has argued that *China Men* generates "polyphony" in that the text's attentiveness to racial inequities is simultaneously woven through with its emphasis on gender exclusions. I argue that this polyphony resonates with other categorical registers so that the scenes of the vanishing and ghostly Indians are invested with a sense of the past that is not fixed or "given" but rather epistemologically capacious. This rendering of the past thus becomes a space for emotional excesses adjacent to settler affective investments in Indigenous dispossession and disappearance.[64] Put another way, the ghostly hauntings of Indigenous peoples in the narrative can be described, via scholar Danika Medak-Saltzman, as the "spirit of an idea" that conveys the logics and erasures of settler racial common sense.[65] I argue that these indeterminacies productively wrack the narrative, unveiling the different relational temporalities and spatialities that are obscured when the sole emphasis is on settler capitalist constructions of time and space.

It is in the context of Kingston's polyphonic narrative that the symbolism of ghosts functions differently; that is, they have a resonant symbolic economy that exceeds the colonialist image of the vanishing Indian trope. In the most elemental terms, ghostly presences explode containers of space, time, and tense. The ghost is simultaneously here and elsewhere, it represents both past and present, and can cue us to anticipate particular visions of futurity.[66] Coupled with the narrative's polyphonic voice, ghostly Native presences cue the readers to consider an elided past, present, and future that is foreclosed by the narrative's own historiographical imperatives. In short, ghostly presences in *China Men* can point toward settler national, alien, *as well as* Indigenous epistemologies of time and space.

This excess of meaning is most apparent in the previously referenced scene in Hawaiʻi, where Bak Goong encounters an abandoned Native village and the ghostly presence of a Native Hawaiian woman. In the scene, Bak Goong is spooked by sounds emanating from deep within the huts and tries to reason that they were only the sounds of some wild animal. Yet the wailings persist, inviting Bak Goong to join in their sorrow. Kingston writes:

He heard sobs, the lamentations of old men and children, thousands of souls wailing in separate voices. He could not make out the quivering words, or it was a language he did not know. . . . He felt like weeping in sympathy; sorrow filled his chest, but he kept the tears back not to blind himself as he ran out of the village.[67]

As he struggles to leave the place, Bak Goong is once again invited to join in the pain—this time by the aforementioned ghostly Native woman who gestures to him to enter the commotion. When she touches him, however, Bak Goong is too unsettled by the "supernatural" to enter and leaves "quickly, rudely."[68] In this moment, Bak Goong is invited to enter a cacophony of sounds, the meanings of which overwhelm him with an abundance of feeling that he refuses to fully acknowledge and process. Rather than being a meaningless site of emotional excess, the ghostly sounds communicate through a language that Bak Goong cannot—and after his refusal to enter, will not—take into consideration. This experience, which takes place on one of his days off from work, illuminates his complicity in obscuring violent settler projects and gives form to the ethical ramifications of such elisions. That is, Bak Goong's refusal to enter the ghostly scene symbolizes his inabilities to acknowledge settler violence on Indigenous lands and peoples as well as his own relationship to such processes. Moreover, his refusal to enter the hut dramatizes not only the obscuring of violent U.S. Asian American and Indigenous convergences within settler histories but also the present and future knowledge that can emerge through the conjuring of such histories. Indeed, what is lost is not solely Bak Goong's attentiveness to settler violation of Kānaka Maoli peoples, and his relationship therein, but the potential knowledge that can be produced when Kānaka Maoli histories "touch" Bak Goong's own histories.

Where Bak Goong refuses to go, however, the double voice in the narrative invites the reader to enter. In this sense, the text conveys the space of what Byrd theorizes as the "cacophony of empire," where hegemonic organizing principles break down to convey alternative epistemologies that are hidden by the settler imperial project.[69] The seemingly illegible scene conjures all-too-legible historical scenes of violent colonial relations, particularly those that led to and resulted from the decimation of Native Hawaiian communities after the revision to the 1848 Hawaiian Land Distribution Act (the Great Mahele) that allowed "foreign residents" to buy and lease land.[70] Bak Goong's presence alludes to the role of Chinese contract labor in this history and positions the U.S. Asian American figure as a complicit participant and witness. Although Bak Goong refuses to enter this space of cacophony, the narrative invokes the absent presence of the potential knowledge and ethical relations that are closed off by his departure.

The scene of cacophony and the narrative's gesture toward it convey not only the spatiotemporalities closed off by settler racial epistemologies but also their structures of feeling. That is, while the repetition of the stock image of "Indianness" often works to congeal affective investments of sympathy for the dying Indian into the time and tense of settler consolidation (as a psychical space through which to mourn and clear the ground for settler notions of belonging), here the double-voicing and ghostly imagery in the scene instead points to and possibly generates emotional ruptures. This is to say, the scene participates in the bracketing of settler racial structures of feeling; the double-voicing and the ghostly imagery forestall the movement of sympathies (both Bak Goong's and the reader's) toward the directionality of settler racial time and tense. With its emphasis on the soundscape of sorrow and Bak Goong's almost uncontainable unease, the narrative conveys the instabilities and failures of settler colonialism as a totalizing hegemonic process. Although Bak Goong moves forward in his day, the reader is invited to enter the space of affective possibilities and potentiality, but with no element of resolution. The haunting scene thus makes visceral the instabilities that can potentially rupture the progression to settler catharsis. Indeed, ruptures of catharsis are the affective element structuring the entire narrative; I argue that these ruptures begin as nascent intensities embedded within and disrupting the settler common sense that permeates Asian immigrant narratives of labor and multiculturalist inclusion into the settler nation. This moment of cathartic denial reveals (albeit only momentarily) opportunities to suspend settler place making that exploits the mourning of the vanishing Indian as U.S. Asian American labor transits through capitalist modes of production and memory making.

These ruptures of settler catharsis also permeate the rest of the narrative. Stories that purportedly highlight the masculine valor and vigor of Maxine's male forebears are repeatedly truncated. From scenes where Maxine's grandfather Ah Goong is cutting down redwood trees to moments where he performs a supposed mastery and sexual dominance over the earth by masturbating and ejaculating into a chasm in the ground, the narrative nods to the violence structuring the heroic tradition and in turn recenters land-based perspectives, histories, and knowledge and opens the opportunity to engage Indigenous-centered land-based epistemologies, or what Glen Coulthard terms "grounded normativity."[71] Of the former scene, Kingston writes: "The tree swayed and slowly dived to earth, creaking and screeching like a green animal. . . . The trunk lay like a red torso; sap ran from its cuts like crying blind eyes. At last it stopped fighting."[72] In these scenes, by anthropomorphizing the land and imagining the trees' death throes, the narrative draws attention to what is lost other than the human. Arguably, the imagery of the "red torso" implies the relationship between the bleeding Earth and the violence enacted on Indigenous communities and lands. Ah Goong witnesses this scene with "awe," forgetting momentarily his work. In this sense, the narrative again reveals the possible affective ruptures along the telos of settler time, space, and structures of feeling, suggesting the openings that are always immanent in the process of settler racial hegemonies.

Images of the ghostly and dying Indian, together with the narrative trope of "taming" the land, seem at first to repeat white settler structures of feeling. However, in Kingston's imagination this repetition is never fully complete. I now turn to how Gerald Vizenor's work grapples with Native and Japanese warrior traditions in the context of occupation-era Japan.

Gerald Vizenor's *Hiroshima Bugi: Atomu 57*

Published in 2003, *Hiroshima Bugi: Atomu 57* depicts the stories and adventures of Ronin Browne, a "*hafu*," or "cross-blood," orphan of a Japanese woman named Okichi and an Anishinaabe soldier called Nightbreaker. Most of Ronin's adventures occur in Japan and center on his abilities to unsettle and critique the multitude of memorials that have been erected in the name of peace and memorials to honor Japanese warriors in the aftermath of World War II. Ronin's protestations of these forms of memorialization in Japan take on an embodied and performative aspect.[73] For Ronin, the memory work that occupies official memorial spaces in Japan hides the complex histories of imperial and colonial wars and thus neutralizes the stories and possibilities of "survivance" for Native, cross-blood or mixed-blood, and other marginalized peoples. Ronin's performances are framed in two narrative points of view. The first is narrated in a densely relational and academic tone that elucidates and expands on the multitudinous references that occupy Ronin's story, while the second is told from Ronin's first-person perspective as it is reconstructed from pieces of his journal writings over the years. The narrator of the former perspective is Nightbreaker's best friend, called Manidoo Envoy, whom Ronin meets at the Hotel Manidoo in Nogales, Arizona, a place of residence for wounded Native veterans. Upon visiting the hotel, while searching for his father (who died only days before), Ronin is inspired to share his personal journals so that the community at the hotel would be able to integrate them into the larger process of "perfect memory" making. Through this narrative frame, the novel invests in expanding memories of World War II beyond national demarcations of space and time.

The connections that Vizenor draws between Asian and Indigenous histories and traditions are not his first. His earlier novel, *Griever: An American Monkey King in China,* emerges from his personal experience in China as a

Fulbright instructor.⁷⁴ In *Hiroshima Bugi: Atomu 57*, however, imaginations of Native presences in Japan reflect Vizenor's personal background in the U.S. Army, and also speak to the prevalence of Native military service for the United States.⁷⁵ In centering Indigenous movements across the Pacific to Japan, Vizenor's work traces the intersections of U.S. settler colonial and imperial technologies, and the often-elided relationalities and intimacies that can be drawn from these material histories. In her reading of the text, Jeanne Sokolowski writes that "Vizenor's narrative coupling of occupation-era Japan with Native American populations draws on the unexpected parallel of their status as 'dependents' of the United States."⁷⁶ She continues:

> Intellectuals of both Japan studies and Native American studies make arguments for an ongoing colonial presence in these locations, suggesting that both Native American nationalists in the United States and Japanese neonationalists (especially during the turbulent 1990s) have struggled and continue to do so against the continuing colonial efforts of the U.S. government in their respective drives for autonomy and assertion of their sovereignty.⁷⁷

In a similar vein, Byrd details how "Vizenor links Japanese and indigenous peoples who are drawn together and pulled apart by imperial, colonialist, and militaristic violences as well as the uranium sourced from American Indian lands and exploded as 'Little Boy' above Hiroshima."⁷⁸ Both critics discuss how these often-obscured histories not only trace relationalities wrought from colonial and imperial wars but also provide a context for thinking through a mode of moral survivance that contains "a vision and vital condition to endure, to outwit evil and dominance, and to deny victimry."⁷⁹ In particular, for Byrd, against facile narratives of victimry, Vizenor illuminates the complicity of Japan and Native Americans in the violent production of empire. In so doing, he creates a "trans-Pacific indigenous ethic that confronts the inherited complicities of globalization."⁸⁰ Furthermore, Vizenor fashions an Indigenous-centered epistemology and aesthetic that can productively confront these spatially expansive and ethically complex histories of empire and settlement.

In conversation with these scholars, I here trace the connections that Vizenor makes between the peace and warrior traditions in both Native American/Indigenous and Japanese nations. In particular, Vizenor's narrative shows how such traditions/memorials collude in the process of "remembering and forgetting" that is central to the constitution of what Jodi Kim calls "liberal capitalist consuming and productive subjects."⁸¹ In conjuring these connections, Vizenor reveals the liberal logics of U.S. settler colonialism and imperialism in a postwar era that is reliant on the extenuated "service" of Native American/Indigenous and Japanese communities through the memorialization of the war. I specifically focus on how these memorials and traditions can reproduce colonial grammars that cordon off the violence of the past from the present, hold the necessity for peace in the future tense, and produce mythic figurations that fuel the desirous circuits of consumption through the cult of celebrity. These tense logics structuring the traditions/memorials are critical to U.S. global economic imperatives and the incorporation of Japan as a "junior partner" during the postwar era.[82]

Adjacent to and present within these memorial sites are figures that destabilize imperial and settler colonial productions of time and tense. The narrative specifically centers ghostly figures, American Indian veterans, and traveling cross-blood figures who carry alternative memories and structures of feeling elided by dominant memorials of war. Emphasizing these figures' embodiments, Vizenor's text conveys the potential for global transformation and Indigenous survivance when the memories of these characters are shared. Taken together, these figures unsettle settler and imperial global capitalist productions of space, time, and tense.

In the novel, the main character, Ronin, is concerned with critically destabilizing both the war *and* peace memorials that are erected in Japan after World War II. This motivation is most evident in the chapters that center on the Atomic Bomb Dome, the adjacent Peace Memorial Museum, and a Shinto shrine called the Yasukuni Jinja, all of which are key memorial sites in Japan. Since they are memorials in the context of Japanese national histories, the narrative most directly implicates Japanese nationalist modes of memory making. However, by framing Ronin's performative critiques through the visionary storytelling of the Native veterans at Hotel Manidoo, the narrative invokes the connections between the memorials in Japan and those that are produced in the United States, particularly those that relate to Native American/Indigenous peoples and histories. Through his embodied mimicry of the memorials, Ronin depicts the ways that memorials across colonial sites can propel the emotional forces of nationalist, imperialist, and settler colonial attachments.

As elucidated by Ronin and the Manidoo Envoy, the story begins with Ronin's presence and actions within the Atomic Bomb Dome—one of the major edifices in Hiroshima that stands in ruins after the bombing. Ronin is one among many who perished at this site and who currently haunt its ruins alongside the ghostly parade of children who "rush their stories under the dome."[83] Declaring the dome his "Rashomon," Ronin immediately represents this space as one in which memories percolate and refract in a multitude of singular, overlapping, and yet contradictory stories.[84] To Ronin, this

"Rashomon" constitutes "a theater of . . . perfect memories" where the experiences of those like Ronin and his friend Oshima (a leper) are indeterminately entangled.[85]

Although these "perfect" memories continue to permeate this space, Ronin traces the Dome's transformation into a political marker of Japanese nationalism and economic enterprise. The effects of this transformation are tragic; it encloses the memories of the past, and Ronin himself, in what he describes as a perpetual "diorama of victimry," which instigates "passive notions of peace."[86] Ronin notes: "My bones were mounted in a museum, with my broken, burned watch beside me, probably as punishment for my resistance and tease of time."[87] As Sokolowski argues, the display of Ronin's body (here blurred with the narrative of his friend Oshima) conjures Native American/Indigenous contestations over how tribal histories, bones, and artifacts are collected and displayed in museum spaces.[88] I agree with Sokolowski and would add that Ronin's emphasis on time signals how the memory work of the museum, and the display of Ronin's body, is implicated in the reproduction of settler time and tense. That is, the novel suggests that the display of Native bones, artifacts, and histories works to demarcate Indigenous pasts, presences, and futurity. The fact that Ronin's body is displayed specifically in Japan, rather than in the United States, allows the reader to draw similarities between the tactics of U.S. settler colonial, imperial, and Japanese nationalist powers.

In this scene, the settler colonial temporality of the display is dramatized via the image of Ronin encased in a "diorama of victimry," set with his watch suspended in time to the date of the atomic bomb. In the museum, Ronin's purpose is simply to be displayed and passively consumed in the name (but not the function) of pacifism. Here Ronin is not meant to change but to forever stay in this perpetual state of annihilation. This diorama functions much like images of Indigenous peoples as "vanishing Indians" taken by Edward S. Curtis in the early twentieth century. Curtis's project sought to preserve their likenesses before they were presumably eliminated altogether. Separated from the viewers and the unfolding passing of time and space, Ronin's annihilation is similarly rendered as a foregone conclusion. He becomes a means through which museumgoers can process, mourn, or lament, and then move forward. This process is iterated in the U.S. and Japanese state relationships to victims and survivors of the atomic bomb, whereby the protracted afterlife of this moment in history, embodied in the scars and medical needs of survivors, is subsumed by the state's need for historical erasure. As Kim writes:

> While the U.S. government engaged in projects . . . conceptualized as gendered racial rehabilitation [that is, in projects of producing ame-

nable Japanese and Japanese American subjects of U.S. capitalist empire], those in actual need of physical and mental rehabilitation—the survivors of the U.S. government's atomic bombings—were denied it.... The U.S. occupation government would not even allow the survivors to talk about their pain or grief publicly.... These silenced survivors were thus rendered effects without a cause and lifted outside of time and history.[89]

Through the display of Ronin, Vizenor exposes similar logics of settler time and tense as they are applied to both American Indian and Japanese survivors of U.S. settler colonialism and imperialism. The display of Ronin draws connections between U.S. and Japanese nationalist tactics of postwar memorialization where the remembrance of those who have died is also a form of forgetting, silencing, or abandoning those who survive.

This production of a settler colonial grammar is also evident in the Peace Memorial Museum. In contrast to the Atomic Bomb Dome, the Peace Memorial Museum is designed as a destructive simulacrum of the former. Constructed in 1955, the Peace Memorial Museum lies within the Peace Memorial Park in Hiroshima. It is in very close proximity to the Atomic Bomb Dome, which can actually be seen from the museum. Built as a memorial of the war and bombing, the museum has become a major visitation site for locals and tourists alike. Among the exhibits within the museum, Ronin takes special issue with a column that displays letters written by an array of political and social actors, all of whom argue for the imperative of peace. Ronin does not, however, believe that these letters demonstrate a true commitment to peace; rather, he reads this display purely as a kind of political mongering whose zero-sum game may best be described as a "greedy scheme."[90] As Ronin narrates through his journals:

> I live with roamers in the real dome, in the ruins of the atomu bomb, and despise the models. The museum is a cynical theme park of human misery, and the miniature letters are testament to the arrogance and deceptions of peacemongers. Hundreds of presidents, prime ministers, pacifists, and worldly mediators write promissory letters that are read by tourists, a column of pretense and duplicity. Come with me, you materialists, and bear a kabuki ghost parade in the ruins.[91]

In calling these documents of peace within the museum "promissory letters," Ronin conjures the economic construct that contributes to the problematic aspects of the museum. He goes on to say that "these letters are the worst of the occasional politics of peace and victimry. The museum elevates the peace letters, the government solicits a free ride on the passive road to peace and, at the same time, there are tricky moves to contract nuclear weapons in the country."[92] While this passage clearly shows the hypocrisy of the peace letters by juxtaposing them with the government's continued efforts to escalate nuclear warfare, I also want to point out the importance of tense in the novel's critique of the memorial site. The promissory note calls an as-yet-unrealized necessity for peace into the very present while holding in abeyance that realization until the future tense. It is thus fitting that Ronin cites an entry in the publicly accessible museum dialogue book, where a visitor named Mary Rose remarks on the connection of the bombing's devastation in the past (at the test sites) into the future (as evident in the continual threat of nuclear warfare). This notion of a written promise in abeyance till the future tense also recalls settler tactics in regard to Indigenous peoples under late liberalism. Indigenous calls for actions in the durative present are often held in suspension until the future, rendering "forms of suffering and dying, enduring and expiring, that are ordinary, chronic, and cruddy rather than catastrophic, crisis laden, and sublime" as conditions of possibility for the continual violence of the settler state.[93] Through Ronin's critiques of the Peace Memorial Museum, the novel reveals similar liberal temporal tactics in the United States and in Japan.

Ronin links the work of the peace memorials to that of war memorials—the subject of Ronin's critique in the later chapters of the novel. His critique of the warrior tradition in Japan is manifest most materially in the chapter on the Yasukuni Jinja shrine and the attendant war museum in Tokyo. According to Ronin, this Shinto shrine "is dedicated to the more than two million warriors who died in domestic and foreign wars over the past century. The shrine was misused by the emperors and then by militarists to unite the nation in colonial wars."[94] For Ronin, the shrine and war museum's veneration of war criminals not only erases the violence wrought by Japan's imperial actions but also masks the nation's responsibilities for the bombings of Hiroshima and Nagasaki.[95] At the shrine, clothed in the U.S. military uniform of his father, Ronin exclaims, "Come out of that shrine you cowards, come out under the tori and face the thousands of children you sacrificed at Hiroshima. The atomu children deserve to be honored more than you or any emperor."[96] When Ronin meets Bogart, an old Japanese "ultranationalist," it is clear that Bogart's dedication to the imperial interpretation of Japan drives his revisionist ideas of history. Of Bogart, Ronin writes: "He never once mentioned the enemy, the atomu bomb, the end of the war, or the occupation of Japan."[97] For Ronin and the Manidoo Envoy, the shrine prevents the constructing of "perfect memories" of the atomic bombing because it protects the spirits of war criminals. In his description of Japanese war criminals during World War II, the Manidoo Envoy writes that "Tojo and more than a thousand other convicted war criminals were enshrined in the Yasukuni Jinja in 1978. The shrine priests honored and protected these war criminals as *gunshin,* war spirits or deities of the shrine."[98] The Envoy suggests that the sentiment of war, sustained into the present, is manifest via the repetition of honor shown by the war veterans who daily visit the shrine and museum. As he describes it:

> Nearby in a new section of the museum a group of war veterans, tiny old men in military uniforms, watched a continuous video presentation on a combat fighter plane, the Mitsubishi Zero. They were moved to tears day after day by war memorials, and sang along with the patriotic sound track on the video docudrama.[99]

Just as Ronin is suspended in his repetition of trauma in the peace museum, the war veterans are suspended in a patriotic repetition made possible by a war video on constant replay. This repetition cuts the veterans off from any awareness of the linkages between past, present, and the future, and allows them an uncanny ability to ignore the consequences of war.

Ronin connects Japanese and Native American warrior traditions by exposing their similar temporal invocations. Through references to both Ira Hayes and Dennis Banks, two well-known Indigenous figures who have gained overwhelming recognition for their U.S. military service, Ronin reveals how the colonial temporalities implicit in the war museum expand outwards toward popular conceptualizations of Native warriors. Hayes is referenced only in passing, when Ronin plays Johnny Cash's famous song "The Ballad of Ira Hayes," but Banks appears both in Ronin's narrative and the Manidoo Envoy's explication. Alluding to the problematic economics of the shrine, where "war trinkets" are commodified and sold, Ronin and the Manidoo Envoy critique how Dennis Banks is mythologized and then re-produced as a figure for capital and symbolic gains via the romanticized allure of the Native warrior tradition. Whereas Ronin gestures to this profiteering through the playful repetition of the name "Banks," our second narrator explicitly names Banks an "ambitious capitalist agent."[100] This critique of Banks's romanticization of the warrior tradition is explicit in Miko, the shrine maiden's, visceral reaction to Ronin's appearance in soldier garb, and the immediate association with Banks: "She read his [Banks's] romantic story, attended his protests and lectures on nuclear peace, and the more she hears the more she wanted his baby."[101] Through this reference to Banks, the novel suggests that the Native American and Japanese warrior traditions, although different in their approaches to the memorialization of empire/empire's ruins, can work together in the production of desires toward capitalist commodification (manifest materially in Miko's sustained involvement in the cult of celebrity that places American Indian warriors in mythic time). It is through this connection that Vizenor's text reveals the reach of U.S. settler colonial and imperial technologies as the settler state works to produce what Jodi Kim terms "junior partners" in the continuation of empire. For Kim, U.S. occupation of Japan after the war led to the fashioning of Japan as a "junior partner" for U.S. global capitalist imperatives. Kim argues that Japan's economic boom following the postwar years, managed by U.S. economic strategies, worked to situate Japan as an economic ally for the United States.[102] Through the text's emphasis on the similarities between Japanese and U.S. commodification of the myth of the warrior, Vizenor reveals U.S. global capitalist influences as a settler and imperial technology.

Rather than mythologizing war veterans in a cult of celebrity, or doing away with their memorialization entirely, Vizenor's text suggests that the veneration of war veterans should work in concert with the memorialization of those who have died and those who continue to carry the injuries from the violence of war (particularly those injured by nuclear devastation).[103] The connections made cannot be contained within any geopolitical boundaries or temporalities. That is, the narrative suggests that memorialization of Native American/Indigenous and Japanese veterans must be enacted simultaneously with the people who have been devastated by the conflicts in which these warriors participate. The relationality drawn between these different figures, the narrative suggests, can explode settler colonial and imperial containers of space and time nourished in the museums. By connecting the warrior tradition to the expansiveness of settler colonial and imperial violence, opportunities for connection and change, and strategies for survival, can be created.

In an early scene at the Atomic Bomb Dome, the narrative symbolically represents the potential for Indigenous survivance through the sharing of memories beyond nationally demarcated time and space. Under the Atomic Bomb Dome, and not its capitalist simulacrum, Ronin is able to share his background with the living and the dead in the ruins produced by U.S. and Japanese empire. Ghosts of dead children and the devastated bodies of those who have been violated by the nuclear bomb all interact together to build what Vizenor calls "perfect memories." By connecting these stories, which span time and space, Ronin's own story is made flesh: "I was surrounded by white bones and burned, puffy bodies. The river was packed with bodies that never floated out to the bay. I was dead, a heap of ancient white bones, and could only reach out for bits of passing flesh to cover my bones, to create a new memory."[104] At the original Atomic Bomb Dome the conjuring of Ronin's traumatic experiences, while painful, is made meaningful through his interactions with the survivors and nonsurvivors that surround him, many of whom are presented as incorporeal, ghastly, or ghostly. Through this sharing of "perfect memories," Ronin's body, which was previously rendered diminished by the bombing, is slowly made into flesh once again. Here the sharing of the past, the grieving of the dead, and the attention to the voices of those presently suffering are rendered as creative.

Like the Atomic Bomb Dome, the Hotel Manidoo becomes a kind of foil or counterexample to the museums and memorials in Japan because there the experiences of veterans are not encased in a display of the past but are, rather, made flesh. It is in Vizenor's concept of "perfect memory making"—the goal of the veterans at the Hotel Manidoo—that the narrative is able to disrupt the ways that Native peoples are often represented within settler historiographies, public memory, and the warrior tradition. In an early scene, the narrative centers the discussions that the veterans have over a meal.[105] Here the presences of the veterans are embodied, not reified and cut off from time and space as they are in museum spaces. The fact that their sharing of memories occurs over a meal marks the connection between such dialogue and the physical nourishment of their bodies. Rather than the singular nationalist narratives captured in the museum's display of the past perfect, which Ronin deems "commerce," the stories that the veterans tell are "elusive teases" that embody the complexities and "variations of stories." While there is repetition in their sharing of the past as they come together five nights a week, their collective remembrances are created over dinner and so point to the memories' palpability in the present. Furthermore, here the repetition opens rather than closes the multitudinous narratives and possible meanings still to be made of the memories of the past. For Ronin and the Manidoo Envoy, it is this particular repetition of sharing through story that allows for moments of improvisation and chance, moments that are the building blocks of Native survivance. The imagery of memory making in the flesh, in this specific scenario, fittingly encapsulates the centrality of time and tense in the forging of new community formations, grounded in Indigenous-centered epistemologies and praxis.

This emphasis on embodied memories emerges too in the description of Ronin's "invisible tattoo," which is a sign of his dedication to remembering those who have died due to the atomic bomb. Of the tattoo, the narrator states: "Ronin wore invisible tattoos, as you know, on his chest and back. Atomu One, Eight Fifteen, printed on his chest, is the time and date of the nuclear destruction of Hiroshima. Atomu One is a new solar calendar that starts with *hibakusha* pain, torment, and misery."[106] On his back are floral designs that include chrysanthemums and wild lettuce.[107] As opposed to the letters that are attached to the metal columns of the peace museum, these tattoos symbolize how the past is a living entity that is connected inextricably to Ronin's very being. The fact that the tattoo is visible when his skin flushes suggests the ways that Ronin's registering of the past inflects his very tactile sensibilities of being in time and space. It is particularly through this tactile embodiment of these intersecting histories that Ronin can avoid having his renderings of the past become flat or closed off. As Ronin himself remarks to the Manidoo Envoy, "The perception of the real must be sincere, yet the sense is ironic, never actual."[108] In short, Ronin's tattoo embodies these histories not simply as clear-cut markers of the past but as nuanced, contradictory, paradoxical, ironic representations that can do justice to the very affective registers through which devastation is experienced and through which its aftermaths permeate. It is particularly these visceral interpretations of the past that provide Ronin with the possibilities for making "chance connections" and "uncommon unions" across different communities.

Through this emphasis on embodiment, the narrative also suggests the possibilities inherent when memory making is mobilized across different geopolitical spaces. Elizabeth Povinelli uses the term "diasporic object" to describe the ways that settler colonialism mobilizes its own logics across different spaces.[109] The narrative suggests that countermemories must also travel accordingly. For example, as previously discussed, Ronin meets a Japanese war veteran, Bogart, who has been hired by nationalists to spread propaganda around town. Vizenor describes Bogart's propaganda as "military music and loud, nasty diatribes that attacked liberal pacifists and foreign deceptions, and always closed with veneration of the emperor."[110] Joining Bogart on his rounds, Ronin convinces him to replace the nationalist music with songs from, among others, Johnny Cash. As Vizenor writes in the novel: "'The Ballad of Ira Hayes' moved everyone on the street, and many worried hearts mourned over the miseries of the Amerika Indian." Indeed, "The Ballad of Ira Hayes" can solidify the narrative of the vanishing Indian through its repetition of the chorus that laments Ira Hayes's alcoholism and death and can summon immediate feelings of "mourning." At the same time, the way this song is conveyed (played loudly in a vehicle that moves through the city) opens up the possibilities for it to "touch" communities and subjectivities differently. The narrative seems to suggest that its effects are manifest in how it travels and finds meaning.

By the end of the novel, the aftermath of Ronin's death illuminates this particular point most palpably. Miko, Ronin's lover, comes first to the White Earth Reservation in Minnesota to share her stories of Ronin and his death, which we learn from the Manidoo Envoy's narration. This moment of unlikely "contact," between figures differently affected by U.S. settlement and empire, dramatizes the difficulties and yet possibilities for enabling forms of memory making beyond national demarcations. At the reservation, Miko attempts to share her memories of Ronin but finds the community to be a resistant audience. Throughout her stay there, the narrative highlights the tensions that emerge when competing epistemologies and narratives of the past are set up against one another. The Envoy notes Miko's initial experience at the reservation:

> She was angry, worried, humiliated, and critical of Ronin. He never told her about reservation manners and politics, and she regretted the journey. Naturally she summoned *kami* spirits, but the native tease was much stronger. Ronin was a mighty teaser, she knew that, but he never resisted her *kami* charms.[111]

After an initial confrontation, in which Miko earns a reputation by shouting at the old woman Miishidoon, an elder in the community, she is accepted, and her stories begin to meld into the community consciousness. This moment of connection is made palpable by the narrative's emphasis on touch. In reaction to Miko's persistence in narrating her memories of Ronin, "Miishidoon turned away, waved her arms, and then burst into wild laughter. Later she reached out to touch the new shouter on the reservation. Miko could hardly bear the stench of her body, but the old woman was truly warm, gentle, and she emanated the lusty scent of a bear. Miko, for the first time, wondered if the woman was a man."[112] Through Miishidoon's touch, Miko is able to experience what the old Native woman is trying to express in her refusal to accept Ronin's death.

This moment opens up a space not for uncritical or uncomplicated forms of memory making, but for the chance that such connections can allow for one community to be changed and simultaneously change the other:

> Miko earned her voice as a shouter, she lived with the old bear woman and told many stories over several days about the adventures of Ronin. The people were moved by his vision of the *atomu* children and laughed over the scenes at Yasukuni Jinja. The last stories of his death, however, were resisted by everyone on the reservation. She learned later that the crane feather was one of his ancestral totem, the signature of his conversion, spiritual motion, and sovereignty of magical flight, but never his death. Miishidoon shouted that he might have vanished, but never died that morning at the waterfront park in Matsue Japan.[113]

Set against the backdrop of this particular community's resistance to accepting Ronin's death, the last scene of the novel reveals the importance of movement, of push and pull, and of concessions and renewed imagination. This dynamism is the critical component activated by memories and feelings that fall outside the temporal and tense structures of settler and imperial memory making—and even those that fall within it. Miko is not only a part of moving the enabling memories of the reservation forward; she is also moved by the reservation's stories and knowledge systems. Her final scene shows that while she works to erect memorials for Ronin at the reservation through her *kami* grammar, she is not unaffected by the tease of Native stories.

Through these final scenes of embodiment, Vizenor's text suggests that memorializations of warrior traditions can be enabling for Indigenous survivance insofar as they are embodied and shared across communities affected by settler colonialism and imperialism. Miko's presence at the White Earth Reservation reveals the possibility of emotional connection between communities affected by the devastation of war, empire, and its aftermaths (indeed, Miko spurs energy and laughter through her *kami* spirits). Her presence also suggests that this kind of sharing of different epistemologies, and shifting from less-sustainable ways of thinking and feeling, can make up the building blocks for Indigenous futurities.

Conclusion

Both Maxine Hong Kingston's *China Men* and Gerald Vizenor's *Hiroshima Bugi: Atomu 57* highlight an enduring and important facet of hemispheric Asian Americanist and Indigenous organizing and criticism—the need to highlight previously obscured histories as a key part of critical liberatory formations and collectivities. Specifically, both narratives suggest that such liberatory formations hinges on the rememorialization of their histories in relationship to the space, time, and tense of the settler nation.

Both novels were published years before the current phase in critical ethnic studies (when these questions of identity and politics, of race, imperialism, and settler colonialism have productively collided), but these moments of imaginations, and their particular emphasis on historiography, affect, and tension, nevertheless reveal the entanglements of settler and imperial processes between the United States, Asia, and the Américas. In addition, the novels' emphasis on memory making highlights the ways that counter-historiography produces structures of feeling that can instigate liberal power's endurance and yet its instabilities.

Kingston's reworking of the U.S. Asian American heroic tradition to engage laboring bodies of settlement in Hawai'i and the United States forges multicultural affective formations that obscure the imperatives of Indigenous sovereignty. Ghostly embodiments haunt the narrative, and I have argued that *China Men* reveals the movements of settler structures of feeling at the same time as they reveal different kinds of affective ruptures that indicate its persistent incompletion. This approach allows us to think through alternative forms of memory making that move outside the given settler logics of space and of time.

Vizenor's text also takes on nationalist memorialization through his critique of memorial spaces in Japan, the United States, and Native communities. In theoretical dialogue with Kingston's work, *Hiroshima Bugi* imagines indeterminacies found in excess of nationalist structures of feeling and how they might produce improvisational sites of chance connections. These chance connections, rendered most palpably in embodied forms of memorialization such as eating, tattooing, and touching reveal unforeseen connections between Indigenous and Asian (American) histories. These embodied forms of memorialization work differently than the museums represented in the novel. Both forms of memory making, whether embodied or institutionalized, reveal their function in inflecting the space, time, and tense of the settler nation. The novel not only imagines the unforeseen connections between settler and imperial productions of power but also asks us to carry this past into our understandings of the present and the future.

2

Legal/Juridical Tensions

*The Affective Temporalities of
Canadian Redress and Reconciliation*

On September 22, 1988, Canadian prime minister Brian Mulroney issued a formal apology on behalf of Parliament to those of Japanese ancestry interned in Canada during World War II. In addition to parliamentary recognition, Mulroney agreed to a settlement with the Japanese Canadian community and provided a monetary compensation of $21,000 to the survivors of internment, 12 million dollars to the Japanese Canadian community as a whole, and 24 million dollars to a newly created Canadian Race Relations Foundation in order to "foster racial harmony and help fight against racism."[1] Spearheaded by the efforts of the Nisei and Sansei (second- and third-generation Japanese Canadians) and headed by National Association of Japanese Canadians (NAJC) president Art Miki, this formal agreement was, according to NAJC legal representative Maryka Omatsu, four long years in the making.[2]

Twenty years later, on June 11, 2008, Prime Minister Stephen Harper's "House of Commons Apology to Inuit, Métis, and First Nations Peoples for Residential Schools" was announced. The apology emerged from the 2006 Indian Residential Schools Settlement Agreement. The agreement provided compensation that was divided into different components, including the Common Experience Payment that provided former students of Indian residential schools $10,000, plus $3,000 for each additional year that they were in attendance. The agreement also allocated money to Healing Funding ($125 million), Truth and Reconciliation Funding ($60 million), Commemoration Funding ($20 million), and funds of an unspecified amount to the Independent Assessment Process. As the largest class-action suit in Canada, this agreement was a culmination of thousands of court cases against the government, which sought not to close but open up a reckoning with Canada's settler colonial past and present, particularly and problematically through the Truth and Reconciliation Commission (TRC).[3]

Recent scholarship has begun to examine these two public apologies in relationship to one another. Such comparative work has the potential to trace the intersecting racial and colonial logics structuring Canada's contemporary policies. In their edited collection *Reconciling Canada,* Jennifer Henderson and Pauline Wakeham read these two public apologies amid a proliferation of state gestures of repentance, gestures that are inconsistent and staggered maneuvers by a variety of state actors that nevertheless have worked to form themselves into a coherent national narrative. They write:

> The state has arguably framed its approach towards reconciliation as a more committed and coherent project than it actually is in order to shore up national mythologies of Canada's dedication to pluralism and to reinforce Canada's international reputation as a peacekeeping, peace-making nation. Like the project of "official multiculturalism" to which it is articulated, reconciliation has been appropriated by hegemonic discursive formations for the purposes of framing the Canadian nation-state as a leader in the "'globalization' of forgiveness," modelling values of civility and tolerance in the world.[4]

As Henderson and Wakeham suggest, these unevenly implemented dialogics, between "'minoritized' constituencies' call for addressing and redressing wrongs" and the state's public remorse, take on narrative coherence relative to one another. The apologies, which emerge out of the movements for redress and reconciliation, can thus be seen as central to the contemporary image production of Canada as a reformed, and renewed, nation—that is, a nation that demonstrates liberal values of civil progress through their investment in state-sanctioned multiculturalism. As Sunera Thobani argues, settler societies like Canada emerge out of the triangulation between the "national," the "immigrant," and the "Aboriginal." She continues, "Given that processes of identity formation are relational, and given that national identity becomes instated in the 'encounters' between national subjects and their various others, the identity of this subject remains inherently and enduringly unstable."[5] Thus, these public apologies become one modality through which to provide a coherence to (civility) and direction for (progress) a national identity under consistent dissolution.[6]

While Mulroney's and Harper's apologies reveal the performative aspects of redress and reconciliation, their emphasis on national remorse and community healing suggests the central role of affect and emotions in this reconstitution of Canadian settler identity. Thobani contends that the history of Canadian national formation hinges on the "exaltation of the national subject," which has "ennobled this subject's humanity and sanctioned the elevation of its rights over and above that of the Aboriginal and the immigrant."[7] Redress and reconciliation thus become, within Canadian multicultural policies, affective means to recover such "exaltation," which has been put under sustained criticism. What becomes clear, through this affective lens, is how Canada's production of itself as a "peacekeeping and peacemaking nation," undergirded by the "innate humanity" of the civil subject, hinges on funneling settler, non-Native communities of color, and Indigenous community sentiments into temporally instantiated narratives of state rupture and national healing. This narrative works to produce community sentiments about the civil progress of the nation, enacted through Canadian multicultural policies. In doing so, the settler state also works to foreclose other transformative feelings and collectivities.[8]

In this chapter, I move from an exploration of historical narratives (the subject of Chapter 1) to an analysis of how redress and reconciliation movements, as legal/juridical forms of resistance by Nikkei and Aboriginal communities, can become incorporated into the settler nation's self-narrative of civil progress. I do so by juxtaposing four cultural productions that all unevenly reckon with Canada's movements for redress and reconciliation: Mulroney's 1988 public apology, Harper's 2008 public apology, Joy Kogawa's novel *Obasan* (1981), and Marie Clements's play *Burning Vision* (2002). Taken together, these cultural productions reveal the critical reliance on the affective formations of Aboriginal and Asian Canadian communities in propelling Canada's narrative of settler reformation. I trace the ways the apologies activate these narratives of progress by pointedly drawing out, nourishing, and redirecting Nikkei and Aboriginal feelings in regard to the nation's present and historic violence. In contradistinction, Kogawa's and Clements's texts, I argue, reveal the emotional excesses embedded in the "culture of redress." The texts suggest that redress and reconciliation do not end, but transform, the logics of settler racial processes.

By suggesting that redress and reconciliation are central to the continuation of the settler racial state, I draw from scholars who have critiqued what Glen Sean Coulthard describes as "a global industry . . . promoting the issuing of official apologies advocating 'forgiveness' and 'reconciliation.'"[9] In an interview, Roy Miki laments that the 1988 apology constitutes a loss for the Nikkei community insofar as the nation-state "strengthened itself by taking ownership of redress" and renarrating it within the official history of Canada.[10] With regard to Indigenous peoples, Coulthard interrogates how the public apology and push for reconciliation can undergird the state's narrative of progress, which works to relegate ongoing inequities into the past tense of history. As Coulthard notes, this "industry of apology" initially emerged from states that were in transition from "openly authoritarian regimes to more democratic forms of rule." For Coulthard, implementing practices of "transitional justice" in settler states such as Canada has the effect of obscuring the continuing structure of coloniality. As such, in his words, "reconciliation takes on a temporal character as the individual and collective process of overcoming the subsequent legacy of past abuse, not the abusive colonial structure itself."[11] This "temporal character" of public apology is connected to what Elizabeth Povinelli calls the "social tense" of settler colonial governance. The contradictions of settler claims are epistemologically resolved through the production of knowledge that splits Indigenous peoples and settlers into two social categories separated by tense: the former occupying the condition of the past perfect and the latter occupying the condition of future potentiality.[12] For Sara Ahmed, this narrative of progress is galvanized through the cultivation of national shame during the public performance of the apologies. She argues that shame offers a temporary affective staging for the reconsolidation and reaffirmation of national love. She writes: "Exposing the failure of the ideal is politically important—and part of what shame can do and has done—but it can also become the grounds for patriotic declarations of love. In such declarations of love, shame becomes a 'passing phase' in the passage towards being-as-nation, where the ideals that the nation 'has' are transformed into what it does."[13]

Connecting these scholars' discussion of public apologies as an affective impetus toward moving the settler state into some promised liberal settler potential, I argue that a comparative reading of the 1988 and 2008 public apologies reveals the ways that such national affective movements are staggered and unevenly projected onto communities positioned differently in relationship to the state.[14] In the first part of this chapter, I focus on how the two official apologies conjure particular emotions that work together to cultivate what I term "settler racial structures of feeling." This is a phrase I reformulated from Mark Rifkin's notion of "settler structures of feeling." The term "settler racial structures of feeling" identifies a settler racial common sense that requires the containment of *both* Nikkei and Aboriginal affective formations in the midst of the culture of redress. Rifkin states that settler common sense comprises the "quotidian ways of (re)producing the givenness of settler jurisdiction, placemaking, and personhood."[15] He compellingly argues that such common sense may not reference Indigenous peoples explicitly, but its formation is contingent on the givenness of Indigenous dispossession and discursive erasures. Expanding Rifkin's theory, I argue that these public apologies reveal a settler racial common sense in crisis—so much so that Indigenous and racialized figures emerge in a central and embodied way as the very condition of possibility for the enactment of Canada's narrative of reformation and civil progress. In my analysis of Mulroney's and Harper's apologies, I contend that their invocations of specific emotions, such as burden and sadness, engage settler racial structures of feeling that unevenly work to compel (and thus contain) these two communities' healing through the terms and directionality of the state.[16]

The last sections of the chapter examine how Joy Kogawa's and Marie Clements's texts grapple with redress and reconciliation as a technology of Canadian settler racial hegemony. In other words, redress and reconciliation are the means through which the Canadian liberal multicultural state draws settler, Asian alien, and Indigenous peoples into collusion with settler narratives of reformation and civil progress. The texts also trace, however, community sentiments and relationalities that cannot be fully foreclosed by this culture of redress. Published *prior to* the respective public apologies, the novel and play imagine the transformative possibilities of what Anne-Marie Reynaud terms "emotional transgressions."[17] In particular, I explore how the relational yet incommensurate communication of grief and melancholia across these two communities can project visions of settler racial technologies of power that are obscured by redress and reconciliation performances. Nikkei and Indigenous relationalities represented in both these texts unsettle settler racial vocabularies and temporalities of harm, and suggest that the foreclosures immanent in redress and reconciliation are always and already unstable and unfinished.

Canada's Public Apologies

The 1988 and 2008 apologies were part of a conglomeration of events separated by decades, sites of enactment, and differences in means and ends. These publicly coordinated testimonies were, according to Henderson and Wakeham, "shaped by the ambivalent domestic forces of a series of different government administrations and policy changes, partisan one-upmanship, and domestic and international political pressure."[18] Yet, as these two scholars compellingly articulate, these events underwrite Canada's narrative of itself as "a peacekeeping, peace-making nation."[19] I read these moments as both grasping for national coherence and yet distinctive in their own right. On the one hand, the state's strategies to manage the unwieldy emotional dynamics across settler, Asian alien, and Indigenous collectivities are deeply invested in the liberal multicultural progress of the state. At the same time, the asymmetrical ways that Asian Canadians and Indigenous peoples are incorporated into the affective temporalities of the settler state reveal the flexible operations of settler racial hegemonies.

Prime Minister Brian Mulroney's 1988 public apology and Prime Minister Stephen Harper's 2008 public apology both employ narratives of progress that position Nikkei internment and Indian residential schools in the past tense of Canadian history, and both mark the apology as inaugurating the future potentiality of the Canadian state. The 2008 apology does so immediately by stating that the "treatment of children in Indian Residential Schools is a sad chapter in our history."[20] Here the grammatically marked national narrative is distilled in the banal metaphor of a book whose shameful chapter has been written, edited, and can ultimately be thought of in the past tense. While the 1988 apology does not employ this specific metaphor, reports after the redress announcements were made reveal similar sentiments. For example, Sergio Marchi, the Liberal Party's Multiculturalism critic, congratulated Mulroney, Art Miki, and the NAJC for closing "the chapter of what was a very sad and sensitive memory in history."[21]

When read comparatively, the apologies work to induct Japanese Canadians and Aboriginal people unevenly, and contradictorily, into the future tense of Canada. In the 1988 apology, the imperative to forget the injuries of the past is communicated through the inclusion of Japanese Canadians in the multicultural promise of the Canadian present and future. The apology encourages both the children of the Canadian government and the children of those interned to forget and forgive the crimes of the past "so that they can walk together in this country, burdened neither by the wrongs nor the grievances of previous generations."[22] Only in forgetting and forgiving can the promise of a multicultural Canada be fulfilled. This imperative of national memory is rhetorically enunciated by Mulroney's declaration, which contradictorily overwrites the past and rewrites the present in order to proclaim the future of Canada:

> We are a pluralistic society. We each respect the language, opinions, and religious convictions of our neighbor. We celebrate linguistic duality and our cultural diversity. We know that the strength of our country lies in the collective energies of its regions. We are tolerant people who live in freedom in a land of abundance. That is the Canada of our ancestors. That is the Canada our ancestors worked to build. That is the kind of country we want to leave to our children.[23]

Here the racist and xenophobic logics of internment are overwritten by the declarative history of a multicultural and accepting Canada of "our ancestors," the very "ancestors" whose actions the apology seeks to redress. The revision of the "sad chapter" is, for the state, accomplished as Japanese Canadians are officially inaugurated into "the Canada of Rights and Freedoms, the new Official Languages Act and the Canadian Multiculturalism Act." Japanese Canadians are further integrated with the future potentiality of Canada when Mulroney declares that "as inadequate as apologies are they are the only way we can cleanse the past so that we may, as best we can, in good conscience face the future."[24]

The settler state's imagination of a multicultural future inclusive of Japanese Canadians is built on erasures beyond that of the trauma and violence of internment, an internment that is here circumscribed as the "mistakes of the past."[25] Indeed, the apology does not simply work to clear the past, it also clears the land, for Canada is deemed the "land of abundance." The phrase evokes the *terra nullius* paradigm, a central narrative of settler states that imagines the land as unoccupied and thus ripe for taking. By evoking the "land of abundance," the public apology assumes the absence of Aboriginal peoples. This erasure of Aboriginal peoples is reiterated when Mulroney proclaims Canada's "solemn commitment and undertaking to Canadians of every origin that such violations will never again in this country be countenanced or repeated."[26] The fact that Indian residential schools continued in operation until the mid-1990s, years after Mulroney's "solemn commitment," reveals how this apology evacuates the presence of Aboriginal peoples and the violations they experienced by the state. Thus, when read in relationship to the 2008 apology for Indian residential schools, the emptiness of the 1988 promise that the violations would never be committed again is apparent.

The 2008 apology operates differently than the 1988 apology, in part because of the different community it addresses but also in the spatiotemporality through which Aboriginal peoples are situated in relationship to the social tense of Canada. Indeed, the narrative of the future potentiality of Canada, promised through the possibilities of multicultural inclusion, the hallmark of the 1988 apology, is less overt in the 2008 apology. The state erases the ongoing structures of settler coloniality by suggesting that Aboriginal struggles emerge solely or primarily from the "event" of harm produced by residential schools. While Harper admits that the violence of the past reverberates in the present, the implication that the continuing problems in Indigenous communities stem primarily from this particular imposition further erases the continuing effects of the structure of coloniality. Harper proclaims that "[residential school] policies ha[ve] had a lasting and damaging impact on Aboriginal culture, heritage and language." He maintains that "the legacy of Indian Residential Schools has contributed to social problems that continue to exist in many communities today."[27] Like the 1988 address, then, the 2008 apology works to overwrite the ongoingness of legal/juridical decisions that affect Aboriginal people. Scholar Sheryl Lightfoot suggests that the 2008 Canadian apology "has compartmentalized the wrongs against Indigenous peoples, confining the apology to the survivors of Residential Schools while remaining silent on the larger processes of colonization, of which residential schools play only a part."[28] For example, as Deena Rymhs discusses, Child Welfare policies in the current moment are not qualitatively different from but a continuation of the settler colonial logics of Canada.[29]

These apologies' repeated references to emotions or affects—in particular sadness, solemnity, burden, and tolerance—suggest the centrality of community emotions in activating the future-oriented settler national narrative; they infer that the clearing of the violent past requires the clearing of the felt life worlds that sustain such structures of violence. In her exploration of the temporal architecture of shame performed during the public apology, Ahmed argues that "the desire that is expressed is the desire to move on, where what is shameful is either identified as past (the 'brutal history') or located in the present only as an absence ('the shame of the absence of shame')."[30] As with shame, the emotions conjured by the 1988 and 2008 apologies also contain temporal architectures, whether in and of themselves or through grammatical sleights of hand, that propel Canada toward its "being-as-nation." The questions of what is allowed to be felt, what must be gotten over, and in what direction must that which cannot be quickly exorcized be moving are addressed unevenly but are oriented toward the future potentiality of the nation-state.

The different ways that affect and emotions are cited in the two apologies reveal, too, the asymmetrical ways these two communities occupy the condition of possibility for Canada's narrative of reformation and progress. *Sadness,* as previously mentioned, is the dominant feeling ascribed to (and prescribed for) the nation in both public apologies. In the apologies, sadness is existent in and oriented toward the past, which implies that sadness does not exist in and need not be directed toward the present juncture of Canadian policies. This invocation of sadness for the past suggests the similarities in how both apologies work to activate the settler state's being-as-nation. Yet, a related feeling, *regret,* works differently in the two apologies with regard to Nikkei and Indigenous communities. The apology for Nikkei internment situates regret temporally in a similar way as sadness. That is, regret is constrained within a grammatically marked narrative. Mulroney, in the formal apology, does not proclaim the nation's regret; rather, he cites the nation's regret as already of the past tense through a direct quotation on the actions he has taken in response to this feeling of regret. He states:

The issue of Japanese-Canadian redress is one which I raised in the House of Commons more than four years ago with the Prime Minister of the day when I was Leader of the Opposition. I said then in this House:

> There is a world of difference between regret and a formal apology. Canadians of Japanese origin had their rights trampled upon. The reputation of this country is besmirched.
>
> Since then, Mr. Speaker, the present Government has sought a settlement with the Japanese-Canadian community to put things right between them and their country.[31]

For Mulroney, regret is inactive; it does nothing. Regret occupies a temporal limbo; for Mulroney, regret goes nowhere. It is what one does with the regret that makes the emotion useful. By citing regret as a *former* state of feeling, Mulroney implies that the nation has actively exorcised the emotion that would forestall the future potential of Canada as a multicultural state.

In the 2008 apology, regret is deployed differently, which reveals the apology's difficulty in bringing full closure through reconciliation. Amid the listing of facts surrounding the legacy of residential schools, Harper declares: "regrettably, many former students are not with us today and died never having received a full apology, from the Government of Canada."[32] Here the feeling of regret is in the present tense and in a context that cannot fully be resolved. While the statement that proceeds from Harper's "regret" asserts the state's active movement toward reconciliation and healing (through the apology), the statement of regret suggests that there is nothing that can be done for those who have died without an apology.

This difference, between the push to move on from the past in the 1988 apology and the acknowledgment in the 2008 apology that it is impossible to do so fully, is even clearer when we look at the different ways each apology engages with the *burden* of the past. The apology for Nikkei internment registers burden as a negative affect, one that must—like regret—be expunged in order that the future potential of the nation can be actuated. Burden carries a temporal, often generational, valence that can reverberate indefinitely. The 1988 apology operates as a kind of performance of the end to such a burden—a pronouncement that such negative feeling must be stopped so that progress can be made for the "children" of Canada. The close relationship of burden to responsibility—they both activate generational inheritances—begs the question of what kind of feeling would be acceptable to carry on from one generation to the next. While responsibility is not explicitly cited in Mulroney's address, it is implied in his mention of tolerance. He declares: "We are tolerant people who live in freedom in a land of abundance."[33] Interestingly both burden and tolerance connote a carrying of a negative weight. What is implied in the transition from burden to tolerance, in the 1988 address, is the removal of the burden of Canada's violent past through tolerance of Canada's Japanese Canadian community. That is, the apology discursively absolves the responsibility the nation has toward its own violent legal and juridical actions and re-emphasizes the necessity of "tolerating" Japanese Canadian presence.

The 2008 apology conveys a different kind of relationship to the burden of the nation's past actions. Whereas the 1988 apology absolves Canada's "children" from the burden of its past violence policies, the 2008 apology expressly takes on this burden. Harper proclaims: "The burden of this experience has been on your shoulders for far too long. The burden is properly ours as a government, and as a country."[34] Harper incites Canadian citizens to feel burden, to carry this with them as a structure of feeling in the re-formation of the settler state. Burden in this sense, however, invokes imperialist fantasies of the "white man's burden" as popularized, for example, by Rudyard Kipling's poem "The White Man's Burden: The United States and the Philippine Island, 1899."[35] Read in this light, the burden that is taken on registers as a continual affective investment in, not the end to, colonial encroachment. For, in the same vein as Kipling's reformulation and justification of colonial encroachment in the Philippines as a spiritual and religious service to the "Natives," the 2008 apology recasts the nation's burden of accounting for its crimes toward Aboriginal peoples to an emphasis on so-called service to Canada's "Natives." This spiritual imperative is emphasized by Harper's closing address: "God bless all of you. God bless our land."[36]

In addition to its spiritual undercurrent, Harper's apology employs pseudoscientific language to encourage this march toward the future potentiality of the nation. That is, the apology assigns the survivor and the perpetrator to two different roles, that of the patient and that of the doctor, respectively. Implied in this categorization is the idea that full reconciliation between Aboriginal and settler Canadian peoples is contingent on these figures' fulfillment of such assigned roles. Residential school survivors are represented as feeling too much, while the apologetic nation is imagined as "solemn," self-reflexive, and available to help. This can be seen in Harper's most direct apology in the address:

> To the approximately 80,000 living former students and all family members and communities, the Government of Canada now recog-

nizes that it was wrong to forcibly remove children from their homes, we apologize for having done this.

We now recognize that it was wrong to separate children from rich and vibrant cultures and traditions, that it created a void in many lives and communities, and we apologize for having done this.

We now recognize that in separating children from their families, we undermined the ability of many to adequately parent their own children and sowed the seed for generations to follow, and we apologize for having done this.

We now recognize that far too often these institutions give rise to abuse or neglect and are inadequately controlled, and we apologize for failing to protect you.

Not only did you suffer the abuses as children, but as you became parents, you were powerless to protect your children from suffering the same experience, and for this we are sorry.[37]

Harper follows this structurally similar series of sentences with the promise that Canada will join in helping Aboriginal peoples "recover from this experience."[38] The repetition of Canada's *recognition*, in juxtaposition to Aboriginal peoples' *suffering*, accentuates the contingency of Canadian reformation and progress on resolving the excess of Aboriginal feelings through settler-prescribed healing. In *Therapeutic Nations,* Dian Million argues:

> Healing encompasses Canada's dialogues with Indigenous peoples, moving the focus from one of political self-determination to one where self-determination becomes intertwined with state-determined biopolitical programs for emotional and psychological self-care informed by trauma. In this context, well-being, physical and mental health, is articulated as a key component in human development within self-determination goals at the same time as an autonomous self-determination is left vague and poorly defined.[39]

In the apology, the state is largely positioned as objective ("recognition" often implying a mental process detached from emotion); Canadian settlers are compelled to feel insofar as they can feel *for* Aboriginal people—such as through the reconfiguration of the settler colonial feeling of "burden."

In examining the two public apologies, one can see the uneven formation of settler racial structures of feeling in Canada's narrative of civil reformation and progress. As symbolic, publicly performed components of redress and reconciliation, the two apologies reveal the centrality of emotions and affect in regenerating the settler state. These formations hinge on asymmetrical yet intersecting affective relations with regard to Japanese Canadian and First Nations, Métis, and Inuit communities. The public apology for Japanese Canadian internment replaces feelings of white settler *burden* (based on the wrongs of the past) with the encompassing feeling of *tolerance* toward the Nikkei community. This affective movement provisionally invites Japanese Canadians into the narrative of national being and belonging, but as an exception. That is, their place within the formation of Canada's being-as-nation is as an unwanted but nevertheless necessary condition for Canada's future potentiality. This invocation of tolerance outlines the affective labor required to "right the wrongs" of the past. This stands in stark contrast to the public apology for Indian residential schools, where the state's invocation of tolerance is absent. Instead, the settler nation encourages its citizens to feel and carry the burden of Aboriginal healing. This call for Aboriginal healing is largely framed, however, through placing Aboriginal people in the role of the patient, and Canada in the role of the objective doctor.

As Patrick Wolfe claims, coloniality operates as a structure and not an event.[40] Thus, these two public apologies are a part of a constellation of legal/juridical maneuvers, symbolic gestures, and public and private events that maintain the structure of settler racial rule. That is, the public apology is but one rhetorical means through which redress and reconciliation comes into being. Thus, while the public apologies enunciate settler racial structures of feeling at the juncture of Canada's reformation, these affective formations are nourished and sustained through a variety of phenomena that constitute a range of possible means toward redress and reconciliation.

With this in mind, I conclude this section by examining how two state projects, the Canadian Race Relations Foundation (CRRF) and Canada's Truth and Reconciliation Commission, can function as settler racial hegemonic continuations of the public apologies. Both of these projects, as part of the redress package for Nikkei internment and residential schools, work to encourage and redirect "excess" affects and emotions that seem to spill over and against the emotions that are called forth in the public apologies.

As part of the redress settlement for Japanese Canadian internment, Canada and the NAJC donated a total sum of 24 million dollars to develop the Canadian Race Relations Foundation. Enacted into law in 1996, under the Canadian Race Relations Act, the foundation seeks to "facilitate throughout Canada the development, sharing and application of knowledge and expertise in order to contribute to the elimination of racism and all forms of racial discrimination in Canadian society."[41] In addition, the foundation is charged to issue a report of its activities at the end of each year. In many ways, CRRF operates not as the agent but as a liaison that supports activities and initiatives that are focused on the elimination of racial discrimination in Canada. The CRRF implicates the limits of the public apology and the necessity for the eradication of racial discrimination as an ongoing project rather than a largely symbolic event. Whereas the 1988 public apology is rife with an excess of emotions in order to compel the nation toward eliminating the *burden* of the past and to urge *tolerance* as the affective inheritance of the nation, the CRR Act and the CRRF annual reports are dominated by bureaucratic language—of facts, numbers, and logistics.[42] This shift suggests that the maintenance of *tolerance* as the prevailing settler racial structure of feeling requires that those implicated in and hurt by the harms of the past must evolve to an objective stance with which to encounter the "problem" of race in Canada. Thus, for the settler state, to maintain the being-as-nation so recently achieved through Nikkei redress is to cleanse the subjective self. This bureaucratic language, and the hailing of the objective citizen, emerges over and against other affective formations that are present and can also be read in the CRRF annual reports.

In contrast to the CRRF report, the TRC Commission and its summary report places feelings at the forefront of the work for reconciliation in the aftermath of the public apology. The report, released in the middle of 2015, marks both the culmination of TRC events, and the uneven, often contradictory, and complex process of reconciliation as part and parcel with Canadian settler reformation. Indeed, the summary report to the TRC Commission activities states at multiple times: "As important as Canada's apology was, it did not simply mark a closure of the past. It also created an opening for Canadians to begin a national dialogue about restoring Aboriginal peoples to a just and rightful place within Canada."[43] While the report asserts a different functionality from—indeed even seems to critique—the 2008 public apology, it continues to uphold a future-oriented narrative of settler national reformation and progress contingent on the language of state care and of Aboriginal healing. As Million states, "Truth commissions operate within an economy of crisis, disclosure, and catharsis."[44] This temporally structured imperative is evident, for example, in the report's framing of residential schooling as a lapse in the promise of Aboriginal and Canadian relations, a promise that emerged during first settler contact. Citing the treaties of settlement, the TRC report narrates the inception of Canada as a settler state that begins with settler-Indigenous relations structured by "mutual support, co-operation, and respect."[45] It is in stating this settler origin story that the abuses in residential schools are implicated as a failure, rather than as the condition of possibility, of Canadian settler formation. The rendering of Canadian and Aboriginal relations as initially healthy suggests that "disclosure" becomes the necessary step toward the enactment of a "catharsis" understood as reconciliation. This enactment of reconciliation as catharsis becomes the primary directionality toward which the TRC tends. The report states:

> Reconciliation is in the best interests of all of Canada. It is necessary not only to resolve the ongoing conflicts between Aboriginal peoples and institutions of the country, but also in order for Canada to remove a stain from its past and be able to maintain its claim to be a leader in the protection of human rights among the nations of the world. Canada's historical development, as well as the view held strongly by some that the history of that development is accurate and beneficent, raises significant barriers to reconciliation in the twenty-first century.[46]

It is only through an affective reformation toward reconciliation that Canada can return to its prior state of wholeness. As a non-Aboriginal person, I do not wish to diminish the effects of the often Indigenous-led organizing of the TRC and events, which have brought about incredible moments of collectivization and reckoning with the settler state. However, although during TRC national events survivors of the residential school system were able to share their various experiences and feelings with regard to the reverberating harm of residential schools, the report often works to ensure that these (unwieldy) affects tend toward the temporal directionality of settler imperatives of civil progress. The process, the TRC report recognizes, may be long, and protracted, but nevertheless must move toward this very progressive narrative. This can be seen in the report's statement about what could manifest if reconciliation is not achieved: "It would not be inconceivable that the unrest we see today among young Aboriginal people could grow to become a challenge to the country's own sense of well-being and its very security."[47] Proffered as a warning rather than a promise, the statement implies that the temporally unwieldy sentiments, particularly of "unrest," as similar to anger, mark the critical limits of acceptable and productive emotions during reconciliation efforts.

What of these feelings that exceed the limits of governmental reform movements typified by redress and reconciliation? As the aftermath of the public apologies reveal, there exist affective formations that are denied, dispersed, or neutralized in the march toward being-as-nation. In the next sections of this chapter, I follow these affective ruptures as they emerge in representations of Nikkei and Indigenous relationalities in Joy Kogawa's *Obasan* and Marie Clements's *Burning Vision*.

Joy Kogawa's *Obasan*

Kogawa's novel was published in 1981, at the beginning of a period in which redress to the Nikkei for their internment, dispossession, and relocation during World War II would become a very public issue. The novel offers a layered voice and intimate resonance to the movements in Canada and the United States.[48] The text thus serves as a public testimony, evidence of the material, social, and psychical damage caused by violent, racialized state policies. Part fiction, part autobiography, and part journalism, *Obasan* includes established legal and juridical language as evidence for the case against state violence. Yet it also values the intimate, legally unintelligible testimony that is equally necessary for the healing of a grieving community.

Kogawa explores the ramifications of the postinternment years through the narrative of Naomi Nakane, a third-generation Japanese Canadian woman whose entire family is broken and dispersed by the internment and relocation brought about by the Canadian government's Order in Council P.C. 1486. We follow Naomi as she returns to her Obasan's (aunt's) house after her uncle (Isamu) passes away, several years after the end of World War II. The story is punctuated by reminiscences from the past, as Naomi strives to make sense of and process her own traumatic memories. This past is, for Naomi, difficult to revisit, given the slipperiness of memory and the recalcitrance of her family in speaking about the loss of her mother, who went missing during the war years. This struggle is symbolized through Obasan's and Aunt Emily's (her maternal aunt's) divergent reactions—the former representing the silent Japanese Canadian community who wanted to forget the past, the latter representing the vocal and activist contingent who sought to make the government directly accountable for its past actions.[49] While much scholarship has explored the possibilities and limits of silence and sound in the process toward healing and justice, it is only recently that readings of *Obasan* have taken a comparative race turn—particularly how the novel explores community grieving and healing through imaginative connections between Nikkei and Aboriginal groups.[50]

Scholars have argued that references to Indigenous figures in both *Obasan* and Kogawa's sequel, *Itsuka,* undergird, in a problematic way, the novel's testimony of injury and demands for justice. For scholar Marie Lo, given the centrality of First Nations–white Canadian relations in Canadian national discourse, Aboriginal figures often serve as what she terms the "model minority" of resistance for Asian Canadian communities. Thus, Aboriginal peoples and their struggles offer examples of resistance to domination, a resistance that is instantiated outside economic rubrics and logics.[51]

Following from Lo's reading, Iyko Day argues that moments of cross-racial identification in *Obasan* assert affinities between the two groups based on similar experiences of dispossession and relocation, "placing Japanese Canadians on a broader colonial continuum that begins with dispossession of indigenous peoples."[52] These representations and affiliations, as both Lo and Day point out, also recite the often repeated trope of "going Native," which amounts to a national claiming of belonging made possible through the symbolic invitation and permission of Indigenous peoples.[53] Day argues that although Kogawa renders these affiliations differently, it is "no less vexing" because "Asian migration to settler colonies has often contributed to the dispossession of indigenous people."[54]

Adding to both Lo's and Day's readings, I examine these cross-community imaginaries through a temporally inflected affective lens. From this perspective, I argue that the social tense through which Kogawa frames Japanese Canadian injury situates the novel as a complicated text that both reiterates and yet moves beyond the colonial narratives of progress that structure the public apology. The cross-racial citations in the narrative reveal affective relationalities and deterritorialized emotions (that is, emotions that might be deemed unproductive for the state) that rupture the settler racial structures of feeling nourished in the public apologies.[55] In particular, Kogawa depicts character relationships that strive for, but perhaps cannot fully articulate, what I consider an "attentive relational communication"—praxes of cross-community acknowledgment that form the groundwork for understanding the intersecting racial and settler colonial dimensions of harm and healing. These fleeting communicative moments constitute what Raymond Williams considers "emergent" affective formations that have yet to be fully realized within the rights-based movements that informed Nikkei mobilization during the 1970s–1980s.[56]

As the story in *Obasan* begins, the case against state violence, embodied here in the breakdown of a cohesive Japanese Canadian family, is made more palpable by memories of familial wholeness and economic vibrancy. Returning to Alberta to visit her Aunt Obasan after the death of Uncle Isamu, Naomi quickly becomes immersed in memories of the past, likening the pre-internment wholeness of her family to the comfort of a blanket. She concludes by proclaiming, "We were the *original* 'togetherness' people."[57] This representation of familial wholeness is further legitimized by Naomi's early depiction of harmony between her family and the local Aboriginal community. In particular, Naomi elaborates on the economic prosperity of the Nakanes and her grandfather's prosperity in the boat business after his arrival in Canada in 1893.[58] Naomi repeats her uncle's narration of the past: "The native Songhies of Esquimalt and many Japanese fishermen came to his boatbuilding shop on

Saltspring Island, to barter and to buy. Grandfather prospered. His cousin's widowed wife and her son, Isamu, joined him."[59] Naomi not only asserts this prior economic wholeness but also gestures to its loss as impacting the future tense of the settler nation. Naomi ruminates: "If we were knit into a blanket once, it's become badly moth-eaten with time. We are now no more than a few tangled skeins—the remains of what might once have been a fisherman's net."[60] Likening what has been lost to a "fisherman's net," Naomi gestures to the tragedy of the loss of not only her grandfather's and uncle's livelihood but also a future potentiality. In registering the loss of the family as loss of the economic prosperity of the nation, the grief and grievances of Naomi's family, and the Japanese Canadian community writ large, become most recognizable *as loss* in the logics of the settler state. Kogawa's problematic depictions reveal how the "coloniality of Japanese internment" extends into the coloniality of Nikkei redress.[61] In particular, the description of Canada as a "land of abundance" in Mulroney's public apology aligns well with the narrative of economic loss and potentiality permeating *Obasan*. As discussed earlier, the apology's invocation of *terra nullius* suggests that the true violence of internment lies in the nation's disruption of the full potential of making use of the land and the people's labor.

Kogawa's inclusion of Indigenous communities in this story of loss not only legitimates Japanese Canadian belonging and portrays a racialized group's "going Native"; it does so by deploying the settler colonial division of social tense. As previously mentioned, Povinelli argues that contradictory settler colonial claims are ameliorated through the production of knowledge that splits Indigenous peoples and European settlers into two social categories separated by tense. She writes:

> As democracy fitfully expanded across Europe and European conquest across the globe, the truth of some would be increasingly judged in terms of a past perfect being—their already having been or, their potential to stop being what they are still in essence—while the truth of others would be judged from their potentiality. The futures of some, or the hopes that they have for their future, can never be a future. They can only drag others into the past.[62]

In regard to the settler state, injury and justice are often recognized by how state action affects the "past perfect" sanctity of Indigenous communities or the future potentiality of citizens of the settler state. By framing her family's loss as interrupted economic potential, Naomi aligns her community along a temporal trajectory with European settlers.

In contrast to the novel's representation of Naomi's family's loss as economic prosperity interrupted, multiple representations of Indigenous figures in *Obasan* mourn the losses of Indigenous communities as the loss of the "past perfect."[63] These grammatically structured assertions are exemplified in Naomi's comparison of Uncle Isamu to the figure of Sitting Bull. In the opening scene of the novel, Naomi and her uncle visit a coulee outside of Granton, Alberta, in 1972. While Uncle Isamu has taken her to that spot every year since 1954, Naomi is unaware of the rationale. After so many years, Uncle Isamu continues his silence, stating that Naomi is "still too young" to know.[64] Contemplating the significance of his taciturnity, Naomi states:

> Uncle could be Chief Sitting Bull squatting here. He has the same prairie-baked skin, the deep brown furrows like dry riverbeds creasing his cheeks. All he needs is a feather headdress, and he would be a picture postcard—"Indian Chief from Canadian Prairie"—souvenir of Alberta, made in Japan.[65]

In this moment of reflection on her uncle's silence, Naomi likens her uncle's trauma to a cultural icon of resistance against Euro-American encroachment and violence. Scholars rightly argue that this moment reflects the problematic conflation of Indigenous and Asian North American experiences, which is further punctuated by the subtle terror that underlies Naomi's comparison. It is at the height of Naomi's anxieties over Uncle's silence that she connects him to Sitting Bull, using this figure as not only a template for Native resistance, as Day argues, but also the ultimate sign of irrevocable loss. Summoning Sitting Bull's image recalls dominant settler conceptions of the vanishing Indian: indeed, he does not speak, and Naomi compares his face to "dry riverbeds." He is, in short, a figure of the "past perfect," one that prominently figures in the novel's (and the mainstream) cultural imaginary of Indigenous dispossession. It is through the perfectly still picture portrait of this Indigenous chief that Indigenous communities have often been lamented and mourned. For Povinelli, and other Indigenous and critical ethnic studies scholars, this temporal configuration of Indigenous cultures continues to abet settler colonial state governance and policies with regard to Indigenous peoples.[66] This framing persists in *Obasan* when, further on in the novel, we hear the story of a town once peopled by but now empty of Indigenous inhabitants. Additionally, the racially ambiguous figure of Rough Lock Bill appears instead of a depiction of the large presence of First Nations people in Canada.

Kogawa's novel reveals the fraught ways that Nikkei demands for social justice rely on the temporalities that organize and make salient the imperatives of the settler state. However, it does not simply and fully reiterate this past perfect picture of Indigenous communities. In fact, even in her depiction of Uncle Isamu as Sitting Bull, Kogawa's text points to how such an image can feed into hegemonic cultural economics. Naomi ponders: "All he needs is a feather headdress, and he would be a picture postcard—'Indian Chief from Canadian Prairie'—souvenir of Alberta, made in Japan."[67] In this statement, Naomi implicates her own complicit role in the economic production of the settler state through the commodified figure of the Indian. Naomi also implicates the power asymmetries between herself and her Aboriginal students in an elementary school in Alberta. While her references to being a teacher of Aboriginal students is fleeting at best, it nevertheless ruptures the colonial telos of the narrative by highlighting Naomi's relationship to the future potentiality of Aboriginal communities.

Kogawa's novel veers even more tellingly away from the social tense of the settler national imagination through its problematizing of griev*ance* as the salve for the griev*ing* of different communities. *Obasan* depicts grief as uncontainable. That is, the Nikkei community's grief as depicted in the narrative is not solely attributed to the *event* of internment; nor are the emotional ramifications of internment registered solely within the living generations of those who are directly harmed. Just as Indigenous communities surface in the novel's articulation of Nikkei grievances, they also figure prominently as a medium through which to express this uncontainable condition of grief in the Nikkei community.[68] I argue that the narrative's representation of affective links between Nikkei and Indigenous identities (that is, the links between Uncle Isamu and Chief Sitting Bull as well as Naomi and Aboriginal students), which often resists locating and harnessing pain to a single time, space, and identity, evoke a different spatiality and temporality for grieving and thus grievance, reparations, and healing. In so doing, these affective crossings unsettle state-sanctioned attempts to alleviate loss through the terms of the settler state and its futurity.[69] It is precisely and ironically through these cross-identity conflations that Kogawa's novel opens up possibilities for a not-yet-articulated ethics of cross-identity recognition and dialogue that moves beyond the temporal limits of national recognition and redress.

Rather than simply measuring one community's grief in relationship to another, these Asian North American and Indigenous affiliations show the impossibilities of fully representing the trauma and grief of *both* communities. Citing scholar Sau-Ling Wong's theoretical formulation of "doubling" in Asian American literature, Day argues that representations of cross-racial affiliations aesthetically work through the affective impasses that prevent the telling of traumatic events or experiences. Day continues, particularly in regard to *Obasan,* that the doubling of Nikkei and Indigenous losses constitutes a narrative strategy for representing trauma through the "terms of survival and resistance."⁷⁰ In her argument, the very character of grief as the aftermath of trauma forestalls its ability to be directly represented. For Day, by representing grief through Asian North American and Indigenous affiliations, the un-representable emerges with both political and psychical meaning.

At the same time as these Asian-Indigenous crossings fashion meaning out of grief of the Nikkei community, I argue that such representations also highlight the challenge of representing Indigenous community trauma. We revisit the moment between Naomi and her Uncle at the coulee: Uncle's silence contains the unshared and unspoken knowledge and thus denial of Naomi's, and perhaps his own, ability to mourn the loss of Naomi's mother. His refrain for withholding this information has always been "Kodomo no tame," or "For the Sake of the Children." Situated between the silent Japanese Canadian community on the one hand and frequently impersonal political language on the other, Naomi's loss and grief are personally unarticulated and politically undervalued. Her comparison of Uncle to Sitting Bull at first seems to provide language and value to Naomi's unknowable and unattended grief. However, rather than allow her to break the silence with a certain kind of telling, her comparison only offers her a doubly displaced inscrutability.⁷¹

In the novel, the pain that will not speak does speak, ironically, in doubly muted language. In a text that considers and interrogates the efficacy of silence, these scenes of simultaneous affective impenetrability suggest something beyond the incommensurability of pain or the impossibilities of cross-racial affinities. In her analysis of "attentive silence" in *Obasan*, scholar King-Kok Cheung explores the multiple and often contradictory resonances of silence in the novel. On the one hand, silence is registered as oppressive and destructive, as can be seen in Naomi's silence about her molestation by Old Man Gower and the silence of the Japanese Canadian community during and postinternment. On the other hand, Cheung argues that Kogawa goes beyond critiquing silence, bringing to bear its enabling aspects, positive manifestations, and healing possibilities. For Cheung, silence enables attentive listening. Furthermore, the silence performed by the aesthetic pauses in the novel incites readers to give pause and critically attend to what is communicated.⁷²

With respect to Kogawa's problematic and often ambivalent representations of the Indigenous, I argue that the doubled silence communicated in the alignment between Uncle Isamu and Sitting Bull incites a more capacious cross-racial ethics of relationality. While this ethics does not, in the novel, fully open toward an open dialogue about the ethics or epistemology of decolonization, it nevertheless reflects a political potentiality for Asian-Indigenous relationships. For example, immediately after describing her uncle's pain through the image of Chief Sitting Bull, Naomi speaks of the silent Aboriginal students that she has taught over the years. Likening them to the Japanese schoolchildren she grew up with in their "animal-like shyness," Naomi allows the silence of her Uncle and the Native chief to connect to the generations.[73] Yet, even in these cross-racial, cross-generational, transnational affiliations, there exists a distance, a resistance to name the likeness as sameness; for example, the schoolchildren "*could* almost pass" for Japanese—but they do not.[74] In these moments, the mirrored scenes establish affinities insofar as they refuse to express pain too singular and painful to be foreclosed through direct expression. As a result, the passage circumvents a kind of empathy for Native communities that would claim that particular community's pain as its own.

Although Kogawa sets up a quiet distance between the grieving of these two communities, and even between those in the same racialized group, the affective links are still palpable. Kogawa does not approximate the fabric or detail of this affective comparative dialogue, but we can certainly piece together its pattern as historical legacy. Thus, in one sense, the novel's ethics of comparativity between Nikkei and Indigenous communities imaginatively carves out what Michel Foucault has theorized as a heterotopic space, one that unsettles preconceived logics of comparison between these two communities. In contrast to Western epistemological divisions between discrete entities (such as national bodies), Foucault posits "heterotopias" as spaces where the analytical separations that structure and order discrete entities become destabilized or fused. Grace Kyungwon Hong and Roderick A. Ferguson argue that heterotopias can be conceived of either as literal spaces or spatial imaginaries that "mark epistemological and discursive failure, disjuncture, or dissonance. They emerge at the moment when epistemological certainties that are required for comparison are undermined."[75] This notion of heterotopia as a spatial *imaginary* has particular salience in Kogawa's representations of Nikkei and Indigenous dialogue. Through this heterotopic vision, Kogawa does not simply render the comparisons between Nikkei and Indigenous communities illegible. Rather, the distances and affinities that the novel invokes (particularly through affect) require an alternative optic for comprehending and understanding these relationships. In such a way, Kogawa's cross-racial connection embodies more specifically what Hong and Ferguson posit as a "heterotopic *somewhere*." They write that this space is one

> where the objects of comparison have an unstable interrelation to each other, because they have changing meanings depending on context. These objects are not merely incongruous, as in Foucault's analysis, and they are not merely uncategorizable under a uniform set of criteria. Their relationality is constantly shifting.[76]

By conjuring the space of Nikkei and Native contact between Naomi, Sitting Bull, and the Native schoolchildren as a "heterotopic *somewhere*," Kogawa's text opens up possibilities for ethical dialogue that go beyond preconceived, and often state-sanctioned, pathways toward justice and healing. In other words, it is through the simultaneous connection and impenetrability made between these two communities in Kogawa's narrative that a justice-oriented *praxis* of cross-racial communication can emerge. In particular, by not harnessing this affective dialogue to one single spatial or temporal narrative (i.e., harm done to one community by another, which produces an effect that is temporally and spatially situated), Kogawa's novel gestures toward the need to cultivate ethical (and political) relationships that attend to the relationalities between multiple shifting referents. The novel's cultivation of a relational sensibility has the capacity to address both the promise and the limits of political recognition and redress.

In the context of Nikkei redress, the novel's affective registers invoke alternative forms of recognition, redress, and healing that do not cede to the temporal logics of the settler state. As such, *Obasan* adds to conversations on the problematics of state recognition that have emerged in hemispheric Asian American and Indigenous scholarship over the last several years. For example, scholar Glen Sean Coulthard has examined the colonial trappings of an Indigenous politics centered on gaining political recognition through the state. For Coulthard, political recognition is ultimately based on the state's terms rather than through a mutual recognition between two parties. This dependence on the language of the colonizer has serious implications for colonized communities seeking self-determination. Through a reading of Frantz Fanon, Coulthard explains how state-led processes of recognition produce colonized subjects whose "psycho-affective" attachment to colonial apparatuses of power undergird the perpetuation of the colonial state and its attendant violence and inequities.

Although these forms of redress might provide short-term gains for Indigenous communities, Coulthard argues that they do not ultimately change the unequal structure of coloniality. In place of a politics that strives for political recognition, Coulthard calls for a different "transformative praxis" that will provide the means and source for empowerment and thus liberation. He writes:

> The empowerment that is derived from this critically self-affirmative and self-transformative process of de-subjectification must be cautiously directed away from the assimilative lure of the statist politics of recognition, and instead be fashioned toward our own on-the-ground

practices of freedom. As the feminist, anti-racist theorist bell hooks explains, such a project would minimally require that we stop being so preoccupied with looking "to that Other for recognition"; instead we should be "recognizing ourselves and [then seeking to] make contact with all who would engage us in a constructive manner."[77]

I argue that Kogawa's text illuminates an ethics of recognition, via attentive silence, that nurtures what I consider a form of attentive relational communication that can set the stage for cross-racial decolonizing practices.

While in Slocan, where she was relocated with her brother and Aya Obasan, Naomi's encounter with the racially ambiguous Rough Lock Bill resonates as an Asian Canadian and Indigenous encounter that performs this "on-the-ground" praxis of attentive relational communication between Indigenous and Asian Canadian/alien communities that goes beyond the codifications of political recognition and legal redress. On first seeing Rough Lock Bill, Naomi describes his presence in relationship to the land itself. She also describes his skin color is as "dark as a walnut," and compares the rest of him to the nonhuman natural world:

> The first things I see are his feet in a pair of sand slippers. One big toe sticks out through a hole in his sock. He is a thin man, skinny as a tree, his face grooved like tree bark. His arm is a knobby branch darker than mine. His hair is scraggly and covers his head like the seaweed on Vancouver beaches draped on the rocks.[78]

As with Sitting Bull, whose face is compared to "dry riverbeds," Rough Lock Bill's presence is inextricable from the natural elements, which suggests his place-based belonging to the wilderness.

The ambiguity of Rough Lock Bill's racial identity is maintained even as he becomes a familiar character to Naomi (and her friend Kenji). In narrating a story of the origins of the town and how it came to be named Slocan, Rough Lock Bill tells of a dying tribe of Indians who moved to Slocan for survival "a long time ago." The cause for their dying is unexplained, although Rough Lock speculates that it might be from "smallpox maybe. Tribe Wars. Starvation. Maybe it was a hex, who knows."[79] Because the time and reason of their arrival are unspecified, their presence in Slocan could have presumably occurred either precontact or postcolonization.

Even as Rough Lock Bill incorporates his own family's presence into this particular history, his racial identity becomes more and not less confusing. He shares this:

"When my Granddad came, there was a whole tribe here." He points to a stick at his cabin. "Right there was the chief's teepee. But last I saw—one old guy past the mine—be dead now probably."[80]

Here, in Rough Lock Bill's story, his grandfather is clearly not part of the originating tribe in Slocan. In addition, he emphasizes that the last of that tribe might have already died, which separates his own presence from this Indigenous community. Yet, although Rough Lock Bill implies that the entire tribe has vanished, he undermines this conclusion with his own statement that in circumstances of extreme hardship, "there's always a few left when something like that happens."[81] Rough Lock Bill's story produces slippages that interrupt the usual narratives of the dying or vanishing Indian, slippages that are invested in the very presence of the teller himself. Indeed, at first, Rough Lock Bill's story seems to position his family as settlers to the town; thus, it could be argued that he is of European descent. However, because the time of arrival of the tribe could have predated colonial incursion, Rough Lock Bill's own grandfather could have been from a different tribal community. Ultimately, however, Kogawa does not clarify Rough Lock Bill's identity. This indeterminacy sets the stage for an encounter between Naomi and Rough Lock Bill that models, albeit fleetingly, a different process of Asian North American and Indigenous recognition and acknowledgment.

Rough Lock Bill's interaction with Naomi demonstrates the impact of Indigenous epistemologies and ways of communicating beyond the bounds of settler discourse. In particular, his subsequent interactions with Naomi model an ethics of attentive relational communication in which each party looks to the other through multiple and shifting frames, languages, and terms. It is an engagement with self and other that drives such a communication, and that requires epistemological deconstruction and reconstruction.

Naomi and Rough Lock Bill's first encounter primarily centers on accessing alternative ways to communicate. Rough Lock Bill's first question, simple as it is, conveys his attempt to acknowledge Naomi's presence: "Whatcher name?" he asks. In response to her silence, Rough Lock turns to her friend, Kenji, for an answer. Although Rough Lock Bill gets an answer from Kenji, he does not move on. Instead, he looks for an alternative way to communicate with Naomi, asking her to write her name in the sand. This alternative mode of communication allows Naomi to break her perceived silence. Likening Naomi's silence to the silence of presumably the last Indigenous inhabitant of Slocan, Rough Lock Bill proclaims that silence is not an absence of communication. Speaking to Naomi, Rough Lock Bill states:

> Don't talk much, do ya? . . . Like that old fella up past the mine. Never said a word. Almost like a mute, he was. But I heard him chirping one time just like a bird. . . . I tell ya, the old man there could talk to the birds as if he was one of them. One time he had the whole forest singing so loud you'd think there was a hootenanny up there. . . . 'Birds could all talk once. Bird language. Now all they can say is their own names. That's all. Can't say any more than their names. Just like some people. Specially in the city, eh? Me, me, me. . . . But smart people don't talk too much. Redskins know that. The King bird warned them a long time ago.[82]

In his narration, Rough Lock creates a triangulated connection between Naomi, the Indigenous inhabitant of Slocan, and a bird. By positioning these three figures in one frame, Rough Lock demonstrates his own attunement to nonhegemonic notions of silence, sound, and language. The Indigenous man's silence is "like" a mute's, but not; humans can and do, in fact, talk with nonhuman nature; and the inability to communicate can even be the domain of those who talk so much ("me, me, me"). Rough Lock's episteme on communication very much informs what is, quite literally in this instance, his "on-the-ground" practices of liberating communication. It is through this epistemologically collaborative recognition that Naomi and Rough Lock come to know one another.[83]

The scene dramatizes the import and impact of Rough Lock Bill's ability to bridge the impasse between Naomi and others—himself included. Following their interchange with Rough Lock, Naomi and Kenji play in the lake near Rough Lock's house. The raft they are on sinks, and Naomi begins to drown. Kogawa narrates Naomi's reaction: "From somewhere in my body, a sound comes out intended as a cry—but deep and guttural like the growl of an animal. Again and again I am plunged and twirled in the frantic dizziness."[84] In that instant, between her drowning and dying, Rough Lock saves Naomi. Connecting Rough Lock's narration about bird language and Naomi's animal-like growl, Kogawa aligns the impossibility of being heard on your own terms with the image of drowning. Thus, on one level Rough Lock literally saves Naomi from drowning in the lake. On another level, the rescuing amounts to her finally being heard.

Naomi cultivates this attentive relational communication throughout the novel. In particular, Naomi's epiphany about her communication with her "wordless" mother marks the apex of this cultivation. After hearing about her mother's agonizing life and death in Japan, Naomi reflects on how her own drive to understand what happened to her mother ironically prevented her from acquiring a fuller knowledge about her mother. Likening herself to a courtroom interrogator, Naomi exclaims:

> The grand inquisitor was carnivorous and full of murder. His demand to know was both a judgment and a refusal to hear. The more he questioned her, the more he was her accuser and murderer. The more he killed her, the deeper the silence became.[85]

Naomi subsequently realizes that "only when he [Naomi as grand inquisitor] enters her [Naomi's mother's] abandonment will he be released from his own."[86] Cheung has argued that it is in that very moment when Naomi most visibly denounces her mother's protective silence that the daughter invokes "attendance" to the silence that allows her to hear her mother's wordlessness as an "absent presence." Cheung notes that "attentive silence" is enabling, through its qualities of "visual sensitivity[,] anticipatory responsiveness [and] intuitive understanding," and a sense of intimate care between listener and the wordless speaker.[87] It is through this attendance that Naomi (and Kogawa) create a space for communion between mother and daughter.

Scholars have read this private imagined moment between daughter and mother as reflecting a transcendental communion. Given the Christian influences and intertextual rhetorical presence in the novel and in Kogawa's own life, such a reading aptly connects this passage to an interior drama that is also outside of the singularly private. I want to emphasize, however, how the use of the metaphor of the courtroom in this passage performs a response to the limits of the juridical, and the need to reach out to different epistemologies of communication, recognition, and justice. Cheung suggests that Naomi's sensibility here comes solely from her Japanese heritage, but I disagree. I assert that this shift in Naomi's communicative style was also directly informed by her encounter with Rough Lock.

At the end of the novel, Naomi returns to the coulee—the place where her uncle Isamu has taken her for years in order to grieve her mother's death. Through these trips to the coulee, Naomi had been grieving without fully knowing what she was grieving for. Her return, in one sense, marks a closure for her: we are told that she now knows why she has been going to that very spot for so many years. The return, then, is presumably a final and knowable reunion with the memory of her mother. At the same time, the return is also in remembrance of her uncle, who has since died. In this scene she is grieving for both her uncle and her mother but, in fact, the limits and knowledge of her grief are still unmappable. Kogawa writes: "The perfume in the air is sweet and faint. If I hold my head a certain way, I can smell them from where I am."[88] This final sentence emphasizes Naomi's embrace of her embodied faculties as central to her practice of attentive relational communication. Rather than read this scene as signifying Naomi's, and Kogawa's, universalizing apolitical impulse, I would like to suggest that Naomi's expansive attunement prepares her to return to the political work of her Aunt Emily. Indeed, we end not with Naomi in the coulee but with a documented "memorandum sent by the Co-operative Committee on Japanese Canadians to the House and the Senate of Canada, April 1946."[89] Through the juxtaposition of Naomi's seemingly private moment in the coulee and this very public document, the narrative calls for the expansion of methodological and discursive means through which to transform the political. While *Obasan* gestures to how this attunement to attentive relational communication can infuse the beginnings of redress, it ultimately leaves this space underexplored.

I now turn to Marie Clements's play *Burning Vision* to examine how the playwright directly engages the limits of public apologies and the push for redress and reconciliation. Like *Obasan*, the play is an evocative exploration, but unlike the novel, the play is more directly in tune with imaginations of decolonial relationships between Nikkei and Aboriginal people. Of course, this has partly to do with the different time periods out of which these two texts emerge and the social and political possibilities that were forged in the political arena during those times. Mona Oikawa writes "[the fact] that Aboriginal Peoples are . . . largely absent from our representations of histories of people of color is noted in the historical literature of Japanese Canadians. Most importantly, what may be missing from this representation is an analysis of colonization in Canada and its critical function in establishing the categories of whiteness and non-whiteness and in making dominant and subordinate subjects."[90] This omission is a consequence of the parameters that made redress even possible. Kirsten Emiko McAllister and Roy Miki both write that even the very possibility for Nikkei redress meant that Japanese Canadians had to represent themselves, to the general public, as loyal Canadian citizens. Miki elaborates that this refashioning of Japanese Canadian identity within the public sphere dialectically produced a citizen subjectivity, which had previously gone unarticulated.[91]

Miki notes, however, the changes within public discourse on citizenship years after redress: "The heightened language of citizenship rights that was heralded in the 1988 redress settlement seems to have lost much of its currency, new meanings of citizenship may be emerging as the borders of nations become zones of conflict and contradictory loyalties."[92] The unsettling of Canadian national borders includes relations between not only settler states but also settler states and First Nations, which has brought about a more distinct dialogue between Nikkei and Aboriginal peoples. Such dialogue has also been made possible by the ways Nikkei redress informed and infused subsequent movements. Indeed, as Jennifer Henderson and Pauline Wakeham write, Nikkei redress in the 1980s influenced the subsequent structuring logics, discourses, and calls for redress/reconciliation among a multitude of Aboriginal and historically marginalized communities.[93] These relationalities across seemingly different movements provide the condition of possibility for the imagination and critique of redress and reconciliation in the contemporary moment.[94]

Marie Clements's *Burning Vision*

Marie Clements's play *Burning Vision* premiered at the Firehall Arts Centre, Vancouver, British Columbia, in 2002. The play has subsequently received positive critical attention, winning, for example, the Japan Canada Literary Award in 2004.[95] Clements's work traces the interconnections of communities across different times and spaces by fusing poetic, musical, and theatrical forms and playing with their limitations and possibilities (for example, the lack of the fourth wall and the breakdown of spatial and temporal borders).[96] In particular, the playwright explores the connection between Canadian Uranium Mining at the Sathu Dene Territory at Great Bear Lake in 1930s–1940s and the U.S. bombing of Nagasaki and Hiroshima in 1945. Woven into her dramatization of these major historical events, Clements depicts stories of lives lost or deferred by the incarceration of men, women, and children through capitalist, racist, and genocidal policies such as Nikkei internment and Indian residential schools. Thus, the very structure of the play challenges the teleological rendering of history as a series of events with delimited cause and effect. In so doing, the play posits what scholar Larissa Lai aptly identifies as a "poetics of relationality" that narrates an "echoing world." Lai suggests that Clements's representation of this echoing world "is always stepping forward to claim responsibility and produce connection, even if, at individual and causal levels, responsibilities are not being taken and connections are not being made."[97]

Building on Lai's analysis of *Burning Vision*, I suggest that Clements's depiction of this "echoing world" addresses the problematics of redress and reconciliation as they are produced and reproduced through a paternalistic nationalism. The play suggests that, instead of enabling processes of healing, the affective character of the public apology binds the aggrieved subject to the sovereign authority of the state and its apparatuses. The play suggests that the public apologies code redress and reconciliation in familial narratives of love and redemption, of individual harm and psychological healing. In place of this paternalistic power dynamic, Clements's play articulates the recalcitrant affective formations that structure but are then expunged from state-sanctioned processes of redress and reconciliation. In particular, Clements suggests that the communication of melancholy—or the refusal to let go of experiences of loss—between Asian and Indigenous communities can produce expansive understandings of settler harm and decolonizing epistemologies of healing.

Clements dramatizes the limits of redress and reconciliation through the representation of the relationship among three pivotal characters: Fat Man, Round Rose, and Little Boy. In the play, these three characters haphazardly form a "nuclear" family, with Fat Man as the self-appointed head of the household. These characters exemplify the relations among settler national, Nikkei, and Indigenous communities. In representing these connections through the language of family, Clements highlights the affective relations that fuel the process of settler racial formation, and the subsequent push for redress and reconciliation. Fat Man, described as "an American bomb-test dummy manning his house in the late 1940s–1950s," typifies dominant U.S. national complacency that leads to the devastating bombings. While both Round Rose and Little Boy occupy the status of "alien" in times of national and geopolitical anxiety, they represent different yet interconnected experiences within the settler racial state. Round Rose is described as a "homely" Japanese American student (the real-life figure of Iva Toguri) falsely accused and imprisoned for treason as "Tokyo Rose," the infamous "propaganda radio personality who aired 'zero hour' broadcasts during the Second World War." On the other hand, Little Boy is described as "a beautiful Native boy. Eight to ten years old. The personification of the darkest uranium found at the centre of the earth."[98] As Lai argues, the play "privilege[s] the evocative over the concretely specific."[99] While Lai is referring specifically to the stage directions, the same could be said of the characters, who conjure a multiplicity of meanings. Round Rose's character represents not only the specific incarceration of Japanese American student Iva Toguri but also the incarceration of the Nikkei community in Canada and the United States. While Little Boy directly refers to the name of the bomb that was detonated in Hiroshima, his characterization also gestures to the residential school experiences of Aboriginal children. Through these evocative descriptions, Clements reveals the gendered racial and settler colonial striations that constitute Canada's national formation.

In presenting the formation of the nation through the violent constitution of a nuclear family headed by Fat Man, Clements enunciates how settler racial logics are produced and coded in the narrative of a reproductive paternal nation-state. Fat Man provisionally incorporates Round Rose and Little Boy into his family but, upon a perceived threat to the settler nation, he retracts and pushes both figures out, blaming their "alien" identity. Fat Man proclaims, "I am a soldier despite myself. I am a living-room soldier. . . . I got a *responsibility* to uphold the fort no matter who the Indian is. I got to defend my country and my family. Even if my family are Indians."[100] In this quotation, which reveals the paradox of national formation itself, Fat Man describes himself as an accidental or unwilling father to a settler nation-state. In turn, he explains his actions through the paternal language of "responsibility," which, as the play reveals later, also structures the conditionality of his subsequent apology to Round Rose and Little Boy. Seeing that his "family" has left him upon his violent expulsion, Fat Man proclaims, "Where is my family? What did I say? I didn't mean you. I didn't mean it. I said it[,] . . . I did it[,] . . . but I didn't mean it! . . . I'm sorry. What did I do wrong?"[101] When Fat Man's "authentic" apology does come, he proclaims that he merely has "matrimonial problems" and that Round Rose will inevitably return. He states:

> She'll come back 'cause we got something real. She's not American but she is sorta. It just shows different cultures can get along if we're willing to sit down and fuck . . . [t]alk. She's a good girl. A hard-working girl. She'll come back[;] . . . you'll see.[102]

Written and performed several years after the public apology for Nikkei redress, Clements's play critiques the power dynamics that structure Canada's statement toward the Nikkei community. In particular, the play's restaging of Mulroney's public apology punctuates the function of the apology that continues to place the Nikkei community within, yet not fully incorporated into, the national body. Fat Man's remark about Round Rose as "a good girl. A hard-working girl" alludes to historical attributions of Asian North American women either as virtuous model minorities or as prostitutes, "dragon ladies," or sexualized deviants. The fragmented sentences that connect these two stereotypes reveal how these two figures are mutually central in the self-affirmation of the paternalistic nation-state as represented by Fat Man. The paternalism of the apology is apparent in not only his sexualized references to Round Rose but also the declarations that frame his apology. *He,* as the "living-room soldier" holds the right to identify *her,* hence the repetition of "she" in his statement. The grammatical structure of his apology situates Fat Man in the place of authority as he works to form the nation into a multicultural state—one that recalibrates but does not reconfigure power relations. Thus, the apology continues to evoke dominant tropes of the submissive and sexualized Asian woman. Even when, later in the play, Fat Man shows sincere remorse, he says he is sorry because he does not "want to die alone," suggesting that his apology is contingent on the holding up of his *"livingroom"*—or, in other words, holding up the continuation of nation-state sovereignty.[103]

In addition to Fat Man's apology, Round Rose's response to it is emphasized as key to the settler state's movement toward redress and reconciliation—which she initially denies. Round Rose, directing her invective to Fat Man—but also to the audience—provides a major, explicit critique of the apology. Closing out the third movement of the play, Round Rose calls out Fat Man:

> Let's be honest, hell, you can't even apologize for the shit you did yesterday never mind fifty years ago. Indian residential schools, Japanese internment camps, hell, and this is just in your neighborhood. . . . Everybody's sorry they got caught sticking it to someone else[;] . . . that's what they are sorry about . . . getting caught. . . . Don't be a sorry ass, be sorry before you have to say you are sorry. Be sorry for thinking about, bringing about something sorry-filled.[104]

In this moment, Clements's play provides an overt critique of the Canadian government's public apology, particularly in its late arrival; that is, the apology comes only when the perpetrators are made accountable for their actions. As she astutely points out in a list of wrongs that should be apologized for, Round Rose suggests that the apology is always already late.

This critique of the apology is also reflective in Round Rose's perpetual state of suspension and irresolution even after receiving an apology. This state of suspension gestures to the affectual imprisonment of Iva Toguri and the Nikkei community even after redress. Clements's play dramatizes this suspension by depicting Round Rose in two phases of her life. As a young woman, Round Rose visits relatives in Japan but is unable to leave after the bombing of Pearl Harbor. To gain reentry, she writes a letter that asserts her "Americanness" and her relinquishment of her Japanese identity: "Dear America, how are you? I am fine. I am waiting for you on Japanese soil. I know you will recognize me when you see me. We will look at each other—one American to another."[105] After signing her letter "your true American daughter, Tokyo Rose," Round Rose continues to wait, proclaiming, "They will recognize me."[106] Later, Round Rose is presented as "an older, middle aged, very Japanese ROUND ROSE" who broadcasts a radio show from her father's Japanese souvenir store. She proclaims to an unnamed audience, "You do not recognize me? Why should you, I do not recognize me. My hope has aged. . . . My notepaper of hope is a disappointed white bird [crane]."[107] In her article on the infamous figuration of Tokyo Rose, Naoko Shibusawa writes that, although Toguri "was vindicated decades later and pardoned in 1976, [she] lived with the notoriety of being 'Tokyo Rose' for the rest of her very long life."[108] Thus, even when she is no longer deemed "criminal," she is marked as such by the general public and must perform perpetually an innocence for which she is never recognized.[109] Similarly, the play suggests that the Nikkei community's desire for recognition by the state, even through definitions of the state, is a lost cause. Thus, despite being set free, this image of Round Rose in a persistent state of arrest points to the paradoxical effects of redress. That is, the play suggests that redress can produce subjects that are more and not less bound to the sovereignty of the settler state's definitions and redefinitions of national identity, allegiance, and innocence. In so doing, the play reveals the limits of the language of redress that rely solely on the familial terms of the state.

Through the representation of Little Boy, and his response to Fat Man's apology, *Burning Vision* represents Indigenous epistemologies that move beyond national rhetoric of familial (paternal) redemption. After being kicked out of Fat Man's house, Little Boy becomes the Dene Seer who, according to Clements's character description, "sang four seer songs over a long night, in the late 1880s."[110] The Dene Seer sees the destructive future by making connections across different times and spaces. He says:

> Can you hear through the walls of the world? Maybe we are all talking at the same time because we are answering each other over time and space. Like a wave that washes over everything and doesn't care how long it takes to get there because it always ends up on the same shore.[111]

In contrast to Round Rose's myopia in her futile quest for state recognition, a myopia engendered by the language of family deployed by Fat Man, the Dene Seer's vision offers a broader familial ecology, one that includes human and nonhuman connections. With this expansive ecological worldview comes too an expansive understanding of the temporality of harm. Harm expands beyond direct contact, as is evident in the reverberating toxicity of uranium across spaces and generations. With his transformation into the Dene Seer, Little Boy embodies an Indigenous-centered epistemology, not a reliance on state-sanctioned forms of redress and reconciliation.[112]

This potential to move beyond state-sanctioned forms of redress and reconciliation is central in but not limited to Indigenous epistemologies. Indeed, through representation of two different characters in the play (a Japanese fisherman named Koji and a Métis woman named Rose), Clements illustrates the potential for a decolonizing praxis of solidarity that can be engaged between these two historically, yet asymmetrically, aggrieved communities. Both figures, like Little Boy, occupy a liminal space: Koji treads the line between life and death after the nuclear detonations in Japan, while Rose is described as walking "between Native and non-Native lines."[113] Although they are separated by time and space, they somehow meet through the recognition of the persistence of war in multiple manifestations as it reverberates physically, affectively, and psychically across different peoples, different communities, and different environments. Rose articulates this when she queries the regeneration of war: "Does it keep going until it ends in us and, when it does, where does it live?"[114] Koji adds to this question and asks, "Where does it have to live to survive."[115] As scholar Rita Wong argues, although Koji and Rose's meeting is "spiritually possible through the chain of uranium that brings them together . . . it is not being made the target of a common enemy that defines their relationship but what they produce out of these circumstances."[116] Wong suggests that Koji and Rose's antiwar stance, and their resolve to have "no enemies," provide a strong foundation for forging a promising world.

Building on Wong's analysis, I suggest that through representation of Rose and Koji's liminal states, Clements's play shows the decolonizing potential of those affective formations that are deemed unproductive to the narrative of healing as it is framed within the predominant discourses of reconciliation and redress. In Clements's rendering, both Rose and Koji refuse to move on, instead continuing to repeat the moment of trauma that marks them, in psychoanalytic terms, as living in states of melancholia. As Sigmund Freud argues, melancholia stands in opposition to mourning as an unproductive form of grieving from loss. The play reveals what may be deemed both Koji and Rose's psychical state of suspension through their respective dialogue. Koji is introduced in a state prior to the detonation of the atomic bomb, repeatedly reminiscing about his childhood memories of his grandmother; he states: "I am riding on my grandmother's back yet I am a man. All man legs and / tall arms. I am a man and yet she is carrying me like I / weigh nothing."[117] Caught between life and death, Koji struggles to hold onto this memory of his grandmother carrying him, knowing that the memory of this moment and her words will somehow allow him to make it through the present devastation. Rose's state of suspension is dramatized by her walking in a circle with her bag of flour spilling as she moves. She is also seen perpetually kneading dough for bread, a food that she says is inherited from her white father. Through this repetition, Rose is largely rendered as dwelling in the trauma of nonbelonging, as her Métis status presumably marks her as *other than* fully Aboriginal. To use psychoanalytic language, both occupy states of trauma and precarity, which would seem to mark their inability either to move on or to live in the present.[118] Yet, it is in their inability to move past the trauma that both Koji and Rose are able to meet, fall in love, and eventually produce a baby boy that offers the final hope in the last scene of the play. Through her representation of these characters' nontrajectory, Clements's play undermines the paternalistic narratives about mental health that permeate the culture of redress. The play instead asks the audience to consider what knowledge might be produced when one reconsiders affects and emotions that are considered nongenerative in settler racial structures of feeling.

Thus, much like the productivity of anger that scholars such as Coulthard have discussed, Clements suggests the decolonizing possibilities inherent in Rose and Koji's states of precarity.[119] Coulthard calls for us to take seriously anger and resentment as an affective production of knowledge about contemporary conditions of coloniality; I would argue that Clements's play similarly suggests that melancholy, often read as the inability to move on, can produce knowledge of the present. Indeed, rather than read Koji and Rose as stuck in their psychical relationship to the past, I suggest that these two are in fact affectively gauging the presence of the past in settler racial processes. Such a reading is further supported by the temporal destabilization that permeates the action of the play. Thus, Clements's play critiques the clinical narratives of individual trauma and mental health that dominate the rhetoric of reconciliation. Refusing to work through trauma in psychoanalytic terms can also be a refusal to obscure the ongoing presence of settler racial violence.

The play sidelines the potential of clinical treatments of trauma to heal and centers instead—like Kogawa—an on-the-ground praxis of communication as the way to enter into a different, decolonizing discourse of healing. Drawing from Lai's "poetics of relationality," I call this a "poetics of healing."[120] That is, there is a thread of hope that emerges from the relationship between Rose and Koji (metaphorically distilled in their son), and it emerges not from a temporally linear national script of healing but from the process of communication that comes from their sharing of similar but noncomparative states of trauma and melancholy. This poetics of healing is further shaped by the dialogue, by calls and responses, as well as the definition and blurring of boundaries between the two characters.[121] Rose's first question to Koji, "where'd you come from?," is rejoined by Koji's question of "where are we?," suggesting both characters' desire to define their surroundings and their relationship to one another.[122] While these characters are separated by a chasm of time and space, Clements emphasizes that their embodied relationality is crucial to both their survival and healing. Upon seeing Koji in a state of distress, Rose asks about and tends to his comfort. In response, amid the encroaching blast of the atomic bomb, which is represented in the destabilized timeline of the play, Rose asserts her own anxieties, to which Koji lends his support:

ROSE
    I can't take it anymore, I can't breathe anymore . . .

KOJI
    Then breathe me in.

KOJI and ROSE sing into each other, merging their voices and bodies.[123]

Here Clements suggests that one's own healing is as contingent on the healing of an-other as within the self. This moment undergirds Clements's ecologically expansive vision of harm and healing, one that both recognizes the asymmetry of Asian/hemispheric Asian American and Indigenous experiences and yet calls for their interconnection. In sharing their felt knowledge, which is made possible within the melancholy of settler racial processes, Koji and Rose's relationship embodies an epistemology that is temporally and spatially expansive.

Conclusion

As I have shown in my readings of the public apologies, Joy Kogawa's *Obasan*, and Marie Clements's *Burning Vision*, the formation of redress and reconciliation emerges not as an end to, but as a continuation of settler racial processes emergent from the activations of settler racial structures of feeling. Such structures of feeling are constituted by the uneven and asymmetrical movements of sadness, tolerance, and burden toward these two differently aggrieved communities. Both Kogawa's and Clements's cultural productions represent this narrative of the settler racial state and critique it. The texts emphasize Nikkei and Indigenous relationalities and reveal the mutually constitutive affective modalities through which these state imperatives for redress and reconciliation are made. In *Obasan,* the metaphorical relationship between Indigenous and Nikkei experiences of trauma provides both an iteration and a marked critique of settler colonial grammars. *Burning Vision* directly engages with redress, revealing how the paternalistic narratives of settler national regeneration continue in the nation's public apologies and reinvigorate settler racial striations of power.

It is, however, precisely through the emphasis on affective formations—particularly as they connect across Indigenous and Asian/American communities—that these cultural productions reveal the instabilities inherent in settler racial hegemonies. Indeed, like Coulthard's and Reynaud's rendering of the productive possibilities of anger and resentment, both Kogawa and Clements imaginatively theorize a poetics of communication and healing that moves outside the constraints of state-sanctioned redress and reconciliation. Representations of Nikkei and Indigenous dialogue that highlight "emotional transgressions," from grief to melancholia (which evade political, legal/juridical, and clinical modes of healing), expand the spatial and temporal registers of communication and harm and, therefore, healing. The two works mark the limits and possibilities of settler racial structures of feeling at the conjuncture of Canadian redress and reconciliation. Through this affective lens, these cultural productions reveal how Canada's narrative of itself as the "leader of forgiveness" is an immanently undone, unfinished project that perpetually strives and yet unavoidably fails to fully compel communities into these narratives of wholeness and healing. The settler racial state's instabilities and failures thus create possibilities for transformative decolonizing collectivities.

3

Economic Tensions

Global Capital and Mestizaje/Mestiçagem
Discourse in Latin América

In the book *The Cosmic Race,* or *La raza cósmica* (1925), Mexican philosopher and writer José Vasconcelos imagines a future where the human race ascends toward a racial universalism through racial mixing, or *mestizaje.* Vasconcelos argues that Latin América, given its history of racial mixing, particularly between Spanish and Indigenous peoples, is ideally situated to produce the primary conditions out of which ascendency to the fifth and final race is possible. Indigenous peoples are referenced throughout Vasconcelos's conception and are rendered as signifiers of a past race that will be disintegrated for the materialization of a new and better race. Vasconcelos also makes multiple mentions of Asians (termed varyingly Mongols and Orientals), as well as ethnic-specific Asian immigrants. While the rendering of the Asian figure is similar to that of the Indigenous figure, in that it will add specific contributions to this future race, the author suggests several times that Asians have a negative propensity to procreate with one another, and an inability to mix with other races, which will lead to their eventual annihilation.

Several years later, anthropologist Gilberto Freyre conceptualized the formation of *mestiçagem,* the Portuguese term for racial mixture, in Brazil. In *The Masters and the Slaves* (1933), Freyre describes Brazil's plantation economy as conducive to a harmonious racial mixing between Indigenous, African, and Portuguese people, who he argues blended more peaceably there than in any other parts of the Américas. Freyre's notion of racial mixture highlights the centrality of black identity even more than Vasconcelos's, given Brazil's history of slavery, the plantation economy, and the African/black cultural presence thereafter. Indigenous peoples are featured in Freyre's concept but continue to be placed along a trajectory of eventual and necessary assimilation into a Portuguese-centered racial mixture. The Asian figure appears but fleetingly in Freyre's first book, although it has a much more meaningful presence in his later book *The New World in the Tropics* (1945), in which Japanese people are listed multiple times as crucially mixing into Brazilian national identity.[1]

Emerging decades later, writers Karen Tei Yamashita's and Leslie Marmon Silko's novels index this settler and racial legacy of *mestizaje/mestiçagem* discourse within their representations of critical resistance to global capitalist encroachment in Latin América. Their novels, *Through the Arc of the Rain Forest* (1990) and *Almanac of the Dead* (1991), narrate the alignments between global capital and the U.S.–Latin American trade agreements that unevenly draw Asian immigrant and Indigenous communities into relationality in the United States, Mexico, and Brazil. Both texts imagine the mobilization of global alliances and solidarities that can effectively confront the human and environmental devastation produced by corporate enterprises. While each of their texts index the limits of the identity-based cultural nationalist movements of the 1960s–1970s, their renewed visions of anticapitalist resistance differ dramatically; these different perspectives reveal the continued settler racial hegemonic logics that structure hemispheric Asian American and Indigenous organizing.

For example, in *Through the Arc of the Rain Forest,* Yamashita represents U.S. and Japanese capitalist encroachment into Brazil as it reaches a crisis point through the ecological devastation of the Amazon rainforest. The text narrates the complicity and eventual reformation of a Japanese immigrant figure, Kazumasa Ishimaru, who unwittingly fuels this disaster by financing and working for a key transnational corporation in the novel, GGG. Kazumasa's reformation is represented in the intimate union between Kazumasa and Lourdes, his Brazilian former maid. In addition to class asymmetries, their union is also problematic because it is preceded by the death of a key Indigenous character named Mané Pena and his entire family. This narrative trajectory indexes a hemispheric Asian Americanist revision of *mestiçagem* ideology, one that incorporates the Asian immigrant into the Brazilian nation's vision of liberation through racial mixture while reiterating settler tropes that dramatize and lament the dying Indian.

Silko's *Almanac of the Dead* contrasts remarkably with the narrative trajectory of Yamashita's novel. In *Almanac,* global capital and environmental devastation are connected to the context of colonial encroachment since 1492. The convergence of various Indigenous-centered decolonial movements (north and south of the United States/Mexico border) promises to counter the neoliberal manifestation of settler power. Amid the global mobilization of alliances and solidarities across different groups, possibilities are raised for a romantic union between two revolutionary figures, a Korean immigrant, Awa Gee, and a mixed-blood Yaqui woman, Zeta, but their relationship is immediately thwarted as undesirable. Silko's story is an imaginative rejoinder to facile celebrations of cross-racial solidarity through racial mixture; that is, the narrative reveals the destructive histories of *mestizaje* discourse for Indigenous peoples and its osmosis within race-based resistance and solidarity movements. In place of state-sponsored *mestizaje* rhetoric, which seeks to dissolve Indigenous peoples within the temporality and directionality of capitalist time and space, *Almanac* posits Indigenous epistemologies and histories as the basis for thinking through the presence of racially mixed Indigenous peoples in the Américas. At the same time, Silko's revision of *mestizaje* seems to pivot on ugly representations of the Korean immigrant figure that wrack earlier *mestizaje* imaginaries.

I have offered this primer on the settler and racial formation of *mestizaje/mestiçagem* discourse to highlight its legacy as a continually reproduced structure of feeling that informs neoliberal capital and concomitant responses within social justice discourse and movements. Published in the contexts of postrevolutionary Mexico (1910–1920) and Brazil (1930), respectively, Vasconcelos's and Freyre's works indicate the centrality of Asian and Indigenous figurations in the consolidation of a national identity articulated most explicitly in the celebration of racial mixture. Such celebrations serve largely as critical rejoinders to the concepts of white racial purity that predominated Euro-settler racial sciences and discourses, from Eugenics to Spencerian Darwinism. In this sense, the ideas of both Vasconcelos and Freyre can be seen as more liberal considerations of colonized and racialized peoples who have served as the degraded lynchpin of white supremacist evolutionary logics. While the two theorists both embrace the incorporation of these two nonwhite communities within what they conceive of as a process of harmonious miscegenation, their works also make clear the roles that Asian and Indigenous *difference* plays in the formation of a liberal modern nation.[2] As such, in the histories and formation of Mexican and Brazilian national identity, the dialectic of inclusion/expulsion of the Indigenous and Asian alien emulates the settler racial formations that also mark the processes of settler colonialism in the United States and Canada—the focus of Chapters 1 and 2.

In Chapters 1 and 2, I examined how alternative historical narratives and redress and reconciliation movements have become incorporated into liberal settler narratives, revealing examples of settler racial hegemonies in the context of British settler colonialism. This chapter turns to the ways that settler racial hegemonies function in the context of Spanish and Portuguese settler histories and presences. In particular, I examine how imaginations of transnational/cross-racial mobilization against global capital in Latin América can become incorporated within or structured by liberal ideologies that problematically center the mixed-race (*mestizo/mestiço*) subject or mixed-race unions as the primary inheritors of the nation. As noted, *Mestizaje/mestiçagem* (mixed-race) discourse has been crucial in propelling both revolutionary and neoliberal economic policies in Mexico and Brazil. Such ideology hails universal inclusion through racial mixture, with a privileging of Indigenous identity (*indigenismo*), and yet has unevenly incorporated and abjected Indigenous and Asian people under Iberian capitalist territorialization, privatization, and development. Through a comparison of Yamashita's *Through the Arc of the Rain Forest* and Leslie Silko's *Almanac of the Dead*, I trace how differing imaginations of cross-community mobilization against global capital can unevenly repeat the settler and racial legacies of *mestizaje/mestiçagem* discourse. The novels trace the transformations of Asian American and Indigenous political mobilization in response to economic changes, transformations that move from identity-based mobilization to transnational and cross-racial connectivity. I argue that representations of Asian-Indigenous intimacies within these imaginations of solidarity reveal the limits of transnational, cross-racial theories of economic resistance as they encounter the settler racial legacies of *mestizaje/mestiçagem* ideologies. At the same time, as performative metanarratives, both novels also open up fraught but necessary lines of discussion about the efficacy of different literary forms, their pitfalls, and their potential, which can help to generate decolonizing collectivities amid the global, neoliberal present.

Settler Racial Teleologies of *Mestizaje* and *Mestiçagem* Discourse

Before analyzing the uneven ways that transnational cross-racial mobilization against neoliberal capital can undergird the settler and racial logics of contemporary *mestiçagem/mestizaje,* I contextualize and examine more critically Vasconcelos's and Freyre's conceptualizations of racial mixture in Mexico and Brazil. While these philosophers' works were circulated decades prior to both the publication of Yamashita's and Silko's texts and the major neoliberal global shifts in the economy, I want to highlight the centrality of both Indigenous and Asian identities in these men's critical visions of *mestiçagem/mestizaje,* which continue to inform present-day global economic discourse and struggles. Highlighting the settler racial logics of *mestiçagem/mestizaje* philosophies in these two settler states allows us to more carefully track its problematic legacy as it shapes Yamashita's and Silko's representations of contemporary hemispheric Asian American and Indigenous resistance to global capital.

Mestizaje *in Revolutionary Mexico (1910–1920)*

In revolutionary Mexico, the concept of *mestizaje* worked together with that of *indigenismo*, or state rhetoric, policies, and programs that sought to center Indigenous communities while also registering such communities as an "Indian problem" impeding the unification of the settler state. While revolutionary Mexican leaders worked to do away with the Eurocentric thinking and narratives of white superiority that were woven through the policies implemented by the prior Porfirio Diaz regime, *mestizaje* during the revolutionary era continued to share a liberal inheritance that registered Indigenous peoples through a narrative telos that demanded assimilation into the national economy and into "modern" citizenry.[3] Despite the complicated rationales that structure *mestizaje* and the related policy of *indigenismo*, they were nevertheless forged from very particular ideas about indigeneity that registered Indigenous communities as weak and unorganized, in need of nourishment and strengthening by the paternal presence of the state. As scholar Alan Knight suggests, these policies emerged out of a nationalist common sense that was inflected by sensibilities toward social justice for Indigenous peoples but was also conditioned by economic interests of national coherency.[4]

This imperative toward economic coherency is also reflected in the revolutionary Mexican state's responses to Asian immigration. Whereas revolutionary *mestizaje* sought to incorporate Indian difference as a way to unify the state, such unification also depended on external limits that were marked meaningfully by anti-Chinese sentiments. As Knight writes: "Sinophobia was the logical corollary of revolutionary *indigenismo*. And the outcome, in Mexico as in Europe, was discriminatory legislation, ghettoization, and expulsion."[5] While anti-Chinese sentiments circulated throughout the hemisphere, they were most visible in U.S.-based Chinese exclusion acts. Mexico often inherited these sentiments and at the same time linked Chinese immigrant relationships to its hemispheric capitalist ties with the United States. That is, Chinese presence, particularly in northwestern Mexico, was seen as an economic threat to the Mexican *petit bourgeoisie*, as well as a stand-in or middleman for U.S. imperial encroachment.[6] Knight's analysis draws on the economic logic of this dialectic of integration and expulsion and suggests that the association of the Chinese with economic threat provided a racial symbol against which revolutionaries could rally.[7]

As a liberal vision of the state, Vasconcelos's conceptualization of *mestizaje* is structured by a telos that seeks to situate Mexico and all other Latin American countries as a preeminent settler colony and therefore as a global imperial power. For Vasconcelos, *La raza cósmica* emerges out of three stages of historical development: (1) materialist, (2) logical, and (3) aesthetic. This progression follows society's move away from logical reasoning as the prime rationale for racial mixing and toward transcendental affinities for the aesthetic or the beautiful. Early in his essay, Vasconcelos cites the necessity for engaging the spirit (rather than materialism or logic) toward this vision of the future race. At the same time, he suggests that the formation of the cosmic race, while stemming from an impalpable sense that veers from the logical or critical realm, is also contingent on the telos, or trajectory, of progress. He maintains again later on in the essay that this spirit must be funneled into a critical directionality for the future of the race to be actuated.[8] While the end goal is the blending of all races into one cosmic universal ideal, Vasconcelos makes clear that this telos begins and is deeply informed by the European colonial imagination and the historical competition between Anglo-Saxon and Latin people. That is, the trajectory toward the formation of the cosmic race, or what Vasconcelos terms the "fifth universal race," relies on European (particularly Latin: Spanish and Portuguese) conquest of the Américas.[9] His text calls for a pan–Latin Américan formation, or a "Latin Confederation," to create the necessary connections across nations in Latin América as the necessary groundwork for his future-tense vision.

Within Vasconcelos's vision of *mestizaje*, Indigenous peoples are rendered as signifiers of a past race that will be developed for the materialization of a new race. He argues that

> the Indian has no other door to the future but the door of modern culture, nor any other road but the road already cleared by Latin civilization. The white man, as well, will have to depose his pride and look for progress and ulterior redemption in the souls of his brothers from other castes. He will have to diffuse and perfect himself in each of the superior varieties of the species, in each of the modalities that multiply revelation and make genius more powerful.[10]

Here Vasconcelos situates the Indian as moving toward "the door of modern culture" and on a "road already cleared by Latin civilization." The image implicates this movement as one of forging Indigenous peoples into the trajectory of modernization wrought from industrialization. So far as Vasconcelos's vision seeks to move Indigenous peoples toward participation in Mexico's modes of production, it does not veer far from the project of *indigenismo* that typified the Porfirian regime. The difference is that, in Vasconcelos's vision, the white race will also no longer exist, since it will inevitably blend into the cosmic race. Despite this seeming difference, the white race and colonial domination continues to be the agent and actor out of which the final race will be actuated. As shown in the above quotation, the white race changes, not from its own movement toward progress but rather in a selective process of "perfecting [it]self" in what amounts to the cultural appropriation of Indigenous peoples.

Vasconcelos's conception of the cosmic race and the rise of the *mestizo* is also contingent on territory as the necessary grounds on which this kind of aesthetic transcendence can be actuated.[11] His repeated proclamation about the abundance of land marks the materialist rationale for the incorporation of Indigenous peoples in his vision of the cosmic race. As he articulates, Latin América serves as a particularly ripe geography out of which the cosmic race might flourish, given the abundance of land that typifies the nations within. Interestingly, rather than articulating land possession as a necessary step to forge a space for the final race, he suggests that territorialization of Indigenous lands is already a foregone conclusion, thus hailing the tense logics of settler colonialism, much as we saw in the public apologies discussed in Chapter 2. In this sense, the prevailing *mestizaje* discourse, represented by Vasconcelos, mobilizes the protection of Indigenous communal holdings at the same time as it naturalizes the state's autochthonous rights to Indigenous lands.[12]

Vasconcelos conceptualizes the Asian or "Oriental" in a conflicted way. That is, the figure operates as a shifting signifier in this trajectory toward the cosmic race. On one hand, as noted by the essay's translator, Dider T. Jaén, Vasconcelos was very much informed by "Oriental thought and religious concepts," particularly from India.[13] The translator also describes how the conceptualization of *mestizaje* as a spiritual movement outside of materialist logics stems from the author's education in Indian religiosity.[14] This impact can be seen in the conclusion, where Vasconcelos sets up India as one of the nations that has the capacity to move, along with the "Ibero-Americas," toward what he conceives as the final destination of humanity.[15] Proceeding from his statement about what aspects of other races should be incorporated—including Indian ancient knowledge and black sensuality—Vasconcelos writes that the cosmic race welcomes "the Mongol, with the mystery of his slanted eyes that see everything according to a strange angle, and discover I know not what folds and newer dimensions."[16] In both instances in which Vasconcelos incorporates an Asian figure into the cosmic race, he emphasizes their mystical and/or mysterious nature.

Vasconcelos seems to oscillate between rendering the Asiatic or Oriental as, on the one hand, one of the multitudes of races that will blend into the fifth race and, on the other, as unassimilable. In both cases, the logical end provides the grounds for their eventual annihilation. Thus, Vasconcelos's commitment to this racial mixing in the essay is fleeting at best; the Asian figure appears and disappears multiple times in his text. This oscillation is most apparent in Vasconcelos's rendering of the Chinese immigrant. In an interesting moment, the author discusses Chinese exclusions prevalent in the United States, presenting it as an example to highlight how U.S. exclusion of the "other" will eventually prove unviable for that settler nation. Vasconcelos argues that Latin América is different than the United States because it is more prepared for and open to racial mixture writ large. At the same time, he argues that the restriction of the Chinese may be necessarily implemented in Mexico. He maintains that while nationalism is parochial, it is sometimes necessary in order to protect the formative nation from foreign encroachment of chaotic elements. Vasconcelos further supports this rationale for Chinese exclusion by suggesting that such a mixture is negative to the fulfillment of the cosmic race, given the Chinese propensity toward isolation and their "zoological" ability to multiply.[17] In his assessment of Chinese exclusion, Vasconcelos leaves open the possibility that it should extend to the context of Latin América. However, he considers this viable not because of any form of economic logic (which he situates as a lower order of feeling) but as a matter of taste, which he argues will spur the formation of the cosmic race.

For Vasconcelos, Asians and Asian immigration not only are situated as both possibilities and threats to internal cohesion; Asian nations also serve as comparisons to Mexican/Latin American imperial prominence. Along with the United States, Japan is described as a possible future imperial power that could undermine Mexican/Latin American cohesion and the solidity of an Iberian empire.[18] Vasconcelos writes that while Latin América does not want to war with these other nations, it will protect itself from their "violent force." Vasconcelos sets up Latin América as implementing world domination through the education of beauty and love, in contrast to the use of imperial force. Relying on a teleological view of history progressing in three stages, Vasconcelos dismisses the possibility of domination by Asian nations. For Vasconcelos, such countries cannot fulfill this "mission" because they are "exhausted" and "lacking in the necessary boldness for new enterprises."[19] Vasconcelos mentions the Malaysian as one example of a race that is irrevocably stuck in the second stage of history, the stage of logic, a view that follows dominant precepts of Asians as "crafty."[20] However, Vasconcelos very quickly neutralizes the notion that the logical (Asian) races could win over "the dreamers and kind at heart." In his scenario, then, like Indigenous peoples in Latin América, Asians belong to the past in his conception of the future.

Although Vasconcelos replaces the white subject for the *mestizo* subject, it is nevertheless apparent that for him Latin América's race toward "progress" continues to hinge on the territorialization of Indigenous lands, the economic assimilation of Indigenous peoples, and the racialization of Asian aliens as signs of imperial encroachment and competition. The role and function of *mestizaje* is to relay this "forward" march as a common sense tied to the naturalized affinities of taste and beauty.²¹ The appreciation of taste and beauty is registered as a transcendental quality and situated in opposition to the lower order of reason. However, his discussion of the formation of the fifth race continues to rely on an armed encroachment on peoples who, and lands that are, at odds with such common sense. Vasconcelos suggests as much as he envisions the future role that Latin América plays globally: "If the fifth race takes ownership of the axis of the future world, then airplanes and armies will travel all over the planet educating people for their entry into wisdom."²² Vasconcelos's theorization of racial mixture is premised on settler colonial and imperial values—reliant as it is on both the hailing and yet obscuring of settler violence. In this it is similar to Freyre's concept of racial mixture in Brazil, although their views are different in methodology and content.

Mestiçagem *in Vargas-Era Brazil (1930–1945)*

In the context of Brazil, *mestiçagem* discourse—which often romanticizes racial mixing and overwrites violent and sexualized histories of colonization and plantation labor—had its roots in the early formation of the Portuguese colony and the subsequent formation of the Brazilian state.²³ During the Getúlio Vargas era, and the official implementation of the *Estado Novo,* the discourse of *mestiçagem* was accelerated by political and economic imperatives of national consolidation and industrialization that sought to connect the industrialized eastern portion of the state to the western hinterlands.²⁴ As historian Seth Garfield highlights, during this period Indigenous peoples were simultaneously considered central to national identity and as communities needing to be conquered or incorporated into a racially mixed nation.²⁵

In addition to incorporative representations of the Indian, the Vargas era saw the unassimilable (Asian) immigrant as a threat to national identity formation and consolidation. Fears of the increasing ethnic diversity of Brazil, tied to the rise of Japanese immigration during the first half of the twentieth century, led to controlled immigration and restrictions on education for Japanese people.²⁶ As with representations of Indigenous peoples, discussions of Japanese immigration and presence were far from monolithic. Interestingly, anti-Japanese activists stressed the unassimilability of these new immigrants, while advocates for Japanese integration into the national body cited blood ties between the Japanese and the Indigenous communities of Brazil. While both camps oscillated in public support, the often underlying sentiment of both camps was that in any form of racial mixing, the white element should be dominant. As such, additional European immigration was encouraged, while the immigration of Asians (particularly the Japanese) was undesirable.[27]

Best known for his anthropological works *The Masters and the Slaves* (1933) and *New World in the Tropics* (1945), Freyre's theory of *mestiçagem* was published in the *durée* of the Vargas era and continues to influence commonsense understandings of Brazilian national identity.[28] Freyre's conceptualization is anchored by the assertion that Brazil is a superior settler colony in comparison to the United States and Spanish-colonized Latin American countries.[29] He highlights Brazil's prominence as a paradise of racial mixture, but it is also evident that Portuguese identity is the central component in this formation. In *The Masters and the Slaves*, Freyre traces a history of Portuguese identity formation and its long process of racial mixture between Europeans, Moors, and Africans as the foundation of miscegenation in Brazil. For Freyre, Portuguese history and propensity for racial mixture, coupled with Portuguese male sexual potency, led to unions between Portuguese men and Indigenous and enslaved African women in the colony. For Freyre, it was this early and sensual mobilization of mixed couplings, at least in comparison to Spanish and British colonization in other parts of the Américas, in conjunction with the tropical climate, that led to the unifying economic structure of the plantation system and the formation of the family unit, which he argued solidified the strength of the settler colony.[30] While it is worth noting that Freyre provides multiple critiques of the violence of colonization, he considers the means justified by what he believes is a productive and positive end.[31] Thus, Freyre romanticizes Brazil as a "hybrid" society, but one in which the European colonizer (dubbed "advanced") continues to appropriate for his benefit what he considers the best of Native and African (dubbed "backward") peoples.[32] Through the dyad of "advanced" and "backward" peoples, and through explaining their relationship to each other as one of "profit" and "value," Freyre's conceptualization of *mestiçagem* is registered along a culturally punctuated capitalist telos whereby incorporation of Indigenous or enslaved African peoples becomes the means by which a mixed yet European-centered "future race" can emerge. The actor and agent of this entire process of miscegenation is the Portuguese, whose sexuality in the tropics is to be celebrated and largely, but not entirely, disentangled from the violence that structures it.

Like Vasconcelos's depiction of *mestizaje*, Freyre's concept of *mestiçagem* depends on representations of Indigenous peoples that position them along the path from savagery to civilization. This temporal placement of the Indigenous continues throughout his work. Freyre conceives of the Brazilian Native peoples, even in contrast to the Aztec and Maya, as "one of the most backward populations," who are like "bands of grown-up children."[33] This "backwardness," Freyre argues, produced less forceful resistance to colonial encroachment. In analyzing Indigenous resistance to colonial force, Freyre both conflates and contrasts Indigenous people with the land. For Freyre, the Indian was "vegetable in his mode of aggression," less resistant to Portuguese invasion than the uncompromising land itself.[34] In aligning Indigenous peoples with the land, Freyre also makes more explicit his concept of Indigenous peoples as the raw materials out of which the nation and national identity will be forged.

Asian figures are not prominent in *The Masters and the Slaves* but are given more attention in Freyre's later book *New World in the Tropics*. In the former book, where Asians or Asian nations are mentioned, they are aligned with their positionality as past or potential countries to be colonized. For example, Freyre mentions Portuguese colonization of India as a point of comparison and condition of possibility for the colonization of Brazil.[35] That is, the extraction of resources in India went hand in hand with the extraction of knowledge from colonies in Asia, which, for Freyre, created the necessary means for a successful Portuguese colonial endeavor in Brazil.[36] For Freyre, the success of this colonial endeavor is especially evident in comparison to U.S. colonization of the Philippines. That is, given the U.S. colonizers' inability to acclimatize to tropical zones, Freyre argues, their efforts were not as quick or virile as those of the Portuguese in the colonization of Brazil.[37] He expands his discussion of Asian presence in his conceptualization of *mestiçagem* in *New World in the Tropics*. In it, Freyre provides an even more extensive catalogue of knowledge accrued in Asian nations (from India to China) that led to the construction of types of architecture that were more amenable to the tropical climate of Brazil.[38] While Japanese immigrants are included in his understanding of *mestiçagem*, it was predominantly Asian culture and form that provided value in Freyre's formulation of a settler paradise.

As both Vasconcelos's and Freyre's works reveal, the formation of *mestizaje/mestiçagem* national identity at key revolutionary and postrevolutionary junctures depended on the dialectic between settler territorialization of Indigenous lands and settler imperial longings and protectionist logics. The co-constitutive representations of Indigenous and Asian (or "Oriental") peoples in Vasconcelos's and Freyre's conceptualizations of *mestizaje/mestiçagem* are organized along a temporal trajectory; both communities play a different role, but both are seen as past cultural formations that will be bypassed by the triumphant formation of an Iberian-centered racial mixture. This progress toward the future nation, and the crucial yet past-tense role of

Indigenous and Asian communities therein, establishes a common sense of national identity that simultaneously recognizes, celebrates, and obscures the violent settler racial processes out of which these future nations come into being.

While critical scholarship on the formation of *mestizaje/mestiçagem* has highlighted the ways that these ideas are contingent on racial/colonial hierarchies and settler logics that incorporate Indigenous peoples and land as raw materials out of which a future race might emerge, very few have explored the ways that they are interlinked with Asian racialization.[39] As we examine the influential writings of Vasconcelos and Freyre, it is clear that these different communities' racialization cannot be considered separately; their presence is mutually interactive in the construction of the settler state and the *mestizo/mestiço* subject therein. Thus, the settler and racial logics that structure *mestizaje/mestiçagem* continue to influence both state economic projects and social justice movements in the contemporary moment.

In the next sections, I examine how critical imaginations of transnational cross-racial mobilization against global capitalist encroachment draw from the settler and racial logics of *mestizaje/mestiçagem* ideology. In Yamashita's and Silko's texts, relationships between Asian and Indigenous characters reveal the complicated ways that revisions of hemispheric Asian American and Indigenous social justice imaginaries can support such settler racial logics. By exposing these problems in their metanarratives, both texts enable dialogue about the complicated role of literary form and formations in helping to incite solidarities and alliances amid the incorporative dynamics of settler racial hegemonies in Latin América.

Karen Tei Yamashita's *Through the Arc of the Rain Forest*

Published in 1990, Karen Tei Yamashita's magical realist novel *Through the Arc of the Rain Forest* addresses global economic changes and the shifts in social movements that can affect nations, communities, and ecologies. Expansive in scope, the narrative crosses three continents (North America, South America, Asia), and depicts characters of a multitude of national, racial, ethnic, gender, and sexual backgrounds. The central action revolves around the fictional site of the Matacão, a broad expanse of supposedly virgin land located in Brazil that is vulnerable to the environmental exploits attached to global capitalist enterprises. The Matacão, mysteriously made out of a plasticlike material, draws the attention of GGG, a multinational corporation based in the United States. GGG relocates to Brazil in order to extract and profit from the plasticlike substance. The commodification of the Matacão's "miracle" substance is propelled by the actions and beliefs of an often-unwitting group of characters. In particular, the lives of a Japanese immigrant (Kazumasa Ishimaru), a Brazilian "everyman" and "everywoman" (Batiste Djapan and Tania Aparecida Djapan), a gay religious icon (Chico Paco), an Indigenous peasant (Mané Pena), and a U.S. American businessman (J. B. Tweep) intersect and contribute to the ecological disaster that concludes the story.

Through this expansive vision, Yamashita reveals how global capitalism redistributes material access across different communities. In addition, the novel engages how the very discourse of social justice can itself provide the conditions of possibility for ecological disaster come the novel's end. In so doing, the narrative has its finger on the pulse of the crisis in the post–civil rights and cultural nationalist era, when social justice movements paradoxically enable the asymmetrical economic mobility of communities of color through capital's co-optation of the language of social and political resistance.[40] As scholar Masao Miyoshi argues, since the 1970s the change in capital's mode of production affirms the autonomy of transnational corporations as it maneuvers across and within geopolitical divides. He argues that the incorporative and flexible accumulation of capital is multifaceted in its reaches, to the point that even discourses of resistance can be reformulated into a profitable package.[41] In the novel, the efforts and ingenuity of various characters begin with intentions for the greater good, only to be repackaged and sold for profit. Such products—from Kazumasa's magical ball, which floats over his head and connects him to different social and physical environments, to Mané Pena's magical feather, which he discovers can heal both psychical and physical ailments—are cheaply reproduced by GGG and then sold for $9.99. Through this quirky rendering, Yamashita's text grapples with the problems of contemporary cultural resistance within the incorporative drive of global capitalism.

Kazumasa's narrative trajectory captures the problems of contemporary trends in hemispheric Asian American critique, trends that emphasize transnational cross-racial mobilization. While attentive to the new forms of economic exploitation, this transformed Asian Americanist critique participates in settler racial hegemonies through its reiteration of *mestiçagem* discourse and its settler racial logics. In my reading of the novel, I argue that this problem of contemporary Asian American critique is highlighted in the relationships between Kazumasa and two key characters: Lourdes, his Brazilian maid-turned-lover, and Mané Pena, an Indigenous peasant-turned-guru. While Kazumasa's story provides a revision of cultural nationalist politics in Asian American critique, it problematically invokes romanticized narratives of *mestiçagem* discourse, which obscure the power asymmetries that persist in the relationship between Lourdes and Kazumasa. In addition, their relationship is set in the aftermath of Mané Pena's death, which links contemporary *mestiçagem* discourse and the elision and death of Indigenous peoples.

These narrative moments highlight the problems inherent in the oversimplified transformations of Asian American political mobilization that fail to attend to the entrenched settler histories that inform the settler racial common sense in Brazil. In her self-reflexive transit through these problematics, Yamashita specifically opens up space to think through the ways literary and cultural forms (specifically the telenovela and the postmodern novel) establish and reestablish settler racial hegemonies in the global neoliberal contemporary moment. It is through literary form that Yamashita grapples with the question of how to move beyond the settler logics that haunt hemispheric Asian Americanist organizing and critique.

Revisions of Asian American Critique in Global Capital

Set amid global economic restructuring in the late twentieth century, Yamashita's novel illuminates shifts in the economies of the United States and Japan and their specific impact in Brazil. In the 1970s, the United States shifted from Fordism toward a system of flexible accumulation that ushered the movement of capital out of the nation into countries amenable to corporations' needs for cheap labor and resources.[42] For Miyoshi, this change in capital's mode of production speaks to the sovereign drive of transnational corporations (TNCs) and their profit-driven maneuverings across and within geopolitical divides.[43] Such changes provide the condition of possibility for U.S. economic encroachment into Brazil, a condition illuminated in the novel by the rise of GGG.

Japan also became increasingly influential in Brazil's economy.[44] In the post–World War II era, Japanese capital investment in and immigration to Brazil grew exponentially.[45] Scholar Jeffrey Lesser writes that these economic relations were shaped by several factors. First, he explains that "Japan's huge capital reserves needed to be invested overseas, and Brazil, with its raw materials and potential growth, was a logical choice. Investment in Brazil also helped Japanese multinationals cut labor costs and export some of their most polluting plants."[46] In addition, given the increasing rate of Japanese immigration to Brazil, the investment of Japanese capital in what was considered a "debtor nation" was spurred by the availability of Japanese Brazilians who were able to take on key managerial and clerical roles.

Yamashita's novel illuminates these economic contexts while grappling with the critical transformations of Asian American politics in ways that can account for the economic ascendancy of Asian immigrant/Asian American communities. As scholar Rachel Lee argues, Yamashita's novel reveals how these economic realities make previous iterations of Asian Americanist, nationally based discourse seem anachronistic. The novel thus calls for an Asian Americanist politics that "might widen the scope of their struggles to de-ethnicize their communal fidelities in order to fight for the poor and oppressed regardless of national origins."[47] For Lee, it is specifically through Kazumasa's marriage to Lourdes that this gesture toward solidarity across national, racial, and class demarcations is apparent. She states: "When Asians become associated less with the laboring bodies of historical memory . . . and more with the ownership of capital and professional occupations[,] . . . Asian American writers may negotiate that financial-economic ascendancy by (re)-claiming proletarian solidarity through the symbolism of marriage."[48] For Lee, this narrative movement symbolically counteracts Asian Americanist desires for class ascendancy through marriage to white and economically privileged people. While Lee highlights the problematically obscured class asymmetries that result from this symbolic political move, I want to highlight how it carries on the settler racial legacy of *mestiçagem* ideology in Brazil. Thus, while Kazumasa's claiming of solidarity through his marriage with Lourdes may undercut the economic rise and desires of an ascendant Asian American/immigrant class, it actively feeds into the settler narratives of *mestiçagem* so prevalent in Brazil and other Latin American countries.

Indeed, while it offers a new narrative of Asian American transnational and cross-racial political commitments and orientations, the love story between Kazumasa and Lourdes also recalls earlier *mestiçagem* narratives that feature relations between the Portuguese male colonizer and the Indigenous woman. Such narratives are perhaps best exemplified in Freyre's conceptualization of Brazil's mixed-race paradise, itself influenced by the legends of *Iracema*. Ella Shohat and Robert Stam write that the narrative of *Iracema* is a romantic fable written in the nineteenth century that "imagines the origins of Brazil as a nation in the fecund heterosexual encounter of European male and indigenous woman, presented as the primal matrix of Brazil's identity."[49] In this narrative, the Portuguese man is a representation of virile masculinity and the Indigenous woman is represented as accommodating and docile.

This regressive national trope is exemplified in one of the final scenes of *Through the Arc*, where Kazumasa and Lourdes reunite on a farm to begin their life together:

> [Kazumasa] immediately moved Lourdes and the children onto a farm filled with acres and acres of tropical fruit trees and vines and

> a plantation of pineapple and sugarcane, sweet corn and coffee. Rubens [Lourdes's son] wheeled happily around the guava orchards, and Gislaine [Lourdes's daughter] sat in the branches of a jaboticaba tree, sucking out the sweet white flesh of its fruit from their purple-black skins. Kazumasa ran around Lourdes like another child, filling her baskets with miniature bananas, giant avocados and mangos, which seemed to him to reflect the sunset. Lourdes put her baskets down on the rich red soil of their land and embraced Kazumasa, who now stood casually with a rather newly formed posture, the sort to accompany, quite naturally, the tropical tilt of his head.[50]

In contrast to the environmental devastation that surrounds them, their farm is lush and teeming with a sexual energy that typifies stereotypical renderings of Brazilian life and specifically Freyre's depiction of the colonial slave plantation. The scene, too, conjures the image of the virile man pursuing the docile woman as Kazumasa "fill[s] her baskets with miniature bananas." Moreover, it is in the insistence that this is "their land" that the scene iterates the cross-racial romantic couple as the originators, and their progeny as inheritors, of the Brazilian nation.

In recalling this earlier trope, however, the novel also provides important revisions. For one, the novel changes the major figures central to the narrative of *Iracema*. In place of the Portuguese male–Indigenous female dyad is a Japanese immigrant male–Latina (presumably mixed-race) female. By replacing the Portuguese colonizer with the Japanese immigrant, the narrative displaces the xenophobia attached to Eurocentric frames of reference that had informed early *mestiçagem* discourse. The narrative thus seems to call for the embrace of the new (alien) immigrant as a key contributor to the formation of Brazil's national identity. Additionally, it must be noted that Lourdes, who is never racially identified, is described only as a "native" of São Paulo. Like Batiste Djapan's identity, which is presented as "Brazilian everyman," Lourdes's Brazilian identity is unmarked (especially interesting in comparison to the codifications that name Mané Pena's "Indianness" and Kazumasa's "Japanese-ness"). Her identity thus signals the naturalization of Brazilian identity as it is presumably informed by histories of racial mixture between African, Indigenous, and Portuguese peoples. Even more interestingly, what marks her identity is her class status in relationship to Kazumasa. By replacing the figure of the Indigenous woman with the Latina woman, the narrative points to the logical end of *mestiçagem*—the racially mixed figure replaces the Indigenous figure as the "natural" inheritor of Brazilian national identity and the land the settler state occupies.

The novel's central romance also revises the class asymmetries that structure past conceptions of *mestiçagem*. In contrast to Freyre's conception of racial mixture as the primary mode through which the Portuguese colonizer and slave owner was able to accomplish his rise in social and economic status, here Kazumasa's love for Lourdes connects him more greatly to the working-class everyday people of Brazil.[51] The novel sets up this distinction most explicitly in the love triangle between Lourdes, Kazumasa, and his cousin Hiroshi. Despite his unwitting role in the rise of the GGG, Kazumasa is for the most part an egalitarian figure with a love for the common people. He stands in stark contrast to Hiroshi, whose immigration to Brazil is associated with a middle-class embrace of leisure and capital accumulation.[52] Kazumasa, too, receives a hero's redemption by the end of the novel when he relinquishes entirely his ties to GGG. Lourdes's sustained love for Kazumasa, rather than Hiroshi, thus represents the common sense of a national ideal that values class equality over class ascendancy.

In addition, while Kazumasa and Lourdes's farm recalls Freyre's trumpeting of the plantation family as the pinnacle of Brazilian national formation, Freyre's paternalistic slant is not strongly present in the scene. In contrast to mainstream understandings of virile masculinity, Kazumasa might be deemed "unmasculine." Indeed, he moves like "another child" and fills Lourdes's basket both with the sexually suggestive "bananas" as well as with the more feminized eroticism of "giant avocados and mangos." Here too, the ideal hemispheric Asian American liberatory subject lives a deeply place-based existence, one that emphasizes his continued commitment to class equity symbolized by Kazumasa "filling [Lourdes's] baskets" with fruit. Overall, these revisions of *mestiçagem* discourse (as distilled in the *Iracema* story) work to envision new collectivities and liberatory subject formations for the global present. Kazumasa's and Lourdes's equitable sexualized union is set up as that of a new emblematic couple ushering in a more hopeful future.

Reiterating the Settler Logics of Mestiçagem

Like past conceptions of *mestiçagem* discourse, however, this new liberatory identity formation for Brazil continues to rely on a settler common sense that has historically structured the formation of Brazil as a settler nation. First, Kazumasa and Lourdes escape to a place that reiterates the idea that Indigenous space/place must be cleared and settled for a new *mestiçagem* future to emerge. By the time they arrive, all that remains of Indigenous presence in the text is a passing reference to the "red earth." Rather than contextualizing how Kazumasa and Lourdes reach the farm, the narrative moves from the devastation of the environment—where all land was seemingly enveloped in the environmental disaster—to Kazumasa and Lourdes's miraculous access to territory. The narrative leap from ecological disaster to pastoral paradise emulates the type of logical leap that structures a settler common sense that continues to naturalize the settler seizing of lands from colonial "contact" to the global contemporary. Such a leap constitutes the kind of colonial amnesia or lapse in logic, what Lisa Lowe terms the "economy of affirmation and forgetting," that continues to structure contemporary liberatory imaginations.[53]

The logics of this supposed amnesia, however, are made visible through the narrative's representation of the primary Indigenous figure in the novel, Mané Pena, whose death precedes Kazumasa and Lourdes's happy ending. Examining Mané's narrative trajectory reveals that it is not a lapse in logic but a deeply processed epistemology and structure of feeling that provides the possibility for Kazumasa to move from ecological disaster to pastoral paradise. We can see through Mané's overall trajectory in the narrative how his narrative path is epistemologically and affectively entangled with Kazumasa and Lourdes's happy ending.

First, Kazumasa and Lourdes's farmland is epistemologically cleared from Indigenous claims of settlement through the narrative devaluation of any notion of "authentic" indigeneity within the context of capitalist commodification. This devaluation is evident in the novel's postmodernist sensibility, which conveys the loss of authenticity in the commodification of peoples and cultures. This postmodernist sensibility sets up the logical trajectory through which Mané's presence and claims to lands become increasingly nullified.

Mané is introduced in the narrative as a forest-dweller type, and his family experiences a series of displacements and shifts in subsistence when first the Brazilian state and then later transnational corporations eye and then seize the land on which his family subsists. Throughout these ordeals, Mané and his family survive through the use of a feather that can magically calm the spirits and cure varying ailments. While initially it is used specifically for his family, Mané's feather catches the attention of GGG, which later reproduces, markets, and sells the feathers as a product for the masses. With the sale of feathers increasing among the public, Mané rises to the status of the "Father of Featherology," the man who can translate the knowledge of the feather to the non-Indigenous public.

A clear reference to a Carlos Castañeda–type figure, Mané experiences a rise to world renown that tracks specifically the ways Indigenous-based epistemologies become commodified and then translated to a non-Indigenous public, thereby implying a lost legitimacy as a knowledge system forged in community. For example, at multiple moments in the text, Mané is compelled to categorize, hierarchize, and legitimize how the feather should be used, emulating objective scientific language to conjure the power of the feather. Over time, Mané's transformed understanding of the feather's power as scientific seems totalizing. For example, in a statement that he issues to forewarn the public about irresponsible uses of the feather, he devalues Indigenous and glorifies Western scientific uses of the feather:

> He and his institute opposed the senseless killing of birds for their feathers for purely decorative uses, such as in costumes, headdresses, or on hats. . . . However, Mané Pena, the official statement read, continued to support the use of feathers for the greater cause of *science and human health*.[54]

Here what might be registered as Indigenous traditional dress is regarded as purely aesthetic, while the value of the feather lies in its scientific properties delineated through academic/scientific language.

The narration traces how, once locked in the discursive parameters and value systems of objectivity and science, Mané is irrevocably vulnerable to its terms. Come the narrative's end, the feathers carry a microorganism that becomes the source of a major typhus epidemic:

> Rickettsia were microorganisms that traveled via a minute species of lice, which in turn traveled via feathers, which, of course, traveled via birds and, of late, humans. The lice that transmitted rickettsia were practically invisible to the naked eye, but they were the nasty creatures that invaded the pores in the ears and around the neck and sucked the skin into a rash.[55]

Mané and his entire family become vulnerable to the epidemic, and the magic of the feather that once helped them through difficult times is neutralized. In this passage, Mané's death is explained through minute attention to, again, scientific language. For Mané, locked in a foreign discursive system, the feather's former powers are rendered useless. He finds that he is unable to forge the invisible lines that once linked him to his family and allowed him to infuse the feather with so much power: "The old couple now clung to each other in complete pity, weeping for an irrecoverable past and for their youngest two children, Beto and Marina, now dead and buried. Cause of death: Typhus."[56] The official statement, "cause of death: Typhus," punctuates the point that the subject's consumption of (the language of) so-called Western science has foreclosed alternative avenues for healing of familial bonds. Through the tragic story of the Pena family, not only is the decimation of Indigenous figures represented; their very status as "authentic" Indigenous peoples is also rendered questionable. Ultimately, the priceless "virgin" land of the Matacão is revealed as a product of the accumulation of trash from the "first world." This postmodernist globalizing of traditional Indigenous lands upends the notion of traditional lands itself.

In addition to the epistemological clearing of Indigenous claims to land, Mané's death also affords an affective clearing of readerly consciences that allows for the emotional investment that structures Kazumasa and Lourdes's happy ending. That is, the affective investment in a mixed-race paradise repeats a settler structure of feeling that is primed by the lamenting of and yet the impossibility of grieving for the dying Indian. The demise of Mané and his family highlights this affective labor. This mourning process is formally and temporally structured: Part 6 (the last part of the novel) begins with Mané's death and concludes with Kazumasa and Lourdes's happy ending. In addition to this placement of Mané's death in the timeline of the plot, the narrative squeezes as much melodrama and pathos as it possibly can out of Mané's and his family's final moments.

Wracked with desperation to save their remaining children, Mané and his wife, Angustia, "desperately" seek different ways to use the feather, but to no effect. Upon the death of their children, Mané and Angustia "clung to each other, weeping for an irrecoverable past." On his deathbed Mané "wept, cried against the deception of his dubious fortune." His death is rendered in spectacular fashion: his ears were so torn from Angustia's desperate attempts to cure him that "morticians were forced to sew the old leathery ears back into place before displaying the body."[57] Through these melodramatic death scenes, the reader is drawn in emotionally to the process of lamenting and mourning Mané and his family's fates. Preceding Kazumasa and Lourdes's reunion, the mourning of the "dying Indian" heightens the tragedy of globalization, making the novel's final emotional apotheosis of hope distilled in a *mestiçagem* futurity all the more effective.

Literary and Cultural Form in the Logics of Settler Racial Hegemonies

Yamashita's metanarrative novel invites discussion on how narrative and cultural forms participate in the reproduction of settler racial hegemonies. *Through the Arc* references several literary and aesthetic forms; in addition to the postmodern novel, it draws on the telenovela form and a Candomblé dance. It is through this emphasis on form that the text opens possibilities beyond the settler racial logics that continue to haunt Asian American literature and critique in the global capitalist present. The "Author's Note" that begins the book indicates that the novel proceeds like a *novela* or telenovela:

constricted by the generalities of the Brazilian soap opera form and yet "changeable through the whims of public psyche and approval."[58] As scholar Mauro Porto argues, telenovelas provide an index and performative mediation of social formation where "broader processes of political, economic, and social change [are] reflected in television fiction's localized representations of the nation." He goes on to say that "*telenovelas* shape these same processes and endow them with new meanings."[59] Through both this prefatory note and her emphasis on the "whims of public psyche," Yamashita suggests that the novel's actions and its political mooring are formed through the commons—its genealogy, its transformations, and its shifting structures of feeling. In the context of Brazil, however, the commons is highly informed by the settler legacies of *mestiçagem* ideology. While the telenovela is arguably a form that reaches and can be influenced by the masses, and therefore egalitarian in form, Yamashita's note also reveals its settler legacy when it claims that it does not and cannot be influenced by "Indians and the very isolated of the frontiers and rural backlands."[60] In this way, in the forging of an Asian American hero under a global capitalist system, the very telenovela form that constructs that hero's triumph is always already limited in its potential to be formed and informed by Indigenous epistemologies that are considered outside the commons.

Interestingly, the novel ends not with the pastoral image of a fruitful earth, but with industrial wreckage, in which the Candomblé dance revives the memory of Kazumasa and Lourdes's story. Candomblé is a syncretic religious and cultural form that fuses Indigenous African and Indigenous American beliefs and is practiced primarily in Brazil. In opposition to *mestiçagem* ideology, which often privileges Portuguese identity even as it glorifies the African and the Native, Candomblé centers Indigenous elements and epistemologies that have emerged out of settler colonialism and enslavement while also incorporating residual forms and formations from Indigenous culture prior to invasion. Although this form is referenced only briefly, this additional framing of the novel within a Candomblé dance opens possibilities for Asian American literature and critique to attend to Indigenous cultural forms and their concomitant epistemologies as a basis for forging a decolonizing Asian American figure that can productively confront settler colonial power in the global capitalist present. In the next section, I examine how Leslie Marmon Silko's *Almanac of the Dead* seems to extend beyond where Yamashita's text leaves off with regard to the forging of a new *mestizaje/mestiçagem* form that includes the possibilities of both Indigenous and hemispheric Asian American critique in the critical movements toward decolonization.

Leslie Marmon Silko's *Almanac of the Dead*

Published in 1991, Leslie Marmon Silko's *Almanac of the Dead* depicts in unrelenting detail the devastating impact of global capitalism and its emergence from the legacies of settler colonialism in the Américas. At more than eight hundred pages and with a cast of more than fifty characters, Silko's narrative depicts the depravities of the colonial order as well as the continuous resurgence of Indigenous-centered resistances. Key Indigenous leaders and non-Native allies meet to plan an already foretold revolution to take back the lands. The novel centers on the converging projects of two sets of revolutionary twins: Lecha and Zeta, Yaqui/mixed-blood women, and Tacho and El Feo, Mayan brothers. Lecha and Zeta are tasked with transcribing the almanac referenced in the book's title, which has been derived from ancient Mayan codices and ancestral knowledge and foretells both settler colonial invasion and its eventual end. The twin brothers, along with a key Mayan character named Angelita La Escapía, work to inspire and prepare for revolution among Indigenous communities in Mexico. In addition to these figures, a Laguna Pueblo man (Sterling), a white woman (Seese), a black Vietnam War vet (Clinton), and a Korean immigrant (Awa Gee), among others, contribute in various ways to revolutionary mobilization across the hemisphere. By the end of the novel, the characters converge in Tucson, Arizona, specifically in Room 1212, to strategize for the end of colonialism.

Like Yamashita's novel, Silko's *Almanac* addresses the limits of nation- and identity-based social justice movements in countering the drive and devastation of contemporary global capitalist processes.[61] Thus, the expansive geographies and cross-racial emphasis of the narrative instigates a move from national to transnational Indigenous collectivities and toward cross-racial connections that can mobilize the masses against what David Harvey has called capital's "accumulation by dispossession."[62] Whereas Yamashita's text indexes the liberal incorporation of contemporary transnational and cross-racial social mobilization into the settler logics of *mestiçagem,* Silko's novel seems to anticipate and then circumvent *mestizaje*'s deleterious effects for Indigenous resurgence. In particular, in the representations of transnational and cross-racial alliances between Indigenous and non-Native allies, the novel curtails a facile romanticization of these alliances and liberal celebrations of racial mixture/*mestizaje* as the key to a decolonial future. This is evident, for example, in the working relationship and precarious alliance between Awa Gee, a computer hacker, and Zeta, an arms dealer. The narrative depicts how, in the past, Awa Gee desired a romantic encounter with Zeta, but the latter refused his attempts. Whereas in *Through the Arc* Kazumasa's liberatory potential is actuated through his marriage to Lourdes, in

Almanac Awa Gee's potential as a decolonial figure is contingent on his romantic distancing from Zeta.

Silko rejects romanticization of liberatory movements through depictions of what I call "ugly alliances," unattractive renderings of decolonizing "heroes" that resist easy romanticization of cross-racial and transnational solidarities. Such monstrous depictions of decolonial efforts, I argue, confront the structures of feeling that often capture liberatory imaginations of resistance against global capitalism. At first glance, Silko's unattractive depiction of Awa Gee, especially his unpalatable sexuality, seems to be another example of the anti-Asian currents that we see in Vasconcelos's conceptualization of *mestizaje*. I engage with this characterization as a heuristic that reveals how Silko's decolonial vision is contingent on a critique of Asian Americanist politics. Like Yamashita, Silko has a self-reflexive engagement with form (particularly her extension of the Mayan codices) that centers the role of literature in confronting settler racial hegemonies.

Ugly Alliances under Economies of Care

In interviews given about her novel, Silko makes clear how local and geopolitical dynamics in the 1980s were formative to her stories. Silko was living in Arizona at that time and saw firsthand the corruption and racialized policing of borders "against anything brown or indigenous." U.S. Air Force helicopters flew over her house in the Abra Valley regularly, and conversations about terrorism in the Middle East and its fueling of Desert Storm were prevalent.[63] Silko explains how the economic focus in *Almanac* was inspired by her reading of Karl Marx and her increasing awareness of the World Bank. These experiences resulted in her depictions of monstrous characters—such as Menardo, Max and Leah Blue, Beaufrey and Serlo—who are identifiable as "destroyers" that directly and unapologetically seek destruction for profit.[64]

Silko's narrative makes clear that the collusion of these characters fuels and shapes the killing, abandoning, and letting die represented in the novel. At the same time, although the novel highlights the impact of these agents of destruction, the forces of colonial degradations do not begin nor end with them. For Silko, the particular machinations of the "destroyers" are linked to what she calls the epoch of the "Death-Eye Dog," emerging from European "contact" in the fifteenth century.[65] By comparing the machinations of neoliberal capitalism to settler colonial violence, Silko brings to our attention what is critically obscured when neoliberalism is viewed as an exception to colonial settler governance, or, in other words, when liberal forms of settler colonial governance are considered the "good guy."

Linking neoliberal global capitalism to liberal forms of rule and care, the narrative self-reflexively queries how the almanac can perform the protective work necessary for the survival of Indigenous and all other beings. Silko's text suggests that survival, for Indigenous peoples, requires being able to recognize and protect the people against the specific forms through which power and violence are manifested, a recognition and resistance enabled by the almanac itself. In a story narrated by Yoeme, grandmother of Zeta and Lecha, the children who are tasked with protecting the almanac are asked to journey northward from the now colonial state of Mexico to the colonial state of the United States. The danger on this journey is not the white colonizers, who are merely spectral presences in the abandoned villages they encounter. Instead, the danger takes the shape and form of a woman in the state of ultimate abandonment, a woman left to die when her community fled the area for refuge elsewhere. Happy to see the children when they arrive at the area called "The Mouth," the old woman is friendly and generous, immediately sharing a pot of stock made from roots she has been foraging from the largely desolate region. Yet, as the days unfold and the children need to continue northward, the old woman's impulse to survive, in any state of degradation, leads her to kill and eat one of the children. It is only because of the literal sustenance of the almanac and the eldest girl's often instinctual actions that she, her other traveling companions, and the almanac survive. The narrative concludes with Yoeme's warning that "the reign of the Death-Eye Dog is marked by people like the [old woman]. She did not start out that way. In the day that belongs to the Death-Eye Dog, the possibility of becoming like her trails each one of us."[66]

Through the story of the old woman's hospitality-cum-violence, Silko raises questions about how the almanac in its present novel manifestation can circumvent the harm that unfolds in various forms in the present moment. Specifically, the narrative raises questions about how to understand the kind of harm that takes the form of care in liberalism. Indeed, in Silko's tableau of neoliberal and liberal permutations of settler coloniality, violence is perpetuated not only directly, through gainful dispossession, but also more insidiously, in seemingly positive affects such as care, hospitality, and even love. In turn, Silko's text allows us to consider questions about what it means to survive and endure when the very ideas that form our understandings of the "good life" produce harm and destruction. If the possibility of "becoming like her trails each one of us," and is imparted through social norms that constitute the otherwise of colonial settler governance, how do we recognize and work against the point where endurance—the impulse to survive and pass on the "good life"—instantiates its own destruction? These questions inform Silko's intimate formation of coalitional politics from the 1980s and into the imagined future.

As my readings of Silko's depictions of ugly Asian-Indigenous alliances show, Silko's novel is a spiritual/affective text—one that does not simply represent the desire and prescription for decolonization but in fact fashions itself as central to the revolution that coincides with the taking up of arms. She shares this:

> These stories work on unconscious levels that we don't have control of and access to by direct everyday means. When I was working with these narratives, I wanted them to have an after-effect in the unconscious, and I knew that things are present in some narratives, especially oral narratives, that make them unforgettable.[67]

It is with this central goal of speaking to readers on a visceral level that Silko reacts almost joyously to negative charges from the mainstream press:

> In the *New Republic* the guy was honest about how viscerally affected he had been [reading the novel], and you could see it in the language. "Aha," I thought, "Something magical *did* happen." I didn't control it, really, but there was something in those narratives that just forced itself to be told through me.[68]

For Silko, the kinds of reactions her text engendered are deemed magical, desirable in a sense, and the consequence of a narrative that she considers not only an almanac but also a "Voodoo Spell" to which she too is beholden.[69]

At the same time, because her text imagines decolonization as a process that must include participants of all races around the world, all of whom occupy different roles, the spiritual upheavals that take place are differentiated. Thus, although Silko's text might, in fact, depict moments of extreme violence to "arouse horror and disgust towards the cruel and extremely egoistic destroyers . . . as well as empathy for the suffering of victims," as Marja-Liisa Helenius suggests, her uneasy and ugly descriptions of even the critical allies to the movement itself demonstrate her attentiveness to the racialization and politics of emotions.[70] Her discussion of *Almanac* as triggering the unconscious, the spirits, the visceral, and the magical affirms the novel's status as an affective decolonial project.

Decolonizing Asian American Critique

It is precisely in this ambiguous distinction between neoliberal and liberal capitalist contexts that Silko's rendering of Awa Gee and the potential of hemispheric Asian American alliances with Indigenous movements emerges as a necessarily messy affair. In the last half of *Almanac,* Silko introduces Awa Gee, a Korean immigrant who has been employed by Zeta, the part-Yaqui underground arms and drugs smuggler who is prophesized to lead the upcoming revolution in the Américas. Awa Gee is a computer hacker and mathematical genius who is paid to help Zeta crack computer codes, reroute phone calls, and create leaks in shipment pipelines of those of Zeta's business associates whom she does not trust. At the same time that he is working for Zeta, Awa Gee has also anonymously linked himself into a network of deep ecologists dubbed Eco-Warriors who are preparing to "destroy all interstate high-voltage transmission lines, power generating plants, and hydroelectric dams across the United States simultaneously."[71] His skills and propensities make Awa Gee critical to the unfolding revolution.

Silko's compelling description of Awa Gee's personality typifies some of the most blatant stereotypes about Asians and Asian Americans: a "strange little yellowish man [with] black slanty eyes," Awa Gee is a mathematical genius, hypersexualized *and* desexualized, and a social outcast. In other words, he possesses the intellectual and social components that make up the figure of the model minority—a general stereotype about Asian Americans in the United States.[72] At the same time, although his profile matches all the key traits of the model minority figure, his orientation, desires, and intentions are far removed from the docility that the discursive model intends to manifest. The novel dramatizes Awa Gee's resistance. During his stint as a researcher at the University of Arizona, one of his many undercover identities, Awa Gee secretly constructed a solar war machine that would eventually destroy the infrastructures of "giants" such as the United States. Rather than working within the economies of U.S. multiculturalism, Awa Gee is fueled by a desire for total destruction of all infrastructures: "He was interested in the purity of destruction[,] . . . in the perfection of complete disorder and disintegration[,] . . . wanted to build nothing[,] . . . wanted nothing at all except for the lights to go out."[73]

Through Awa Gee, the narrative stakes out a particular Asian American positionality that is attuned to a hemispheric vision of decolonization. For one, Awa Gee has no strong attachments nor affinity to a U.S. national identity. Indeed, one of Awa Gee's specialties involves his ability to forge "new identities complete with passports, driver's licenses, social security numbers—everything obtainable through computer records."[74] His activities mark his recognition of the construction and precariousness of state identities, perpetually vulnerable to infiltration and annihilation with one push of a button. Awa Gee not only is particularly adept at this line of business—infiltrating official and classified government documents—he enters into it with a glee and intimacy that speaks to his connection to it beyond employment or economic gain. He confesses to Zeta, "The dead are my friends. . . . I go to find birth dates on the gravestones or in the newspaper, then I write to the state capital for a new birth certificate."[75] The novel suggests that this *dis*affiliation with a U.S. national identity is *compelled* by a particular racial experience in the United States. Indeed, Silko depicts Awa Gee as being driven by rage and indignation that are directed toward a United States that denied him government research funding in favor of those he considered "intellectual imbeciles."[76] The novel's satirization of his indignation echoes accounts by Asian Americans of the fiction of the model minority and the reality of the glass ceiling.

The novel imagines that a decolonizing Asian American politics is one that draws from and is mobilized by these felt indignities of national exclusion and racialization. At the same time, the complex characterization of Awa Gee emphasizes the need to read that experience in relationship to U.S. geopolitics and imperialism. As a Korean immigrant, it is not just U.S. racial injustice that drives his anger but also the geopolitical dynamics and economic logics that have shaped his migration to the United States.

> The United States had been different when Awa Gee had first arrived from Seoul by way of Sonora. Awa Gee remembered that back then the world economy had still been riding on the big wave; to Americans, Awa Gee looked Japanese. Back then, all the Americans had been able to talk about were Japanese cars this and Japanese cars that. Love-hate between Japan and the United States, two countries that Awa Gee had despised for their racism and imperialism.[77]

Awa Gee's abhorrence of Japan and the United States is anchored in twentieth-century global politics: the Japanese colonization of Korea since 1910; the division of Korea at the thirty-eighth parallel in 1945, with the Soviet Union occupying the North and the United States occupying the South between 1945 and 1948; and finally U.S. military and epistemological involvement in the Korean War from 1950 to 1953.[78] In *Ends of Empire*, Jodi Kim argues that the Korean civil conflict that followed Japanese and U.S. colonial occupation can be "seen as an arrested project of decolonization."[79] She argues that the "context of Cold War geopolitics and logics that were rapidly congealing as the dominant structure of feeling and knowledge" overwrote readings of the conflict as a continued struggle toward decolonization. Kim also explains that the postwar period resulted in U.S. military investment and aid to South Korea, which in turn boosted Japan's economy, the domestic racial effects of which we see in Silko's narration.[80] In the novel, the U.S. domestic racial logics—part and parcel of Kim's formulation of Cold War geopolitics as epistemological project—threaten but fail to overwrite Awa Gee's embodied memories. Indeed, as a structure of feeling, Awa Gee's *anger* traces the genealogy of his arrival to the United States in the aftermath of colonialism, imperialism, and a circumvented although perpetual impulse toward decolonization. It is precisely from this position, in its embodiments of history, that Awa Gee becomes critically aligned with the global movements toward decolonization that Silko narrates in *Almanac*.

Silko's characterization of Awa Gee has deep implications for the theorization of a politically viable hemispheric Asian American politics. Her narrative reframes Asian American historicization and critique, moving from sole focus on nationalist logics of inclusion and exclusion toward what Jodi Kim terms the imperial logics of "expulsion."[81] This move has a couple of effects. First, attending to the geopolitical dynamics of "expulsion" allows the Asian American subject to address and also move beyond the U.S. nation as the sole site where injuries are to be registered and redressed. Simultaneously, this reframing allows for a reflective analysis of how Asian Americanist cultural productions, as they are connected to a settler structure of feeling, may feed into imperialist and colonial logics.[82] Silko implies that an Asian American struggle that stops at the history of civil rights and national inclusion can enable a kind of forgetting that flattens ethnic particularities and its geopolitical attachments. Awa Gee experiences a form of racist love that is contingent on and overwrites the unequal political and economic alliance between Japan and the United States after World War II—a love whose embrace would also effectively erase Awa Gee's own presence as metonym for Korea's presence within these geopolitical dynamics.[83] His internalization of this structure of feeling via the narrative of inclusion would have meant a form of geopolitical forgetting that Kim argues is at the crux of Cold War knowledge productions. Yet, Silko's Korean American character resists the racial dynamics that lead to this form of historical amnesia.

This resistance to historical amnesia figured in Awa Gee requires attention to the permutations and imbrications of racial formations and geopolitics, an abstract critical lens that he possesses:

> He was most relaxed, most "at home," with his own thoughts and the numbers. Numbers are alive to Awa Gee; some numbers "sang," while others flashed complex patterns of iridescent colors as if they were exotic blossoms or jungle birds. Numbers were his companions, his roommates, and his allies. One morning the "big cheeses" would wake up to discover how the numbers had suddenly all added up to zeroes for them. The power of numbers would reside with the poor and the dispossessed.[84]

For Awa Gee, home and belonging are not harnessed to any nation but to numbers themselves—that is, to an abstraction not yet reified or solidified but one that will always "reside with the poor and dispossessed." The numbers serve as Awa Gee's way of reading and thus situating himself in the world, a political mooring for the hemispheric Asian American subject that is compatible with Silko's vision of decolonization.[85]

Interestingly, although Silko makes explicit how Awa Gee's experience of imperial "expulsion" and national "exclusion" attunes him to the network of the poor and dispossessed, she is careful to distance this particular optic from an affinity with Indigenous experiences in the Américas. It is through the relationship between Zeta and Awa Gee that we see this disentanglement being made. Although Zeta and Awa Gee have a productive working relationship, it works precisely because both recognize and accede to the other's boundaries. Although Awa Gee has confessed his love for Zeta, both are happy to maintain their platonic relationship, and they both concede that friendship will keep them both "safe." Awa Gee is content with what he perceives as Zeta's trust and understanding of "what he can do with computers and numbers."[86] At the same time that Zeta extends a degree of trust to Awa Gee, she also maintains a critical distance from him. Zeta listens to what she calls Awa Gee's "freewheeling discourse" not with full understanding but "amazement [as] his black, slanty eyes twinkled."[87] As he discusses the secure networks he is hacking, Zeta simply shakes her head, alternating from confusion to bemusement. When Awa Gee assures her that he is respecting her privacy, Zeta nods in agreement but thinks privately that she "didn't want to bet on it."[88] In short, although Zeta and Awa Gee are pleasant with one another, they lack the intimacy and understanding that typically form the basis of solidarity movements.

This distance is further established by the narrative's unflattering rendering of Awa Gee as an idiosyncratic man, a perpetual foreigner who does not have a home in the Américas and whose "rightful" place, if it ever comes down to it, is in Korea. In this way the narrative depicts a heroic Asian immigrant figure who—according to American cultural nationalist rubrics—would be deeply undesirable to emulate. Rather than read Silko's representation diagnostically, assessing how it plays up "yellow peril" and may exacerbate dominant conceptions of the Asian American as the perpetual foreigner, I want to understand it heuristically, that is, to ask what this representation of an "ugly alliance," an "uneasy solidarity" suggests about Silko's hemispheric decolonial vision and the place of Asian America in maintaining its coherency.

In her representation of Awa Gee and Zeta, Silko attends to the historical affinities between hemispheric Asian American and Indigenous communities who have experienced the violent collusion between imperial powers and state violence. At the same time that she emphasizes the importance of these affinities, she preserves a particular kind of Native-settler-alien triad that is central to her articulation of decolonial social and environmental justice, one that responds especially to the state- and corporate-sponsored violence attached to neoliberalism and globalization.[89] Silko asserts an Indigenous place-based attachment to land that registers a deep history at the same time that she rejects desires for return to a mythical premodern past. Awa Gee's critique of the deep ecologists he has allied himself with enunciates this particular point:

> To Awa Gee, such a longing for the distant past was a symptom of what had become of Europeans who had left their home continent to settle in strange lands. Awa Gee estimated it took two or three thousand years before migrant humans were once again comfortable on a continent. But Eco-Grizzly and the others were truly aliens because Awa Gee could always return to Korea, but they could not get back to the Pleistocene. Not unless something cataclysmic happened, and if something cataclysmic occurred, they would still not find the pristine planet their Pleistocene ancestors had enjoyed.[90]

Consistent with his obsession with numbers, Awa Gee calculates the amount of time (two or three thousand years) that would be necessary to obtain true attachment to a particular area of land. Although the numerical variability in his approximation reveals the impossibilities of evaluating the relationship between time and belonging, Awa Gee marks the qualitative difference between such assertions and the deep ecologists' desires and attachments to a prehistoric past. Here Silko reasserts the integrity of Indigenous epistemologies and identities produced out of a temporal relationship to space and place, at the same time as she counteracts notions of Indigenous cultures as belonging strictly to the past. This particular kind of claim to autochthony—contingent on the relationship among time, land, and identity—harnesses the tensions between the currents of Native American studies' transnational/hemispheric and national politics that Silko is navigating in the novel. That is, land claims to belonging, so deeply central to Native American national projects, are reiterated, but without the claims to essentialism embedded in Native-settler binaries. For Silko, whose vision of decolonization is contingent on environmental and social justice, place-based knowledge and experience must hold a central place.[91] As a result, Silko's own political moorings require configuring the Asian immigrant figure as alien to the continent.

This configuration of the Asian (American) as alien provides both a latent critique and circumvention of the structures of feeling produced by antiracist and anticolonial solidarity movements of the 1950s–1970s and associated movements in Mexico that have shaped *mestizaje* discourse. Indeed, Silko's narration of Awa Gee suggests her divestment from particular kinds of cross-racial solidarity movements that emphasize the symmetrical experiences of racial and colonial violence across communities of difference. Given that Zeta is herself a mixed-blood woman, the narrative does not depict an outright rejection of racial mixture (as if it were even possible in imaginations of decolonization) but works to counteract the diminishment of Indigenous decolonization as the force of U.S. liberal multiculturalism infuses its way into formations of Indigenous-centered and grounded *mestizaje* movements across the hemisphere. Such an abjection of Awa Gee as a desirable figure then reveals the novel's work to circumvent the liberal narratives of U.S. neocolonial encroachment and the role of Asian Americanist formations in its midst.

This divestment is made most explicit when we compare the representation of hemispheric Asian Americans in *Almanac* with such representations in Silko's previous novel, *Ceremony*. In her 1977 work, Silko writes about the experiences of Tayo, a World War II veteran returning from a veterans' care facility to the Laguna reservation. In the story, Silko depicts Tayo's struggle through various cross-racial affinities between Indigenous peoples and Asians/Asian Americans. This narrative technique suggests that healing begins by recognizing the interconnected experience of loss and violence wrought out of the "witchery" of the European colonial legacy of the fifteenth century. As such, Silko's earlier novel reflects the possibilities and dialogues associated with the 1960s and 1970s civil rights, antiwar, and Third World Liberation Movements.

In comparison to *Ceremony*, *Almanac* marks a shift in the representation of intimate connections between hemispheric Asian (Americans) and Indigenous peoples, while still acknowledging the links in their experiences produced by the legacy of European colonialism and Enlightenment values.[92] Rather than suggesting that Japanese American and Native American/Indigenous experiences are commensurate, *Almanac* draws attention to Japan's role as a global superpower and implies, although subtly, the material effects that it has had on Asian American racialization. The dynamics of race, racial hierarchies, and racial discourse are captured in distinct yet linked "chronotopes"—one imagined after World War II, and one speculatively imagined in the 1990s United States.[93] Given that the two texts emerge out of different spatiotemporal racial moments, Silko's later revisioning of Asian-Native affinities in *Almanac* could be interpreted in various ways. (1) It might suggest Silko's recognition that given the changing global dynamics of power and capital and the proliferating dominant understandings of the Asian American as the "model minority," Asian American experiences can no longer be understood on the same trajectory as Native American/Indigenous experiences. (2) Alternatively, and more compellingly, given that Silko calls the novel a "spiritual text," Silko's shifts in representing Native-Asian affinities acknowledge the limits of a platform of cross-racial resistance based on shared struggle—namely, the ways such platforms occlude the specificities of Indigenous struggles.[94]

Conclusion

Both Leslie Marmon Silko's *Almanac of the Dead* and Karen Tei Yamashita's *Through the Arc of the Rain Forest* engage with processes of global capitalism, emphasizing how mobilities brought about by transnational capitalism must necessarily open the scope of national optics for critique. Through representations of cross-racial/colonial contact between the Asian and Indigenous figures in the hemisphere, the narratives reveal the possibilities as well as the seemingly impossible tensions that can emerge in these epistemological reconsiderations of power in the contemporary moment. These texts thus distill the problematic intersections between hemispheric Asian American and Indigenous organizing as they hinge on the legacies bound in critical/theoretical discourses, and the hauntings of the settler racial ideologies of *mestizaje/mestiçagem*. Yet, it is by engaging with these figurations and the critical problems that emerge that we are able to assess these seemingly impossible tensions. For both novels, self-reflexive approaches to these problems provide opportunities for further exploration of the formal and affective excesses that always percolate within settler racial hegemonies.

4

Biopolitical Tensions

*The Work of Shame and Anxiety
in Native-Asian Mixed-Blood Narratives*

In a 2012 interview, Larry Grant, an elder of mixed Musqueam (First Nation) and Chinese Canadian background, recalls early feelings of nonbelonging when he was "boarded out" to (in other words, taken under the care of) a Chinese family while his cousins and other Aboriginal children were sent to Indian Residential Schools in Canada.[1] In frustration, he asked his mother the rationale for this unfairness: "I used to ask why we can't go to school with our cousins, you know, they're going to Mission City, they're going to St. Mary's in Mission. Why can't we go? We're Indian just like our cousins." In reply to his query, his mother tells him: "the government say you're Chinese, so you can't go. You don't belong in the Indian school." Grant concludes, "So that was my first not belonging and my second not belonging was being boarded out to a Chinese couple."[2]

Born in the Musqueam Indian Reserve, Larry Grant was one of the children born from the marriage of his Chinese father, Hong Tim Hing, and his Musqueam mother, Agnes Grant. After arriving in Canada in the 1920s, Hong Tim Hing met Agnes Grant while working on the Lin On Farm at the Musqueam Indian Reserve No. 2. Unbeknownst to the Department of Indian Affairs, the Musqueam nation had rented out their lands to Chinese immigrants prior to 1906, which led to relationships that continue to the present day. While Grant and his siblings were raised within Musqueam traditions, they were designated as Chinese, thus leading him to the feelings of exclusion and nonbelonging that he mentions above. At the same time, they shared feelings of exclusion from the Chinese family with whom they had stayed.

Through the narration of his birth and experiences, Grant reveals the often-untold histories of Chinese immigrant relationships with Aboriginal communities in Canada and the intimacies that these meetings produced. Historian Lily Chow writes that cross-racial relationships between Chinese and Aboriginal communities (such as in Grant's story) have a long and dense history, dating back to the mid-nineteenth century, when Chinese labor was employed in Canada to build the Canadian Pacific Railroad.[3] This history set the context for the development of friendships and working partnerships between Chinese and Aboriginal peoples from the canneries in the Skeena region to the freight/wagon trains business, to the hop farms in areas such as Langley, Chilliwack, and Kamloops. Since Chinese immigrants were predominantly male, and since anti-miscegenation laws restricted Chinese men from marrying white women, romantic unions between Chinese men and Aboriginal women occurred frequently. At the same time, Aboriginal women were restricted regarding whom they could marry under the Indian Act, a set of governing documents that consolidated the Canadian settler state's policies concerning Aboriginal peoples.[4] Under the Indian Act, the state determined the definition of "Indian," implementing "status" and "non-status" designations across Aboriginal communities. Status Indians were legally recognized as Indian by the settler state, based on prior treaties with the Crown, and accorded certain economic and land rights and restrictions. A key component of the act stripped Aboriginal women of their Indian status if they were to marry nonstatus men. While the law seemed to target Aboriginal women's unions with white men, the Indian Act also restricted these women's unions with other non-Indian men. It was amid these intersecting regulations and the choices and actions of Chinese and Aboriginal peoples that stories such as that of Grant's parents emerged.[5]

In addition to revealing the conditions that lead to Asian-Aboriginal relationships, Grant's discussion also exposes how the social and political forces that produced the bodily regulations of Aboriginal peoples and Chinese immigrants also influenced how Grant, as a mixed-blood person, was registered in the eyes of the settler state. As scholar Bonita Lawrence maintains, both Indian women and their children were stripped of their Indian status if the women married nonstatus men. These restrictions persisted until 1985, when changes to the Indian Act through Bill C-31 worked to lift gendered discrimination and to restore status to women and their children.[6] Because Grant and his family were stripped of their Indian status, they had to move outside of the reserve to Vancouver during Grant's childhood.[7] The state's management strategies through the Indian Act emerged from a long history of colonial anxieties about the presence of mixed-blood people, whose existence destabilized imperatives of white settler futurity and the colonial categorizations that undergirded white settler endurance in Canada. Regarding unions between white men and Aboriginal women, sociologist Renisa Mawani writes that the mixed-race progeny of such unions during the colonial era "were [seen as] in urgent need of legal governance because they complicated racial taxonomies and orders of rule that were invested in maintaining distinctions between Indians and whites."[8] Colonial management of mixed-blood people, however, ran up against a paradox. On the one hand, if they were designated as non-Indian, they were seen as polluting the racial taxonomy of the colonial state and deemed ungovernable according to racist precepts of mixed-blood people at the time. Such designation would thus destabilize the precarious balance of white settler power. On the other hand, if designated as Indian, colonial authorities feared that they "might make fraudulent claims to land and resource rights that would hold serious implications for territorial control."[9] While discourses surrounding mixed-blood people have changed since the colonial era, Mawani's comments reveal how designations of mixed-blood people have been central in the management and yet the destabilization of race and racial difference. Such management of mixed-blood identity, from colonial times to the present, is connected to the colonial state's imperatives for white settler futurity and land acquisitions. In Grant's case, his designation as Chinese circumvented this colonial paradox because it simultaneously restricted him from claiming land and resources designated for Indians and placed him within the governmental restrictions and discipline to which Chinese persons were also subject.

In addition to illuminating the governmental restrictions placed on the biological lives and choices of both Asian and Indigenous communities, Grant's testimony centers his own emotions in relationship to his background and upbringing. By centering such feelings, Grant provides a window into the impact of these restrictions on the two communities, and thus on his own sense of personhood. This is to say that the critical emotions that he documents in his interview allow us to trace the intersections between Asian and Indigenous community responses to these settler racial restrictions, community responses that culminate in the very tensions within his own body. His centering of his feelings also documents his abilities to elude the biopolitical and sovereign imperatives of the state. As Mawani argues via Michel Foucault, racialized settler states (like the United States and Canada) operate through both biopolitical and sovereign power. That is, the simultaneous use of "liberal" technologies that extend or manage the life and longevity of subjects (biopolitical) and the use of "illiberal" practices that police and punish those deemed exterior (sovereignty) define the power employed by the settler state. Against settler state biopolitics that sought to disconnect mixed-blood people from their Indigenous communities, in what amounts to a mass-scale cultural genocide, Grant specifically highlights his own and his siblings' endurance to connect and persist.[10] In the same interview, after he describes his feelings of nonbelonging, he continues: "Not quite belonging makes you really strive or quit, so we [Grant and his siblings] didn't quit. And that's the part that I think was really good for us." Currently a Musqueam Nation Language and Culture Consultant, Grant continues work toward the resurgence of the Musqueam nation and, at the same time, helps to convey the historical ties between Chinese and Aboriginal peoples. Thus, rather than accede to the state's attempts to annihilate Aboriginal and Chinese presence, and their intersecting histories, Grant works to make visible the relationships (which were often deemed infractions) between Chinese and Aboriginal communities that led to his birth in the first place.

I begin with this expanded discussion of Grant's feelings, and the critical knowledge that they convey about settler racial rule in Canada, in order to highlight the potential of testimonies by mixed-blood people to expose and destabilize contemporary (neo)liberal celebrations of mixed-race identity. The critical work that Grant's life story produces is especially urgent in contemporary Canada and the United States, where celebrations of the mixed-race subject as the face of the future nation (like *mestizaje/mestiçagem* in Chapter 3) can be deployed within liberal and neoliberal discourse to obscure the continuing colonial and racial imposition of the settler state. While the history of racial mixture, and thus mixed-race discourse, emerges differently across these settler states, they nevertheless "all originate in the European Enlightenment systems of racial taxonomy and legacies of colonialism."[11] Indeed, in our current moment, prevalent celebrations of mixed-race identities in the United States and Canada have become part of the dominant discourse, and structure of feeling, that imagines racial blending as the key to postracial harmony.[12] While centralizing a nonwhite identity as the future subject of the nation, such celebrations also amount to the evacuation of racial and ethnic particularity and difference—an assimilatory vision that recalls earlier strategies to integrate Indigenous peoples into the settler state in order to take their lands. Under (neo)liberalism, mixed-race or multiracial identity is often positioned in the mainstream media as depoliticized from historical contexts and aestheticized as a desirous identity for the liberal capitalist consuming individual. Such depoliticization individualizes race as a private property, or commodity, of the (neo)liberal person. In addition to obscuring racial and settler colonial inequities, such discourse often upholds a liberal multicultural or colorblind rhetoric that works to dismantle affirmative action, civil rights claims, and decolonial movements.[13] As such, dominant rhetoric of mixed-race identities can amount to a kind of discursive allotment that emphasizes (and indeed celebrates) racial difference of mixed-race individuals, only to attribute to them value as private, future-oriented, individuals of the settler nation.

In the U.S. context, scholar Jared Sexton registers both liberal and conservative multiracial movements as stemming from the devaluation of black politics and the maintenance of normative heterosexuality. Sexton argues that calls for recognition of multiracial identity (through the lobbying for a multiracial category in the 1990 census) elides histories of discriminatory racial structures and presents racial harm solely as a condition of nonrecognition registered through the multiracial individual's psychical or emotional pain. He writes:

> It is telling that the multiracial movement refrained from putting forth any substantive arguments regarding either a history of discrimination or a violation of the civil rights of multiracial people per se. Instead, the demand to alter the existing classification scheme was grounded in a nebulous "right to recognition," a pseudolegal claim buttressed by the specious contention that the physical, mental, and emotional health of the multiracial community, and the self-esteem of multiracial children most especially, hinged on this form of official acknowledgement.[14]

For Sexton, the movement to include multiracial as a category did not emphasize questions of structural inequities but, rather, emphasized individualism through the language of mental health and the right to choose.[15] This has a profound effect on racial rights movements in the United States, where census categories based on race were employed in the post-1960s in order to monitor civil rights infractions.[16]

In Canada, as Iyko Day maintains, the push toward multiracial categorization (most visibly first by Métis during the 1960s) did not produce the same issues as in the United States. She writes:

> In Canada, because minority rights hinge on membership in an aggregate visible minority population, the political mobilization of panethnic groups to maintain or increase numbers for rights and recognition—often in competition with other groups—has not become controversial. Although there are clearly problems with an aggregate visible minority classification, most obviously in its misleading approach to racial minorities as a culturally and economically undifferentiated bloc who experience race relations in identical ways, it has nevertheless prevented the formation of competitive racial and ethnic blocs that have formed in the US.[17]

Thus, while mixed-race discourse can function to weaken the numbers of racial categories necessary for the ongoing struggles for racial parity (as in the case of the United States), it also has, in the case of Canada, worked to enable the visibility of communities of color in the strengthening of numbers under the "visible minority" category and the recognition of Métis people.[18] Yet, at the same time, in the context of both these countries, the celebration of the image of the multiracial figure under (neo)liberal multiculturalism has been coopted in ways that elide the power dynamics (particularly the territorial claims and temporal trajectory of the settler state) that historically and continuously inflect cross-racial unions and the treatment of their children.

I here expand on my previous analysis of racial mixture in Latin América by examining the knowledge produced within writings by mixed-blood (specifically, Asian-Indigenous) authors in Canada and the United States. Through readings of literature and critical works by Dorothy Christian and Greg Sarris, and interviews by community leaders such as Larry Grant, I trace how mixed-blood figures can illuminate the biopolitical and sovereign logics and instabilities of the United States and Canada. Through the centering of their life stories, the writers convey the uneven implementation of anti-miscegenation, adoption, and assimilation policies that bring Asian and Indigenous communities into political, economic, and intimate relationships. Such convergences reveal the different and yet entangled ways that both Asian and Indigenous communities were restricted bodily in order to protect the territorial claims and temporal longevity of the category of whiteness.[19]

In addition to illuminating these settler racial imperatives, the narrators' emphasis on their shame and anxiety in relationship to their mixed-blood identity, I argue, provides insight into the role of emotions in both revealing and inflecting the biopolitical and sovereign logics of the settler state. On the one hand, such feelings of shame and anxiety about their mixed-blood background, which is a product of histories and presences of racial and colonial degradation, work to produce silences and disconnections between the narrators and both their Asian and Indigenous families and communities. This disconnection of mixed-blood children with their families and communities has historically been a strategy for the actuation of white settler futurity. At the same time, through the form that both texts take on—a hybrid of life writing and critique—the narrators analyze how such emotions can track both the incommensurabilities and the affinities between Asian and Indigenous communities. Through the analysis of their emotions, these writers convey a mixed-blood epistemology that draws on their elided backgrounds in order to illuminate the complicated terrains and yet possible avenues through which to forge Asian and Indigenous solidarities against the eliminatory logics of the biopolitical and sovereign state. As such, rather than reading these texts' emphasis on emotions as a move toward the privatizing of mixed-race experiences, we see that these writers open up the meaningful histories and relationships between Asian and Indigenous communities in ways that can productively confront contemporary settler racial hegemonic processes in the Américas.

Dorothy Christian's "Articulating a Silence"

Appearing in *Ricepaper Magazine* in 2012, Dorothy Christian's autobiographical essay "Articulating a Silence" traces her experiences growing up Aboriginal-Asian in the Secwepemc-Syilx (Okanagan-Shuswap) Indian community in British Columbia's North Okanagan Valley.[20] Born to a Chinese father and an Aboriginal mother, Christian grew up having only vague memories of meeting her father once in her life. She had long sensed but was never directly told the identity of her father. Throughout the essay, Christian speaks out about her community's silences about her family history and the negative feelings that such silence produced throughout her life. Christian initially "came out" as half Chinese in 2002 at a conference at the University of Western Washington, and her essay works to draw out the often-silenced connections between Asian and Aboriginal communities in Canada. In so doing, the essay provides knowledge about the connections and tensions between the two communities and, at the same time, serves as crucial step toward Christian's self-acceptance.

Throughout the essay, Christian describes her feelings of shame, which emerged as she got closer to moments when her background surfaced. Additionally, she speculates on the shame that both sides of her family carry in regard to the intimate histories of Aboriginal-Chinese relations. Rather than register shame solely as a pathological product of the history of colonial and racial degradation, Christian's essay traces the role of these emotions in both unveiling and inflecting the power asymmetries that exist between the settler state, Chinese Canadian/immigrant people, and Aboriginal communities. Christian links the shame that she feels to the shame that both of her communities carry in relationship to the histories of exploitation produced by the settler state's gendered legislations. In doing so, Christian's essay works toward connecting these two communities' often incommensurate feelings of shame, revealing how the emotions that have pushed these two communities away from dialogue with one another can provide the connection toward more meaningful sites of discussion about cross-community responsibility and solidarity against the ongoing legacies of settler colonial and racialized harm. Thus, Christian offers an Asian-Indigenous mixed-blood epistemology (one that specifically centers Indigenous sovereignty and survival) that cites negative emotions, such as shame, as a catalyst in relation to the biopolitical and sovereign imperatives of the settler racial state.

Like Grant, Christian offers glimpses of the history of Chinese and Aboriginal relations in Canada, and the impossible choices that were made because of the legislative restrictions placed on both the communities. Given the national and community silences that obscure the full picture of her family history, Christian works to piece it together from hints and incomplete fragments of information from her family. Through this process, Christian discusses what she calls the "shared oppression" of Native and Chinese peoples that took the form of the Indian Act (discussed earlier) and the Chinese Head Tax (repealed 1949), respectively. Whereas the Indian Act designated, and circumscribed the lives of, those who were and were not considered "Indian" (based on recognized treaties), the Chinese Head Tax restricted Chinese immigration by according a fixed fee to those who wanted to enter the settler state. Coupled with anti-miscegenation laws that restricted Chinese men from marrying white women and laws that restricted Chinese women from immigrating to Canada, the Chinese Head Tax worked to circumvent the lives and growth of Chinese communities in Canada. As Christian notes, these acts restricted both these communities biologically, socially, politically, and economically.

Christian also highlights how these circumstances forged important moments of interactions. While identity, immigration, and anti-miscegenation legislation sought to curtail the growth of these two communities, they also created the condition of possibility for critical "alliances" for mutual survival. She writes:

> Natives taught the Chinese how to hunt and fish on the land, and where to find edible wild berries. Chinese men, who were neither allowed to bring their wives from China, nor permitted to have any kind of relationship with white women, befriended the Native community. Thrown together by legislation and circumstance, it was natural for the two groups to turn to each other. It was out of these alliances that I entered the world.[21]

Such alliances can be tracked throughout Asian alien and Aboriginal histories. For example, as Lily Chow noted in her history of relationships between these two groups, fears of Chinese miners supplying arms to First Nations peoples during the Canyon War were recorded as early as 1858. In addition, there were records of First Nations peoples teaching Chinese miners how to trap animals in the 1900s.[22] Like Christian, Chow highlights how the connections between these two communities were enacted via the sharing of foodways.[23]

In addition to their "shared oppressions," Christian also discusses the incommensurabilities of Asian and Aboriginal experiences in relationship to the settler state. For one, in 1947 the Chinese were enfranchised with voting rights, which was earlier than Aboriginal peoples, who were not able to vote in Canada until 1960, and 1969 in Quebec.[24] Even the condition of enfranchisement for Aboriginal peoples in Canada was often contingent on the stripping of their Indian status. Christian notes, for example, that after World War II, Aboriginal soldiers seeking benefits from the state lost their Indian status. This policy was connected to the Gradual Civilization Act of 1857, which sought to remove Aboriginal people's ties to their tribal communities through access to Canadian citizenship. Lawrence writes that "through various changes in the legislation over the years, Native people could be enfranchised for acquiring an education, for serving in the armed forces, or for leaving their reserves for long periods of time to maintain employment.... This legislation was openly aimed at the elimination of Indigenous peoples as a legal and social fact."[25] As noted earlier, the Indian Act stripped Aboriginal women of their Indian status if they married a "non-status" man and prohibited them from land and community connections that Indian status might entail. For scholar Beth Piatote, this dispossession of Aboriginal women of their Indian status was also often rendered as a form of voluntary enfranchisement into whiteness were the women to marry white men. Piatote writes that "in the United States and Canada indigenous populations are bound to not one national domestic but two: the tribal-national and the settler-national."[26] For Piatote, the Indian Act's gendered restrictions utilized legal definitions of marriage as "one mechanism, among others, that could move land and individuals out of the tribal-national and into the settler-national."[27] The dispossession of Aboriginal women under the Indian Act's marriage policy engaged in settler colonial imposition and coercion while hiding behind the language of consent and enfranchisement toward the settler-national in the form of giving Aboriginal women white status were they to marry white men.[28] Thus, whereas the goals of Asian immigrants/generations often center on equality and enfranchisement within the settler state, Aboriginal peoples' encounters with settler state enfranchisement coalesced with tribal dispossession.

The differing experiences of the Chinese and Aboriginal communities in relationship to the settler state can also be seen in the unequal economic relationship between the two communities. Such inequalities provided the condition of possibility for Christian's parents' encounter, where her mother was sold to her father. Christian writes: "In this world, my family worked in the many fields that belonged to the Chinese, because Chinese farms were the only places that would hire Native people."[29] Christian later finds out that her father was an employer of her mother's family, and so it was in the context of an unequal economic relationship that her mother was "traded to [Christian's] Chinese father at age 16."[30] Not knowing the full details of this seeming "trade" until later, Christian learns this information only by hints and indirect means from the people in her tribal community. One of the most startling implications of this interaction comes from Rosalind Williams, whom Christian deems the knowledge keeper of the tribal community. In a recollection of a conversation Christian had with Williams, the latter implores: "You have to remember that there was an employer/employee relationship.... Our people were going through hard times, and many of our women had to prostitute themselves to feed their children."[31] Williams does not directly say that Christian's mom was sold to her dad; instead, she describes the circumstances for many women in the community. The most explicit information about her mother came from Christian's sisters: "My mother, during her visits with them in their foster home, had told of how she was traded to my Chinese father at age 16. I was born when she turned 17, the result of a forced liaison."[32] Through these moments of disclosure, Christian learns how her mother's situation emerges out of the settler racial asymmetries of the state, where Indigenous dispossession and the endurance of colonial rule can be enacted via another historically oppressed group (that of the Chinese). Of this, Christian attests: "I realized then, that Native oppression did not just end with colonial rule. Even between two communities that were both oppressed, we still drew the shorter draw." She concludes, "My burden of shame felt heavier than ever."[33]

Throughout her essay, Christian reveals how shame and silence worked in tandem to disconnect her from both her father and her mother, and their respective communities. The relationship between silence and shame is evident throughout this essay, especially where the force of one emerges in response to the force of the other. It is the shame of the impossible choices—choices made in the matrix of these intersecting histories—to which Christian attributes her community's silence regarding her mother and father's union. Yet it is also that community's silence that produces her private shame, which leads to her past secrecy about her background.[34]

The result of this cycle of silence and shame can be seen in Christian's early denial both of her father's background and of her mother's experiences. Christian recalls a moment in her childhood eating with a Chinese man (married to her great-aunt on her mother's side) who was acquainted with her father. Knowing that Christian was part Chinese, this man at first tries to encourage and later to discipline her into using chopsticks.

> "Your father would want you to know how to eat with chopsticks," He said. Even then, my natural response was to resist his instruction. "You can't have any supper unless you eat with these," he countered. I went hungry that day.[35]

Similarly, when Christian recounts a vague memory of meeting her father on the farm, she describes her negative reaction to his offer of ginger candy: "It is spicy, and I spit it out as quickly as I put it in my mouth. Ginger candy. I grow up not liking ginger."[36] In these two scenes, Christian reveals how her shame about and rejection of her Chinese identity emerges in the most elemental embodiment: eating.

Christian's essay suggests that the refusal of her Chinese background can also overwrite her mother's experiences. More specifically, in her rejection of her father, Christian potentially obscures the biopolitical and sovereign histories that produced the gendered colonial violence her mother experiences. Furthermore, this denial can potentially erase the strategies through which her mother navigates these difficult terrains. It is only when Christian punctures the silence about her background that she is able to see her mother's actions as part and parcel of the vexed struggle for what Gerald Vizenor describes as Indigenous survival and resistance, or "survivance":[37]

> I often wonder why my mother was willing to accept her fate with my father. Now, my [maternal] uncle reveals something else: my mother had been the knowledge keeper of our family lineage. During his dating days, my uncle had to consult her before making any advances towards a girl. My mother would consult with the Elders and determine whether it was alright for the couple to get together. At only sixteen years old, it was her duty to preserve our family lineage, her duty to be responsible to the collective.[38]

Christian concludes this passage by speculating as to whether this sense of responsibility for the family lineage made her mother decide to have children with her father. Christian explores her mother's experiences not simply through the lens of gendered colonial coercion but through Indigenous epistemologies of responsibility, choice, and endurance. Christian's erasure of her father's background thus erases her mother's movements between what Piatote calls the "tribal-national" and "settler-national." By confronting her shame, Christian opens up space in which to consider her mother's movements and choices within the relations between two sovereign national bodies. For example, Christian reveals that her parents never married, speculating that perhaps her mother chose not to do so in order to maintain Indian status or as an outright rebellion against the coercion of her body.[39]

While silence and shame are central to the imperatives of settler racial rule in that they disconnect Christian from both her communities, her critical focus on them opens for her the possibility for these actions and emotions to do different kinds of work toward the destabilization of settler racial hegemonies. Christian reveals how silence is not always the effect of shame and how her sense of shame is not traceable to a single originary site or moment. She mentions, for instance, how her tribal community kept its silence about her mother's relationship with her father for so many years in part because of their particular respect for her mother. She writes, "Respect for my mother prevents the knowledge keepers in my Native community from talking about my father."[40] In this statement, Christian suggests particular tribal protocol in relationship to the sources and movement of information. It is the "knowledge keepers" who make particular choices about the dissemination of community and personal history. Thus, as she works through the community's silence, she uncovers different logics, tribal epistemologies that fueled the silence about her mother's past. As Christian implies, the community's silence could have emerged from the community's respect for her mother as much if not more than from a sense of shame about her mother's experiences and their own sense of complicity. While the impact of the silence and the shame on Christian as a child is unchanged, this unraveling of cause and effect, of shame necessarily leading to silence, allows Christian to rethink the settler state's capacity to fully inform Aboriginal community actions. In other words, her speculation that silence might be linked to the tribe's respect for her mother conveys her recognition that tribal actions and concomitant protocols of knowledge dissemination work in response to and yet in excess of the settler state.

Christian is interested in exploring not only the silence and shame of her tribal community but also the silence and shame of her Chinese Canadian family. She writes: "But would my father's family prefer to continue the silence? Are they ashamed too?"[41] Her sense of detachment from the Chinese Canadian community limits her understanding of why there is silence about the intimacies between her father and mother. She is thus in the realm of speculation as it pertains to her understanding of her Chinese Canadian family and community. As with her conjectures about her own tribal community, Christian questions whether shame was the primary agent that drove her father's family toward secrecy. While she may suspect that shame leads to silence, her question raises the possibility that other emotions or intentions may have been an agent. In addition, as her own experience with shame suggests, even if shame contributed to her Chinese family's detachment from her, the object of that shame is unclear. That is, for Christian, the object of her own shame shifts throughout the narrative—from shame about her mixed background, to shame about her father's Chinese identity, to shame about her mother's experiences as an Aboriginal woman, to shame about being Aboriginal. The fact that shame has many possible objects raises further questions in regard to her Chinese family's shame: Is her family ashamed of their own circumstances and oppression that led to the history of Asian-Native relations? Is her family ashamed of their complicity in forging unequal relationships with Native communities? Both the answers to such questions and the questions themselves remain unspoken, again silent. Still, in her questioning of her Chinese family's silence and potential shame, Christian opens up dialogue about Chinese community expressions and choices that may emerge in response to and yet move beyond the biopolitical and sovereign imperatives of the settler state.

While her sense of shame about her background can work to produce silence and disconnection between Christian and both Chinese and Aboriginal communities, it is paradoxically these very emotions that lead her toward the search for and the knowledge about her background. This potential of emotions to lead to knowledge emerges from its ability to create an effect on the subject prior to or in excess of verbal and conscious knowledge. Throughout the text, Christian accesses the foreclosed knowledge of her background through her emotions and senses. While tribal family members worked to hold the secret during her childhood, community emotions nevertheless seep out from beneath the seal of secrecy. She writes:

> Growing up, I knew that my father was Chinese. However, no one ever spoke about it openly. Through the hushed murmurings of my childhood, I somehow found out that my father was Chinese. . . . The tone of the adults would change, and they would say, "you kids go outside and play," before lowering their voices to whispers and speaking in another language.[42]

Here Christian recounts how she guessed her father's Chinese identity from the tone that those around her used when talking about him and from their attempts to exclude her from the conversation. Christian was able to pick up the critical information not despite the lowered registers and switch in language but because of them. The emotions of the adults around her exceeded spoken language, and it was this nonverbal excess that moved Christian toward desire to understand.

Two additional moments in the essay shows how emotions often precede conscious knowledge. Christian describes an experience while she was a student at the University of Toronto, when her roommate's relationship with his daughter caused her to react unexpectedly:

> I cried for hours after they left the apartment. I initially did not understand why I was crying. But delving deeper into my emotions, I realized that I was grieving a relationship that I never had. I had never known the love of a father. That experience opened a gaping wound that I couldn't articulate in words.[43]

Her feelings in this moment register and precede what she herself cannot acknowledge, and again opens the desire for further exploration. The second instance of deep emotion preceding understanding occurs when, while studying, Christian encounters a page in a book, which she does not ultimately identify, that includes the statement "NO INDIANS, NO CHINAMEN AND NO DOGS ALLOWED." In seeing this text, Christian reacts viscerally: "Paralyzed with what vaguely felt like fear, I sat with my book open to the tell-tale page."[44] She then narrates why she felt paralyzed and felt so much fear: that her secret about her mixed Asian-Indigenous background is fully reflected on the page. In this moment, Christian relays her feelings first, before explaining what caused her to feel such paralysis and such fear. The very structure of the narration thus emulates how emotions have the capacity to precede conscious understanding.

With the recognition that confronting her own shame can lead her toward greater connection to and knowledge about herself and her two communities, Christian also mobilizes the potential that can emerge when shame becomes communicated, and shared, across Chinese Canadians and Aboriginal peoples. Christian illuminates this potential when she discovers the history of Chinese women's experiences as sex workers. In a section of the essay entitled "Parallel Suffering," Christian writes:

> While watching *Under the Willow Tree,* A National Film Board production directed by Dora Nipp, I learned that some Chinese women pioneers in Canada had also been traded and sold into servitude. As I listened to the daughters of these women talk, I learned about their mother's hardships, toils and troubles. Their stories made me grateful: Throughout my humiliation and shame, I had thought that my

mother was alone. It is terrible to admit but I was relieved to know that Aboriginal women weren't the only ones who had been treated this way.[45]

Here recognizing a shared source of potential shame, that both Chinese and Aboriginal women have been bodily coerced under the settler state, leads to the possible solidarity between the two communities—the possibility, that is, to feel that she, and her own mother, were not alone. In addition, the sharing of this source of shame moves the feeling of shame into feelings of gratefulness and then feelings of relief. While Christian states that it is "terrible to admit" that she was relieved, she also conveys that the relief stems not from others' suffering but from the knowledge of a kind of shared history.

This form of shared shame, I suggest, can lead to potential cross-racial discussions on how to activate or renarrate shared community emotions toward mutual decolonizing and antiracist knowledge and movements. Here, I gesture to Sean Kiccumah Teuton's concept on "learning to feel."[46] For Teuton, tribal communication and interpretation of emotions and feelings are crucial to developing politically empowering Indigenous futurity. Citing scholar Satya Mohanty, Teuton writes that "emotions are profoundly mediated, yet, few will doubt, indispensable for understanding ourselves and our place in the world. Their importance in social struggles is enormous; indeed, without drawing on emotions, we would be incapable of claiming our painful pasts or transforming ourselves politically for our futures."[47] Because emotions do not come fully formed outside of us, "waiting to be released," inchoate feelings of shame, when shared, might potentially lead to other politically mobilizing emotions, such as anger.[48] Christian's essay reveals how this potential for sharing shame across differently positioned communities in the settler state can conjure other, perhaps more politically mobilizing, emotions that may lead to previously undiscussed knowledge about settler and racial domination.

Given the potential knowledge that Christian sees in the sharing of what scholar Sianne Ngai designates as "ugly feelings," that is, noncathartic feelings such as shame, Christian concludes her essay with a call to break the silence. For Christian, breaking the silence means taking "ownership of the Chinese in [her]."[49] In this claim to "take ownership," Christian suggests that embracing her background and honoring both her bloodlines will amount to the disruption of the imperatives of the settler state to erase Indigenous and Chinese identities, and their relationships. This ownership includes accessing and communicating (owning up to) the emotions that she has previously connected to her mixed-blood identity. While she fears what she might lose if she connects more fully to her Chinese family, the essay suggests the potential connection will only lead her closer to her Aboriginal identity.

I now turn to Greg Sarris's biography *Mabel McKay* to examine how the author conveys and works through his sense of shame and anxiety about his mixed-blood identity. Whereas Christian's essay directly confronts her shame about her mixed-blood background, Sarris's experiences of shame (and also anxiety) about his background emerge specifically through the form of his biography. That is, the shame and anxiety about his Asian-Indigenous-white identity (which is often registered through a Native-white binary) manifests in the formal containment of his biographical subject, the Pomo doctor Mabel McKay, and the elision of Sarris's own Filipino background throughout the narrative. Through Sarris's depiction of his struggle with using a typical form for writing a biography, and through the book's self-reflexive blending of biography, autobiography, and critique—his text provides a mixed-blood epistemology that conveys the knowledge and connections between Asian and Indigenous communities and thus provides a blueprint for critical conversations across these communities.

Greg Sarris's *Mabel McKay: Weaving the Dream*

Published in 1994, Greg Sarris's *Mabel McKay* is a biography of the famous Pomo basket weaver. Sarris depicts Mabel's life as a member of the Long Valley Cache Creek Pomo tribe and her experiences as a Dreamer and sucking doctor (a healer) within her community.[50] As Sarris explains in his critical work *Keeping Slug Woman Alive,* Dreamers emerged out of an anticolonial resistance movement during the 1870s: "Dreamers were guided by their dreams, and they inculcated an impassioned Indian nationalism in the homes and roundhouses."[51] Through her dreaming, Mabel was also taught to treat patients by sucking illness out of their mouths and spitting it into her baskets. Told through Sarris's perspective as a mixed-blood Asian-Indigenous-white adoptee from the Santa Rosa region of California, Mabel's stories and speaking style defy normative literary forms and boundaries, particularly those of typical biographical storytelling. That is, Mabel's stories are nonlinear in style, often moving from one topic to another without thematic connection. In an early interaction between the two, Sarris proclaims, "See Mabel, that's the problem. Your stories go all over the place. I can't write them like that. It's too hard for people to follow. I don't know where to start. . . . Mabel, people want to know about things in your life in a way they can understand. You know, how you got to be who you are. There has to be a theme."[52] In response, Mabel states, "Well, theme I don't know nothing about. That's somebody else's rule."[53] Through Mabel's invitation to depart from the conventions that typify biographies—including objective narration, authorial distancing, and linear narrative progression—Sarris presents

Mabel's life story as it is intertwined with those of her friends and family (particularly her grandmother Sarah), and with the biographer himself.[54]

Throughout the biography, Sarris weaves together his own interactions with Mabel, his experiences of adoption and foster care, and his discovery of his Pomo-Miwok and Filipino background. Through his sometimes-vexed interactions with Mabel, moments of tension between Sarris and Mabel that at first seem to be attributed to Mabel's reluctance to communicate reveal instead the biographer's anxieties about his own identity and place within the community. These anxieties, I argue, expose how biopolitical technologies of the state—including anti-miscegenation laws, adoption policies, and blood quantum measurements (which amounted to the exclusion of U.S. Asian Americans and the genocidal elimination of Indigenous peoples)—continue to impact personal and community understandings about mixed-blood people's identity and authenticity. I examine how emotions and states of feeling such as shame and anxiety provide insight into and propel Sarris's struggles with his own identity and his sense of family amid these eliminatory logics. These emotions reveal the tensions specifically between Sarris's Indigenous and White identities. Interestingly, in contrast to Christian's essay, the lack of tension that Sarris represents between the Filipino and Pomo-Miwok communities seems glaring. I suggest that this omission specifically reveals the white-nonwhite logics of the U.S. settler state, which obscures the settler racial asymmetries that constitute the colonial state. The narrative nevertheless hints at moments of Asian and Indigenous crossings that provide ruptures of these binary logics.

Sarris's conception story and the silences that are produced around it reveal the histories of U.S. Asian American, Indigenous, Mexican, and white intimacies in California, and the ways these histories generated community sentiments of shame. As Sarris notes, he finds out late in his life that his biological mother was Bunny Hartman, a white (Irish-German-Jewish) woman from an economically well-to-do family in Laguna Beach, and that his biological father was Emilio Hilario, a Kashaya Pomo, Coast Miwok, and Filipino man who had an affair with and impregnated Bunny when she was in high school. His paternal grandmother was of Pomo-Miwok background, while his paternal grandfather was Filipino (manong), from Cebu. Because of his maternal grandmother's shame about her daughter's illegitimate pregnancy by a nonwhite man, Bunny was taken to the north of Laguna Beach to deliver the child. Shortly after Sarris's birth, Bunny died of a botched blood transfusion. His maternal grandmother covered up the entire pregnancy and gave Sarris up for adoption to a white couple in Santa Rosa, Mary and George Sarris.

Sarris's family story emerges out of the history of anti-miscegenation laws and their effects, which forged the connections between his paternal grandfather and paternal grandmother, and then his mother and father. In an interview, Sarris says of his grandparents:

> I learned then—and I had some knowledge before—that it was very common for the manongs to marry American Indian women in the 1920's, 30's, and 40's. America had passed the anti-miscegenation laws, whereby a Filipino could not get a marriage license. There was much prejudice here against Filipinos in those days.[55]

As in Canada, these laws focused on the restriction of marriages between Asian men and white women, thereby opening up more possibilities for connection between Filipino men and nonwhite women, including American Indian women. As legal scholar Leti Volpp argues, anti-miscegenation laws that restricted marriages by Filipino men were fueled by discourses about a "third Asian invasion." For Volpp, this hateful rhetoric depicted Filipino men as ruining wage work for white men, threating the biological health of the community with Filipino diseases, and tainting the sexual purity of white and Mexican women.[56] Compared to Chinese and Japanese men, who had also been restricted from marrying white women since the 1850s, Filipino men were considered more sexually passionate and sexually exploitative by anti-immigration and anti-miscegenation proponents.[57] Volpp writes:

> While Chinese and Japanese were also considered sexually depraved—and, perhaps more sexually perverse—Filipinos appeared to be specifically characterized as having an enormous sexual appetite, as more savage, as more primitive, as "one jump from the jungle."[58]

Volpp cites several different rationales for why Filipino men were sexualized differently from their "Mongolian" brethren, including the fact that Filipino sexuality was often aligned with black male sexuality and the influence of Latin culture on Filipino sexual mores. In addition, Volpp cites the behaviors of sexual aggressiveness and possessiveness that Filipino men were said to exhibit in the infamous dance halls of the 1920s–1930s (where Filipino men paid to dance with white women). These cited behaviors lent credibility to the representation of Filipino men as hypersexualized and dangerous.

While anti-miscegenation laws in California were lifted in 1948 by the decision in the *Perez v. Sharp* Supreme Court of California case, the laws were not taken out of the California Civil Codes until 1959. Sarris's biography reveals how antagonistic sentiments toward Filipino men, and indeed all men of color, persisted well into the years of Sarris's parents' meeting and his own birth and adoption in 1952.[59] He writes of his father's racialization in Laguna Beach:

> Emilio Hilario, the boy all the girls loved because he wasn't like the other boys they knew. Emilio. Dark, dangerous, sexual. Forbidden fruit. A Filipino kitchen worker's son. And that standoffish Indian woman named Evelyn. Emilio, exulted town athlete. Town n——r.[60]

Through the dramatic repetition of his biological father's name—Emilio—Sarris highlights the racial objectification and exoticization of his mixed-blood father. The description reveals how the exoticization of Emilio emerged from the conflation of racial stereotypes about Filipino, American Indian, and black men. On the one hand, Emilio's dangerous sexuality derived from stereotypes that, as stated above, hypersexualized Filipino men. On the other, this exoticization is similar to the stereotypes of American Indian and black men. Scholar Margaret D. Jacobs writes that while intimacies between white men and Native women were generally met with disapproval, they did not inspire the vitriol that unions between white women and Native men created. This latter "unnatural" union was seen as "violating the hierarchical order that developed between European Americans, African Americans, and American Indians."[61] At the same time, white women's perceptions of Indigenous men started to shift at the turn of the twentieth century when, amid the rise of anthropology and the theory of cultural relativism, a "growing primitivist sentiment [fueled by modernism's nostalgia for a simple past] among many white Americans in the 1920s" rendered the Native (American Indian and black) male figure as more superior, sexual, and masculine, than the white man.[62] It is from out of the often conflated representations of these figures (the Filipino, the American Indian, and the black) that Emilio's rendering as "dark, dangerous, sexual" emerges.

Emilio also conjures anxieties of racial mixing given his unidentifiable race. In describing Emilio's racialization as a "town n——r," Sarris's text not only reveals histories of racial conflation but also the placement of mixed-race people among the lowest rungs in the U.S. white supremacist racial hierarchy. This denigration of mixed-race people emerges from the long history of U.S. slavery and colonization, as well as U.S. white supremacist comparisons to other nations' histories of racial mixing. For example, Volpp cites how major public figures of the 1920s–1930s "warned of 'race mingling' which would create a 'new type of mulatto,' an 'American Mestizo.'"[63] She notes that anxiety about miscegenation emerged in the comparisons to Mexico and the Philippines; that is, opponents of racial mixing cited Mexico's *mestizo* nation and

Filipino people mixing with the Spanish to show the deleterious effects of white unions with racial others.[64] Court cases against marriage between whites and nonwhites were thus built on the perceived negative effects that the characters of people with "impure" mixed-race blood can have on a whole nation. Conversations about racial mixing between white and American Indian peoples were inflected by the rise in eugenics, which saw mixed-bloods as encompassing "the vices of both races and the virtues of neither."[65] As Jacobs states, "Already ranking Indians and blacks far below whites, some theorists believed race mixing would result in progeny with even worse genetic makeups than full-blood Indians or pure blacks."[66]

Certainly, these beliefs about the "impurity" of mixed-blood people impacted Bunny's mother's reactions and responses to her daughter's pregnancy, compounded by the fact that this was an illegitimate teenage pregnancy. The embarrassment that Sarris's maternal grandmother felt (about both the illegitimate birth and Bunny's secret relationship with Emilio) drove her first to isolate Bunny from their local white community and then to legally erase the progeny of this union via adoption. While Sarris's case is different from the adoption policies that forcibly removed Indigenous children from their traditional homes (which ended only after the passage of the 1978 Indian Child Welfare Act), his maternal grandmother's move to put him up for adoption nevertheless performs a similar erasure of Sarris's Indigenous identity. Thus, early anti-miscegenation laws (which were supposedly dispelled by the courts by the time of Sarris's birth in 1952) and mixed-blood discourses continued to invoke feelings and actions that worked in tandem with policies of Indian adoption and forced assimilation. These forces converged as a means to eliminate Indigenous cultural identities and thus Indigenous claims to territory.

U.S. biopolitical and sovereign technologies that worked to eliminate Indigenous cultural identity manifested also in the post-1960s, the time period in which Sarris's own life story is set. That is, Sarris's struggle with his identity is set against the history of blood-quantum measurements, whereby the Indian status of Indigenous peoples were often defined by settler state measurement of Indian ancestry/blood.[67] Blood quantum is determined by the percentage of the person's forebears who were full-blooded. J. Kēhaulani Kauanui states, "Blood quantum is a fractionalizing measurement—a distance in relation to some supposed purity to mark one's generational proximity to a "full-blood" forebear.... Blood quantum logic presumes that one's 'blood amount' correlates to one's cultural orientation and identity."[68] Blood quantum measurements often have the effect of undercutting tribal definitions of Indianness, eliminating the tribal identity of those who do not meet the requirements and affecting relational ties in American Indian communities. Kauanui argues, "In considering the racialization of indigenous peoples, especially through the use of blood quantum classification, a genocidal logic of disappearance is tied to the project of selective assimilation for those Natives who still exist yet do not measure up for entitlements or benefits."[69] Given blood quantum restrictions, mixed-blood people are especially vulnerable to the logics of elimination via assimilation into the settler state.

In addition to the impact of blood quantum and its effects on relationships in tribal communities, the post-1960s era also saw the rise of white people "playing Indian" through the resurgence of primitivism via the hippie and New Age movements.[70] This fascination with "going Native" also affects Indigenous struggles to maintain tribal identity. As Lorenzo Veracini and other settler colonial studies scholars have argued, settler logics of elimination include the push toward becoming Native in order to eliminate the Native.[71] These contexts haunt Sarris's relationships within the Pomo community. In particular, the anxiety and shame that often typify his interactions with Mabel and other community members reveal the effects that histories of whites "playing Indian" have on Indigenous community relationships with mixed-blood individuals. That is, mixed-blood people who have been in one way or another disconnected from their families and tribal identities, and may phenotypically present as Caucasian, may be met understandably with suspicion from tribal communities. At the same time, by self-reflexively highlighting these moments of uneasy connection, Sarris's biography also reveals Pomo epistemologies of relationality (that is, genealogical and kinship ties) that defy and refuse the settler state's goals of eliminating Indigenous peoples through blood politics.

Sarris indicates his own struggle, and disconnection, with his Pomo cultural identity through the struggles that he has with the form that the biography takes on. That is, in the narrative, Sarris depicts himself acceding to white commonsense understandings of biographical form, which stands in opposition to Mabel's resistances to such formal restrictions. His attempts to weave Mabel's stories and interviews into a recognizable biographical form leads to moments of tension. At first, Sarris considers his difficulties with Mabel as a result of the biographical subject's obstinacy ("She is maddening, puzzling," he writes early on in the book). Yet, the narrative slowly unveils the fact that Mabel's refusal to accede to Sarris's formal demands is due to the force of narrative form in the containment of Mabel's tribal identity and philosophy.

Mabel's resistance to accede to white settler logics and values is seen during her lecture at Stanford University. The lecture, one of many that Mabel holds in order to share her knowledge about basket weaving, seemingly becomes derailed during a Q&A portion. Among a largely white audience of students and professors, Mabel refuses to change her style of interaction in order to accede to their expectations of her as a kind of Native informant. When asked by an audience member when it was that her basket weaving reached "perfection," Mabel says that she does not comprehend the question and has to turn to Sarris for clarification. When pushed about whether plants talk to her and what they say to each other, Mabel proclaims, "I don't know. Why would I be listening?"[72] For Sarris, Mabel's refusal to assimilate to the rhythms and expectations embedded in the conversation "baffles" him. Such refusal typifies also her response to Sarris's interview questions for the biography and leaves him at a loss as to how to tell her story as a coherent whole. During a long drive together, Sarris voices his frustrations: "See Mabel, that's the problem. Your stories go all over the place. I can't write them like that. It's too hard for people to follow. I don't know where to start."[73] In response, Mabel closes off her body by placing her hands "resolutely over her purse," a position that signals her resolution not to give into Sarris's organizational demands. After an argument about theme, she concludes: "You just do the best way you know how. What you know from me."[74] Her resistance persists through to the end of Sarris's text.[75]

Sarris's desire to order Mabel's biography is opposed to Mabel's worldview as a Bole Maru Dreamer, a worldview that does not see clear distinctions in the parameters of settler time and space. Of the Dreamers, Sarris writes: "In the winter of 1871–1872 the revivalist Bole Maru (Dream Dance) cult started and spread throughout Pomo and Miwok territory. Local cult leaders, known as Dreamers, organized their respective tribes around this cult. Dreamers were guided by their dreams, and they inculcated an impassioned Indian nationalism in the homes and roundhouses."[76] Taught by Essie Parrish, the last known Kashaya Pomo Dreamer, Mabel is said to have been the last to carry the Dreamer philosophy. During another exchange about the form of the biography, Mabel asks Sarris how he is planning to write her book. In response, Sarris announces that he just needs to get the "exact dates and figures" in order to correctly order the events. To this Mabel proclaims, "I don't know about dates. It's everlasting what I'm talking about."[77] This resistance to linear time is repeated when, in an effort to place events in Mabel's life on a recognizable timeline, and into recognizable categories, Sarris asks Mabel when she began having the prophetic dreams. Mabel responds with incredulity: "It didn't have no start. It goes on." When Sarris suggests that she might be confusing spirit with dreams, Mabel proclaims "same thing." In an attempt to resituate the conversation on what he perceives to be more solid ground, Sarris suggests: "Maybe we should start with the baskets. That's what people know you best for." Again, Mabel matter-of-factly states, "Well, same thing." After a beat, Mabel observes: "You try to do things white way. On account you're all mixed up. You don't know who you are yet. But you're part of my Dream. One day you'll find out."[78] In this instance, Mabel connects Sarris's struggle with form and his struggle over his own identity and sense of tribal belonging.

Sarris's anxieties around identity and belonging can also be seen in the hesitations that occur throughout his interactions with Mabel's friends and family. In a moment between Sarris and Parrish's daughter Violet and niece Anita, their inference of his whiteness leads him to feel "unnerved."[79] Rather than let them know immediately that he was in fact mixed-blood, despite his "fair skin and blue eyes," Sarris begins talking about Native friends he had known growing up. He later signals his part-Pomo identity to Anita and Violet, but only when they ask him to explain why he knows the Native people who are considered in the community as "the gutter snipe, the lost Indians."[80] This hesitation to share his background continues in another scene when Sarris meets up with Mabel, Violet, and Anita. In the midst of sharing her stories, Mabel urges Sarris to get his tape recorder. In response, Sarris confesses:

> I sat there. I didn't say anything, not even no. If I had halfway convinced anyone that I was an Indian, how could they believe me? Anthropologists, white people, carry tape recorders, for godsakes.[81]

At her continued prodding, Sarris goes to his car to get the tape recorder, but he is suspicious that the three were talking about him while he was gone. Here in this moment, Sarris is self-conscious about being seen as an anthropologist (and, by default, white). The tape recorder especially typifies a key technology that anthropologists use in order to record and place Indigenous knowledge in time and space, with the assumption that their culture will soon disappear. Thus, while recording Indigenous peoples in the durative present, the use of the tape recorder assumes that such present is already of the past tense and must be archived in order for its knowledge to be available for the uses of settler culture in the future. The role of the recorder, like the form of the biography that Sarris seems to extol, seeks to lock Mabel into settler colonial logics of time and tense.

The rationale for his anxiety and hesitation can be illuminated in a later moment in the text when Sarris describes white folks whom Mabel cannot stand because of their disrespectful mode of "playing Indian," or appropriating Indian culture for the white community's own political self-articulation. Given his own relatively light skin, his status as an academic working with Indigenous peoples, and his vague and unknown background due to his adoption, Sarris is in close proximity to this long history of white appropriation:

> Mabel was generally patient with people and their endless questions. If anything, it was her answers that made others impatient. But one group of visitors who came regularly to Dexter Street [presumably her home] annoyed her, so much so that she asked them to leave. They were students from junior college. A few claimed they were Indian, part Cherokee. They wore beads and feathers, open leather vests showing their bare chests.[82]

Mabel's feelings about people who choose to consume "Indianness" through aesthetic means are revealed here, but this particular scene also sets Sarris apart from these students. Their conspicuous performance of Indianness ("beads and feathers") is directly different from his inconspicuous demeanor and hesitation to claim his Pomo-Miwok background. Seen in the context of this brief scene, the hesitations that seem to condition Sarris's relationship with Mabel and her relatives are responses to the present histories of assimilation policies, blood quantum regulations, and white appropriation, all of which seek to eliminate Indigenous identities and claims to land. That is, Sarris's tense exchanges within the Pomo community are the affective responses to the long history of settler imperatives to disconnect Indigenous peoples from their community and culture.

It is clear in Sarris's biography, though, that what Sarris perceives to be the community's judgment about his behavior is also an internalized self-regulation—one that is explicit through both his actions and his embodied reactions. While Christian's essay traces the work of shame in separating herself from her own history, Sarris's sense of shame is less overtly expressed—often emerging in indirect ways. In a key scene, while he drives Violet home after a long interview with Mabel, Violet acknowledges that he is "part of the gang." Rather than accept Violet's inclusion of him in this sense of community, Sarris hesitates for a minute, given Violet's denigration of the Native folks that she deems "gutter snipe." Sarris's first impulse is to attribute Violet's comment to creating a separation between good Indians and bad Indians, which propels him to defend the Native people he grew up with in Santa Rosa. Thinking of the group he grew up with, the group that Violet calls "gutter snipe," Sarris puts up his guard.[83] Immediately after this thought, however, Sarris recalls Mabel's story about standing naked (after a game of strip poker) in front of strangers. In the story, while Mabel initially covered parts of her body with her hands, the others tell her to "put [her] hands down," inspiring her to expose herself without embarrassment or shame. By referencing Mabel's story, Sarris suggests that this moment with Violet is, for him, a moment of exposure that causes perhaps some sense of embarrassment or shame. His recall of Mabel's story also, however, suggests his desire to put down his defenses, to be vulnerable no matter how strong the desire to protect himself.

This self-regulation can also be seen in Sarris's repetition that he is a "stranger." After driving Violet back to her house, she invites him to stay on the couch instead of taking a trip to his adoptive mother's house so late at night. His hesitation spurs Violet to comment casually, "quit acting like a stranger." Sarris responds:

> The word ["]stranger["] hit a nerve. I stiffened, then came through the doorway.... Seeing Violet working over the sofa, I felt awkward, more ridiculous than ever. Like salt rubbed in the wound of my frightened, hardheaded life. Of course Violet meant what she said. She cared for me.[84]

Later, in another conversation in which Sarris details his family history, Violet and Anita ask him how he feels, knowing that he is related to the Native folks with whom he grew up. After some back and forth, they assess that he still does not feel like he has family and state that he is still a "stranger to himself."[85]

Linking Sarris's struggle with genre and his struggle with identity, the form that his biography of Mabel takes on emulates Sarris's ultimate confrontation with the settler racial demarcations and delimitations of Indigenous identity and community. That is, although he lays bare his conflicts and his struggles with Mabel about the form of the biography, the structure ultimately coalesces with a kind of mixed-blood epistemology, one that conveys the knowledge and histories that make up Sarris's experiences as mixed-blood, and yet attends deeply to Mabel's (an Indigenous-centered) ethos of identity and of family. Thus, even as Mabel rejects discussions about theme, the coalescing theme of the piece speaks to a centering of Pomo sovereignty and epistemology specifically about family and community—that is, the movement from settler-national to tribal-national configurations of the "intimate domestic."[86] Rather than begin with Mabel's birth, for example, the biography opens with her grandmother Old Sarah's perspectives and struggles. The biography also weaves in Sarris's own adoption story, thus emphasizing the connection between his identity and Mabel's. In addition, Sarris takes pains to emphasize Mabel's own adoption into multiple Native and non-Native communities and families. First, Mabel was adopted by her grandmother Sarah then by Mary Wright, a Cortina woman who came to adopt her when she became too sickly for Sarah to take care of. Sarris later describes how Mabel told of being adopted by her good friend and fellow medicine woman Essie Parrish: "She was quiet for a long time with the tape recorder just running. Then she started talking about Essie, about how Essie adopted her in at Kashaya [a neighboring Pomo tribe], the stories about her first trip there and the incident of the Kashaya woman who stole her bone whistle."[87] Sarris also emphasizes the continuity of adoption when he mentions meeting Mabel for the first time via her adopted son, Marshall.[88]

Interestingly, Sarris's Filipino background does not figure as largely in the narrative—instead, it is minimized as he seeks to engage his Pomo-Miwok identity. Such minimization reveals the racial binaries that permeate discourses of race and settlement in the United States. Early in the biography, Sarris mentions his father's identity as an "unknown non-white," a phrase that suggests that racialization pivots on the classification of white/nonwhite despite the racial asymmetries of settler, alien/arrivant, and Native histories.[89] Like Christian, Emilio seems to be phenotypically unidentifiable, being mistaken for a "town n——r" in one instance and a "Hawaiian-type guy" in another.[90] Also, given Sarris's light-skinned appearance, his attention to the white-Native binary infuses his relationships with different Native community members throughout the book and provides the central pivot of the narrative tensions, anxieties, and (formal) resolutions. In this sense, his overwhelming feelings of anxiety and shame (particularly about his white identity) seem to overwrite attention to the linkages (and possible tensions) between Indigenous and Filipino communities. Thus, the binary racial logics of the United States produce a kind of state-produced silence, an overriding structure of feeling, that circumvents the potential to fully and explicitly engage direct discussions about Asian-Indigenous connections and potential for solidarities amid the biopolitical technologies of the settler racial state.

While he does not fully address his Filipino background, the biography does include several instances in which Mabel engages with people of Asian descent. In these scenes of interaction, the narrative provides glimpses of Asian-Indigenous connections and alliances. An early childhood memory of Mabel's was going to a Chinese herbalist who was able to cure her of her inability to gain weight.[91] Mrs. Spencer, a white woman who also adopted Mabel when she was a child, takes Mabel to visit the herbalist's shop for the first time:

> Mrs. Spencer and Alice [her daughter] ushered Mabel into a small house on the edge of town. The place was set up as a doctor's office. The front room served as a waiting room, the bedroom as an examination and consulting room. While they waited, Mrs. Spencer and Alice browsed through books and journals on Chinese herbs and other kinds of unusual medicines. Mabel had no idea how unconven-

tional the old woman and her tall, straight-haired daughter were at the time.⁹²

This moment, built on Mabel's account, outlines the alternative economies within which the Chinese herbalist operates: he lives on the "edge of town" and his home is his place of work. On examination of Mabel, the herbalist, a "tiny balding Chinese man," concludes that Mabel has "weak blood" and assigns her an eating program and key herbs and tinctures to consume. The doctor's prescribed diet made Mabel less emaciated—indeed, made her "fat" and "stout"—but her condition of falling asleep (an undefined lethargy that plagued her throughout her life) continued on. Another example of Mabel's interaction with Asian people in the United States is when Mabel was living in San Francisco and working at a Japanese restaurant later in her life. As she recalls: "'My work is washing dishes in a Japanese restaurant. Geary and Fillmore streets. Fifty cents a day and food. I have a room by there. Ten dollars a month.'"⁹³

Placed in juxtaposition, these two scenes interestingly align these two communities along two settler racial temporalities: one of "old world" knowledge and the other of "modern" economic life. The fact that Mabel juxtaposes the two as nonmutually exclusive occurrences reveals the narrative's own push to destabilize settler racial designations of Asian and Indigenous peoples as existing in distinct temporalities. In the first instance, Mabel's scene with the Chinese herbalist allows for cross-community dialogue about "alternative," non-Western, or "Old World" medicine. While white doctors could not cure Mabel, this Chinese doctor was able to assist—to a certain extent. That is, Mabel is able to gain weight but continues to have a mysterious kind of lethargy. Sarris's representation of the Chinese doctor's role and limits provides an opportunity to open up discussions about sharing non-Western and traditional forms of medical knowledge. This brief reference conjures possibilities for further dialogue between Chinese and Pomo medicine—that is, the possibility for these two knowledge systems to mutually benefit one another. Mabel's story reveals how this mutual benefit need not come out of the full alignment between Asian and Indigenous knowledge systems or temporalities. The Chinese doctor's world, so spatially and temporally removed from Mabel's own, can nevertheless impact Mabel's health and life. The second example, of Mabel's work at a Japanese restaurant, places Mabel within the contemporary economic infrastructure via her relationality with the Nikkei community in San Francisco. Taken together, these two moments show the role of the U.S. Asian American presence in potentially enabling Pomo health and economic life.

These all-too-brief scenes of Asian-Indigenous connections do not disrupt the binary white-nonwhite logics that primarily drive Sarris's struggle with his Native identity. At the same time, they do offer glimpses of possibilities for connection between Asian and Indigenous peoples. That is, through these scenes of interaction, the narrative reveals the multiple yet incommensurate temporalities that undercut settler delineations of Asian and Indigenous communities in time and space. Thus, Sarris conveys converging and adjacent temporal sites where these two communities can potentially and perhaps briefly connect. It is specifically through Sarris's partially giving over to Mabel's narrative form (that is, by attending to stories that seemingly go nowhere) that these temporal ruptures are made present to the reader. Ultimately, Sarris's emphasis on moments of anxiety and shame, which manifest in his struggle with the biographical form, provides insights into how emotions, as social forces, can both reveal and inflect the conditions of settler racial hegemonies in the United States.

Conclusion

As Christian suggests, the silence surrounding Asian and Indigenous relationships and the implicit refusal to recognize their mixed-blood progeny can foreclose productive critiques of settler racial biopolitics that are perpetuated through an uneven racialized and colonial regulation of Indigenous and Asian bodies. In Sarris's text, this silence is produced by the overriding focus on white-nonwhite logics that structure the narrator's anxieties about his Indigenous identity. The silence can obscure the variety and techniques of cross-racial relationalities and solidarities that can emerge when these two communities' converging histories are attended to. In the cases of Christian, Sarris, and the Grants, assertions of Indigenous identity and heritage serve as critical refusals of the logic of elimination that structure the biopolitical and sovereign technologies of the state against Indigenous peoples—such as antimiscegenation laws, adoption policies, and blood quantum regulations. Their critical voices suggest that this refusal to accede to Indigenous annihilation can be possible, not in spite of but through attention to their Asian backgrounds. By drawing on their backgrounds, these scholars convey the intersecting settler and racial technologies of domination that bring these two communities together and yet might drive them into critical tension. At the same time, conveying these crossings provides opportunities for direct and indirect dialogue about Asian-Indigenous responsibilities, solidarities, and strategies to unsettle settler racial space, time, and tense. In each of these texts about mixed-blood individuals, such figures actively seek connection with their Indigenous roots. Through this deep connection, these mixed-blood writers draw on (to varying degrees) the responsibilities of Asian communities in recognizing their placement within and in working toward a decolonized future.

As I mention in the introduction to the chapter, along with their entire family, Howard and Larry Grant serve as community leaders of the Musqueam nation. For Howard Grant, despite his fond memories of his father and his pride in being Chinese, "there was no lifeline provided to [him] from [his] Chinese side."[94] As I also mentioned, under the Indian Act, the Grants' Aboriginal identity would not have been recognized. The Musqueam nation's continued connection to the Grant children, despite settler state demarcations of "Indianness," suggests the nation's sustained refusal to fully accede to settler state biopolitical technologies of Indigenous disappearance. That is, while not recognized by the settler state as Indigenous people, the Grant children's integration into the tribal national community reveals the continued prominence of tribal definitions of belonging. It is with this strong grounding in his Musqueam identity that Larry Grant makes connections with his Chinese heritage and the Chinese Canadian community writ large.

For Christian, her discussion of "coming out" as part Chinese does not diminish but, rather, opens up her possession of Secwepemc-Syilx (Shuswap-Okanagan) knowledge and lifeways. Knowing her background allows her insight into the survival strategies of her mother and their tribal community in relationship to white and nonwhite settlers. As part of the assimilation policies known as the "sixties scoop," where Aboriginal children were taken from their families to be placed in foster care or for adoption, Christian reveals how the settler state's push toward Indigenous erasures was not simply a past but a present and ongoing technology. As with the Grant family, the fact that Christian identifies fully with her tribal nation reveals the limits of settler biopolitics to extinguish Indigenous sovereignty and self-determination. Thus, as Christian begins to accept her Chinese father's existence, she does so in order to more fully embody her Indigenous identity and the difficult work for self-determination and decolonization. That is, her movement from shame to acceptance (or acceptance through shame) allows her to imagine her mother's decisions and actions within the perspective of Indigenous survivance, amid a more complicated terrain of race and settlement in Canada.

In her later essay on Canada's Truth and Reconciliation Report, Christian continues this reflection and work. Christian acknowledges the complicated settler racial terrains and the shared histories and oppressions that Chinese and Indigenous peoples have experienced. At the same time, Christian emphasizes the work of decolonization and the responsibility to Indigenous peoples and Indigenous lands on which settlers of color live. Citing a 2007 conference panel in which she participated entitled "Women, Resistance, and

Cultural/Community Activism—Catalyzing Agents: The Ethics of Doing 'Asian Canadian,'" Christian writes: "At the end of my presentation, I asked them [Asian communities] *when* they were going to start giving back to the lands they had chosen as their new home and, also, *what* they would give back."[95] In this inquiry, Christian employs the concept of "giving back," which is central to many Indigenous traditions. Addressing transnational ties forged by Asian Canadians and immigrants with their country of origin, Christian queries the responsibilities to the land on which they settle:

> Settler peoples come from all over the world to these lands to reap the benefits of this land of milk and honey, and they send their financial and other resources to their homelands. What do they give back to the Original Peoples of these lands? Do they ever take the time to learn about the Indigenous people whose lands they occupy?[96]

Through this discussion, Christian calls for ethical work (and the time taken) among the Asian Canadian community to respatialize and retemporalize Asian Canadian identity in relationship to their embodied presence on *present* Indigenous lands and with Indigenous peoples.

Coda

Of comparative work, Shu-mei Shih writes, "If one places three related terms under the pressure of triangulation, new insights emerge. The ethical question, however, pivots on the choice of what three terms to place under pressure, on the selective valorization of these three terms over others, and on the consequence of diminishing returns for interracial solidarities."[1] Throughout this book, I have made the argument that centering the relations between Asian and Indigenous peoples in the Américas provides much-needed insight into the *tense* liberal logics of settler colonialism that enjoin these two communities into active, passive, and resistive participation. I have traced how scenes of Asian-Indigenous crossings in the literary archives of these two communities reveal and grapple with (often problematically) the life, transformations, and endurance of what I have termed "settler racial hegemonies." Settler racial hegemonies names the process through which political, cultural, and social articulations from Native and non-Native communities of color have been incorporated and thus neutralized under the liberal imperatives of the settler state.

Given the diametrical positions of these two communities within the spatiotemporal constructions of settler national identity, I have argued that this comparative scope (or triangulation between Asian, Indigenous, and white settler) provides a way to understand settler racial hegemonies as persisting through the production of settler racial tense. Settler racial tense encapsulates how accommodation to (often registered as resistance to) settler colonial power comes to be activated by the deployment of a settler grammar that unevenly conjugates differently racialized and colonized communities into settler racial constructions of time and space. Such constructions, as I have shown, are mobilized and yet also disrupted by the emotional or affective economies embodied within Asian and Indigenous communities. In examining the affective currents through which this participation manifests, this book works toward capturing the contradictions and incompletions that persist in the interstices of settler colonialism. As such, while the narratives I examine all confront the inherited problems of meaningful solidarities across the liberal logics of racial, imperial, and colonial formations, they nevertheless contain glimpses of emotional "excesses" that haunt the peripheries of settler racial hegemonies. These affective excesses constitute nascent, yet-to-be-formed, structures of feeling.

I have employed a hemispheric lens to trace how settler racial hegemonies as a matter of tense emerge across different settler colonial boundaries in the Américas, therefore linking the processes of settler colonial imposition across British, Spanish, and Portuguese empires. This book reveals how these differentiated empires operate through the uneven tensions across Indigenous and alien communities, as these communities' cultural and political articulations become funneled into liberal imperatives grounded in settler acquisition and maintenance of territory and oriented toward settler futurity and longevity. Each of the chapters focused on different colonial apparatuses of power in distinct geographies—from historiography in the United States to legal/juridical performances in Canada, economic maneuverings in Mexico and Brazil, and biopolitical governance across the United States and Canada. Taken together, these chapters reveal the diversity and yet malleability of settler technologies of power. Yet, what remains consistent across these settler state apparatuses are their shifting yet continual reliance on the asymmetrical positioning of Asian and Indigenous peoples with relation to settler constructions of place and time. For example, across these settler states, the legitimation of settler claims to territory is often contingent on the placement of Indigenous communities in the past tense of the modern and future-oriented nation. This placement occurs through different technologies—from the settler state's positioning of Indigenous anger/melancholy in regard to settler violence as limiting Indigenous growth in the future (as is the case in Canada's public apologies) to the dissolution of the "authentic Indian" through the celebration of mixed-race futurity (as in the case of Mexico and Brazil)—but can be seen as a sustained and malleable requirement for settler legitimacy. In like manner, the settler state often fashions the Asian alien as in tune with settler constructions of time—from their inclusion as laborers for the modern nation (United States) to their ability to forgive racialized crimes of the settler state (Canada)—but still situates Asian belonging as a supplement to normative settler identities and thus out of step with settler belonging in place. For example, Canada's public apology for Nikkei internment rendered the Nikkei community as in step with the future orientation of the nation (through their getting over the crimes of the past) yet continues to render Nikkei communities as subjects only "tolerated" by the settler state, positioning them asymmetrically in relationship to the legitimate settler subject. This book reveals how such uneven yet enduring positionings depend on these two communities' mutual yet uneven participation in the colonial and racialized logics of settler temporalities and territoriality. Ultimately, I suggest that the understanding of continuities of settler empires in the Américas that can be drawn from *Unsettled Solidarities* can help to provide a groundwork toward meaningful dialogue on racial formations and relationships that speak beyond the spatial and temporal delimitations of the settler liberal present.

Still, this relational hemispheric focus, and the insights it yields, leave unanswered the question of why I have chosen this particular comparative work over others. Early in the Introduction I explained my "selective valorization" of comparison between the Asian and Indigenous as stemming from my own background as a Vietnamese refugee woman occupying the traditional lands of Cheyenne and Arapahoe peoples. My own movements through the world have brought me to places where the violent intimacies of racialization, empire, and settlement are both partially embodied and intentionally left hidden by the various communities of which I am a part. I have moved to and lived in colonial spaces from San Diego, California; to Denver, Colorado; to Santa Barbara, California; and, currently, Tampa, Florida. Within each of these spaces, there are varying scales through which the presences of Indigenous peoples have been violently conjugated or completely erased. My decision to engage Asian and Indigenous crossings, then, has its roots in my desire to make sense of my own tense embodiments (as a Vietnamese refugee, U.S. Asian American, cisgender woman of color) and ethical relations within the traditional homelands of the Juaneno, Luiseno, Cahuilla, Cupeno, Kumeyaay, Northern Diegueño, Cheyenne, Arapahoe, Chumash, Tocabaga, Seminole, and Miccosukee.

However, the knowledge that emerges is inevitably haunted by that which is occluded. This is to say, the critical knowledge that we gain by this uneasy triangulation cannot be complete. The epistemological critique and ethical considerations of placing Asian and Indigenous communities in relationality is simultaneously haunted by questions of what is still illegible in the project. At the time of my writing this book, addressing these limits becomes ever more urgent as the lives of black and brown communities continue to be under siege from the violence of police brutality, border surveillance, and the dismantling of families and relationships. Indeed, I have moved to settler colonial spaces peopled by communities of color that are continuously under siege from U.S. policies that reach back to the legacies of the settler colony's inception. In addition, these communities are critically central to the spatial, temporal, and affective reproduction of settler colonial imposition. Amid these conditions, I want to conclude the book by asking: In what ways can this project also provide a lens into Asian and Indigenous relationality to the legacy of racial oppression—of anti-blackness, Islamophobia, and the mass deportations of Latinx people—that is inextricably stitched into the histories of the Américas? In addition, how might this study's attentiveness to Asian and Indigenous presence in the Américas productively inflect struggles and protests for black lives and immigrant rights? On the other hand, how might attentiveness to black and Latinx communities' articulations and struggles provide additional insights into the work of solidarities and alliances crucial in the destabilization of settler colonialism in the Américas? Although my emphasis on Asian-Indigenous relations may implicate some kind of abandonment of these questions, I suggest that what has been gleaned from this study can bring us all the more closer to thinking through these critical relationships during these critical times.

More specifically, despite the elisions that come from the comparative work that has been central to this book, I do suggest that the concept of settler racial hegemonies (as a matter of tense) is a malleable heuristic that can be applied to the considerations of these different relationalities. That is, this concept of settler racial hegemonies can serve as a lens through which to read relationships across all different geometries (and intensities) of identities and power in the Américas. It is a lens that is not bound to some geometric triangulation but rather a barometer that allows one to grasp the pressures or tensions across an array of relationalities. This barometer centers the settler and racial asymmetries that structure the lives of all communities. It urges the reader toward spatial and temporal readings of these cross-racial relationships as they both exist within and yet in excess of liberal consolidation of settler territories and temporalities. In addition, this lens works to capture the felt experiences of such relationalities and conditions to access both settler racial structures of feelings and elided affective formations that persist through the conditions of harm and power that differently racialized and colonized communities experience. As a barometer of relationality and power, my conceptualization of settler racial hegemonies thus does not occlude but invests in thinking through the relationality across *all* communities of color, to think through identity formation and political articulations as they reverberate across differently positioned communities across the Américas. However, this lens also calls for the recognition of the discrete spatial and temporal separations wrought out of the uneven histories of colonization, imperialism, and racialization—histories that bespeak not only the asymmetries of communities but also the possibilities and limits for cross-racial connections and futurities.

To illuminate settler racial hegemonies as heuristic/lens/barometer, I turn back to a key character in one of the literary texts that has been the focus of my book: Clinton, a black-Cherokee Vietnam War veteran represented in Leslie Marmon Silko's *Almanac of the Dead*. While *Unsettled Solidarities* emphasizes close readings of Asian-Indigenous relationalities, and the logics and instabilities of power that they reveal, the literary texts imagine full and complicated worlds with various characters that are of different racial and ethnic backgrounds living in the Américas. In addition to Clinton, there are other differently racialized characters in these texts, from brief references to a black relative in Maxine Hong Kingston's *China Men* to the presence of Mexican communities in Greg Sarris's *Mabel McKay*. These texts reveal the varying identities, connections, and tensions that make up the legacy of settler colonialism in the Américas. Such representations also speak to the very magnitude of settler racial hegemonies, and our own relationships and responsibilities within these processes. Thus, while this book centers Asian-Indigenous connections in order to articulate a conceptualization of settler racial hegemonies as a matter of tense, the texts themselves reveal how this dynamic captures *all* communities of color.

In *Almanac,* Clinton's often freewheeling perspective and critique demonstrate the knowledge that can be gleaned and the relationalities activated through a critical barometer of settler racial hegemonies. Through this lens, Clinton provides insight into the linkages between settler colonial and imperial violence as well as the relationship among struggles for emancipation, sovereignty, and place that emerge among differently positioned communities of color. As a black-Cherokee Vietnam War veteran, Clinton's presence in the novel merges histories of settler colonial violence, enslavement, and imperial wars across the Pacific. Affectively embodying and verbally conjuring these histories throughout the narrative, Clinton works to raise an army of homeless people who can mobilize against settler colonial productions of violence. In addition, Clinton has been recording radio programs, which he plans to disseminate in order to mobilize the masses. Working with Roy, a white veteran, Clinton breaks into and temporarily lives in abandoned vacation homes in Tucson. While there, Clinton intercepts credit cards and bank account information sent to homeowners too rich and busy to track the movement of their money. Clinton and Roy slowly siphon money out of these intercepted accounts to build the funding for the Army of the Homeless (or what Clinton calls "the Army of Justice"). Silko's text suggests that this army is a crucial component to the formation of hemispheric Indigenous resistance against settler colonial expansion and violence.

On first encountering Clinton, the reader becomes immediately privy to his distinct perspective: he centers the asymmetries and yet relationships among present histories of settler colonialism, imperial wars, and enslavement. Moreover, he highlights the complicit incorporation and participation of Native and non-Native communities of color in these asymmetrical processes. Of the Vietnam War, for example, Clinton writes: "It had been easy to see it was a white man's war; the colored man was sent to do the dangerous, dirty work white men were too weak to perform."[2] As scholar Sharon P. Holland notes, the use of black service in U.S. wars can be seen also in the histories of the Buffalo Soldiers, "who were enlisted to do the most dangerous job of bringing about white law, order, and settlement to tribal lands known to American as the 'frontier.'"[3] While highlighting the complicit participation of black communities in destroying "indigenous populations," Clinton also describes the histories of Native American participation in the enslavement of black communities. Drawing from the knowledge of his own family's background, Clinton cites Cherokee slaveholders:

> Clinton had not got over the shock and wonder of it. He and the rest of his family had been direct descendants of wealthy, slaveowning Cherokee Indians. That had been before Georgia white trash and president Andrew Jackson had defied the U.S. Supreme Court to round up all Indians and herd them west. Clinton had liked to imagine these Cherokee ancestors of his, puffed up with their wealth of mansions, expensive educations, and white and black slaves. How "good" they thought they were! No ignorant, grimy cracker-men dare touch them! So pride had been their fall. That was why a people had to know their history, even the embarrassments when bad judgment had got them slaughtered by the millions.[4]

Clinton does not fall into the trap of rendering these processes as commensurate with European colonization. For example, while acknowledging enslavement in Africa, Clinton highlights its critical difference as one of scale: "Where a tribe might capture fifty slaves in ten years, the demand for slave labor in Spanish and Portuguese colonies of the New World greatly increased tribal warfare for the procurement of slaves. Hundreds and finally thousands of slaves were needed in the gold mines and plantations that were worthless without slave labor."[5] What he seems to emphasize is slavery's reverberating effects on the magnification of white settler colonial power.

Clinton not only highlights the complicit participation of communities of difference in the reproduction of settler colonial, imperial, and racialized power; he also points out how such participation lends to the spatial and temporal consolidation of the United States as a settler and imperial state. In his reveries on the Vietnam War, Clinton recounts the taking of Vietnamese lands and also the war's relationship to the taking of black spaces and futurities. He declares:

> Black people all knew deep down the Vietnam War had been aimed at them to stop black riots in U.S. cities. The war had destroyed some of their best young men. The war had destroyed two generations of hopefulness and cultural pride. A dangerous generation had emerged from the Korean War. Black warriors and warrior women who sat down at the lunch counters and refused to ride at the back of the bus had changed the face of America. Efficiently, the white man had sent sons and daughters to burn down Vietnam instead of Detroit, Miami, Watts. Vietnam had been designed to stop the black man in America.[6]

Here he links the violence perpetrated on Vietnamese lands to the degradation of predominantly black urban spaces from Detroit, Michigan, to Miami, Florida, and Watts, California. Moreover, he exposes how this process continues to cycle across the histories of the Américas through settler racial commonsense renderings of space, time, and tense. That is, the connections that Clinton makes across these different spatial and temporal histories are often rendered by Roy and even people of color as nonlogical, paranoid, and simply crazy. This dismissal of Clinton's worldview reveals the reigning dominance of settler space, time, and tense where discrete historical moments are partitioned according to liberal classifications of what constitutes a meaningful event.[7] By recognizing this common designation of his insanity, Clinton exposes how such forms of violence, through settler racial hegemonies, become actuated through the matter of tense.

Destabilizing the spatial and temporal delineations of these seemingly discrete events across racialized and colonized communities, Clinton works toward drawing out the felt experiences and affective forces emerging from communities affected by these interconnected histories and events. That is, drawing on these histories and their connections provides the potential to conjure the critical emotions that can enliven collective formation toward decolonization and racial justice. Specifically, for Clinton, making the linkages between histories of black enslavement and the colonization of Indigenous peoples can provide the grounds to conjure past, present, and future affinities that have the potential to create collective insurgence against settler colonial and racialized violence. Clinton cites, for example, the insurgence of African and Indigenous spirits in the Caribbean islands, where both communities joined together to survive collectively and fight against the colonizers.[8] For Clinton, these connections reach back not only to conditions stemming from European colonization but also toward emphasis on Indigenous/tribal worldviews across continents. Connecting these histories, which are produced out of cross-community complicities also provides space to move beyond simple romanticization of solidarity toward critical expression and responsibility for how one community's actions can affect the other. While Clinton does not fully go into detail about the affective spirits that might be conjured by Vietnamese/Vietnamese refugees, black communities, and Indigenous peoples in the Américas, the reference to Indigenous insurgence in Vietnam suggests that similar connections can potentially be drawn.

The lens through which Clinton reads the connection between seemingly discrete "events" of racialized or colonized harm has the potential to nuance, problematize, and thus build on critical movements and seemingly liberatory structures of feeling in our current moment. Here I expand the optics from black-Indigenous-Asian connections to gesture specifically toward the continuation of the killing, containment, and deportation of brown communities that stem from the racialized legacies of settler colonialism. Critical mobilization against mass deportation has often hinged on the common expression that "we are a nation of immigrants," obscuring the continued presence of Indigenous peoples. Moreover, critical expressions among Chicanx organizers, asserting, "We didn't cross the borders/the borders crossed us," cite the 1848 Treaty of Guadalupe Hidalgo, which expressly privileges the sovereignty of Spanish colonial regimes at, again, the elision of the violent Spanish encroachment on Indigenous lands. Even more disconcerting are liberal expressions of fatigue with U.S. governance and threats to move to the more beneficent governance of Canada, which erases not only the privilege of border crossing but also the continued circumvention of Aboriginal community lives and livelihoods. Through the barometer of settler racial hegemonies, the elisions of these critical expressions would be made ever present in ways that critically confront our settler racial divisions of space, time, and tense and how these divisions inform our affective attachments to vexingly oppressive expressions of liberation. This critical lens can provide both spatiotemporal disruptions and emotional mobilizations against the rupture of immigrant communities in ways that continue to acknowledge the lives of communities disrupted by present histories of settler colonialism, imperialism, and racialization.

Crucially, however, as a lens that must be physically embodied by different people, communities, and movements, the centering of settler racial hegemonies as an *embodied* barometer also connotes the limits that are immanent in the critical perspectives in the solidarity work toward decolonization. Indeed, Clinton's perspective is rife with problems and contradictions that infuse it with the kind of ugly solidarity work that Silko's novel represents. Indeed, his critique spills over into sexist rhetoric against all women as well as a kind of detachment from any forms of affection to human and nonhuman others.[9] His characterization highlights the limits of, yet does not foreclose, critical perspectives when they are necessarily employed on the ground. Employing settler racial hegemonies as a lens thus must also acknowledge the critical and emotional messiness and incompletion that such a barometer provides; such a lens calls forth a humbling approach in the work of solidarity toward decolonization. Here, I want to invoke Eve Tuck's and K. Wayne Yang's clarification that solidarity "cannot be too easy, too open, too settled. Solidarity is an uneasy, reserved, and unsettled matter that neither reconciles present grievances nor forecloses future conflict."[10]

In sum, the notion of settler racial hegemonies not only describes the conditions of complicity and its excesses in the context of racialization, settlement, and empire but also illuminates how such complicities and their excesses are produced through settler colonial grammars that are wielded by and lived within the emotional lives of all communities. Engaging settler racial hegemonies also provides a barometer with which to read space and place and to see and feel Indigenous and alien critical perspectives that have ongoing salience in the materialization of settler colonial worlds and their instabilities. As an intimately embodied process, my centering of settler racial hegemonies reveals the inchoate refusals that persist in what might seem to be the most compromised aspects of cultural and political articulations within community formations. Finally, the concept of settler racial hegemonies suggests that solidarities are not programmatic across different times and spaces and are indeed messy affairs that find meaning through the dynamic processes and peoples that comprise the particularities of colonial and anticolonial power.

Notes

NOTE ON TERMINOLOGY

1. M. Bianet Castellanos, Lourdes Gutiérrez Nájera, and Arturo J. Aldama, eds., *Comparative Indigeneities across the Américas* (Tucson: University of Arizona Press, 2012), 15.

INTRODUCTION

1. From Simon J. Ortiz, *from Sand Creek* (1981; repr., Tucson: University of Arizona Press, 2000), 15. Copyright © 2000. The Arizona Board of Regents. Reprinted by permission of the University of Arizona Press.

2. See Colorado Department of Human Services, "Country of Origin of Colorado Refugee and Refugee Eligible Population," Colorado Office of Economic Security, Division of Refugee Services, https://sites.google.com/a/state.co.us/cdhs-refugee/about-refugees/data-and-arrival-information.

3. For a discussion of the 1.5 generation, see Sucheng Chan, ed., *The Vietnamese American 1.5 Generation: Stories of War, Revolution, Flight, and New Beginnings* (Philadelphia: Temple University Press, 2006). For a discussion of the Cheyenne and Arapahoe, see Donald J. Berthrong, *The Cheyenne and Arapaho Ordeal: Reservation and Agency Life, 1875–1907* (Norman: University of Oklahoma Press, 1976). On the Sand Creek massacre, see Ward Churchill, *A Little Matter of Genocide: Holocaust and Denial in the Americas 1492 to the Present* (San Francisco: City Lights Publishers, 2001).

4. Asian and Indigenous "crossings," in the texts that I examine, emerge in both literal and discursive ways. Thus, this book examines "crossings" where Asian and Indigenous characters meet (literal crossings) and where dominant discourses about Asian and Indigenous peoples emerge, such as figurations of the "perpetual foreigner" or the "vanishing Indian" (discursive crossings). I also discuss crossings in the affective sense, where Asian-Indigenous convergences produce often vexed emotional states. Engaging these manifold crossings specifically in novels, plays, essays, biographies, and cultural

and political discourses, this book traces the co-constitution of hemispheric Asian American and Indigenous inclusion and participation in the processes of settler colonialism.

5. Lisa Lowe, *The Intimacies of Four Continents* (Durham, NC: Duke University Press, 2015), 3.

6. Gramsci insists that without hegemony, the state's stability can best be described as tenuous. Delineating the formation of the national Risorgimento in Italy, Gramsci writes that "these forces took power and united in the modern Italian State, in struggle against specific other forces and helped by specific auxiliaries or allies. In order to become a State, they had to subordinate or eliminate the former and win the active or passive assent of the latter. A study of how these innovatory forces developed from subaltern groups to hegemonic and dominant groups must therefore seek out and identify the phases through which they acquire: 1. autonomy *vis-à-vis* the enemies they had to defeat, and 2. support from the groups which actively or passively assisted them; for this entire process was historically necessary before they could unite in the form of the state." He elaborates that occasionally states forge power "unilaterally," eliding the two necessary steps through which to actuate this dominant or hegemonic formation. In this case, and in the example of Italy, these forces are "incapable of uniting the people around itself," and this was the cause of its defeats and the interruptions in its development. Antonio Gramsci, *Selections from the Prison Notebooks,* ed. Quintin Hoare and Geoffrey Nowell Smith (New York: International Publishers, 1971), 53.

7. As Viet Thanh Nguyen argues regarding the post-1960s United States: "Hegemony is the political process by which the dominant class of a society extracts the political consensus of the subordinate classes whose interests may be contradicted by the dominant class. As an aspect of hegemony, then, contemporary racial identities involve some type of consensus to the dominant political order. Therefore, Asian America is not simply or only a mode of opposition to this order. It also participates in political struggles over the meaning of citizenship and subjectivity within the American body politic, assuming a variety of possible positions that range from opposition and contestation to acquiescence and consensus with the dominant body politic." He continues, "The last moments of unstable equilibrium ended with the crisis brought about by the civil rights movement, a crisis finally brought under control by the state in the 1970s, shifting the United States to a new period of unstable equilibrium in which we are still living. In this state of equilibrium, racial difference is no longer *principally* policed by violent coercion (although that is still used), but is instead primarily maintained and negotiated through the consent of racial minorities. Omi and Winant borrow the term 'hegemony' from Antonio Gramsci in order to characterize the post–civil rights era and argue that 'hegemony operates by including its subjects, incorporating its opposition.' Part of that incorporation is the bureaucratization of race through civil rights, the census, and affirmative action." Viet Thanh Nguyen, *Race and Resistance: Literature and Politics in Asian America* (Oxford: Oxford University Press, 2002), 13, 15.

8. In using the term "hegemony" to identify contemporary processes of settler racial power, I am not assuming that forms of power have moved from a telos of coercion to consent. Citing Frantz Fanon and Achilles Mbembe, Sunera Thobani critiques the applicability of Foucault's notion of "biopower" as a form of consent that is applicable to Indigenous peoples in relationship to the Canadian settler state. She maintains that both Fanon and Mbembe "refute the notion of a linear and complete transition from a regime of overt

violence to bio-power. Instead, [they recognize] that the colonized subject/object was formed—and lives—within the soul-destroying brutality that was/is the colonial order." Sunera Thobani, *Exalted Subjects: Studies in the Making of Race and Nation in Canada* (Toronto, Canada: University of Toronto Press, 2007), 12. As Michael Omi and Howard Winant write: "Racial rule can be understood as a slow and uneven historical process that has moved from despotism to democracy, from domination to hegemony. In this transition, hegemonic forms of racial rule—those based on consent—eventually came to supplant those based on coercion. *But only to some extent only partially*" (my emphasis). They continue: "What form does racial hegemony take today? In the aftermath of the epochal struggles of the post–World War II period, under the conditions of chronic crisis of racial meaning to which U.S. society has grown accustomed, we suggest that a new and highly unstable form of racial hegemony has emerged, that of colorblindness." Michael Omi and Howard Winant, *Racial Formations in the United States: From the 1960s to the 1990s* (New York: Routledge, 1994), 132.

9. See Jodi Byrd, *The Transit of Empire: Indigenous Critiques of Colonialism* (Minneapolis: University of Minnesota Press, 2011); J. Kēhaulani Kauanui, "Colonialism in Equality: Hawaiian Sovereignty and the Question of Civil Rights," *South Atlantic Quarterly* 107.4 (2008): 635–650; Jean O'Brien, *Firsting and Lasting: Writing Indians Out of Existence in New England* (Minneapolis: University of Minnesota Press, 2010); Mark Rifkin, *Settler Common Sense: Queerness and Everyday Colonialism in the American Renaissance* (Minneapolis: University of Minnesota Press, 2014); Andrea Smith, *Native Americans and the Christian Right: The Gendered Politics of Unlikely Alliances* (Durham, NC: Duke University Press, 2008); Eve Tuck and K. Wayne Yang, "Decolonization Is Not a Metaphor," *Decolonization: Indigeneity, Education, and Society* 1.1 (2012): 1–40. See also: Cari Carpenter and K. Hyoejin Yoon, eds., "Asian/Native Encounters," special issue, *College Literature* 41.1 (2014); Beenash Jafri, "Desire, Settler Colonialism, and the Racialized Cowboy," *American Indian Culture and Research Journal* 37.2 (2013): 73–86; Paul Lai and Lindsey Claire Smith, eds., "Alternative Contact: Indigeneity, Globalism, and American Studies," special issue, *American Quarterly* 62.3 (2010); Karen J. Leong and Myla Vicenti Carpio, eds., "Carceral States: Converging Indigenous and Asian Experiences in the Americas," special issue, *Amerasia Journal* 42.1 (2016); Danika Medak-Saltzman and Antonio T. Tiongson Jr., eds., "Racial Comparativism Reconsidered," special issue, *Critical Ethnic Studies Association Journal* 2.1 (2015); Shaista Patel, Ghaida Moussa, and Nishant Upadhyay, eds., "Complicities, Connections, and Struggles: Critical Transnational Feminist Analyses of Settler Colonialism," special issue, *Feral Feminisms* 4 (2015).

10. With regard to Hawai'i, see Candace Fujikane, "Sweeping Racism under the Rug of 'Censorship': The Controversy over Lois-Ann Yamanaka's *Blu's Hanging*," in "Whose Vision? Asian Settler Colonialism in Hawai'i," ed. Candace Fujikane and Jonathan Okamura, special issue, *Amerasia Journal* 26.2 (2000): xv–xxii; Haunani-Kay Trask, *From a Native Daughter: Colonialism and Sovereignty in Hawai'i* (Honolulu: University of Hawai'i Press, 1999); and Dean Itsuji Saranillio, "Why Asian Settler Colonialism Matters: A Thought Piece on Critiques, Debates, and Indigenous Difference," *Settler Colonial Studies* 3.3–4 (2013): 280–294. With regard to Canada, see Iyko Day, *Alien Capital: Asian Racialization and the Logic of Settler Colonial Capitalism* (Durham, NC: Duke University Press, 2016) and "Alien Intimacies: The Coloniality of Japanese Internment in Australia, Canada, and the US," *Amerasia Journal* 36.2 (2010): 107–124; Larissa Lai, "Epistemolo-

gies of Respect: A Poetics of Asian/Indigenous Relations," in *Critical Collaborations: Indigeneity, Diaspora, and Ecology in Canadian Literary Studies,* ed. Smaro Kamboureli and Christl Verduyn (Waterloo, Canada: Wilfrid Laurier University Press, 2014), 99–126; Marie Lo, "Model Minorities, Models of Resistance: Native Figures in Asian Canadian Literature," *Canadian Literature* 196 (2008): 96–112; Malissa Phung, "Asian-Indigenous Relationalities: Literary Gestures of Respect and Gratitude," *Canadian Literature* 227 (Winter 2015): 56–72; Thobani, *Exalted Subjects*; Bonita Lawrence and Enakshi Dua, "Decolonizing Anti-racism," *Social Justice* 32.4 (2005): 120–143; and Rita Wong, "Decolonizasian: Reading Asian and First Nations Relations in Literature," *Canadian Literature* 199 (Winter 2008): 158–180. For a discussion of Alaska, see Juliana Hu Pegues, "Rethinking Relations: Interracial Intimacies of Asian Men and Native Women in Alaskan Canneries," *Interventions: International Journal of Postcolonial Studies* 15.1 (2013): 55–66.

11. For a discussion about the uneasy history of solidarity, see David Roediger, "Making Solidarity Uneasy: Cautions on a Keyword from Black Lives Matter to the Past," *American Quarterly* 68.2 (June 2016): 223–248. In this article, Roediger complicates easy understandings and declarations of solidarity. Tracing the usage of the term, particularly in labor history, and citing recent works on labor history at the intersection of Indigenous studies, Roediger points out how solidarity among laborers (of different races) has historically hinged on the goal of territorial possession of Indigenous lands. See also Glen Sean Coulthard and Leanne Betasamosake Simpson, "Grounded Normativity/Place-based Solidarity," *American Quarterly* 68.2 (June 2016): 249–255. In their response to Roediger's address on making solidarity uneasy, Coulthard and Simpson highlight the necessity of centering the struggles of protecting Indigenous territories and returning Indigenous bodies to traditional lands. For both, this emphasis on Indigenous struggles provides the basis for the sustenance of what they term "grounded normativity" or the "ethical frameworks provided by these Indigenous place-based practices and associated forms of knowledge" (254). According to Coulthard and Simpson, grounded normativity is the grounds on which Indigenous peoples practice solidarity with Indigenous and non-Indigenous peoples. They write: "Our relationship to the land itself generates the processes, practices, and knowledges that inform our political systems, and through which we practice solidarity. To willfully abandon them would amount to a form of auto-genocide" (254). See also Tuck and Yang, who call for solidarity within education/schools but articulate the necessary uneasiness of solidarity. Tuck and Yang, "Decolonization Is Not a Metaphor," 3.

12. Byrd writes specifically in regard to Indianness operating as a meme: "Indianness can be felt and intuited as a presence, and yet apprehending it as a process is difficult, if not impossible, precisely because Indianness has served as the field through which structures have always been produced. Within the matrix of critical theory, Indianness moves not through absence but through reiteration, through meme, as theories circulate and fracture, quote and build." Byrd, *Transit of Empire*, xviii.

13. Ibid., xiii; Lowe, *Intimacies of Four Continents*, 16.

14. There have been literary studies that connect multiple configurations of Native and non-Native ethnic communities. See, for example, Leslie Bow, *Partly Colored: Asian Americans and Racial Anomaly in the Segregated South* (New York: New York University Press, 2010); Byrd, *Transit of Empire;* Shona N. Jackson, *Creole Indigeneity: Between Myth and Nation in the Caribbean* (Minneapolis: University of Minnesota Press, 2012); Helen Jun, *Race for Citizenship: Black Orientalism and Asian Uplift from Pre-Emancipation to*

Neoliberal America (New York: New York University Press, 2011); James Kyung-jin Lee, *Urban Triage: Race and the Fictions of Multiculturalism* (Minneapolis: University of Minnesota Press, 2004); Julia H. Lee, *Interracial Encounters: Reciprocal Representations in African and Asian American Literatures, 1896–1937* (New York: New York University Press, 2011); Crystal Parikh, *An Ethics of Betrayal: The Politics of Otherness in Emergent U.S. Literature and Culture* (New York: Fordham University Press, 2011); Vijay Prashad, *Everybody Was Kung Fu Fighting: Afro-Asian Connections and the Myth of Cultural Purity* (Boston: Beacon Press, 2002); Cathy Schlund-Vials, *Modeling Citizenship: Jewish and Asian American Writing* (Philadelphia: Temple University Press, 2010).

15. Settler colonial studies in the Américas often center on U.S. settler and racial formation. The emphasis on U.S. formations at the expense of transnational co-constitution or the specificities emergent in other geographical zones can be seen in the use of the term "America" to stand in for the United States, which leaves out the majority of the hemisphere. U.S.-based theorization of racialization and settlement often occludes the differential processes that occur in other sites. U.S. racial discourse often operates through binary logics, with a strong focus and emphasis on black-white relations. As Iyko Day writes, "unlike other white settler colonies like Canada, where colonial dispossession is the paradigmatic signifier of white settler supremacy, in the continental United States it has been the legacy of slavery and anti-black racism. This is certainly not to say that the ongoing dispossession of Indigenous peoples in the United States goes completely unacknowledged but rather to appreciate the fact that alongside recent Indigenous sovereignty movements such as Idle No More in Canada or the BDS movement in Occupied Palestine, it has been Ferguson in the United States." Iyko Day, "Being or Nothingness: Antiblackness and Settler Colonial Critique," *Critical Ethnic Studies* 1.2 (2015): 103. The elisions that arise out of this sole focus on black-white binaries have long been critiqued within critical ethnic studies scholarship, which calls for highlighting other racialized and Indigenous formations and relationalities. Such calls are sought in order to rethink and reconfigure how U.S. racial formation and settler colonial governance come into being.

16. For a discussion of the term "arrivant," to distinguish between settlers and Indigenous communities, see Byrd, *Transit of Empire*, xxx. For a discussion of the triangulation of native, alien, and settler positions, see Day, *Alien Capital*, 18–25.

17. This is what Day describes, quoting Patrick Wolfe, as "the logic of elimination." Day, *Alien Capital*, 25.

18. Byrd, *Transit of Empire*, xvii.

19. Shu-mei Shih, "Comparative Racialization: An Introduction," special issue, *PMLA* 123.5 (2008): 1349–1350; Robert Blauner, "Internal Colonialism and the Ghetto Revolt," *Social Problems* 16.4 (1969): 393–408; Grace Kyungwon Hong and Roderick Ferguson, eds., *Strange Affinities: The Gender and Sexual Politics of Racialization* (Durham, NC: Duke University Press, 2011).

20. Hong and Ferguson, *Strange Affinities*, 8.

21. Claire Jean Kim, "The Racial Triangulation of Asian Americans," *Politics and Society* 27.1 (1999): 105–138.

22. In her examination of racial triangulation, Shih emphasizes the political implications in choosing one set of groupings over another. Shih writes: "The calls to go beyond black-white binary in American race studies are more likely to result in new insights on Asian Americans and Latinas/os (Alcoff) than on other people of color, especially Native

Americans. In other words, some terms may appear more readily triangulatable than others, while some may just disappear or fade into the background, as happened with the binary model. For instance, the call to transcend the binary has not brought the case of Native Americans into sustained triangulation; rather, a sanctioned ignorance persists regarding how issues of Native American rights, land, and cultural preservation must unsettle the framing and articulation of minority issues." Shih, "Comparative Racialization," 1351.

23. Here I align with Byrd, who maintains: "This conflation masks the territoriality of conquest by assigning colonization to the racialized body, which is then policed in its degrees from whiteness. Under this paradigm, American Indian national assertions of sovereignty, self-determination, and land rights disappear into U.S. territoriality as indigenous identity becomes a racial identity and citizens of colonized indigenous nations become internal ethnic minorities within the colonizing nation-state." Byrd, *Transit of Empire*, xxiv. See Kauanui, "Colonialism in Equality"; O'Brien, *Firsting and Lasting*; Rifkin, *Settler Common Sense*; Tuck and Yang, "Decolonization Is Not a Metaphor."

24. As early as *Custer Died for your Sins* (1969), Vine Deloria Jr. argues that the movements for Indian rights position the Indian's legal status relative to the U.S. state. As such, Deloria invokes the problems inherent in Indigenous engagements with civil rights struggles insofar as the struggle calls for integration into the cultural and political fabric of white América. Published years later, Deloria's *God Is Red: A Native View of Religion* (1994) continues to caution against what amounts to the colliding imperatives emergent in Indigenous and civil rights movements where the calls for antidiscriminatory actions might lead to the dispossession of Indigenous communities' status as treaty nations. Vine Deloria Jr., *Custer Died for Your Sins: An Indian Manifesto* (1969; repr., Norman: University of Oklahoma Press, 1988) and *God Is Red: A Native View of Religion* (Golden, CO: Fulcrum Publishing, 1994).

25. Rifkin, *Settler Common Sense*, 10.

26. On race and settler colonialism, see also Aileen Moreton-Robinson, *The White Possessive: Property, Power, and Indigenous Sovereignty* (Minneapolis: University of Minnesota Press, 2015).

27. Haunani-Kay Trask maintains that Asian settlers not only must recognize their presence as settlers in Hawai'i; they also must "criticize other Asian attempts to undermine sovereignty leaders." Haunani-Kay Trask, "Settlers of Color and 'Immigrant' Hegemony: 'Locals' in Hawai'i," in *Asian Settler Colonialism: From Local Governance to the Habits of Everyday Life in Hawai'i*, ed. Candace Fujikane and Jonathan Y. Okamura (Honolulu: University of Hawai'i Press, 2008), 11. Political alliances with Asian groups in Hawaiian sovereignty struggles are necessary, but such collaborations must be directed by Hawaiian leadership.

28. Candace Fujikane and Jonathan Y. Okamura, eds., *Asian Settler Colonialism: From Local Governance to the Habits of Everyday Life in Hawai'i* (Honolulu: University of Hawai'i Press, 2008), 20. In response to charges that Asian settler colonialism may reinvest in the flattening of complex colonial arrangements, Fujikane writes that "Asian settlers who argue that the identification of Asian as settlers 'oversimplifies' historical nuances actually register the ways that Asian settler complicity becomes lost in demands of 'complexity'" (20–21).

29. Ibid.

30. Ibid.

31. Byrd conceptualizes the space where different communities, histories, and knowledge meet via writer LeAnne Howe's literary imagination of the *haksuba*. This world is represented as chaos, as cacophony, but not as meaningless. The *haksuba* conveys the space where such transits of empire cannot be made legible via Western paradigms of comparativity, but that which already has presence and salience within southeastern Indigenous lenses. Byrd, *Transit of Empire*, xxvii; LeAnne Howe, "The Chaos of Angels," *Callaloo* 17.1 (1994): 108–114.

32. Byrd, *Transit of Empire*, 53.

33. Day writes: "The degree of forced or voluntary migration or level of complicity with the settler state is ultimately secondary to their subordination under a settler colonial mode of production driven by the proprietorial logics of whiteness." *Alien Capital*, 24.

Of this notion of intentionality, Zanaib Amadahy and Bonita Lawrence write: "Even in situations in Canada where Black people, after slavery, attempted settlement as free peoples, the process has been fraught with dispossession and denial of access to land. The reality then is that Black peoples have not been quintessential 'settlers' in the White supremacist usage of the word; nevertheless, they have, as free people, been involved in some form of settlement process. What seems more important than the semantics about whether or not individuals should be called settlers is the question of the relationships that Black 'settlers' have, by virtue of their marginality, with those whose lands have been taken, and what relationships they wish to develop, *at present*, with Indigenous peoples." Bonita Lawrence and Zanaib Amadahy, "Indigenous Peoples and Black People in Canada: Settlers or Allies?" in *Breaching the Colonial Contract: Anti-Colonialism in the US and Canada*, ed. Arlo Kempf (Berlin/Heidelberg, Germany: Springer Science, 2009), 107.

34. Day, *Alien Capital*, 24.

35. I use the term "relationality" interchangeably with "intersubstantiation" to highlight the connectivity between communities, human and nonhuman. The term "intersubstantiation" is posited in distinction from "cosubstantiation" to be inclusive of nonhuman beings. For a discussion of cosubstantiation, see Elizabeth Povinelli, *Economies of Abandonment: Social Belonging and Endurance in Late Liberalism* (Durham, NC: Duke University Press, 2011). For a discussion of intersubstantiation, see Aileen Moreton-Robinson, ed., *Sovereign Subjects: Indigenous Sovereignty Matters* (Crows Nest, Australia: Allen and Unwin, 2007), 2. For a connection between the two, see Byrd, *Transit of Empire*, 211. For a discussion of relationality, see Hong and Ferguson, *Strange Affinities*. Hong and Ferguson highlight the example of Cherríe Moraga's well-known train ride, narrated in *This Bridge Called My Back*, to illuminate their argument. In her introductory meditation to this anthology, Moraga emphasizes the need for an efficacious analytic that can allow her to connect the relationship between her and the various persons who are unequally privileged, profiled, and violated on that very train. It is precisely in the ability to see this relationality that Moraga finds the critical and affective groundwork for the forging of alliances and ethical relations. For instance, Hong and Ferguson point out that Moraga is *indignant*, not relieved, by the realization of her relative privilege in going unmolested on the train. Such visceral reactions stem from her lived recognition of the contingencies of her shifting positionalities in the metaphoric train ride of the racialized police state. Cherríe Moraga and Gloria Anzaldúa, eds., *This Bridge Called My Back: Writings by Radical Women of Color* (New York: Kitchen Table, 1983).

36. Byrd, *Transit of Empire*, 53.

37. My emphasis on literary productions hinges on the argument that literature offers a central site for revealing the logics and contradictions embedded in contemporary material conditions. Scenes of Asian and Indigenous relationalities point to not only the role of these two communities but also the works' own cultural participation within the asymmetries of power. Rather than solely attributing to these texts aspects of complicity or resistance to domains of power, I track the complicated nexus through which characters and the texts themselves work to reveal and resolve cross-community complicities and collisions wrought out of settler colonialism. As Helen Jun argues: "We can read culture not merely to identify ideological shortcomings (or, conversely, signs of resistance) but to understand that irrespective of intention and impulse, every text can be read for the inevitable contradictions it attempts to manage or reconcile." Jun, *Race for Citizenship*, 5.

38. In so doing, this book joins other scholarship that calls for the move from treating Asian and Indigenous peoples as objects of study to subjects of critique. Scholars have argued that the centering of Indigenous and Asian figures can expose the material and epistemological resonances of settler colonialism, however unevenly. For example, for Byrd, given the centrality of "Indianness" in both settler and alternative liberatory discourses, a centering of Indigenous phenomenology and cultural formations can provide critical mappings and alternative ways of reading contemporary colonial logics. For Lowe, the material histories of Asian American racial formations set this community apart from the cultural formations of the mainstream (U.S.) nation, where obscured histories can come to the fore. Lowe claims that "this distance preserves Asian American culture as an alternative site where the palimpsest of lost memories is reinvented, histories are fractured and retraced, and the unlike varieties of silence emerge into articulacy." Lisa Lowe, *Immigrant Acts: On Asian American Cultural Politics* (Durham, NC: Duke University Press, 1996), 6. *Unsettled Solidarities* brings together Byrd's centering of Indigenous phenomenology and cultural productions and Lowe's conceptualization of Asian American culture as an "alternative site," with the goal of exploring the unique critical knowledge that a more sustained conversation between hemispheric Asian American and Indigenous epistemologies provide.

39. Povinelli, *Economies of Abandonment*, 26.

40. Ibid., 30.

41. Interestingly, Day conceives of black and Native communities as occupying this diametrically opposing positionality. Day, *Alien Capital*, 25.

42. See Ronald Takaki, *Iron Cages: Race and Culture in 19th Century America* (1979; repr., New York: Oxford University Press, 2000), for various depictions of Asian Americans in the nineteenth century as they are racialized relative to African Americans and Native Americans.

43. For critiques of the Bering Strait theories and how they help to legitimize Euro-settler theft of Indigenous land, see Vine Deloria Jr., *Red Earth, White Lies: Native Americans and the Myth of Scientific Fact* (Golden, CO: Fulcrum Publishing, 1997); David Hurst Thomas, *Skull Wars: Kennewick Man, Archaeology, and the Battle for Native American Identity* (New York: Basic Books, 2001); Maria Shaa Tláa Williams, "Alaska and Its People: An Introduction," *The Alaska Native Reader: History, Culture, Politics*, ed. Maria Shaa Tláa Williams (Durham, NC: Duke University Press, 2009).

44. In addition, the moments of cross-community convergences reveal how the governance of tense in settler racial domination binds these two community bodies in its "interarticulation," whether directly or through mediated association, with one another. This term is borrowed from Susan Koshy's discussion of comparative racialization in "Why the Humanities Matter for Race Studies Today," *PMLA* 123.5 (October 2008): 1542–1549. In this piece, Koshy emphasizes the necessity to center the "interarticulation" between groups of color, rather than solely examining the internal dialogues within the boundaries of racialization.

45. For a meticulous groundwork account and reading of the series of laws and treaties between the United States and different Native nations, see Deloria, *Custer Died for Your Sins*. Deloria's minute reading of these treaties reveals the gap between popular conceptions of Indians' relationships to the United States (as lazy dependents or freeloaders who don't pay tax) and the actualities of Indian Nations' relationship to the United States through a series of treaties/contracts (agreed on primarily in the nineteenth century) that the United States has broken repeatedly and unceremoniously. Deloria frames his discussion of the U.S. history of fraudulence and broken treaties by first talking about the U.S. comments on its war in Vietnam. Deloria pinpoints the hypocrisy of the statement that the United States cannot relinquish its commitments to Vietnam because it does not want the world to lose faith in U.S. promises. For Deloria, the legacy of the U.S. government is based on a series of broken promises aided by the Christian Church. Vietnam is not the first or the most current. For Deloria, "Vietnam is merely a symptom of the basic lack of integrity of the government, a side issue in comparison with the great domestic issues which must be faced—and justly faced—before this society destroys itself." Deloria, *Custer Died for Your Sins*, 53. By viewing the United States in relationship to Indian Nations and broken treaties, Deloria reveals the United States as nothing like what it represents itself as: just.

46. See Mark Rifkin, *Beyond Settler Time: Temporal Sovereignty and Indigenous Self-Determination* (Durham, NC: Duke University Press, 2017).

47. Native Hawaiian activist Haunani-Kay Trask remarks that "politically, the vehicle for Asian ascendency is statehood," which effectively positions the construction and consolidation of Asian Hawaiian (and by extension American) and Native Hawaiian (American) communities in mutually exclusive terms. For Trask, the growing power among Asian settler groups in Hawai'i is contingent on the continuing facilitation and maintenance of U.S. colonial state apparatuses. In its discursive and perhaps more "liberal" forms, a term such as "local" is utilized to fight against dominant (white) power structures, through civil rights claims, but simultaneously occludes Native presence on the island and their calls for decolonization. "Settlers of Color and 'Immigrant' Hegemony," 47.

48. Linda Tuhiwai Smith, *Decolonizing Methodologies: Research and Indigenous Peoples* (London: Zed Books, 1999), 27–28. See also Ashis Nandy, *The Intimate Enemy: Loss and Recovery of Self under Colonialism* (Delhi: Oxford University Press, 1989).

49. Wendy Brown, *Regulating Aversion: Tolerance in the Age of Identity and Empire* (Princeton, NJ: Princeton University Press, 2006), 20.

50. Povinelli, *Economies of Abandonment*, 13.

51. Lowe, *Intimacies of Four Continents*, 41.

52. Critical scholarship in Asian American and Indigenous studies has emphasized the material work of emotions. That is, in addition to comprising an embodied episte-

mology of power, affect and emotions are central to the reproduction and re-formation of power relations. In the context of U.S. settlement, Rifkin discusses how the givenness of settler colonial presence as a surface or boundary is produced and reproduced through the "the ordinary 'emotional knowledges' of nonnatives[, which] work to circulate, instantiate, and normalize settler sovereignty." Rifkin continues that these "settler structures of feeling" often do not reference Indigenous peoples or the process of settlement distinctly but nevertheless perform "a set of routine orientations that arise from and propel the extension of claims of Native lands and dismissal of Native politics." Dian Million, quoted in Rifkin, *Settler Common Sense*, 12. Glen Sean Coulthard highlights how emotions such as anger within Indigenous communities not only trace the manifold logics of settlement but also fuel the critical response toward the formation of Indigenous collectivities and decolonial movements. *Red Skin, White Masks: Rejecting the Colonial Politics of Recognition* (Minneapolis: University of Minnesota Press, 2014). For Jeffrey Santa Ana, Asian American "racial feelings" are a critical inflection of the racialized violence that structures liberal individualism. *Racial Feelings: Asian America in a Capitalist Culture of Emotion* (Philadelphia: Temple University Press, 2015).

These emotions often circulate through the cultural formations of these two communities and offer an archive with which to trace and from which to draw. Million links the "felt theory" of Indigenous community formations to Indigenous narratives where "the stories, unlike data, contain the affective legacy of [Indigenous] experiences. They are a felt knowledge that accumulates and becomes a force that empowers stories that are otherwise separate, to become a focus, a potential for movement." Dian Million, "Felt Theory: An Indigenous Feminist Approach to Affect and History," *Wicazo Sa Review* 24.2 (2009): 31–32. For James Kyung-jin Lee, the glimmerings of a "subcultural presence" in Asian American cultural life, politics, and praxis continue to nourish the "conviction" of social justice that often operates under the sign of Asian America and yet works across racial imaginaries. James Kyung-jin Lee, "Asian Americans," in *The Cambridge Companion to Modern American Culture*, ed. Christopher Bigsby (Cambridge: Cambridge University Press, 2007), 190. Citing cross-racial activism by Asian Americans across racial lines, Lee suggests that, although small, these moments offer a necessary counternarrative to the perhaps overwhelming quantitative evidence of Asian Americans "ascending" into domination. In a later piece, Lee draws from illusory scenes in literary works (*The White Boy Shuffle, No-No Boy*) that maintain glimpses of "the 'needs and aspirations of an ineluctably differentiated humanity.'" For Lee, the continued promise of Asian American (literary) studies lies in the possibility of "build[ing] an archive of feeling that might become the capacity to compel you and others to do things you and they would not do on their own." Indeed, Lee infers that such an archive requires, registers, and provides the very affective possibility to continue the legacies of and for social justice. Nikhil Pal Singh, quoted in James Kyung-jin Lee, "The Transitivity of Race and the Challenge of the Imagination," special issue, *PMLA* 123.5 (2008): 1555.

53. Sara Ahmed, *The Cultural Politics of Emotions* (New York: Routledge, 2004), 10. See also "Collective Feelings: Or, the Impressions Left by Others," *Theory, Culture, and Society* 21.2 (2004): 25–42.

54. In this way, I am adding to the scholarship on affect in Native American/Indigenous and Asian American studies. Given how colonial and racial imposition depends on the production and control of intimate relations, focusing my attention on this domain

can reveal the unforeseen ways that settler colonialism operates. As Ann Laura Stoler writes, "The matters of the intimate are critical sites for the consolidation of colonial power, that management of these domains provides a strong pulse on how relations of empire are exercised, and that affairs of the intimate are strategic empire-driven states." Ann Laura Stoler, "Intimidations of Empire: Predicaments of the Tactile and Unseen," in *Haunted by Empire: Geographies of Intimacy in North American History*, ed. Ann Laura Stoler (Durham, NC: Duke University Press, 2006), 4. Thus, rather than assume that the affective embodiments of these communities are simply the effect of the force of dispossession under empire, such emotions constitute critical epistemologies of settler and racial power relations. Million reads against colonial tendencies to render the felt experiences of Indigenous peoples as pathological or strictly within the domain of the personal. Instead, she argues that the felt experiences of Indigenous women are a "felt theory," a "sixth sense about the moral affective heart of capitalism and colonialism." "Felt Theory," 54. Similarly, Santa Ana traces a series of Asian American cultural productions that convey what he terms "racial feelings," or Asian American felt experiences within the context of U.S. capitalism. He writes: "By articulating negative emotions of alienation, anger, ambivalence, and shame in their works, Asian Americans register the historical signification and containment of Asians in America as economic subjects." *Racial Feelings*, 22. See also Cari Carpenter, *Seeing Red: Anger, Sentimentality, and American Indians* (Columbus: Ohio University Press, 2008); Anne Anlin Cheng, *The Melancholy of Race: Assimilation, Psychoanalysis, and Hidden Grief* (Oxford: Oxford University Press, 2000); David L. Eng, *The Feeling of Kinship: Queer Liberalism and the Racialization of Intimacy* (Durham, NC: Duke University Press, 2010); Christine Kim, *The Minor Intimacies of Race: Asian Publics in North America* (Urbana: University of Illinois Press, 2016); Chrissy Yee Lau, "Ashamed of Certain Japanese: The Politics of Affect in Japanese Women's Immigration Exclusion, 1919–1924," in *Gendering the Trans-Pacific World: Diaspora, Empire, and Race*, ed. Catherine Ceniza Choi and Judy Tzu-Chun Wu (Leiden, Netherlands: Brill Press, 2017); erin Khuê Ninh, *Ingratitude: The Debt-Bound Daughter in Asian American Literature* (New York: New York University Press, 2011); Lily Wong, *Transpacific Attachments: Sex Work, Media Networks, and Affective Histories of Chineseness* (New York: Columbia University Press, 2018).

While these aforementioned scholars have tracked the ways that alternative cultural productions reveal and inflect conditions of inequities in the present, this scholarship has often left out the mutual constitution of race and settlement. In other words, the emphasis on the force of emotions as the thing that mobilizes power may capture linear movements between white-Indigenous or white-nonwhite relations, but such attention to linear movements cannot reveal what Lowe terms the "intimacies of four continents." In Lowe's framework, the formation of (white) liberal personhood, as the privileged life form of empire, is produced through the disavowed relationships across discontinuously racialized and colonized communities. This has been particularly noticeable in the gaps of dialogue across Asian and Indigenous relations. Lowe, *Intimacies of Four Continents*.

55. Raymond Williams, *Marxism and Literature* (Oxford: Oxford University Press, 1977), 132.

56. In the *OED*, "tension" is defined as "a strained condition of feeling or mutual relations which is for the time outwardly calm, but is likely to result in a sudden collapse, or in an outburst of anger or violent action of some kind."

57. Here I cite Raymond Williams's distinctions between feeling and a given ideology: "The term is difficult, but 'feeling' is chosen to emphasize a distinction from more formal concepts of 'world-view' or 'ideology.' It is not only that we must go beyond formally held and systematic beliefs, though of course we have always to include them. It is that we are concerned with meanings and values as they are actively lived and felt, and the relations between these and formal or systematic beliefs are in practice variable (including historically variable), over a range from formal assent with private dissent to the more nuanced interaction between selected and interpreted beliefs and acted and justified action." Williams, *Marxism and Literature*, 132.

Similarly, Povinelli articulates the relationship between an idea and an affect by drawing from Gilles Deleuze: "An idea represents something while an affect does not. An affect is not nothing, but it is also not something in the same way as an extrinsic or intrinsic idea. An affect is a force of existing (*vis existendi*) that is neither the realized thing (an idea), nor the accomplishment of a thing (an act, *potentia agendi*). This perspective on the force of existing is clearly engaging Spinoza's claim that things, finite and determinate kinds of existence, strive (*conatus*) to persevere in being. For Deleuze, the perpetual variation between *vis existendi* and *potentia agendi*—between striving to persevere and any actual idea or action that emerges from this striving—provides a space of potentiality where new forms of life can emerge." Povinelli, *Economies of Abandonment*, 9.

58. Indeed, another definition of tense/tension names the "condition of strain produced by anxiety, need, or by a sense of mental, emotional, or physical disequilibrium." *OED*.

59. Asian-Indigenous crossings provide a site through which we can trace the intimacies of settler racial hegemonies, precisely because these two communities are both central to but radically distanced from settler productions of the private, liberal, possessive individual. As scholars situated within hemispheric Asian American and Indigenous studies have argued, settler colonialism's demarcations of intimacy are made manifest in the breakdown of familial units and are implemented through compulsory definitions through which variances come to be deemed criminal. For Asian alien communities, anti-immigration, anti-miscegenation, and land laws inflected the familial composition of Asian immigrant groups and refigured Asian immigrant/generational personhood as outside of heteropatriarchal norms and ideals. This breakdown of the familial unit as a precursor for the reconsolidation of empire's power can also be seen in the context of U.S. wars in Asia and the radical effects on the microdynamic and spatial movements of families. For Indigenous communities, implementation of federal policies—such as Indian residential or boarding schools, allotment, and forced adoption programs—sought to destabilize Native familial definitions and relationships as a precondition of Native genocide. In Canada, these policies congealed under the jurisdiction of the Indian Act, one of the foundational laws that defined and regulated settler and Indigenous relations. Million argues that "an intimate realignment with Indian social relations through the Indian Act was the core of what colonization meant in practice." For example, "the strongly gendered training in residential schools coupled with the 1876 Indian Act radically reorganized Indigenous familial relations to conform to a uniform, patriarchal order." Dian Million, *Therapeutic Nations: Healing in an Age of Indigenous Human Rights* (Tucson: University of Arizona Press, 2013), 56. Meaningfully, the implementation of colonial and racialized rule and terror not only worked to reorder

the composition of hemispheric Native and Asian American families but also sought to affect the felt life worlds of Asian alien and Indigenous peoples.

60. Sara Ahmed, *The Promise of Happiness* (Durham, NC: Duke University Press, 2010), 40.

61. Ibid., 41.

62. In her discussion of social worlds and social projects, Povinelli writes: "No social world is simply organized or unorganized, coherent or incoherent, unified or fractured. Instead, social worlds are multiply partially organized and thus always multiply partially disorganized. Social projects disaggregate aspects of the social worlds and aggregate individual projects into a more or less whole—a definable and describable thing. But social projects are not fixed things. Indeed, they are not 'things' so much as aggregating practices, incessantly fixing phenomena and cosubstantiating practices." *Economies of Abandonment*, 8.

63. Williams, *Marxism and Literature*, 134.

64. Ibid., 132.

65. Lowe, *Intimacies of Four Continents*, 39.

66. Maxine Hong Kingston, *China Men* (1980; repr., New York: Ballantine Books, 1981).

67. Williams highlights this structure of feeling as constantly in process, a "preformation" that often emerges at significant conjunctures to be provisionally defined as and by a generation. *Marxism and Literature*, 134.

68. Drawing from the transnational turn in American studies writ large, this book emphasizes how national delineations are porous and form through relationships across nations' shifting demarcated boundaries. However, while transnational American studies often has as its focal point and mode of concern the interconnections across the Pacific and Atlantic, *Unsettled Solidarities* shifts toward a hemispheric American framework that emphasizes connections north and south within the hemisphere. For a discussion of the transnational turn in American studies, see Shelley Fisher Fishkin, "Crossroads of Cultures: The Transnational Turn in American Studies—Presidential Address to the American Studies Association, November 12, 2004," *American Quarterly* 57.1 (2005): 17–57; and Janice Radway, "What's in a Name?," *American Quarterly* 51.1 (1999): 1–32. For a discussion of the hemispheric turn in American studies, see Ralph Bauer, "Hemispheric Studies," *PMLA* 124.1 (2009): 234–250; Caroline F. Levander and Robert S. Levine, eds., *Hemispheric American Studies* (New Brunswick, NJ: Rutgers University Press, 2007); Claudia Sadowski-Smith and Claire Fox, "Theorizing the Hemisphere: Inter-Americas Work at the Intersections of American, Canadian, and Latin American Studies," *Comparative American Studies* 2.1 (2004): 5–38. For Latinx contexts, see José David Saldívar, *The Dialectics of Our America: Genealogy, Cultural Critique, and Literary History* (Durham, NC: Duke University Press, 1991).

69. For discussions on Indigenous formations transnationally and across the hemisphere, see M. Bianet Castellanos, Lourdes Gutiérrez Nájera, and Arturo J. Aldama, eds., *Comparative Indigeneities across the Américas*; Chadwick Allen, *Trans-Indigenous: Methodologies of Global Native Literary Studies* (Tucson: University of Arizona Press, 2012); Hsinya Huang, Philip Deloria, Laura Furlan, and John Gamber, eds., "Charting Transnational Native American Studies: Aesthetics, Politics, Identity," special forum, *Journal of Transnational American Studies* 4.1 (2012): n.p., https://escholarship.org/uc/acgcc_

jtas/4/1; Robert Warrior, "Native American Scholarship and the Transnational Turn," *Cultural Studies Review* 15.2 (2009): 119–130; Robin Maria DeLugan, "Indigeneity across Borders: Hemispheric Migrations and Cosmopolitan Encounters," *American Ethnologist* 37.1 (2010): 83–97; Shari M. Huhndorf, *Mapping the Americas: The Transnational Politics of Contemporary Native Culture* (Ithaca, NY: Cornell University Press, 2009).

70. See Isabel Altamirano-Jiménez, *Indigenous Encounters with Neoliberalism: Place, Women, and the Environment in Canada and Mexico* (Vancouver, Canada: University of British Columbia Press, 2013); Pablo González Casanova, "Colonialismo interno (una redefinición)," *Revista Rebeldía* 12 (2003), www.revistarebeldia.org/revistas/012/art06.html; Anibal Quijano, "Coloniality of Power, Eurocentrism, and Latin America," *Nepantla: Views from the South* 1.3 (2000): 533–580; Silvia Rivera Cusicanqui, "Pachakuti: The Historical Horizons of Internal Colonialism," published as "Aymara Past, Aymara Future" in *NACLA* 25.3 (1991): 18–23.

71. M. Bianet Castellanos, "Introduction: Settler Colonialism in Latin America," *American Quarterly* 69.4 (2017): 778. See also Shannon Speed, "Structures of Settler Colonialism in Abya Yala," *American Quarterly* 69.4 (2017): 783–790. In the essay, Speed writes similarly: "the land–labor binary, the importance of which Wolfe elaborated in most of his works and reasserted in the recent *Traces of History* (2016), has become an often-unspoken and largely unexamined premise of the settler state in ways that occlude significant complexity and foreclose recognition of settler structures" (783).

72. In her study of indigeneity in Canada and Mexico, Isabel Altamirano-Jiménez engages a distinction between settler colonialism in Canada versus extractive colonialism present in Mexico. She writes: "Settler and extractive colonialism pursued different strategies, modes of governance, and operation. As a specific type of colonialism, settler colonialism relied on a logic of racial disappearance and spatial seclusion. As a 'structure,' settler colonialism relied heavily on the acquisition of land. Mythical notions such as 'vacant land,' 'empty land,' and 'wilderness' erased prior Indigenous connections to the land. In contrast, in Mexico, extractive colonialism implied that Indigenous peoples were recognized as *subjugated peoples* who had to render tribute and pay taxes to the colonial authority." *Indigenous Encounters with Neoliberalism*, 8.

73. See also Richard Gott, "Latin America as White Settler Society," *Bulletin of Latin American Research* 26.2 (2007): 269–289.

74. For a discussion of hemispheric Asian American studies, see Kandice Chuh, "Of Hemispheres and Other Spheres: Navigating Karen Tei Yamashita's Literary World," *American Literary History* 18.3 (2006): 618–637; Lane Ryo Hirabayashi, Akemi Kikumura-Yano, and James A. Hirabayashi, eds., *New Worlds, New Lives: Globalization and People of Japanese Descent in the Americas and from Latin America in Japan* (Palo Alto, CA: Stanford University Press, 2002). For a historical perspective, see also Evelyn Hu-DeHart, "Introduction: Asian American Formations in the Age of Globalization," in *Across the Pacific: Asian Americans and Globalization*, ed. Evelyn Hu-DeHart (Philadelphia: Temple University Press, 1999); Erika Lee, "Orientalism in the Americas: A Hemispheric Approach to Asian-American History," *Journal of Asian American Studies* 8.3 (2005): 235–256; Jason Oliver Chang, *Chino: Anti-Chinese Racism in Mexico 1880–1940* (Urbana: University of Illinois Press, 2017).

75. While in Latin American contexts an emphasis on Asian racial formation is not as prevalent as Indigenous-settler relations, there has been crucial work to empha-

size Asian racial formation as an inflection of the formation of *mestizaje/mestiçagem* in Mexico and Brazil. That is, emphasis on Asian racial formation in Latin América is not simply an additive discourse to narratives of national identity but constitutive of its colonial logics and processes. In *Chino*, for example, Jason Oliver Chang argues for the constitutive role of Chinese racialization, or "anti-chinismo," in the consolidation of *mestizaje* in the postrevolutionary era. He argues that anti-Chinese movements helped to mobilize and consolidate the *mestizo* identity, which hinged on the incorporation of Indigenous peoples into the postrevolutionary capitalist state reforms and the abjection of the Asian foreigner. What becomes evident, in readings of proponents of *mestizaje*, such as Manuel Gamio and José Vasconcelos, is that such abjection emerges through not only the state's vulnerable economic relations to the United States and across the Pacific but also its protracted longings for an imperial presence. See Manuel Gamio, *Forjano patria: Pro-nacionalismo (Forging a Nation)* (1916; repr., Boulder: University Press of Colorado, 2010); and José Vasconcelos, *The Cosmic Race/La raza cósmica* (1925; repr., Baltimore: John Hopkins University Press, 1979).

76. Sau-ling C. Wong, "Denationalization Reconsidered: Asian American Cultural Criticism at a Theoretical Crossroads," *Amerasia Journal* 21.1–2 (1995): 1–27.

CHAPTER 1

1. Within the intervening seventy-six years that separate these two occasions, the United States had lamented the closing of the frontier, which led settlers violently westward. The United States had effectually re-opened the frontier across the Pacific, for example, in the case of U.S. occupation of the Philippines after the Spanish American War in 1898.

2. Lisa Lowe, *The Intimacies of Four Continents* (Durham, NC: Duke University Press, 2015), 2.

3. Maxine Hong Kingston, *China Men* (1980; repr., New York: Ballantine Books, 1981); Gerald R. Vizenor, *Hiroshima Bugi: Atomu 57* (Lincoln: University of Nebraska Press, 2003).

4. While Kingston's *China Men* emphasizes veterans of war (specifically the narrator's brother in Vietnam), I choose here to focus on the Chinese laborer, given that this figure has been highly debated and discussed within Asian American criticism. My discussion of the debate between Frank Chin and Maxine Hong Kingston illuminates this point.

5. While some cultural theorists have articulated tradition as a "surviving past" and thus inert, Raymond Williams sees it as "powerfully operative in the process of social and cultural definition and identification," and often finds itself defined "in the interest of the dominance of a specific class." In addition, Williams argues that tradition is carried on only insofar as it is made salient to the present conditions as ties to "practical continuities." Raymond Williams, *Marxism and Literature* (Oxford: Oxford University Press, 1977), 115–116. For both Asian Americanist and Indigenous counterhistoriographical works, the re-writing of history is thus also the forging of intimate collectivities in its engagement with the palpability of dominant racial and settler formations. While speaking from a different geographical perspective, Linda Tuhiwai Smith argues not only that writing history from an Indigenous perspective reveals the erasures

manifest in dominant historical narratives but also that it does so by registering and restoring "a spirit, to bring back into existence a world fragmented and dying." *Decolonizing Methodologies: Research and Indigenous Peoples* (London: Zed Books, 1999), 28.

6. Benedict Anderson, *Imagined Communities* (1983; repr., London: Verso, 1996). Anderson elaborates on Walter Benjamin's notion of "homogenous empty time," 24.

7. See Dipesh Chakrabarty, *Provincializing Europe: Postcolonial Thought and Historical Difference* (Princeton, NJ: Princeton University Press, 2000). Lowe writes of History 1 and History 2: "Chakrabarty distinguishes what he calls History 1, or the given uniperspectival linear narrative of the rise of national capitalist modernity and its spread, and History 2, which consists of the broad, uneven conditions out of which History 1 is written. We may consider History 2, not as a process outside, or prior to History 1, but rather simultaneous with it." *Intimacies of Four Continents*, 186.

8. For an illuminating discussion of the politics of recognition versus the politics of decolonization, see Glen Sean Coulthard's "Subjects of Empire: Indigenous Peoples and the 'Politics of Recognition' in Canada," *Contemporary Political Theory* 6.4 (2007): 437–460; see also *Red Skin, White Masks: Rejecting the Colonial Politics of Recognition* (Minneapolis: University of Minnesota Press, 2014).

9. See Frank Chin et al., eds., *Aiiieeeee! An Anthology of Asian American Writers* (Washington, DC: Howard University Press, 1974).

10. Frank Chin, "Come All Ye Asian American Writers of the Real and the Fake," in *The Big Aiiieeeee! An Anthology of Chinese American and Japanese American Literature*, ed. Jeffrey Paul Chan et al. (New York: Meridian, 1991), 1–92.

11. As many scholars have discussed, and as noted earlier, this erasure is made most palpable when viewing the famous photograph that memorialized the completion of the Transcontinental Railroad in 1865. The image, often known as the "Golden Spike Photograph," was initially seen as celebrating the culmination of a major technological feat in the United States. However, despite the many people present in the photograph, Chinese laborers (who made up an astounding percentage of the workforce) were tellingly absent. The rationale for such visible erasures can be tied to the continued hegemony of discourses centering white national ingenuity, and the increasing anxieties of reconciling with the rise of the Chinese presence within the national body, even after their labor has been deemed no longer necessary.

12. Julia H. Lee, "The Railroad as Message in Maxine Hong Kingston's *China Men* and Frank Chin's 'Riding the Rails with Chickencoop Slim,'" *Journal of Asian American Studies* 18.3 (2015): 265–287.

13. See Viet Thanh Nguyen, *Race and Resistance: Literature and Politics in Asian America* (Oxford: Oxford University Press, 2002); King-Kok Cheung, "The Woman Warrior versus the Chinaman Pacific: Must a Chinese American Critic Choose between Feminism and Heroism?," in *A Companion to Asian American Studies*, ed. Kent A. Ono (Boston: Blackwell, 2005), 157–174; Jinqi Ling, *Narrating Nationalisms: Ideology and Form in Asian American Literature* (Oxford: Oxford University Press, 1998).

14. Ling, *Narrating Nationalisms*, 118–119.

15. For an analysis of the exultation of Chinese immigration and labor in the United States from a comparative race context, see also Caroline H. Yang, "Indispensable Labor: The Worker as a Category of Critique in *China Men*," *Modern Fiction Studies* 56.1 (2010): 63–89.

16. See Iyko Day, *Alien Capital: Asian Racialization and the Logic of Settler Colonial Capitalism* (Durham, NC: Duke University Press, 2016).

17. Haunani-Kay Trask, *From a Native Daughter: Colonialism and Sovereignty in Hawai'i* (Honolulu: University of Hawai'i Press, 1999), 47.

18. Candace Fujikane and Jonathan Y. Okamura, eds., *Asian Settler Colonialism: From Local Governance to the Habits of Everyday Life in Hawai'i* (Honolulu: University of Hawai'i Press, 2008), 2.

19. Ronald Takaki, *Iron Cages: Race and Culture in 19th Century America* (1979; repr., New York: Oxford University Press, 2000), 220.

20. Maxine Hong Kingston, *The Woman Warrior: Memoirs of a Girlhood among Ghosts* (1976; repr., New York: Vintage International, 1989).

21. Becca Gercken writes that "Crazy Horse is the most complex figure and idea in *Fancydancing*: he is both real and surreal, he is historical and a-temporal, he is Lakota and pan-tribal. The great war leader and visionary of the Oglala Sioux is best known for his role in the Battle of the Little Big Horn and the ignominious circumstances of his 1877 murder at Ft. Robinson, Nebraska." "The Business of Crazy Horse: Indian Honor and Masculinity in Sherman Alexie's *Fancydancing*," *North Dakota Quarterly* 76.4 (2009): 39.

22. Ibid., 44.

23. Gerald Vizenor, *Manifest Manners: Narratives on Postindian Survivance* (Lincoln: University of Nebraska Press, 1999), 154.

24. Ibid.

25. Ibid.

26. See, for example, Tom Holm, *Strong Hearts, Wounded Souls: Native American Veterans of the Vietnam War* (Austin: University of Texas Press, 1996); Al Carroll, *Medicine Bags and Dog Tags: American Indian Veterans from Colonial Times to the Second Iraq War* (Lincoln: University of Nebraska Press, 2008).

27. Carroll, *Medicine Bags and Dog Tags*, 11.

28. Here Carroll cites conversations he had with Steve Russell. Ibid., 227.

29. Ibid., 228.

30. Ibid., 229.

31. In the context of Hawai'i, Noenoe K. Silva writes, "Colonial historiography . . . does not simply rationalize the past and suppress the knowledge of the oppressed. . . . For those of us living with the legacies and the continuing exercise of power characteristic of colonialism, it is crucial to understand power relations in order to escape or overcome their effects." Noenoe K. Silva, *Aloha Betrayed: Native Hawaiian Resistance to American Colonialism* (Durham, NC: Duke University Press, 2004), 9.

32. Carroll, *Medicine Bags and Dog Tags*, 13.

33. Linda Hutcheon, *Poetics of Postmodernism: History, Theory, Fiction* (London: Routledge, 1988), 5. See also Linda Hutcheon, "Historiographic Metafiction: Parody and the Intertextuality of History," in *Intertextuality and Contemporary American Fiction*, ed. P. O'Donnell and Robert Con Davis (Baltimore, MD: Johns Hopkins University Press, 1989), 3–32. Hutcheon writes: "Historiographic metafiction works to situate itself within historical discourse without surrendering its autonomy as fiction. And it is a kind of seriously ironic parody that effects both aims: the intertexts of history and fiction take on parallel (though not equal) status in the parodic reworking of the textual past of both the 'world' and literature." She continues: "Historiographic metafiction challenges

... both any naive realist concept of representation and any equally naive textualist or formalist assertions of the total separation of art from the world." "Historiographic Metafiction," 4, 6.

34. History as construct is mutually entangled with what Jodi Kim calls the "dialectic of remembering and forgetting" where "the inevitability of forgetting [is set] against the obvious necessity of remembering." *Ends of Empire: Asian American Critique and the Cold War* (Minneapolis: University of Minnesota Press, 2010), 97.

35. For a discussion of the controversies surrounding the attribution of Kingston's text as an autobiography or memoir, see Sau-ling Wong, "Autobiography as a Guided Chinatown Tour," in *Maxine Hong Kingston's* The Woman Warrior: *A Casebook*, ed. Sau-ling Cynthia Wong (Oxford: Oxford University Press, 1999), 29–56. In her essay, Wong traces critiques by writers such as Jeffrey Chan, Frank Chin, and Benjamin Tong, who argue that Kingston and her publishers pass off what they consider to be obviously fiction as fact. For more on Chin's contention with Kingston, see Chin, "Come All Ye Asian American Writers of the Real and the Fake."

36. The early glimmerings of this heroic literary tradition can be seen in Chin et al., *Aiiieeeee! An Anthology of Asian-American Writers*.

37. See Ling, *Narrating Nationalisms*. As Jinqi Ling argues, Kingston's project problematizes a heroic tradition that was central to the construction of a U.S. Asian American group identity during the 1960s and 1970s. He goes on to say that through this self-reflexive narrative voicing, the text resists full incorporation into the U.S. narrative of national progress and the "masculine valor" that such a claiming entails. Ling argues that Kingston's work instead illuminates how the celebration of Chinese male laborers can simultaneously elide the violence structuring that very experience as it renders invisible women's voices in the conception of an Asian American group identity. In so doing, Ling distinguishes his reading from two strands of criticism that are prevalent in scholarship about the book. The first reads *China Men* as a "retribution and compensation" for the suffering that Chinese male laborers experienced; the second reads *China Men* as a balanced critique of American racism and Chinese American sexism. Ling argues that this "feminist renegotiation" of U.S. Asian America's cultural nationalist project "turns a romanticized past into a prologue for the emergence of alternative histories and narrative subjects" (128).

38. For an elaboration of Kingston's assertion, see Arturo Islas and Marilyn Yalon, "Interview with Maxine Hong Kingston," in *Conversations with Maxine Hong Kingston*, ed. Paul Skenazy and Tera Martin (Jackson: University Press of Mississippi, 1998), 21–32.

39. Louis Owens, *Mixed-Blood Messages* (Norman: University of Oklahoma Press, 1998), 127. Similarly, Jace Weaver writes that "of course even the few rude, scattered tribes could not be allowed to survive in the myths of conquest. To allow their survival would be to pose an impediment to Amer-European designs on the continent. Extinction is a superior means of creating indigeneity. If all the indigenes are dead, there is no one to dispute the claim. In fact, guilt for wrongs done to the indigenous peoples in the past does not allow them to be other than *of* the past. Thus the myth of the vanishing Indian was born." Jace Weaver, *That the People Might Live: Native American Literatures and Native American Community* (Oxford: Oxford University Press, 1997), 17.

40. First presented and published in 1893, historian Frederick Jackson Turner's "The Significance of the Frontier in American History" argues that in order to study U.S. his-

tory and its distinct character, one must study the frontier encounter and its geographically defined institutional outcomes. For Turner, the frontier in its different waves of settlement westward, defining itself anew with each wave, marks the move increasingly away from its European roots. This new character is what Turner argues is distinctly American. This essay later appeared as the first chapter of Turner's book. See Frederick Jackson Turner, *The Frontier in American History* (New York: Henry Holt, 1920). Owens writes about the distinction between the frontier and the territory: "Seen from the stock Euramerican perspective, the frontier is the cutting edge of civilization. Beyond the frontier is the incomprehensible 'other.' To inhabit that frontier is to somehow accommodate a radical alterity, the internalization of which leads dangerously in the direction of psychic disintegration or schizophrenia. To make that space inhabitable, it is necessary to map it—that is, figuratively to appropriate it and imagine fixed boundaries, make it conform to a metanarrative." Owens, *Mixed-Blood Messages,* 44–45.

41. Kingston, *China Men,* 98.
42. Owens, *Mixed-Blood Messages,* 117, 125.
43. Kingston, *China Men,* 88.
44. Ibid., 108.
45. Owens, *Mixed-Blood Messages,* 125. These two scenes provide the discursive grounds on which the chapter can signify a belonging to the island beyond the rhetoric of citizenship, from which the Chinese were historically excluded. The scene between Bak Sook Goong and his Native family, then, serves as an alternative means through which to make visible a presence not made available in terms of settler colonial notions of legality; in so doing, Kingston covertly critiques the racialized Chinese exclusion laws that proceeded this imagined moment in Asian American history.
46. Kingston, *China Men,* 142.
47. The narrative's conflation of the "Injun" with a deer and a rabbit conjures multiple significations. This scene, in my reading, implies Kingston's critique of U.S. colonial enterprises as they affect Natives and the land.
48. Turner, *The Frontier in American History.*
49. Kingston, *China Men,* 133, 144.
50. Ibid., 146, 138.
51. Takaki, *Iron Cages,* 175.
52. Custer, quoted in ibid., 178.
53. Takaki, *Iron Cages,* 179.
54. Ibid.
55. Turner, *The Frontier in American History.*
56. Kingston, *China Men,* 142.
57. Jodi Byrd, *The Transit of Empire: Indigenous Critiques of Colonialism* (Minneapolis: University of Minnesota Press, 2011), xviii.
58. Ibid.; Day, *Alien Capital.*
59. Kingston, *China Men,* 99.
60. Ibid.
61. Accounts where Kingston *does* assert a blood relation to Native Hawaiian communities are simultaneously rendered indeterminate, as in the case of her half-black cousin living in China. In Chadwick Allen, *Blood Narrative: Indigenous Identity in American Indian and Maori Literary and Activist Texts* (Durham, NC: Duke University Press, 2002),

the author comments on the politics of blood quantum: "A standard of racial identification, blood quantum originally served as a device for documenting 'Indian' status for the federal government's dividing and subsequently alienating collectively held Indian lands. Blood quantum enshrines racial purity as the ideal for authentic Indian identity; tabulations of blood quantum thus highlight the genetic hybridity of most contemporary U.S. citizens who claim Indian status. In effect, mixed-blood Indians are considered genetically estranged from their full-blood indigenous ancestors once a certain 'degree' of mixing with Europeans, White Americans, African Americans, or others has passed" (176).

62. Candace Fujikane, "Sweeping Racism under the Rug of 'Censorship': The Controversy over Lois Ann Yamanaka's *Blu's Hanging*," *Amerasia Journal* 26.2 (2000): 166.

63. Although Kingston's narrative provides space for the articulation of this "local" claiming, and instigates the problems therein, her aesthetic of indeterminacy also emerges, as scholar Shirley Geok-lin Lim points out, through the foregrounding of the conditional, ironic, and liminal spaces that consistently destabilize her assertions. See Shirley Geok-lin Lim, "The Native and the Diasporic: Owning America in Native American and Asian American Literatures," *Women's Studies Quarterly* 34 (2006): 295–307.

64. King-Kok Cheung, *Articulate Silences: Hisaye Yamamoto, Maxine Hong Kingston, Joy Kogawa* (Ithaca, NY: Cornell University Press, 1993).

65. Medak-Saltzman argues that theories of haunting in postcolonial and cultural studies have a problematic resonance when seen from the perspective of Indigenous studies. Given the proliferating representation and theories about the disappearing/dying Indian, the image of Native hauntings can potentially perpetuate such discourses rather than provide layered critiques of settler histories and presences. In response to tendencies in the deployment of haunting in postcolonial and cultural studies, Medak-Saltzman advocates for a more "theoretically compelling concept of haunting" that "invert[s] the familiar directionality of postcolonial haunting that locates the source of ghostly agency as emanating from the experiential realities of racialized subjects and situates haunting as a consequence of these complicated histories." In diverting understandings of the source of haunting not as the "absent presence" of Indigenous peoples but as "the spirit of an idea" that is settler colonial power and logics, the article suggests that one can define the crucial logics and erasures that maintain the persistent, yet always penetrable, veil of settler common sense. "Empire's Haunted Logics: Comparative Colonialisms and the Challenges of Incorporating Indigeneity," *Journal of the Critical Ethnic Studies Association* 1.2 (2015): 16.

66. Thank you to the Cornell Asian American studies and American Indian studies program faculty and students for your keen insights on the ghostly.

67. Kingston, *China Men*, 110–111.

68. Ibid., 111.

69. For Jodi Byrd, "understanding colonialism as a cacophony of contradictorily hegemonic and horizontal struggles offers an alternative way of formulating and addressing the dynamics that continue to affect peoples as they move and are made to move within empire." *Transit of Empire*, 53.

70. This historic convergence coincided with the implementation of the Big Five Sugar Companies and the decimation of Native Hawaiian communities. In 1853, Native Hawaiians accounted for 96 percent of the population; by 1923, they accounted for only 16.3 percent. See Ronald Takaki, *Pau Hana: Plantation Life and Labor in Hawaii* (Hono-

lulu: University of Hawai'i Press, 1984); see also Haunani-Kay Trask, *From a Native Daughter*.

71. Thanks to Iyko Day for highlighting Coulthard's notion of "grounded normativity" as operative within the text. See Coulthard, *Red Skin, White Masks*. Many critics have analyzed the dynamics of power enveloped in this latter symbolic scene in *China Men*. See, for example, David Leiwei Li, "Maxine Hong Kingston and the American Canon," *American Literary History* 2.3 (1990): 482–502; Gary Y. Okihiro, *Margins and Mainstreams: Asians in American History and Culture* (Seattle: University of Washington Press, 1994); Cheung, *Articulate Silences*; Tomo Hattori, "China Man Autoeroticism and the Remains of Asian America," *NOVEL: A Forum on Fiction* 31.2 (1998): 215–236.

72. Kingston, *China Men*, 128.

73. Vizenor, *Hiroshima Bugi*, 175. Ronin stages protests against spaces such as the Hiroshima Peace Memorial Museum and the Yasukuni Jinja memorial dedicated to Japanese warriors.

74. Gerald R. Vizenor, *Griever: An American Monkey King in China* (Minneapolis: University of Minnesota Press, 1987).

75. Vizenor was part of the U.S. military in Japan during the Korean War.

76. Jeanne Sokolowski, "Between Dangerous Extremes: Victimization, Ultranationalism, and Identity Performance in Gerald Vizenor's *Hiroshima Bugi*, *American Quarterly* 62.3 (2010): 719.

77. Ibid., 720.

78. Byrd, *Transit of Empire*, 213.

79. Ibid.

80. Ibid., 219.

81. Kim, *Ends of Empire*, 103.

82. While Kim is primarily focused on Japanese American texts that show the process of gendered racial rehabilitation as a trans-Pacific phenomenon that "domesticates" Japanese Americans, Japanese nationals, and Japan itself, Vizenor's text suggests this imperial project is intimately connected with the settler colonial logics and processes that incorporate Native American/Indigenous relations.

83. Vizenor, *Hiroshima Bugi*, 1.

84. For an analysis of "Rashomon" references in the novel, see Byrd, *Transit of Empire*.

85. Vizenor, *Hiroshima Bugi*, 2.

86. Ibid., 3.

87. Ibid.

88. Sokolowski, "Between Dangerous Extremes," 722.

89. Kim, *Ends of Empire*, 116.

90. Vizenor, *Hiroshima Bugi*, 80.

91. Ibid., 80–81.

92. Ibid.

93. Elizabeth Povinelli, *Economies of Abandonment: Social Belonging and Endurance in Late Liberalism* (Durham, NC: Duke University Press, 2011), 13.

94. Vizenor, *Hiroshima Bugi*, 143.

95. For further discussions of Japanese imperialism and its collusion with U.S. settlement and empire, see Setsu Shigematsu and Keith Camacho, eds., *Militarized Currents: Toward a Decolonized Future in Asian and the Pacific* (Minneapolis: University

of Minnesota Press, 2010; Kim, *Ends of Empire*; and Lisa Yoneyama, *Cold War Ruins: Transpacific Critique of American Justice and Japanese War Crimes* (Durham, NC: Duke University Press, 2016).

96. Vizenor, *Hiroshima Bugi,* 159.
97. Ibid., 167.
98. Ibid., 159.
99. Ibid., 168.
100. Ibid., 166.
101. Ibid., 153.
102. Kim, *Ends of Empire*, 98–99.
103. For example, Ronin insists that the *kami* (spirits) of dead children in the war memorial and the ghosts of the Atomic Bomb Dome are the voices that must be heard. From the novel: "The *honden,* or main shrine, was the sacred space of the *kami,* the spirits of more than two million dead soldiers. The entrance to the shrine and the inner sanctuary was decorated with the seals of the emperor on a great chrysanthemum cloth. The hewn cedar beams and polished wooden panels created a sense of eternal peace and a natural presence, an imperial reverence and silence that inspired ravens, mongrels, and tricksters. . . . The children of the *atomu* ruins must be enshrined with the *kami* spirits of other children in the main sanctuary, and by their presence, virtue, and decency, the nationalists would be shamed for their dominance." Vizenor, *Hiroshima Bugi,* 149–150.
104. Ibid., 3.
105. From the novel: "Five nights a week we came together for dinner and to create our perfect memories. The marvelous, elusive tease of our many stories, and variations of stories, became concerted memories. Our tricky metaphors were woven together day by day into a consciousness of moral survivance. More than the commerce of reactive survivalists, mere liturgy, ideology, or the causative leverage of a sworn witness, survivance is a creative concerted consciousness that does not arise from separation, dominance, or concession nightmares. Our stories create perfect memories of survivance." Ibid., 9.
106. Ibid., 103.
107. Ibid., 109.
108. Ibid., 69.
109. Povinelli, *Economies of Abandonment.*
110. Vizenor, *Hiroshima Bugi,* 169.
111. Ibid., 207.
112. Ibid., 208.
113. Ibid.

CHAPTER 2

1. Maryka Omatsu, *Bittersweet Passage: Redress and the Japanese Canadian Experience* (Toronto, Canada: Between the Lines, 1992), 20. While controversial, the government worked with the National Association of Japanese Canadians (NAJC) as the representative of the Japanese Canadian community.

2. Omatsu, *Bittersweet Passage.* For readings on the Canadian redress movement, see also Roy Miki, *Redress: Inside the Japanese Canadian Call for Justice* (Vancouver, Canada: Raincoast Books, 2004); Arthur K. Miki, *The Japanese Canadian Redress Legacy: A*

Community Revitalized (Winnipeg: National Association of Japanese Canadians, 2003); Momoye Sugiman, ed., *Japanese Canadian Redress: The Toronto Story* (Toronto, Canada: HpF Press, 2000); and Roy Miki and Cassandra Kobayashi, eds., *Justice in Our Time: The Japanese Canadian Redress Settlement* (Vancouver, Canada: Talonbooks/NAJC, 1991) and *Spirit of Redress: Japanese Canadians in Conference* (Vancouver, Canada: Talonbooks/NAJC, 1989). For an exploration of redress in the works of Joy Kogawa, see Julie McGonegal, "The Future of Racial Memory: Forgiveness, Reconciliation, and Redress in Joy Kogawa's *Obasan* and *Itsuka*," *Studies in Canadian Literature* 30.2 (2005): 55–78. For the Nikkei redress movement in the United States, see Roger Daniels, Sandra C. Taylor, and Harry H. L. Kitano, eds., *Japanese Americans: From Relocation to Redress* (Salt Lake City: University of Utah Press, 1986); Yasuko I. Takezawa, *Breaking the Silence: Redress and Japanese American Ethnicity* (Ithaca, NY: Cornell University Press, 1995); Leslie T. Hatamiya, *Righting a Wrong: Japanese Americans and the Passage of the Civil Liberties Act of 1988* (Palo Alto, CA: Stanford University Press, 1994); and Nobuya Tsuchida, *American Justice: Japanese American Evacuation and Redress* (Minneapolis: Asian/Pacific American Learning Resource Center, University of Minnesota, 1988).

3. For a discussion of Canada's Truth and Reconciliation Commission, see Ronald Niezen, *Truth and Indignation: Canada's Truth and Reconciliation Commission on Indian Residential Schools* (Toronto, Canada: University of Toronto Press, 2013); Jennifer J. Llewelyn, "Bridging the Gap between Truth and Reconciliation: Restorative Justice and the Indian Residential School Truth and Reconciliation Commission," in *From Truth to Reconciliation: Transforming the Legacy of Residential Schools,* ed. Marlene Brant Castellano, Linda Archibald, and Mike DeGagné (Ottawa, Canada: Aboriginal Healing Foundation, 2008), 183–204; Anne-Marie Reynaud, "Dealing with Difficult Emotions: Anger at the Truth and Reconciliation Commission of Canada," *Anthropologica* 56.2 (2012): 369–382; Roger I. Simon, "Towards a Hopeful Practice of Worrying: The Problematics of Listening and the Educative Responsibilities of Canada's Truth and Reconciliation Commission," in *Reconciling Canada: Critical Perspectives on the Culture of Redress,* ed. Jennifer Henderson and Pauline Wakeham (Toronto, Canada: University of Toronto Press, 2013), 129–142.

4. Jennifer Henderson and Pauline Wakeham, "Introduction," in *Reconciling Canada: Critical Perspectives on the Culture of Redress,* ed. Jennifer Henderson and Pauline Wakeham (Toronto, Canada: University of Toronto Press, 2013), 7.

5. Sunera Thobani, *Exalted Subjects: Studies in the Making of Race and Nation in Canada* (Toronto, Canada: University of Toronto Press, 2007), 18.

6. For crucial discussions of immigrant, Aboriginal, and settler triangulations in Canada, see Bonita Lawrence and Enakshi Dua, "Decolonizing Anti-Racism," *Social Justice* 32.4 (2005): 120–143; see also Bonita Lawrence and Zanaib Amadahy, "Indigenous Peoples and Black People in Canada: Settlers or Allies?," in *Breaching the Colonial Contract: Anti-Colonialism in the US and Canada,* ed. Arlo Kempf (Berlin/Heidelberg, Germany: Springer Science, 2009), 105–136.

7. Thobani, *Exalted Subjects,* 9

8. For a discussion of liberal multiculturalism in Canada, see also Daniel Coleman, *White Civility: The Literary Project of English Canada* (Toronto: University of Toronto Press, 2008); and Smaro Kamboureli, *Scandalous Bodies: Diasporic Literature in English* (Waterloo: Wilfrid Laurier University Press, 2009).

9. Glen Sean Coulthard, *Red Skin, White Masks: Rejecting the Colonial Politics of Recognition* (Minneapolis: University of Minnesota Press, 2014), 106.

10. Guy Beauregard, "After Redress: A Conversation with Roy Miki," *Canadian Literature* 201 (2009): 72.

11. Coulthard, *Red Skin, White Masks,* 108.

12. Elizabeth Povinelli, *Economies of Abandonment: Social Belonging and Endurance in Late Liberalism* (Durham, NC: Duke University Press, 2011), 127–128.

13. Sara Ahmed, *The Cultural Politics of Emotions* (New York: Routledge, 2004), 113.

14. Ahmed contends that "the effects of that declaration depend on who speaks the apology—and what prior authorisation they have—as well as who receives it, and how they are interpellated as witnesses to the speech act. And so what an apology is doing in the moment of its utterance goes through a passage of the undecidable, both opening the past, and keeping open the future." Ibid., 116.

15. Mark Rifkin, *Settler Common Sense: Queerness and Everyday Colonialism in the American Renaissance* (Minneapolis: University of Minnesota Press, 2014), 10.

16. For recent discussions of affect and emotions in Indigenous studies, see Cari Carpenter, *Seeing Red: Anger, Sentimentality, and American Indians* (Columbus: Ohio University Press, 2008); Coulthard, *Red Skin, White Masks*; Dian Million, *Therapeutic Nations: Healing in an Age of Indigenous Human Rights* (Tucson: University of Arizona Press, 2013) and "Felt Theory: An Indigenous Feminist Approach to Affect and History," *Wicazo Sa Review* 24.2 (2009): 53–76; Reynaud, "Dealing with Difficult Emotions." For recent discussions of affect and emotions in Asian American studies, see Anne Anlin Cheng, *The Melancholy of Race: Assimilation, Psychoanalysis, and Hidden Grief* (Oxford: Oxford University Press, 2000); Jeffrey Santa Ana, *Racial Feelings: Asian America in a Capitalist Culture of Emotions* (Philadelphia: Temple University Press, 2015); David L. Eng, *The Feeling of Kinship: Queer Liberalism and the Racialization of Intimacy* (Durham, NC: Duke University Press, 2010); Christine Kim, *The Minor Intimacies of Race: Asian Publics in North America* (Urbana: University of Illinois Press, 2016).

17. Reynaud, "Dealing with Difficult Emotions," 370.

18. Henderson and Wakeham, *Reconciling Canada,* 7.

19. It is also important to note Henderson and Wakeham's demystification of rendering the state itself as a coherent singular subject. They write: "If the view of the redressing state as increasingly enlightened and magnanimous is ideologically and methodologically problematic, so also is the comparable view of the state as acting with the intentionality of a cynical and manipulative individual. One of the unpredictable effects of the culture of redress may be its sustaining of this very illusion of the state as the coherent subject orchestrating political practice, whether cynically or in good faith—a fantasized abstraction that Begoña Aretxaga calls the 'imagined national state.'" Ibid.

20. Stephen Harper, "House of Commons Apology to Inuit, Métis, and First Nations Peoples of Residential Schools, 2008," reprinted in ibid., 335.

21. Quoted in Omatsu, *Bittersweet Passage,* 26.

22. Brian Mulroney, "House of Commons Apology to Japanese Canadians, 1988," reprinted in *Reconciling Canada: Critical Perspectives on the Culture of Redress,* ed. Jennifer Henderson and Pauline Wakeham (Toronto, Canada: University of Toronto Press, 2013), 436.

23. Mulroney, "House of Commons Apology to Japanese Canadians, 1988," 436–437.

24. Ibid., 437.
25. Ibid.
26. Ibid.
27. Harper, "House of Commons Apology to Inuit, Métis, and First Nations Peoples of Residential Schools, 2008," 335–336.
28. Sheryl Lightfoot, "Settler State Apologies to Indigenous Peoples: A Normative Framework and Comparative Assessment," *Native American and Indigenous Studies* 2 (2015): 33.
29. Deena Rymhs, *From the Iron House: Imprisonment in First Nations Writing* (Waterloo, Canada: Wilfrid Laurier University Press, 2008), 11–12.
30. Ahmed, *Cultural Politics of Emotions*, 111.
31. Mulroney, "House of Commons Apology to Japanese Canadians, 1988," 436.
32. Harper, "House of Commons Apology to Inuit, Métis, and First Nations Peoples of Residential Schools, 2008," 336.
33. Mulroney, "House of Commons Apology to Japanese Canadians, 1988," 426–437.
34. Harper, "House of Commons Apology to Inuit, Métis, and First Nations Peoples of Residential Schools, 2008," 336.
35. Rudyard Kipling, "The White Man's Burden: The United States and the Philippine Island, 1899," *McClure's Magazine* 12 (February 1899).
36. Harper, "House of Commons Apology to Inuit, Métis, and First Nations Peoples of Residential Schools, 2008," 337.
37. Ibid., 336.
38. Ibid.
39. Million, *Therapeutic Nations*, 6.
40. Patrick Wolfe, *Settler Colonialism and the Transformation of Anthropology: The Politics and Poetics of an Ethnographic Event* (London: Cassell, 1999), 2.
41. Canadian Race Relations Foundation (CRRF), "First Annual Report," 1997–1998, http://www.crrf-fcrr.ca/images/stories/annual_report/annual_report_1998_-_English.pdf, 5.
42. For a discussion of the Canadian Race Relations Foundation, see Audrey Kobayashi, "The Japanese-Canadian Redress Settlement and Its Implications for 'Race Relations,'" *Canadian Ethnic Studies* 24.1 (1992): 1–19.
43. Truth and Reconciliation Commission of Canada (TRC), "Honoring the Truth, Reconciling for the Future," Summary of the Final Report of the TRC, 2015, http://www.trc.ca/websites/trcinstitution/index.php?p=890, 216.
44. Million, *Therapeutic Nations*, 3.
45. TRC, "Honoring the Truth," 212.
46. Ibid., 183.
47. Ibid., 184.
48. For a discussion on the transnationality of Nikkei incarceration during World War II, see Iyko Day, *Alien Capital: Asian Racialization and the Logic of Settler Colonial Capitalism* (Durham, NC: Duke University Press, 2016) and "Alien Intimacies: The Coloniality of Japanese Internment in Australia, Canada, and the US," *Amerasia Journal* 36.2 (2010): 107–124. See also Karen M. Inouye, *The Long Afterlife of Nikkei Wartime Incarceration* (Palo Alto, CA: Stanford University Press, 2016). Inouye discusses both the temporal and spatial "afterlife" of incarceration. Inouye writes that "although afterlife

as conceived of in this study begins with lingering, complex feeling, it also encompasses actions and statements that are purposefully detectable. . . . Afterlife manifests itself idiosyncratically, but one can trace it across temporal, generational, and geographical lines" (11–12).

49. For a reading of Naomi's maternal figures, see Shirley Geok-lin Lim, "Japanese American Women's Life Stories: Maternality in Monica Sone's *Nisei Daughter* and Joy Kogawa's *Obasan*," *Feminist Studies* 16.2 (1990): 288–312.

50. For critical analyses of silence and sound in Joy Kogawa's works, see, for example, Helena Grice, "Reading the Nonverbal: The Indices of Space, Time, Tactility and Taciturnity in Joy Kogawa's *Obasan*," *MELUS: Multi-Ethnic Literature of the U.S.* 24.4 (1999): 93–105; King-Kok Cheung, *Articulate Silences: Hisaye Yamamoto, Maxine Hong Kingston, Joy Kogawa* (Ithaca, NY: Cornell University Press, 1993); and Gayle K. Fujita, "'To Attend to the Sound of Stone': The Sensibility of Silence in *Obasan*," *MELUS: Multi-Ethnic Literature of the U.S.* 12.3 (1985): 33–42. For comparative race and transnational readings of Kogawa's works, see Day, "Alien Intimacies"; Marie Lo, "Model Minorities, Models of Resistance: Native Figures in Asian Canadian Literature," *Canadian Literature* 196 (2008): 96–112; and "Passing Recognition: *Obasan* and the Borders of Asian American and Canadian Literary Criticism," *Comparative American Studies* 5.3 (2007): 307–332.

51. See Lo, "Model Minorities."

52. Day, "Alien Intimacies," 112.

53. With regard to the politics of settlers "going Native," Day cites Shari Huhndorf. Day, "Alien Intimacies," 112. See Shari Huhndorf, *Going Native: Indians in the American Cultural Imagination* (Ithaca, NY: Cornell University Press, 2001). Lo argues that these narratives symbolically legitimate the settler colonial state and elides decolonization struggles. "Model Minorities," 103–104.

54. Day, "Alien Intimacies," 112. Day refers specifically to the presence of Asian settler colonialism in Native Hawaiian struggles for sovereignty.

55. For a conceptualization of deterritorialization and reterritorialization, see Gilles Deleuze and Felix Guattari, *Anti-Oedipus: Capitalism and Schizophrenia* (Minneapolis: University of Minnesota Press, 1983).

56. Williams, *Marxism and Literature*, 121–127.

57. Joy Kogawa, *Obasan* (1981; repr., New York: Anchor Books, 1994), 24, my emphasis.

58. For accounts of early Nikkei immigration to Canada, see Michiko Midge Ayukawa, *Hiroshima Immigrants in Canada 1891–1941* (Vancouver, Canada: University of British Columbia Press, 2008); Patricia E. Roy, *A White Man's Province: British Columbia Politicians and Chinese and Japanese Immigrant, 1858–1914* (Vancouver, Canada: University of British Columbia Press, 1989); Gordon G. Nakayama, *Issei: Stories of Japanese Canadian Pioneers* (Toronto, Canada: NC Press, 1984); Yuko Shibata, Hayashi R. Matsumoto, Rintaro Hayashi, and Shotaro Iida, *The Forgotten History of Japanese-Canadians*, vol. 1 (Vancouver, Canada: New Sun Books, 1966); and Ken Adachi, *The Enemy That Never Was: A History of Japanese Canadians* (Toronto, Canada: McClelland and Stewart, 1976).

59. Kogawa, *Obasan*, 21.

60. Ibid., 25.

61. See Day, "Alien Intimacies," 107, for the phrasing "the coloniality of Japanese internment."

62. Povinelli, *Economies of Abandonment*, 27–28.

63. Ibid., 11–16. Povinelli argues that Indigenous communities and cultures are often (unevenly) registered as artifacts of the "past perfect," providing the grammatical tense through which colonial governance in late liberalism interacts with these very communities.

64. Kogawa, *Obasan*, 3.

65. Ibid., 2.

66. For analyses of the trope of the vanishing Indian, see Gordon M. Sayre, *The Indian Chief as Tragic Hero: Native Resistance and the Literatures of America, from Moctezuma to Tecumseh* (Chapel Hill: University of North Carolina Press, 2005); Louis Owens, *Mixed-Blood Messages* (Norman: University of Oklahoma Press, 1998); Jace Weaver, *That the People Might Live: Native American Literatures and Native American Community* (New York: Oxford University Press, 1997); Renato Rosaldo, *Culture and Truth: The Remaking of Social Analysis* (Boston: Beacon Press, 1993); and Brian Dippie, *The Vanishing American: White Attitudes and U.S. Indian Policy* (Lawrence: University Press of Kansas, 1982). For an analysis of this trope in the formation of Canadian nationalism, see Len M. Findlay, "Spectres of Canada: Image, Text, Aura, Nation," *University of Toronto Quarterly* 75.2 (2006): 656–672.

67. Kogawa, *Obasan*, 2.

68. See Judith Butler's *Precarious Life: The Powers of Mourning and Violence* (New York: Verso, 2004), for a discussion of grief as a condition of ineluctable relationality.

69. This representation of the uncontainable facet of grief works in contradistinction to how the public apologies work to siphon community sentiments into the imperatives of the state. In her recounting of the history of Nikkei redress, Maryka Omatsu illuminates the pivotal role of the racialized other in projecting the coming into existence of a multicultural and inclusive state. She specifically points to redress as an affectively reparative event that attempts to siphon community sentiments and healing into national narratives of progress. Although Omatsu's text seems to affirm this narrative, her embedded critique of the process of redress implies that such sentiments cannot be neatly ordered. Omatsu's critique of the process of redress was due to its autocratic implementation, since the events leading up to the public apology were disclosed to only a few people. Omatsu, *Bittersweet Passage*, 26–27.

70. Day, "Alien Intimacies," 115.

71. These displaced representations of trauma are mirrored in a different text authored by a Laguna Pueblo writer: Leslie Marmon Silko, *Ceremony* (1977; repr., New York: Penguin Books, 2006).

72. Cheung, *Articulate Silences*, 126–167.

73. Kogawa, *Obasan*, 3. Naomi later implies that the silent ones are the ones that you should be worried about.

74. Ibid., my emphasis.

75. For a discussion of Foucault's notion of "heterotopia" in relation to comparative racialization, see Grace Kyungwon Hong and Roderick A. Ferguson, eds., *Strange Affinities* (Durham, NC: Duke University Press, 2011), 5; Michel Foucault, *The Order of Things: An Archaeology of the Human Sciences* (New York: Routledge Classics, 2004).

76. Ibid., 10. Hong and Ferguson refer to Cherríe Moraga's passage through the subway system in Boston to illustrate this notion of a "heterotopic *somewhere*."

77. Coulthard, *Red Skin, White Masks*, 48, citing bell hooks.
78. Kogawa, *Obasan*, 170.
79. Ibid., 172.
80. Ibid., 173.
81. Ibid., 172.
82. Ibid., 173–174.
83. This connection between self/other, human/nonhuman, emulates an ethics of both what Povinelli terms "cosubstantiation" and what Aileen Moreton-Robinson terms "intersubstantiation." Of the difference, Byrd writes: "Where Povinelli emphasizes the kinship responsibilities of cosubstantiation, Aileen Moreton-Robinson makes the point that the multidirectionality of *inter*substantiation inherent in indigenous sovereignty involves ancestral beings, humans, and land." *Transit of Empire*, 211.
84. Kogawa, *Obasan*, 176.
85. Ibid., 273.
86. Ibid., 274.
87. Cheung, *Articulate Silences*, 146.
88. Kogawa, *Obasan*, 296.
89. Ibid., 297–300.
90. Mona Oikawa, "Connecting the Internment of Japanese Canadians to the Colonization of Aboriginal Peoples in Canada," in *Aboriginal Connections to Race, Environment, and Traditions,* ed. R. Riewe and J. Oakes (Winnipeg, Canada: Aboriginal Issues Press, 2006), 18.
91. Miki writes: "In the process, Japanese Canadians were themselves formed by the call for redress. They shaped their unredressed identity out of the racialized national boundaries that had disenfranchised them. . . . To read themselves into that nation as 'citizens,' they had to situate themselves in the narrative of nation building as a collective of 'citizens' to which they belonged through the rights and responsibilities of citizenship." Roy Miki, *Redress: Inside the Japanese Canadian Call for Justice* (Vancouver: Raincoast Books, 2004), 323. See also Kirsten Emiko McAllister, "Narrating Japanese Canadians in and out of the Canadian Nation: A Critique of Realist Forms of Representation," *Canadian Journal of Communication* 24 (1999): 79–103.
92. Miki, *Redress*, 323.
93. Henderson and Wakeham write: "The political and cultural reverberations of Japanese Canadian redress have expanded beyond such narrow claims to the 'same deal,' however. Today, they encompass a discursive formation frequently organized around the pursuit of reparations for specifiable historical injuries and for reconciliation of social divides framed as stemming from those injuries." *Reconciling Canada*, 6.
94. For a discussion of the context of Nikkei internment, redress, and reconciliation, see also Mona Oikawa, *Cartographies of Violence: Japanese Canadian Women, Memory, and the Subjects of Internment* (Toronto, Canada: University of Toronto Press, 2012), and Kirsten Emiko McAllister, *Terrain of Memory: A Japanese Canadian Memorial Project* (Vancouver: University of British Columbia Press, 2010).
95. Rita Wong, "Decolonizasian: Reading Asian and First Nations Relations in Literature," *Canadian Literature* 199 (Winter 2008)," 168.
96. Radio waves permeate the play, as well as poetically inflected dialogue.
97. Larissa Lai, "Epistemologies of Respect: A Poetics of Asian/Indigenous Rela-

tions," in *Critical Collaborations: Indigeneity, Diaspora, and Ecology in Canadian Literary Studies*, ed. Smaro Kamboureli and Christl Verduyn (Waterloo, Canada: Wilfrid Laurier University Press, 2014), 125.

98. Marie Clements, *Burning Vision*, 6th ed. (Vancouver, Canada: Talonbooks, 2012), 1.

99. Lai, "Epistemologies of Respect," 115.

100. Clements, *Burning Vision*, 84–85, my emphasis.

101. Ibid., 90, first two ellipses in original.

102. Ibid., 98, ellipses in original.

103. Ibid., 109.

104. Ibid., 91, second and third ellipses in original.

105. Ibid., 39.

106. Ibid., 40.

107. Ibid., 99–100.

108. Naoko Shibusawa, "Femininity, Race and Treachery: How 'Tokyo Rose' Became a Traitor to the United States after the Second World War," *Gender and History* 22.1 (April 2010): 170.

109. In having Round Rose also play Iva Toguri, Clements suggests how settler state formations, from Canada to the United States, evoke similar paternalistic narratives.

110. Clements, *Burning Vision*, 1.

111. Ibid., 65.

112. Produced at the juncture of reconciliation for Indian residential schools, the play's emphasis on affect indexes the extension of, not the end to, carceral logics embedded within the apology as it unevenly affects Nikkei and Aboriginal communities. As Oikawa argues, the euphemistic renaming of Nikkei internment as an "evacuation" or "relocation" covers over "how the design of the internment in Canada and the sites chosen mask the carceral." In so doing, it also "serves to recreate a more humane image of Canada" and hides the ways that its technologies function to support settler colonial hegemonies. Oikawa, *Cartographies of Violence*, 40. For scholar Deena Rymhs, Indian residential schools are part of a continuum of the settler state's carceral system, a kind of prototype that prefigures Canada's child welfare system and correctional facilities, in which Aboriginal people make up the largest group. She writes that although Indian residential schools did not result from "violations of the Criminal Code, their operations resembled those of prisons." Rymhs, *From the Iron House*, 2. Both Oikawa and Rymhs emphasize the reverberations of incarceration, resisting the tendency to cordon off these histories from their pasts and their presences. The play adds to these scholars' critical trajectories, revealing how the temporal structure of the public apology attempts to evoke "a more humane image of Canada" by covering over but not disrupting the continuum of the carceral state. It is precisely through tracing the "psycho-affective attachments" that Round Rose/Tokyo Rose/Iva Toguri has to the state that Clements reveals redress not as an end to but as a transformation and extension of settler racial hegemonies. The play's rendering of Round Rose/Tokyo Rose/Iva Toguri amounts to a call for Nikkei communities to critique and recalibrate the grand narrative that posits Nikkei redress as a watershed moment that ushers settler nation-states (including Canada and the United States) into a new era of being and feeling.

113. Clements, *Burning Vision*, 2.

114. Ibid., 84.
115. Ibid., 85.
116. Wong, "Decolonizasian," 168–169.
117. Clements, *Burning Vision*, 20.
118. They occupy what Sianne Ngai terms "ugly feelings," which are noncathartic in nature. See Sianne Ngai, *Ugly Feelings* (Cambridge, MA: Harvard University Press, 2007).
119. Coulthard, *Red Skin, White Masks*. See also Carpenter, *Seeing Red*.
120. Lai, "Epistemologies of Respect," 125.
121. Clements, *Burning Vision*, 81–89.
122. Ibid., 81, 82.
123. Ibid., 89.

CHAPTER 3

1. José Vasconcelos, *The Cosmic Race/La raza cósmica*, trans. Didier T. Jaén (1925; repr., Baltimore: Johns Hopkins University Press, 1979); Gilberto Freyre, *The Masters and the Slaves: A Study in the Development of Brazilian Civilization* (1933; repr., Berkeley: University of California Press, 1986); Gilberto Freyre, *New World in the Tropics: The Culture of Modern Brazil* (1945; repr., New York: Alfred A. Knopf, 1959). While Asian identities do not appear so centrally in *The Masters and the Slaves*, Freyre emphasizes the racial mixing of the Portuguese with the Moors, a romanticization that, according to scholars Ella Shohat and Robert Stam, operate as an early form of Orientalism in the Américas. See Ella Shohat and Robert Stam, "Genealogies of Orientalism and Occidentalism: Sephardi Jews, Muslims, and the Americas," *Studies in American Jewish Literature* 35.1 (2016): 13–32.

2. For a discussion of Indian difference, see María Josefina Saldaña-Portillo, *The Revolutionary Imagination in the Americas in the Age of Development* (Durham, NC: Duke University Press, 2003).

3. As Saldaña-Portillo argues, *mestizaje* as a "primary process for identification for the revolutionary nation" has had residual effects today in the major decline in communities that identify as Indigenous since 1910. She writes that "this precipitous decline cannot be explained by overall growth or a dramatic increase in interracial marriages. Instead . . . it reflects the partial success of the discourse of mestizaje as a process of identification." Ibid., 322.

4. See Alan Knight, "Race, Revolution, and *Indigenismo*: Mexico, 1910–1940," in *The Idea of Race in Latin America, 1870–1940*, ed. Richard Graham (Austin: University of Texas Press, 1990), 71–114. In this essay, Knight writes: "*Indigenistas* argued, in so many words, for positive discrimination, which would protect the weak unorganized Indian population. Formal equality before the law, the old liberal nostrum, was meaningless so long as the Indians were denied education, political access, and economic development. The night watchman state had to give way to the *estado papa*, the paternalistic state. This shift, of course, responded to state self-interest as well as to considerations of social justice, but it nevertheless involved a repudiation of the strict social Darwinism of the Porfiriato" (84).

5. Ibid., 97. Knight continues, "During the 1920s, politicians courted support by advocating, and implementing, anti-Chinese measures: economic controls, taxes, ghet-

toization, and ultimately expulsion. Such campaigns were conducted with the panoply of xenophobic racism. The Chinese were stereotyped as filthy, disease-ridden, money-grubbing, parasitic, and sexually threatening. They spread sickness, gambling and drug-addiction" (96).

6. Knight maintains, "The Chinese, originally brought into the country to provide cheap labor, soon became highly successful shopkeepers, traders, and businessmen, especially in the booming Northwest. In particular, they established a profitable symbiotic liaison with the big U.S. mining companies, such as the Cananea Company, for whom they provided many of the basic retailing services and, in doing so, squeezed out Mexican competitors." Ibid.

7. Knight writes: "Another relevant parallel suggests itself: the expropriation by nationalist regimes in East Africa of Asian traders and middlemen, who had prospered in symbiosis with colonial business interests, as the Chinese had in symbiosis with the big U.S. companies in Northern Mexico. In both cases, conscious nationalism justified an attack on an 'alien' petite bourgeoisie, an attack that promised short-term political and economic advantages to the new nationalist elites (in both cases, too, the symbiotically linked corporate business interests both escaped racist obloquy and weathered economic nationalist pressures pretty well)." Ibid., 111n.

8. Vasconcelos, *Cosmic Race*, 28–29.

9. Vasconcelos writes that "the white race has brought the world to a state in which all human types and cultures will be able to fuse with each other. The civilization developed and organized in our times by the white has set the moral and material basis for the union of all men into a fifth universal race, the fruit of all the previous ones and amelioration of the past." *Cosmic Race*, 9.

10. Ibid., 16.

11. Ibid., 23.

12. However, as Saldaña-Portillo argues, communal land holdings or the townships that mark contemporary Indigenous collective formations are in fact resonating effects of the colonial encounter and the implementation of the *encomienda* system. Writing on Manuel Gamio's influential works, Saldaña-Portillo traces the rationale of *Indigenismo* from the colonial encounter to the contemporary moment, arguing that it was implemented to unify the nation and to legitimize minority rule. *Revolutionary Imagination in the Americas*, 205.

13. Jaén notes Vasconcelos's publication of *Estudios indostanicos* in 1916. Vasconcelos, *Cosmic Race*, xxi.

14. Didier T. Jaén writes that "even in these days, in the midst of all the intellectual and political fervor, the mystical thought of India had already caught the attention of Vasconcelos and his contemporaries. In his *Estudios indostanicos*, Vasconcelos recalls that it was in those meetings of the Ateneo de la Juventud that they began to read and be stimulated by Indian philosophy." Vasconcelos, *Cosmic Race*, xxi.

15. It must be noted that Vasconcelos separates Indian from other "Orientals" in the text, revealing the racial formation of the Asian as anything but neat.

16. Vasconcelos, *Cosmic Race*, 22. Interestingly, the Mongolian is separated from the Hindu or Muslim.

17. Ibid., 19–20. Vasconcelos writes: "It may happen sometimes and, in fact, it has already happened, that economic competition may force us to close our doors, as is done

by the Anglo-Saxons, to an unrestrained influx of Asians. But, in doing so, we obey reasons of economic order. We recognize that it is not fair that people like the Chinese, who, under saintly guidance of Confucian morality multiply like mice, should come to degrade the human condition precisely at the moment when we begin to understand that intelligence serves to refrain and regulate the lower zoological instincts, which are contrary to a truly religious conception of life. If we reject the Chinese, it is because man, as he progresses, multiplies less, and feels the horror of numbers, for the same reason that he has begun to value quality." Ibid.

18. Ibid., 25.

19. Ibid., 38.

20. Vasconcelos writes: "If in order to constitute the fifth race we should proceed according to the law of the second period, then a contest of craftiness would ensue, in which the astute ones and those lacking in scruples would win the game over the dreamers and kind at heart. Probably, then, the new humanity would be predominantly Malaysian, for it is said that no one surpasses them in caution and ability, and even, if necessary, in perfidy." Ibid., 37.

21. Vasconcelos writes: "We shall see that the work of racial fusion is going to take place in the Ibero-American continent according to a law derived from the fruition of the highest faculties. The laws of emotion, beauty, and happiness will determine the selection of a mate with infinitely superior results than that of a eugenics grounded in scientific reason, which never sees beyond the less important portion of the love act. Above scientific eugenics, the mysterious eugenics of aesthetic taste will prevail." Ibid., 30.

22. Ibid., 25.

23. Scholar Seth Garfield cites nineteenth-century thinkers who glorified Indigenous and white couplings, 1920s modernist artists who centered a form of primitivism, and Freyre's inclusion of Indigenous presence in Brazilian cultural formation. *Indigenous Struggle at the Heart of Brazil: State Policy, Frontier Expansion, and the Xavante Indians, 1937–1988* (Durham, NC: Duke University Press, 2001), 36–37.

24. Garfield writes that the Vargas era was "marked by import-substitution industrialization, political centralization, labor populism, rural-urban migration, frontier expansion, and World War II mobilization." Garfield, *Indigenous Struggle*, 34. At the heart of westward expansion during this time was the state-led project and discourse of development deemed the "March to the West," which sought to connect the highly populated and industrialized East to the western hinterlands. For Garfield: "During the *Estado Novo*, images of the Indian served to justify the arrogation of indigenous land and sociocultural subordination in the context of western frontier expansion. Moreover, the images allayed elite fears regarding the nation's racial composition and military unpreparedness during a period of world war, which Brazil would formally enter in 1942." *Indigenous Struggle*, 37.

25. Ibid., 39.

26. See Jeffrey Lesser, "In Search of the Hyphen: Nikkei and the Struggle over Brazilian National Identity," in *New Worlds, New Lives: Globalization and People of Japanese Descent in the Americas and from Latin America in Japan,* ed. Lane R. Hirabayashi, Akemi Kikumura-Yano, and James A. Hirabayashi (Stanford, CA: Stanford University Press, 2002), 37–58.

27. Lesser writes: "When the proto-fascist *Estado Novo* (New State) dictatorship was established in 1937, one of its major new policies was the *brasilidade* (Brazilianization)

campaign. This state-driven homogenization program sought to preserve an idealized national identity from the encroachment of ethnicity. New legislation controlled immigrant entry and prevented resident aliens from congregating in farming colonies. Decrees required that all schools be directed by native-born Brazilians and that all instruction be in Portuguese and include 'Brazilian' topics." Jeffrey Lesser, *A Discontented Diaspora: Japanese Brazilians and the Meanings of Ethnic Militancy, 1960–1980* (Durham, NC: Duke University Press, 2007), 7. Anti-Japanese sentiment was exacerbated when Vargas cut diplomatic ties with Japan in 1942 and when Brazil declared war with Japan in 1945. This anti-Asian sentiment was not too different from the years prior to the dictatorship: a number of Asian immigration restrictions were already in place.

28. Freyre's conception of racial mixture, and celebration of plantation labor as less brutal than in the United States, has gained increasing currency throughout the years and provided a context for prevailing sentiments about Brazil's racial identity. See Jan Hoffman French, *Legalizing Identities: Becoming Black or Indian in Brazil's Northeast* (Chapel Hill: University of North Carolina Press, 2009). As French writes, "Freyre's iteration [of racial mixture] became so widespread that Brazilians, on a regular basis, continue to repeat his assertations: that Brazilian slavery was more benign than the U.S. version and that this had led to better relations between black and white people in Brazil allowing for miscegenation and strong kinship bonds across racial lines ('racial democracy')" (212–213).

29. Perhaps considered a hemispheric figure, Freyre's educational background included stints in the United States punctuated by his training under Franz Boas and his work at Stanford University. Unsurprisingly, this experience influenced his comparative approach to race relations; he explicitly juxtaposes Brazilian racial and colonial formations to those of the United States. Like Vasconcelos, Freyre argued against dominant racial perceptions of white/European superiority that held sway across Latin América. See Richard Drayton, "Gilberto Freyre and the Twentieth-Century Rethinking of Race in Latin America," *Portuguese Studies* 27.1 (2011): 43–47.

30. Central to his discussion of Brazilian racial formation is the romanticization and eroticization of racial mixture, which he posits as a combination of Portuguese male virility and Indigenous and enslaved African female licentiousness. Even more so than Vasconcelos, Freyre emphasized the sexualized elements of colonial contact that amounted to the rendering of Brazil along erotic and sensuous terms. For Freyre, it is this "fleshly" aspect of attraction between Portuguese colonizers and Indigenous and Black women that lead to the racial mixture that he posits as the necessary groundwork for *mestiçagem*. Ripe with contradictions throughout, Freyre's book conceptualizes Portuguese men as sexually desirable and yet violent, and Native women as willing and desperately lascivious, and yet always vulnerable to rape. Highlighting that Indigenous-black unions are results of rape, Freyre places Portuguese men above black men in the scale of sexual attractiveness. In addition, Freyre often attributes Portuguese male sexuality to the culture's Moorish past, which he says has provided a necessary inheritance in the tropics.

31. Of the mixed society in Brazil, Freyre writes: "Hybrid from the beginning, Brazilian society is, of all those in the Americas, the one most harmoniously constituted so far as racial relations are concerned, within the environment of a practical cultural reciprocity that results in the advanced people deriving the maximum of profit from the values and experiences of the backward ones, and in a maximum of conformity between

the foreign and the native cultures, that of the conqueror and that of the conquered." *The Masters and the Slaves*, 83.

32. Ibid.

33. Ibid., 81–82.

34. Ibid.

35. In one instance, Freyre argues that the economic investments of India were necessarily diverted to be invested in the colony of Brazil. He writes: "For the formidable task of colonizing so extensive a tract as Brazil, sixteenth-century Portugal had to avail itself of what man-power was left it after the adventure in India." Ibid., 85.

36. Freyre writes: "In the case of Brazil (we are dealing with a seventeenth-century phenomenon), the Portuguese colonizer had in his and the colony's favor all the wealth and the extraordinary variety of experiences that had been accumulated during the fifteenth century, in Asia and in Africa, in Madeira and in Cape Verde, among those experiences being a knowledge of useful plants, good to eat and pleasing to the palate, which were to be successfully transplanted to Brazil, certain advantages of the Asiatic mode of building that were adaptable to the American tropics; and the ascertained capacity of the Negro for agricultural labor." Ibid., 31.

37. Ibid., 18–19.

38. While the conceptualization of the Asian figure is largely absent in *The Masters and the Slaves*, Freyre does in fact infuse his discussion of Brazilian national identity with Orientalist depictions that emphasize the influence of Jews and Moors in the formation of Portuguese identity. Early on in the book, Freyre conveys how the history of mixing with the Jews and Moors has positively influenced the Portuguese character and provided the condition of possibility for the Portuguese to acclimate nicely to the racial diversity and mixing that would characterize their colonial encounters with Indigenous peoples in the Américas. He asserts that the productive antagonisms that are emergent in the crossings of two or more different cultural groups had existed in Portugal long before its movement toward the tropics. See Shohat and Stam, "Genealogies of Orientalism and Occidentalism."

39. See, as an exception, Jason Oliver Chang, *Chino: Anti-Chinese Racism in Mexico, 1880–1940* (Urbana: University of Illinois Press, 2017).

40. As Susan Koshy argues, the gains of the civil rights movement brought a "redistribution of economic, social, and cultural capital in and between racial groups, genders, and sexual identities" to the extent that "the axis of stratification has multiplied and shifted so that it runs within and between marginalized and dominant identities, reconfiguring them in unprecedented ways." "Why the Humanities Matter for Race Studies Today," *PMLA* 123.5 (October 2008): 1547.

41. He writes, "Even local resistance and nativist resentment are open to the seduction of consumerism, as can be seen in the history of graffiti art and rap music. New meanings are attached to all cultural products through aestheticization and/or pricing." Masao Miyoshi, "Sites of Resistance in the Global Economy," *boundary 2: an international journal of literature and culture* 22.1 (1995): 69.

42. See David Harvey, *The Condition of Postmodernity: An Enquiry into the Origins of Cultural Change* (London: Blackwell, 1989); and Miyoshi, "Sites of Resistance in the Global Economy."

43. Miyoshi writes: "TNCs were far more autonomous, and as they grew more pow-

erful and elusive from governmental control, they split the nation-state, appropriated the state apparatus to their own advantage, and jettisoned the nation (that is, the aggregate of citizens and public space) to its own devices." "Sites of Resistance in the Global Economy," 64.

44. In the 1960s Japan was globally deemed to have a "miracle economy." Scholar Mitchell W. Sedgewick writes that "Japan's late-twentieth-century global interactions are dominated by the spread of Japanese capital in a mercantilist form driven by business-state coalitions. In other words, Japanese corporations are the central filter through which 'Japan' interacts with the world, collectively surpassing the Japanese state as an actor in international affairs." Mitchell W. Sedgewick, *Globalisation and Japanese Organisational Culture: An Ethnography of Japanese Corporations in France* (New York: Routledge, 2007), 43.

45. Lesser asserts, "As Japan reemerged as an economic powerhouse after World War II, Nikkei throughout the Americas were linked to international capital in ways that changed identity construction. Japan's position on the world stage meant that Nikkei were simultaneously viewed as 'radically Other' and as part of a 'common capitalist identity.'" *A Discontented Diaspora*, 1. The postwar period also saw the continuation of Japanese emigration to the Américas. Due to its immediate vulnerability in the post–World War II economy, Japan initiated several emigration programs to Latin América. Most notable were the continuation in 1952 of an emigration program to Brazil and the arrival in 1973 of the Nippon Maru to Latin América, which brought the last of this wave of Japanese emigrants. In his discussion of Japan's post–World War II economic growth and its increasing political ties with the United States, scholar Harumi Befu considers this major wave of emigration as coming from a group of people he deems "Those Who Have Forsaken Japan." For Befu, these expats left Japan due to dissatisfaction with their work conditions in Japan and/or desire to explore "exotic places, or because they were bored with life in Japan." "Globalization as Human Dispersal: Nikkei in the World," in *New Worlds, New Lives: Globalization and People of Japanese Descent in the Americas and from Latin America in Japan*, ed. Lane R. Hirabayashi, Akemi Kikumura-Yano, and James A. Hirabayashi (Stanford, CA: Stanford University Press, 2002), 15.

46. Lesser, "A Discontented Diaspora," 12.

47. Rachel Lee, *The Americas of Asian American Literature: Gendered Fictions of Nation and Transnation* (Princeton, NJ: Princeton University Press, 1999), 119.

48. Ibid.

49. Shohat and Stam, "Genealogies of Orientalism and Occidentalism," 17, citing Doris Sommer.

50. Karen Tei Yamashita, *Through the Arc of the Rain Forest* (Minneapolis, MN: Coffee House Press, 1990), 211.

51. For a discussion of the "proletarian solidarity" of the transnational Japanese figure, see Lee, *Americas of Asian American Literature*.

52. Indeed, Hiroshi wanted to move to Brazil because he thought of the people in the country as "bronzed-skinned" and carefree.

53. Lisa Lowe, *The Intimacies of Four Continents* (Durham, NC: Duke University Press, 2015), 39.

54. Yamashita, *Through the Arc*, 154, my emphasis.

55. Ibid., 198.

56. Ibid., 184.

57. Ibid., 184–185.

58. Ibid., n.p.

59. Mauro Porto, "Telenovelas and Representations of National Identity in Brazil," *Media, Culture, and Society* 3.1 (2011): 56.

60. Yamashita, *Through the Arc,* n.p.

61. For discussions on the national/transnational scope of the novel, see Elizabeth Cook-Lynn, "The American Indian Fiction Writers: Cosmopolitanism, Nationalism, the Third World, and First Nation Sovereignty," in *Nothing but the Truth: An Anthology of Native American Literature,* ed. John Purdy and James Ruppert (Upper Saddle River, NJ: Prentice Hall, 2001), 23–38; Shari Huhndorf, *Mapping the Americas: The Transnational Politics of Contemporary Native Culture* (Ithaca, NY: Cornell University Press, 2009); and James H. Cox, *The Red Land to the South: American Indian Writers and Indigenous Mexico* (Minneapolis: University of Minnesota Press, 2012).

62. David Harvey, *A Brief History of Neoliberalism* (New York: Oxford University Press, 2007).

63. Ray Gonzales, "The Past Is Right Here and Now: An Interview with Leslie Marmon Silko," in *Conversations with Leslie Marmon Silko,* ed. Ellen L. Arnold (Jackson: University Press of Mississippi, 2000), 101.

64. According to critic Miriam Schacht, the destroyers "represent the forces of colonialism and multinational corporate capitalism. Generally part of government, high finance, or the real estate industry (or all three), these characters include Menardo, a Mexican businessman selling insurance to large corporations against any kind of disaster, whose secret shame is that his grandfather was one of 'the Indians'. . . . On the U.S. side of the border we find Max and Leah Blue, a pair of real-estate developers trying to usurp the land and water rights of Indigenous peoples in order to squander the valuable resources on desert golf courses. There are also a number of gay men, most of whom pathologically link sex and death, like Beaufrey and Serlo, two aristocrats whose only pleasure comes from the destruction of others. In addition, the Destroyers include an assortment of military officers, weapons and organ dealers, and pornographers, for whom sex, death, and commerce have become inextricably intertwined." "Movement Must Be Emulated by the People: Rootedness, Migration, and Indigenous Internationalism in Leslie Marmon Silko's *Almanac of the Dead,*" *SAIL* 21.4 (2009): 56.

65. It is no small coincidence that the year of publication of Silko's novel was also the five-hundred-year anniversary of Columbus's arrival to the Américas.

66. Leslie Marmon Silko, *Almanac of the Dead* (1991; repr., New York: Penguin Books, 1992), 253.

67. Quoted in Linda Niemann, "Narratives of Survival," in *Conversations with Leslie Marmon Silko,* ed. Ellen L. Arnold (Jackson: University Press of Mississippi, 2000), 108.

68. Ibid.

69. Laura Coltelli, "*Almanac of the Dead*: An Interview with Leslie Marmon Silko," reprinted from *Native American Literature Forum* 4–5 (1992–1993): 65–80, in *Conversations with Leslie Marmon Silko,* ed. Ellen L. Arnold (Jackson: University Press of Mississippi, 2000), 120.

70. Marja-Liisa Helenius, "Darker Side of Mediation: Violence and Its Emotional Effects in Leslie Marmon Silko's *Almanac of the Dead,*" *Electronic Journal of the Depart-*

ment of English at the University of Helsinki 5 (2005), https://blogs.helsinki.fi/hes-eng/volumes/volume-5/darker-side-of-mediation-violence-and-its-emotional-effects-in-leslie-marmon-silko%E2%80%99s-almanac-of-the-dead-marja-liisa-helenius/.

71. Silko, *Almanac of the Dead*, 729.
72. Ibid., 680, 686.
73. Ibid., 683.
74. Ibid., 682.
75. Ibid.
76. Ibid., 681.
77. Ibid., 729. Claudia Sadowski-Smith writes that Silko's representation of Awa Gee and his undocumented status creates linkages between Indigenous rights and immigration rights struggles: "The fate of this undocumented immigrant points to the larger historical and contemporary intersections of struggles for indigenous rights with anti-immigration initiatives that have also weakened the abilities of indigenous peoples to cross borders freely. Even though the similarities among Aboriginal peoples and other cultures have historically been insufficient to create alliances Silko expresses the hope that they will do so in the future." *Border Fictions: Globalization, Empire, and Writing at the Boundaries of the United States* (Charlottesville: University of Virginia Press, 2008), 97. She footnotes, however, that these linkages are not fully fleshed out in the way that Yamashita's work fleshes them out.
78. See Jodi Kim's *Ends of Empire: Asian American Critique and the Cold War* (Minneapolis: University of Minnesota Press, 2010).
79. Ibid., 147.
80. Ibid. Kim continues: "In perhaps one of the many tragedies of the Cold War in Asia, Japan's continued and rapid economic development, and by extension that of the U.S. global capitalism, was made possible by American military orders (called offshore procurements or Special Procurements Program) in the Korean and Vietnam Wars. Virtually every sector of Japan's economy was enlisted in America's war efforts and proved to be a critical boom. Indeed, the governor of the Bank of Japan encapsulated the significance of the Korean War to Japan's economic recovery by calling the U.S. government's procurement program 'divine aid.' This 'divine aid' or 'gift from the gods' would continue throughout the protracted Vietnam War not only for Japan but also, especially, for Korea. While U.S. imperialist intervention in Vietnam was guided by Cold War efforts to maintain Southeast Asia as a regional market and source of raw materials for Japan, the intervention or war itself turned out to 'aid' Japan. Michael Schaller concludes that 'these expenditures cemented the relationship between Japanese recovery and American security policy throughout Asia.'" Ibid., 108.
81. Ibid., 20.
82. Kim directly addresses this dynamic in relationship to Cold War productions of knowledge: "The dominant inclusion-exclusion dyad governing Asian American immigration history tends to elide a critical analysis of imperialism as a catalyzing force of displacement and migration. This elision abets the Cold War as a dominant structure of feeling and knowledge that needs to forget its own imperial longings and tactics, and how such longings and tactics are subtended by a gendered racial architecture. Such a concealment is effected via an abstract universalism and an espousal of 'democracy' defined as individual rights and universal right to own private property." Ibid., 20.

83. Of this unequal alliance, Kim writes: "Though formally called the Allied Occupation of Japan, it was in effect a U.S. occupation. In what Dower calls a 'neocolonial revolution from above' in the specific form of a 'neocolonial military dictatorship,' MacArthur and his command ruled Japan like colonial overlords who were beyond criticism and as inviolate as the emperor and his officials had been." Ibid., 104.

84. Silko, *Almanac of the Dead*, 683.

85. Awa Gee's intimacy with numbers deploys the stereotype of Asians being good at math.

86. Silko, *Almanac of the Dead*, 686.

87. Ibid.

88. Ibid., 687.

89. Multiple scholars have pointed out how Silko's Army of Justice and Redistribution presages the 1994 Zapatista Army of National Liberation (EZLN) uprising in Chiapas. Silko has previously noted her awareness of the Zapatistas while she was writing her book.

90. Silko, *Almanac of the Dead*, 689.

91. Silko identifies the history of displacements from sacred homelands as a premise and stage for pan-tribal alliances of resistance to colonialism and exploitation. These hemispheric affinities are punctuated, whereas Awa Gee's experience of displacement is distantiated. This is due to Silko's incorporation of current movements, interconnections, and collaborations within the larger framework of pre-Columbian linkages, a move that frames identity formations within a cyclical, nonlinear, non-Eurocentric notion of time and space.

92. On the differences between *Ceremony* and *Almanac*, Silko declares: "I go farther with my thinking about the power of narrative in *Almanac* when I consider the writings of Marx." Coltelli, "*Almanac of the Dead*: An Interview with Leslie Marmon Silko," 131.

93. Laura Pulido writes about racial hierarchies: "A racial hierarchy is a specific configuration of power relations in a given place and time based on racial ideology. Racial hierarchies are the mapping of power relations." *Black, Brown, Yellow, and Left: Radical Activism in Los Angeles* (Berkeley: University of California Press, 2006), 25. Shu-mei Shih writes: "Bakhtin's notion of chronotope provides a way for us to emphasize how each conjunction of time and place specifically produces race and the experience of racialization without losing sight of neoliberal globalization's capacity to perpetuate and reactivate universalizing colonial content, that everywhere and in every instance an asymmetry of power structures racialization." "Comparative Racialization: An Introduction," special issue, *PMLA* 123.5 (2008): 1354.

94. As Shari Huhndorf writes: "Native America exposes U.S. identity, from its origins to the present, as constituted through conquest, the imposition of political control, and the appropriation of indigenous lands. Contained by neither geographic region nor time period, this ongoing process cannot be marginalized; *it implicates all non-indigenous peoples in that conquest*. . . . Furthermore, Native histories upset conventional *resistance narratives*, since every wave of immigration, whether forced or voluntary, dispossesses indigenous peoples, whatever complicated social relationships emerge from these interactions." *Mapping the Americas*, 16–17, my emphasis. Huhndorf continues by maintaining that Indigenous land disputes also emerge among Native communities themselves, revealing contradictions embedded in pan-tribal alliances.

CHAPTER 4

1. Larry Grant is Elder-in-Residence at the University of British Columbia's First Nations House of Learning.

2. This short interview was produced by Chinese Canadian Stories, an initiative of the University of British Columbia: https://acam.arts.ubc.ca/community-projects/chinese-canadian-stories/. See also *All Our Father's Relations*, directed by Alejandro Yoshizawa (Canada: Right Relations Production, 2016). This film follows the Grant children from British Columbia to China to trace their father's familial history.

3. Chow notes, for example, that the Chinese laborers were taught how to trap from First Nations peoples. *Sojourners in the North* (Prince George, BC, Canada: Caitlin Press, 1996), 102. For discussions of the relationship between Chinese men and Aboriginal women, see also Jean Barman, "Beyond Chinatown: Chinese Men and Indigenous Women in Early British Columbia," *BC Studies* 177 (2013): 39–64.

4. For discussions of the Indian Act, see Bonita Lawrence, *"Real" Indians and Others: Mixed-Blood Urban Native Peoples and Indigenous Nationhood* (Lincoln: University of Nebraska Press, 2004); Jo-Anne Fiske, "Political Status of Native Indian Women: Contradictory Implications of Canadian State Policy," *American Indian Culture and Research Journal* 19.2 (1995): 1–30; Joyce Green, "Towards a Détente with History: Confronting Canada's Colonial Legacy," *International Journal of Canadian Studies* 12 (1995): 85–105; Sunera Thobani, *Exalted Subjects: Studies in the Making of Race and Nation in Canada* (Toronto, Canada: University of Toronto Press, 2007). Thobani writes of the Indian Act: "Creating a framework for the governance of Indians on the basis that that they needed protection and could be civilized through assimilation, the Act defined which Native peoples were to be eligible for Indian status and which were to be denied such status. The act made the status and rights of Native women within their communities directly dependent upon their relationships to men: Native women and their children would lose status upon marriage to non-status men" (48–49).

5. This history reveals two moments of defiance by both communities. First, Grant reveals how the Indian Department did not initially know of this economic relationship between Chinese immigrants and the Musqueam nation, in which Chinese farmers rented land. Second, while the Indian Act at the time did not allow non-Indians to marry Aboriginal peoples, Grant's parents nevertheless united and had four children together.

6. Lawrence, *"Real" Indians and Others*, 64. As Lawrence argues, these changes had incredible limitations, including the fact that women who were restored status could pass their status on to only one generation.

7. See Yoshizawa, *All Our Father's Relations*.

8. Renisa Mawani, *Colonial Proximities: Crossracial Encounters and Juridical Truths in British Columbia, 1871–1921* (Vancouver, Canada: University of British Columbia, 2009), 176.

9. Ibid.

10. Lawrence, *"Real" Indians and Others*, 55–56. Lawrence writes: "Some sources have estimated that by far the majority of the twenty-five thousand Indians who lost status and were externalized from their communities between 1876 and 1985 . . . did so because of ongoing gender discrimination in the Indian Act. But it is not simply a matter of twenty-five thousand individuals. If one takes into account the fact that for every

individual who lost status and had to leave her community, all of her descendants (many of them the products of nonstatus Indian fathers and Indian mothers) also lost status and for the most part were permanently alienated from Native culture, the numbers of individuals who ultimately were removed from Indian status and lost to their nations may, at the most conservative estimates, number between one and two million. By comparison, in 1985, when Bill C-31 was passed, there were only 350,000 status Indians still listed on the Department of Indian Affair's Indian register.... In comparing the potential numbers of people lost to their Native communities because of loss of status with the numbers of individuals still considered Indian in 1985, the scale of cultural genocide caused by gender discrimination becomes visible." Ibid.

11. G. Reginald Daniel, Laura Kina, Wei Ming Dariotis, and Camilla Fojas, "Emerging Paradigms in Critical Mixed Race Studies," *Journal of Critical Mixed Race Studies* 1.1 (2014): 27. They write: "When we speak of mixedness or *mestizaje* in the Latin American context, this is inseparable from the history of European conquest and colonization (e.g., Spanish, Portuguese, French, Dutch, Danish, and English), the migration of Asian and Semitic populations, the enslavement of Africans, and the subsequent reframing of the mixed Spanish-Euro/African/Native/Asian people of Latin America as *La raza cósmica*. Canada also has a distinct multiracial Aboriginal population, such as the Métis. Moreover, issues pertaining to mixed race and mixed ethnic identities are framed within a vocabulary of 'visible minorities.' Both Latin American and Canadian racial history is notably different than the US framework of hypodescent and dominant black/white polarization, yet they all originate in the European Enlightenment systems of racial taxonomy and legacies of colonialism." Ibid.

12. This notion about the "browning of America" is punctuated, for example, by the election of Barack Obama to the presidency in 2008 and the mainstream declarations of the beginnings of a "postracial society."

13. See Jared Sexton, *Amalgamation Schemes: Antiblackness and the Critique of Multiracialism* (Minneapolis: University of Minnesota Press, 2008). Sexton writes: "In this light, multiracialism can be read, as suggested previously, as an element of the ascendant ideology of colorblindness ... but it is not thereby identical to it. Its target is not race per se, since multiracialism is still very much a politics of racial identity (one often enough holding up multiracial identity as exceptional and exemplary), but rather the categorical sprawl of blackness in particular and the insatiable political demand it presents to a nominally postemancipation society" (6).

14. Ibid., 45.

15. The census now allows multiracial people to check more than one category.

16. Iyko Day, "Must All Asianness Be American? The Census, Racial Classification, and Asian Canadian Emergence," *Canadian Literature* 199 (2008): 45–70. As Day argues, "For many groups in the US, the option of multiple checking registers a major defeat against institutionalized racism. For race-based political lobbying groups, multiple race checking reduces numbers and puts in jeopardy civil rights monitoring and enforcement" (62).

17. Ibid., 62–63.

18. While mixed-race discourse in the United States and Canada is different from in Latin América, current changes in racial demographics and the increase in cross-

racial unions in the United States and Canada have led to some scholars, such as Eduardo Bonilla-Silva, proclaiming the "Latin Americanization of racial stratification in the USA." Eduardo Bonilla-Silva, "We Are All Americans! The Latin Americanization of Racial Stratification in the USA," *Race and Society* 5 (2002): 3–16.

19. Mawani argues that "the management of encounters across racial divides was motivated by biopolitical concerns over the life and longevity of white settlement." *Colonial Proximities*, 15. As such, while the conversations around the management of Indigenous and Asian populations were not monolithic, such concerns often hinged on the temporal figuration of whiteness in the telos of settlement.

20. In the same special issue of *Ricepaper Magazine* 17.3–4 (2012), see also Sharel Wright's "Granddaughter Will Remember," 52–56; Anderson Lee's "A Mother's Memories," 56; and Bessie Chow's *"Cedar and Bamboo,"* 58–61.

21. Dorothy Christian, "Articulating a Silence," *Ricepaper Magazine* 17.3–4 (2012): 16.

22. Lily Chow, *Sojourners in the North*, 102.

23. For convergences via foodways, see Brandy Lien-Worrell, *Eating Stories: A Chinese Canadian and Aboriginal Potluck* (Vancouver: Chinese Canadian Historical Society of British Columbia, 2007).

24. Christian, "Articulating a Silence," 16.

25. Lawrence, *"Real" Indians and Others*, 31.

26. Beth Hege Piatote, *Domestic Subjects: Gender, Citizenship, and Law in Native American Literature* (New Haven, CT: Yale University Press, 2013), 22.

27. Ibid., 23.

28. These restrictions emerged through not only miscegenation and mixed-race fears by white settlers but also the anxieties of Native communities whose numbers and lands were under siege. Mawani discusses, for example, an early attempt by the Lillooet band, of the Central Interior-Fraser Canyon within British Columbia, to petition the governor general to authorize the Lillooet leadership to bring "back the erring ones [women marrying non-status men], and if necessary by force, without subjecting our service to fine and imprisonment." Cited in Mawani, *Colonial Proximities*, 173.

29. Christian, "Articulating a Silence," 15.

30. Ibid., 16.

31. Ibid., 17.

32. Ibid.

33. Ibid.

34. Ibid., 16.

35. Ibid., 15.

36. Ibid.

37. Gerald Vizenor, *Manifest Manners: Narratives of Postindian Survivance* (Lincoln: University of Nebraska Press, 1999).

38. Christian, "Articulating a Silence," 19.

39. Ibid., 17.

40. Ibid.

41. Ibid., 18.

42. Ibid., 15.

43. Ibid.

44. Ibid.

45. Ibid., 18–19.

46. Sean Kiccumah Teuton, *Red Land, Red Power: Grounding Knowledge in the American Indian Novel* (Durham, NC: Duke University Press, 2008).

47. Ibid., 125. See also Satya Mohanty, *Literary Theory and the Claims of History: Postmodernism, Objectivity, Multicultural Politics* (Ithaca, NY: Cornell University Press, 1997).

48. Mohanty, *Literary Theory and the Claims of History*, 206. Teuton discusses the movement from shame to anger, rendering anger as more politically mobilizing. Christian's essay suggests that shame itself produces a meaningful, potentially enabling, albeit often disabling, effect on tribal communities.

49. Sianne Ngai, *Ugly Feelings* (Cambridge, MA: Harvard University Press, 2007); Christian, "Articulating a Silence," 19.

50. He introduces her as "World-renowned Pomo basketmaker with permanent collections in the Smithsonian and countless other museums. The last Dreamer and sucking doctor among the Pomo peoples. The last living member of the Long Valley Cache Creek Pomo tribe." Greg Sarris, *Mabel McKay: Weaving the Dream* (Berkeley: University of California Press, 1994), 3.

51. Greg Sarris, *Keeping Slug Woman Alive* (Berkeley: University of California Press, 1993), 10.

52. Sarris, *Mabel McKay*, 4, 5.

53. Ibid., 5.

54. Sarris elaborates on this in his critical text, *Keeping Slug Woman Alive*.

55. "Greg Sarris: A Native American Finds His Roots," *FilamStar: The Newspaper for Filipinos in Mainstream America*, April 21, 2016, https://filamstar.com/greg-sarris-a-native-american-finds-his-filipino-roots/.

56. Leti Volpp, "American Mestizo: Filipinos and Anti-Miscegenation Laws in California," *UC Davis Law Review* 33.4 (2000): 805–806.

57. In California between 1850 and 1948, all "Mongolians" were restricted from marrying white women. In 1948 the *Perez v. Sharp* Supreme Court of California case repealed the state ban on interracial marriage. It had not been until 1933 that Filipinos were officially considered in the "Mongolian" category and were thus restricted from marrying.

58. Volpp, "American Mestizo," 809–810.

59. Volpp writes that "while California subsequently became the first and only state after Reconstruction to rule that it's state's antimiscegenation laws were unconstitutional in the 1948 case Perez v. Sharp, in 1948, the legislature refused to expunge the invalidated laws from the California Civil Code until 1959." Ibid., 823–824.

60. Sarris, *Mabel McKay*, 139.

61. Margaret D. Jacobs, "The Eastmans and the Luhans: Interracial Marriage between White Women and Native American Men, 1875–1935," *Frontier* 23.3 (2002): 31.

62. Ibid., 46.

63. Volpp, "American Mestizo," 809. Volpp cites leaders from the Commonwealth Club as well as the Immigration Studies Commission.

64. Citing an infamous 1925 case about whether a Filipino man should be desig-

nated Mongolian and barred from cross-racial marriages, Volpp writes: "Counsel for the state discussed the evil effects of miscegenation generally, and pointed to Mexico as a specific example of the effects of race mixture. 'We see the result that the Mexican nation had not had the standing, had not the citizens as it would otherwise if it had remained pure." Ibid., 815.

65. This was a common sentiment, cited in Jacobs, "The Eastmans and the Luhans," 38.

66. Ibid., 37.

67. The measurement of blood quantum was implemented since the Dawes Allotment Act of 1887.

68. J. Kēhaulani Kauanui, *Hawaiian Blood: Colonialism and the Politics of Sovereignty and Indigeneity* (Durham, NC: Duke University Press, 2008), 2.

69. Ibid., 25.

70. For a discussion of "playing Indian," see Philip Deloria, *Playing Indian* (New Haven, CT: Yale University Press, 1998).

71. Lorenzo Veracini, *Settler Colonialism: A Theoretical Overview* (Basingstoke, UK: Palgrave, 2010).

72. Sarris, *Mabel McKay*, 2.

73. Ibid., 4.

74. Ibid., 5.

75. For a discussion of Indigenous refusal, see Audra Simpson, "Consent's Revenge," *Cultural Anthropology* 31.3 (2016): 326–333.

76. Sarris, *Keeping Slug Woman Alive*, 10.

77. Sarris, *Mabel McKay*, 136.

78. Ibid., 31.

79. Sarris writes: "All their talk in Indian and Violet's '*we* Indians,' whether meant to exclude me or not, unnerved me. I was a twelve-year-old kid again. I began talking about the Indians I knew, the people I grew up with in Santa Rosa." Ibid., 57.

80. Ibid.

81. Ibid., 60.

82. Ibid., 130.

83. Ibid., 67.

84. Ibid., 139.

85. Ibid., 143.

86. As Piatote argues, "The interconnected workings of the intimate domestic, the tribal-national domestic, and the foreign domestic of the settler state become clear, as these laws seek to align Native American subjectivity with the settler state and in the process abrogate the territorial and political status of the tribal-national domestic. Through the regulation of intimate domesticity, settler-national domestication goals are accomplished." *Domestic Subjects*, 19.

87. Sarris, *Mabel McKay*, 147.

88. Ibid. 46.

89. Ibid., 47.

90. Ibid., 139, 140.

91. Ibid., 37.

92. Ibid., 36–37.

93. Ibid., 63.

94. Quoted in Diane E. Leung and Kamala Todd, dirs., *Cedar and Bamboo* (Moving Images Distribution, 2010).

95. Dorothy Christian, "Reconciling with the People and the Land?," in *Cultivating Canada: Reconciliation through the Lens of Diversity,* ed. Ashok Mathur, Jonathan Dewar, and Mike DeGagné (Ottawa, Canada: Aboriginal Healing Foundation, 2011), 75. The conference was entitled "The 1907 Race Riots and Beyond: A Century of TransPacific Canada," sponsored by University of Victoria, University of British Columbia, and Simon Fraser University. The conference was held at the downtown campus of Simon Fraser University.

96. Ibid., 76.

CODA

1. Shu-mei Shih, "Comparative Racialization: An Introduction," special issue, *PMLA* 123.5 (2008): 1351.

2. Leslie Marmon Silko, *Almanac of the Dead* (1991; repr., New York: Penguin Books, 1992), 407.

3. Sharon P. Holland, "'If you Know I have a History, You Will Respect Me': A Perspective on Afro-Native American Literature," *Callaloo* 17.1 (1994): 350. Holland cites William Loren Katz's *The Black West.*

4. Silko, *Almanac of the Dead*, 415.

5. Ibid., 407.

6. Ibid., 408.

7. For a discussion of settler production of eventfulness, see Elizabeth Povinelli, *Economies of Abandonment: Social Belonging and Endurance in Late Liberalism* (Durham, NC: Duke University Press, 2011).

8. Silko, *Almanac of the Dead*, 416.

9. Ibid., 405.

10. Eve Tuck and K. Wayne Yang, "Decolonization Is Not a Metaphor," *Decolonization: Indigeneity, Education, and Society* 1.1 (2012): 3.

Bibliography

Adachi, Ken. *The Enemy That Never Was: A History of Japanese Canadians.* Toronto, Canada: McClelland and Stewart, 1976.
Ahmed, Sara. "Collective Feelings: Or, the Impressions Left by Others." *Theory, Culture, and Society* 21.2 (2004): 25–42.
———. *The Cultural Politics of Emotions.* New York: Routledge, 2004.
———. *The Promise of Happiness.* Durham, NC: Duke University Press, 2010.
Allen, Chadwick. *Blood Narrative: Indigenous Identity in American Indian and Maori Literary and Activist Texts.* Durham, NC: Duke University Press, 2002.
———. *Trans-Indigenous: Methodologies of Global Native Literary Studies.* Minneapolis: University of Minnesota Press, 2012.
Altamirano-Jiménez, Isabel. *Indigenous Encounters with Neoliberalism: Place, Women, and the Environment in Canada and Mexico.* Vancouver, Canada: University of British Columbia Press, 2013.
Anderson, Benedict. *Imagined Communities.* 1983. Reprint, London: Verso, 1996.
Ayukawa, Michiko Midge. *Hiroshima Immigrants in Canada 1891–1941.* Vancouver, Canada: University of British Columbia Press, 2008.
Barman, Jean. "Beyond Chinatown: Chinese Men and Indigenous Women in Early British Columbia." *BC Studies* 177 (2013): 39–64.
Bauer, Ralph. "Hemispheric Studies." *PMLA* 124.1 (2009): 234–250.
Beauregard, Guy. "After Redress: A Conversation with Roy Miki." *Canadian Literature* 201 (2009): 71–86.
Befu, Harumi. "Globalization as Human Dispersal: Nikkei in the World." In *New Worlds, New Lives: Globalization and People of Japanese Descent in the Americas and from Latin America in Japan,* edited by Lane R. Hirabayashi, Akemi Kikumura-Yano, and James A. Hirabayashi, 5–18. Stanford, CA: Stanford University Press, 2002.
Berthrong, Donald. *The Cheyenne and Arapaho Ordeal: Reservation and Agency Life, 1875–1907.* Norman: University of Oklahoma Press, 1976.

Blauner, Robert. "Internal Colonialism and the Ghetto Revolt." *Social Problems* 16.4 (1969): 393–408.
Bonilla-Silva, Eduardo. "We Are All Americans! The Latin Americanization of Racial Stratification in the USA." *Race and Society* 5 (2002): 3–16.
Bow, Leslie. *Partly Colored: Asian Americans and Racial Anomaly in the Segregated South.* New York: New York University Press, 2010.
Brown, Wendy. *Regulating Aversion: Tolerance in the Age of Identity and Empire.* Princeton, NJ: Princeton University Press, 2006.
Butler, Judith. *Precarious Life: The Power of Mourning and Violence.* New York: Verso, 2004.
Byrd, Jodi. *The Transit of Empire: Indigenous Critiques of Colonialism.* Minneapolis: University of Minnesota Press, 2011.
Canadian Race Relations Foundation (CRRF). "First Annual Report." 1997–1998. http://www.crrf-fcrr.ca/images/stories/annual_report/annual_report_1998_-_English.pdf.
Carpenter, Cari. *Seeing Red: Anger, Sentimentality, and American Indians.* Columbus: Ohio University Press, 2008.
Carpenter, Cari, and K. Hyoejin Yoon, eds. "Asian/Native Encounters." Special issue, *College Literature* 41.1 (2014).
Carroll, Al. *Medicine Bags and Dog Tags: American Indian Veterans from Colonial Times to the Second Iraq War.* Lincoln: University of Nebraska Press, 2008.
Castellanos, M. Bianet. "Introduction: Settler Colonialism in Latin America." *American Quarterly* 69.4 (2017): 777–781.
Castellanos, M. Bianet, Lourdes Gutiérrez Nájera, and Arturo J. Aldama, eds. *Comparative Indigeneities across the Américas.* Tucson: University of Arizona Press, 2012.
Chakrabarty, Dipesh. *Provincializing Europe: Postcolonial Thought and Historical Difference.* Princeton, NJ: Princeton University Press, 2000.
Chang, Jason Oliver. *Chino: Anti-Chinese Racism in Mexico, 1880–1940.* Urbana: University of Illinois Press, 2017.
Chang, Sucheng, ed. *The Vietnamese American 1.5 Generation: Stories of War, Revolution, Flight, and New Beginnings.* Philadelphia: Temple University Press, 2006.
Cheng, Anne Anlin. *The Melancholy of Race: Assimilation, Psychoanalysis, and Hidden Grief.* Oxford: Oxford University Press, 2000.
Cheung, King-Kok. *Articulate Silences: Hisaye Yamamoto, Maxine Hong Kingston, Joy Kogawa.* Ithaca, NY: Cornell University Press, 1993.
———. "The Woman Warrior versus the Chinaman Pacific: Must a Chinese American Critic Choose between Feminism and Heroism?" In *A Companion to Asian American Studies,* edited by Kent A. Ono, 157–174. Boston: Blackwell, 2005.
Chin, Frank. "Come All Ye Asian American Writers of the Real and the Fake." In *The Big Aiiieeeee! An Anthology of Chinese American and Japanese American Literature,* edited by Jeffrey Paul Chan, Frank Chin, Lawson Fusao Inada, and Shawn Wong, 1–93. New York: Meridian, 1991.
Chin, Frank, Jeffrey Paul Chan, Lawson Fusao Inada, and Shawn Wong, eds. *Aiiieeeee! An Anthology of Asian-American Writers.* Washington, DC: Howard University Press, 1974.
Chow, Bessie. "*Cedar and Bamboo.*" *Ricepaper Magazine* 17.3–4 (2012): 58–61.
Chow, Lily. *Sojourners in the North.* Prince George, BC, Canada: Caitlin Press, 1996.

Christian, Dorothy. "Articulating a Silence." *Ricepaper Magazine* 17.3–4 (2012): 14–19.
———. "Reconciling with the People and the Land?" In *Cultivating Canada: Reconciliation through the Lens of Diversity*, edited by Ashok Mathur, Jonathan Dewar, and Mike DeGagné, 69–80. Ottawa, Canada: Aboriginal Healing Foundation, 2011.
Chuh, Kandice. "Of Hemispheres and Other Spheres: Navigating Karen Tei Yamashita's Literary World." *American Literary History* 18.3 (2006): 618–637.
Churchill, Ward. *A Little Matter of Genocide: Holocaust and Denial in the Americas 1492 to the Present*. San Francisco: City Lights Publishers, 2001.
Clements, Marie. *Burning Vision*. 6th ed. Vancouver, Canada: Talonbooks, 2012.
Coleman, Daniel. *White Civility: The Literary Project of English Canada*. Toronto: University of Toronto Press, 2008.
Colorado Department of Human Services. "Country of Origin of Colorado Refugee and Refugee Eligible Population." Colorado Office of Economic Security, Division of Refugee Services. https://sites.google.com/a/state.co.us/cdhs-refugee/about-refugees/data-and-arrival-information.
Coltelli, Laura. "*Almanac of the Dead*: An Interview with Leslie Marmon Silko." Reprinted from *Native American Literature Forum* 4–5 (1992–1993): 65–80. In *Conversations with Leslie Marmon Silko*, edited by Ellen L. Arnold, 119–134. Jackson: University Press of Mississippi, 2000.
Cook-Lynn, Elizabeth. "The American Indian Fiction Writers: Cosmopolitanism, Nationalism, the Third World, and First Nation Sovereignty." In *Nothing but the Truth: An Anthology of Native American Literature*, edited by John Purdy and James Ruppert, 23–38. Upper Saddle River, NJ: Prentice Hall, 2001.
Coulthard, Glen Sean. *Red Skin, White Masks: Rejecting the Colonial Politics of Recognition*. Minneapolis: University of Minnesota Press, 2014.
———. "Subjects of Empire: Indigenous Peoples and the 'Politics of Recognition' in Canada." *Contemporary Political Theory* 6.4 (2007): 437–460.
Coulthard, Glen Sean, and Leanne Betasamosake Simpson. "Grounded Normativity/Place-Based Solidarity." *American Quarterly* 68.2 (June 2016): 249–255.
Cox, James H. *The Red Land to the South: American Indian Writers and Indigenous Mexico*. Minneapolis: University of Minnesota Press, 2012.
Daniel, G. Reginald, Laura Kina, Wei Ming Dariotis, and Camilla Fojas. "Emerging Paradigms in Critical Mixed Race Studies." *Journal of Critical Mixed Race Studies* 1.1 (2014): 6–65.
Daniels, Roger, Sandra C. Taylor, and Harry H. L. Kitano. *Japanese Americans: From Relocation to Redress*. Salt Lake City: University of Utah Press, 1986.
Day, Iyko. *Alien Capital: Asian Racialization and the Logic of Settler Colonial Capitalism*. Durham, NC: Duke University Press, 2016.
———. "Alien Intimacies: The Coloniality of Japanese Internment in Australia, Canada, and the US." *Amerasia Journal* 36.2 (2010): 107–124.
———. "Being or Nothingness: Antiblackness, and Settler Colonial Critique." *Critical Ethnic Studies* 1.2 (2015): 102–121.
———. "Must All Asianness Be American? The Census, Racial Classification, and Asian Canadian Emergence." *Canadian Literature* 199 (2008): 45–70.
Deleuze, Gilles, and Felix Guattari. *Anti-Oedipus: Capitalism and Schizophrenia*. Minneapolis: University of Minnesota Press, 1983.

Deloria, Philip. *Playing Indian*. New Haven, CT: Yale University Press, 1998.
Deloria, Vine, Jr. *Custer Died for Your Sins: An Indian Manifesto*. 1969. Norman: University of Oklahoma Press, 1988.
———. *God Is Red: A Native View of Religion*. Golden, CO: Fulcrum Publishing, 1994.
———. *Red Earth, White Lies: Native Americans and the Myth of Scientific Fact*. Golden, CO: Fulcrum Publishing, 1997.
DeLugan, Robin Maria. "Indigeneity across Borders: Hemispheric Migrations and Cosmopolitan Encounters." *American Ethnologist* 37.1 (2010): 83–97.
Dippie, Brian. *The Vanishing American: White Attitudes and U.S. Indian Policy*. Lawrence: University Press of Kansas, 1982.
Drayton, Richard. "Gilberto Freyre and the Twentieth-Century Rethinking of Race in Latin America." *Portuguese Studies* 27.1 (2011): 43–47.
Eng, David L. *The Feeling of Kinship: Queer Liberalism and the Racialization of Intimacy*. Durham, NC: Duke University Press, 2010.
Findlay, Len M. "Spectres of Canada: Image, Text, Aura, Nation." *University of Toronto Quarterly* 75.2 (2006): 656–672.
Fishkin, Shelley Fisher. "Crossroads of Cultures: The Transnational Turn in American Studies—Presidential Address to the American Studies Association, November 12, 2004." *American Quarterly* 57.1 (2005): 17–57.
Fiske, Jo-Anne. "Political Status of Native Indian Women: Contradictory Implications of Canadian State Policy." *American Indian Culture and Research Journal* 19.2 (1995): 1–30.
Foucault, Michel. *The Order of Things: An Archaeology of the Human Sciences*. New York: Routledge Classics, 2004.
French, Jan Hoffman. *Legalizing Identities: Becoming Black or Indian in Brazil's Northeast*. Chapel Hill: University of North Carolina Press, 2009.
Freyre, Gilberto. *The Masters and the Slaves: A Study in the Development of Brazilian Civilization*. Berkeley: University of California Press, 1986.
———. *New World in the Tropics: The Culture of Modern Brazil*. 1945. New York: Alfred A. Knopf, 1959.
Fujikane, Candace. "Sweeping Racism under the Rug of 'Censorship': The Controversy over Lois-Ann Yamanaka's *Blu's Hanging*." *Amerasia Journal* 26.2 (2000): 159–194.
Fujikane, Candace, and Jonathan Y. Okamura, eds. *Asian Settler Colonialism: From Local Governance to the Habits of Everyday Life in Hawai'i*. Honolulu: University of Hawai'i Press, 2008.
Fujita, Gayle K. "'To Attend to the Sound of Stone': The Sensibility of Silence in *Obasan*." *MELUS: Multi-Ethnic Literature of the U.S.* 12.3 (1985): 33–42.
Gamio, Manuel. *Forjano patria: Pro-nacionalismo (Forging a Nation)*. 1916. Reprint, Boulder: University Press of Colorado, 2010.
Garfield, Seth. *Indigenous Struggle at the Heart of Brazil: State Policy, Frontier Expansion, and the Xavante Indians, 1937–1988*. Durham, NC: Duke University Press, 2001.
Gercken, Becca. "The Business of Crazy Horse: Indian Honor and Masculinity in Sherman Alexie's *Fancydancing*." *North Dakota Quarterly* 76.4 (2009): 37–48.
Gonzales, Ray. "The Past Is Right Here and Now: An Interview with Leslie Marmon Silko." In *Conversations with Leslie Marmon Silko*, edited by Ellen L. Arnold, 97–106. Jackson: University Press of Mississippi, 2000.

González Casanova, Pablo. "Colonialismo interno (una redefinición)." *Revista Rebeldía* 12 (2003). www.revistarebeldia.org/revistas/012/art06.html.
Gott, Richard. "Latin America as White Settler Society." *Bulletin of Latin American Research* 26.2 (2007): 269–289.
Gramsci, Antonio. *Selections from the Prison Notebooks*. Edited by Quintin Hoare and Geoffrey Nowell Smith. New York: International Publishers, 1971.
Green, Joyce. "Towards a Détente with History: Confronting Canada's Colonial Legacy." *International Journal of Canadian Studies* 12 (1995): 85–105.
"Greg Sarris: A Native American Finds His Roots." *FilamStar: The Newspaper for Filipinos in Mainstream America*, April 21, 2016. https://filamstar.com/greg-sarris-a-native-american-finds-his-filipino-roots/.
Grice, Helena. "Reading the Nonverbal: The Indices of Space, Time, Tactility and Taciturnity in Joy Kogawa's *Obasan*." *MELUS: Multi-Ethnic Literature of the U.S.* 24.4 (1999): 93–105.
Harper, Stephen. "House of Commons Apology to Inuit, Métis, and First Nations Peoples of Residential Schools, 2008." In *Reconciling Canada: Critical Perspectives on the Culture of Redress*, edited by Jennifer Henderson and Pauline Wakeham, 335–337. Toronto, Canada: University of Toronto Press, 2013.
Harvey, David. *A Brief History of Neoliberalism*. New York: Oxford University Press, 2007.
———. *The Condition of Postmodernity: An Enquiry into the Origins of Cultural Change*. London: Blackwell, 1989.
Hatamiya, Leslie T. *Righting a Wrong: Japanese Americans and the Passage of the Civil Liberties Act of 1988*. Palo Alto, CA: Stanford University Press, 1994.
Hattori, Tomo. "China Man Autoeroticism and the Remains of Asian America." *NOVEL: A Forum on Fiction* 31.2 (1998): 215–236.
Helenius, Marja-Liisa. "Darker Side of Mediation: Violence and Its Emotional Effects in Leslie Marmon Silko's *Almanac of the Dead*." *Electronic Journal of the Department of English at the University of Helsinki* 5 (2005). https://blogs.helsinki.fi/hes-eng/volumes/volume-5/darker-side-of-mediation-violence-and-its-emotional-effects-in-leslie-marmon-silko%E2%80%99s-almanac-of-the-dead-marja-liisa-helenius/.
Henderson, Jennifer, and Pauline Wakeham, eds. *Reconciling Canada: Critical Perspectives on the Culture of Redress*. Toronto, Canada: University of Toronto Press, 2013.
Hirabayashi, Lane Ryo, Akemi Kikumura-Yano, and James A. Hirabayashi, eds. *New Worlds, New Lives: Globalization and People of Japanese Descent in the Americas and from Latin America in Japan*. Palo Alto, CA: Stanford University Press, 2002.
Holland, Sharon P. "'If You Know I Have a History, You Will Respect Me': A Perspective on Afro-Native American Literature." *Callaloo* 17.1 (1994): 334–350.
Holm, Tom. *Strong Hearts, Wounded Souls: Native American Veterans of the Vietnam War*. Austin: University of Texas Press, 1996.
Hong, Grace Kyungwon, and Roderick A. Ferguson, eds. *Strange Affinities: The Gender and Sexual Politics of Racialization*. Durham, NC: Duke University Press, 2011.
Howe, LeAnne. "The Chaos of Angels." *Callaloo* 17.1 (1994): 108–114.
Huang, Hsinya, Philip Deloria, Laura Furlan, and John Gamber, eds. Special forum on "Charting Transnational Native American Studies: Aesthetics, Politics, Identity." *Journal of Transnational American Studies* 4.1 (2012): n.p. https://escholarship.org/uc/acgcc_jtas/4/1.

Hu-Dehart, Evelyn. "Introduction: Asian American Formations in the Age of Globalization." In *Across the Pacific: Asian Americans and Globalization*, edited by Evelyn Hu-Dehart, 1–28. Philadelphia: Temple University Press, 1999.

Huhndorf, Shari. *Going Native: Indians in the American Cultural Imagination*. Ithaca, NY: Cornell University Press, 2001.

———. *Mapping the Americas: The Transnational Politics of Contemporary Native Culture*. Ithaca, NY: Cornell University Press, 2009.

Hutcheon, Linda. "Historiographic Metafiction: Parody and the Intertextuality of History." In *Intertextuality and Contemporary American Fiction*, edited by P. O'Donnell and Robert Con Davis, 3–32. Baltimore, MD: Johns Hopkins University Press, 1989.

———. *Poetics of Postmodernism: History, Theory, Fiction*. London: Routledge, 1988.

Inouye, Karen M. *The Long Afterlife of Wartime Incarceration*. Palo Alto, CA: Stanford University Press, 2016.

Islas, Arturo, and Marilyn Yalon. "Interview with Maxine Hong Kingston." In *Conversations with Maxine Hong Kingston*, edited by Paul Skenazy and Tera Martin, 21–32. Jackson: University Press of Mississippi, 1998.

Jackson, Shona. *Creole Indigeneity: Between Myth and Nation in the Caribbean*. Minneapolis: University of Minnesota Press, 2012.

Jacobs, Margaret D. "The Eastmans and the Luhans: Interracial Marriage between White Women and Native American Men, 1875–1935." *Frontier* 23.3 (2002): 29–54.

Jafri, Beenash. "Desire, Settler Colonialism, and the Racialized Cowboy." *American Indian Culture and Research Journal* 37.2 (2013): 73–86.

Jun, Helen. *Race for Citizenship: Black Orientalism and Asian Uplift from Pre-Emancipation to Neoliberal America*. New York: New York University Press, 2011.

Kamboureli, Smaro. *Scandalous Bodies: Diasporic Literature in English*. Waterloo, Canada: Wilfrid Laurier University Press, 2009.

Kamboureli, Smaro, and Christl Verduyn, eds. *Critical Collaborations: Indigeneity, Diaspora, and Ecology in Canadian Literary Studies*. Waterloo, Canada: Wilfrid Laurier University Press, 2014.

Kauanui, J. Kēhaulani. "Colonialism in Equality: Hawaiian Sovereignty and the Question of Civil Rights." *South Atlantic Quarterly* 107.4 (2008): 635–650.

———. *Hawaiian Blood: Colonialism and the Politics of Sovereignty and Indigeneity*. Durham, NC: Duke University Press, 2008.

Kim, Christine. *The Minor Intimacies of Race: Asian Publics in North America*. Urbana: University of Illinois Press, 2016.

Kim, Claire Jean. "The Racial Triangulation of Asian Americans." *Politics and Society* 27.1 (1999): 105–138.

Kim, Jodi. *Ends of Empire: Asian American Critique and the Cold War*. Minneapolis: University of Minnesota Press, 2010.

Kingston, Maxine Hong. *China Men*. 1980. Reprint, New York: Ballantine Books, 1981.

———. *The Woman Warrior: Memoirs of a Girlhood among Ghosts*. 1976. Reprint, New York: Vintage International, 1989.

Kipling, Rudyard. "The White Man's Burden: The United States and the Philippine Island, 1899." *McClure's Magazine* 12 (February 1899).

Knight, Alan. "Race, Revolution, and *Indigenismo*: Mexico, 1910–1940." In *The Idea of Race in Latin America, 1870–1940,* edited by Richard Graham, 71–114. Austin: University of Texas Press, 1990.

Kobayashi, Audrey. "The Japanese-Canadian Redress Settlement and Its Implications for 'Race Relations.'" *Canadian Ethnic Studies* 24.1 (1992): 1–19.
Kogawa, Joy. *Obasan*. 1981. Reprint, New York: Anchor Books, 1994.
Koshy, Susan. "Why the Humanities Matter for Race Studies Today." *PMLA* 123.5 (October 2008): 1542–1549.
Lai, Larissa. "Epistemologies of Respect: A Poetics of Asian/Indigenous Relations." In *Critical Collaborations: Indigeneity, Diaspora, and Ecology in Canadian Literary Studies,* edited by Smaro Kamboureli and Christl Verduyn, 99–126. Waterloo, Canada: Wilfrid Laurier University Press, 2014.
Lai, Paul, and Lindsay Claire Smith, eds. "Alternative Contact: Indigeneity, Globalism, and American Studies." Special issue, *American Quarterly* 62.3 (2010): 407–436.
"Larry Grant: Intertwining Cultures." Chinese Canadian Stories. Citizenship and Immigration Canada, University of British Columbia, Simon Fraser University. December 30, 2016. https://acam.arts.ubc.ca/community-projects/chinese-canadian-stories/.
"Larry Grant: Not Belonging." Chinese Canadian Stories. Citizenship and Immigration Canada, University of British Columbia, Simon Fraser University. December 30, 2016. http://ccs.library.ubc.ca/en/videos/ccs_intertwining_cultures.html.
Lau, Chrissy Yee. "Ashamed of Certain Japanese: The Politics of Affect in Japanese Women's Immigration Exclusion, 1919–1924." In *Gendering the Trans-Pacific World: Diaspora, Empire, and Race,* edited by Catherine Ceniza Choy and Judy Tzu-Chun Wu, 196–220. Leiden, Netherlands: Brill Press, 2017.
Lawrence, Bonita. *"Real" Indians and Others: Mixed-Blood Urban Native Peoples and Indigenous Nationhood*. Lincoln: University of Nebraska Press, 2004.
Lawrence, Bonita, and Zanaib Amadahy. "Indigenous Peoples and Black People in Canada: Settlers or Allies?" In *Breaching the Colonial Contract: Anti-Colonialism in the US and Canada,* edited by Arlo Kempf, 105–135. Berlin/Heidelberg, Germany: Springer Science, 2009.
Lawrence, Bonita, and Enakshi Dua. "Decolonizing Anti-racism." *Social Justice* 32.4 (2005): 120–143.
Lee, Anderson. "A Mother's Memories." *Ricepaper Magazine* 17.3–4 (2012): 56.
Lee, Erika. "Orientalism in the Americas: A Hemispheric Approach to Asian-American History." *Journal of Asian American Studies* 8.3 (2005): 235–256.
Lee, James Kyung-jin. "Asian Americans." In *The Cambridge Companion to Modern American Culture*, edited by Christopher Bigsby, 174–193. Cambridge: Cambridge University Press, 2007.
———. "The Transitivity of Race and the Challenge of the Imagination." Special issue, *PMLA* 123.5 (2008): 1550–1556.
———. *Urban Triage: Race and the Fictions of Multiculturalism*. Minneapolis: University of Minnesota Press, 2004.
Lee, Julia H. *Interracial Encounters: Reciprocal Representations in African and Asian American Literatures, 1896–1937*. New York: New York University Press, 2011.
———. "The Railroad as Message in Maxine Hong Kingston's *China Men* and Frank Chin's 'Riding the Rails with Chickencoop Slim.'" *Journal of Asian American Studies* 18.3 (2015): 265–287.
Lee, Rachel. *The Americas of Asian American Literature: Gendered Fictions of Nation and Transnation*. Princeton, NJ: Princeton University Press, 1999.

Leong, Karen J., and Myla Vicenti Carpio, eds. "Carceral States: Converging Indigenous and Asian Experiences in the Americas." Special issue, *Amerasia Journal* 42.1 (2016): vii–xvii.

Lesser, Jeffrey. *A Discontented Diaspora: Japanese Brazilians and the Meanings of Ethnic Militancy, 1960–1980*. Durham, NC: Duke University Press, 2007.

———. "In Search of the Hyphen: Nikkei and the Struggle over Brazilian National Identity." In *New Worlds, New Lives: Globalization and People of Japanese Descent in the Americas and from Latin America in Japan*, edited by Lane R. Hirabayashi, Akemi Kikumura-Yano, and James A. Hirabayashi, 37–58. Stanford, CA: Stanford University Press, 2002.

Leung, Diane E., and Kamala Todd, dirs. *Cedar and Bamboo*. Moving Images Distribution, 2010. Film.

Levander, Caroline F., and Robert S. Levine, eds., *Hemispheric American Studies*. New Brunswick, NJ: Rutgers University Press, 2007.

Li, David Leiwei. "Maxine Hong Kingston and the American Canon." *American Literary History* 2.3 (1990): 482–502.

Lien-Worrall, Brandy. *Eating Stories: A Chinese Canadian and Aboriginal Potluck*. Vancouver: Chinese Canadian Historical Society of British Columbia, 2007.

Lightfoot, Sheryl. "Settler State Apologies to Indigenous Peoples: A Normative Framework and Comparative Assessment." *Native American and Indigenous Studies* 2 (2015): 15–39.

Lim, Shirley Geok-lin. "Japanese American Women's Life Stories: Maternality in Monica Sone's *Nisei Daughter* and Joy Kogawa's *Obasan*." *Feminist Studies* 16.2 (1990): 288–312.

———. "The Native and the Diasporic: Owning America in Native American and Asian American Literatures." *Women's Studies Quarterly* 34 (2006): 295–307.

Ling, Jinqi. *Narrating Nationalisms: Ideology and Form in Asian American Literature*. Oxford: Oxford University Press, 1998.

Llewelyn, Jennifer J. "Bridging the Gap between Truth and Reconciliation: Restorative Justice and the Indian Residential School Truth and Reconciliation Commission." In *From Truth to Reconciliation: Transforming the Legacy of Residential Schools*, edited by Marlene Brant Castellano, Linda Archibald, and Mike DeGagné, 183–204. Ottawa, Canada: Aboriginal Healing Foundation, 2008.

Lo, Marie. "Model Minorities, Models of Resistance: Native Figures in Asian Canadian Literature." *Canadian Literature* 196 (2008): 96–112.

———. "Passing Recognition: *Obasan* and the Borders of Asian American and Canadian Literary Criticism." *Comparative American Studies* 5.3 (2007): 307–332.

Lowe, Lisa. *Immigrant Acts: On Asian American Cultural Politics*. Durham, NC: Duke University Press, 1996.

———. *The Intimacies of Four Continents*. Durham, NC: Duke University Press, 2015.

Mawani, Renisa. *Colonial Proximities: Crossracial Encounters and Juridical Truths in British Columbia, 1871–1921*. Vancouver, Canada: University of British Columbia, 2009.

McAllister, Kirsten Emiko. "Narrating Japanese Canadians in and out of the Canadian Nation: A Critique of Realist Forms of Representation." *Canadian Journal of Communication* 24 (1999): 79–103.

———. *Terrain of Memory: A Japanese Canadian Memorial Project.* Vancouver: University of British Columbia Press, 2010.
McGonegal, Julie. "The Future of Racial Memory: Forgiveness, Reconciliation, and Redress in Joy Kogawa's *Obasan* and *Itsuka*." *Studies in Canadian Literature* 30.2 (2005): 55–78.
Medak-Saltzman, Danika. "Empire's Haunted Logics: Comparative Colonialisms and the Challenges of Incorporating Indigeneity." *Journal of the Critical Ethnic Studies Association* 1.2 (2015): 11–32.
Medak-Saltzman, Danika, and Antonio Tiongson Jr., eds. "Racial Comparativism Reconsidered." Special issue, *Critical Ethnic Studies Association Journal* 2.1 (2015).
Miki, Arthur K. *The Japanese Canadian Redress Legacy: A Community Revitalized.* Winnipeg: National Association of Japanese Canadians, 2003.
Miki, Roy. *Redress: Inside the Japanese Canadian Call for Justice.* Vancouver, Canada: Raincoast Books, 2004.
Miki, Roy, and Cassandra Kobayashi, eds. *Justice in Our Time: The Japanese Canadian Redress Settlement.* Vancouver, Canada: Talonbooks/NAJC, 1991.
———, eds. *Spirit of Redress: Japanese Canadians in Conference.* Vancouver, Canada: Talonbooks/NAJC, 1989.
Million, Dian. "Felt Theory: An Indigenous Feminist Approach to Affect and History." *Wicazo Sa Review* 24.2 (2009): 53–76.
———. *Therapeutic Nations: Healing in an Age of Indigenous Human Rights.* Tucson: University of Arizona Press, 2013.
Miyoshi, Masao. "Sites of Resistance in the Global Economy." *boundary 2: an international journal of literature and culture* 22.1 (1995): 61–84.
Mohanty, Satya. *Literary Theory and the Claims of History: Postmodernism, Objectivity, Multicultural Politics.* Ithaca, NY: Cornell University Press, 1997.
Moraga, Cherríe, and Gloria Anzaldúa, eds. *This Bridge Called My Back: Writings by Radical Women of Color.* New York: Kitchen Table, 1983.
Moreton-Robinson, Aileen, ed. *Sovereign Subjects: Indigenous Sovereignty Matters.* Crows Nest, Australia: Allen and Unwin, 2007.
———. *The White Possessive: Property, Power, and Indigenous Sovereignty.* Minneapolis: University of Minnesota Press, 2015.
Mulroney, Brian. "House of Commons Apology to Japanese Canadians, 1988." In *Reconciling Canada: Critical Perspectives on The Culture of Redress,* edited by Jennifer Henderson and Pauline Wakeham, 435–437. Toronto, Canada: University of Toronto Press, 2013.
Nakayama, Gordon G. *Issei: Stories of Japanese Canadian Pioneers.* Toronto, Canada: NC Press, 1984.
Nandy, Ashis. *The Intimate Enemy: Loss and the Recovery of Self under Colonialism.* Delhi, India: Oxford University Press, 1989.
Ngai, Sianne. *Ugly Feelings.* Cambridge, MA: Harvard University Press, 2007.
Nguyen, Viet Thanh. *Race and Resistance: Literature and Politics in Asian America.* Oxford: Oxford University Press, 2002.
Niemann, Linda. "Narratives of Survival." In *Conversations with Leslie Marmon Silko,* edited by Ellen L. Arnold, 107–112. Jackson: University Press of Mississippi, 2000.
Niezen, Ronald. *Truth and Indignation: Canada's Truth and Reconciliation Commission on Indian Residential Schools.* Toronto, Canada: University of Toronto Press, 2013.

Ninh, erin Khuê. *Ingratitude: The Debt-Bound Daughter in Asian American Literature.* New York: New York University Press, 2011.
O'Brien, Jean M. *Firsting and Lasting: Writing Indians Out of Existence in New England.* Minneapolis: University of Minnesota Press, 2010.
Oikawa, Mona. *Cartographies of Violence: Japanese Canadian Women, Memory, and the Subjects of Internment.* Toronto, Canada: University of Toronto Press, 2012.
———. "Connecting the Internment of Japanese Canadians to the Colonization of Aboriginal Peoples in Canada." In *Aboriginal Connections to Race, Environment, and Traditions,* edited by R. Riewe and J. Oakes, 17–27. Winnipeg, Canada: Aboriginal Issues Press, 2006.
Okihiro, Gary Y. *Margins and Mainstreams: Asians in American History and Culture.* Seattle: University of Washington Press, 1994.
Omatsu, Maryka. *Bittersweet Passage: Redress and the Japanese Canadian Experience.* Toronto, Canada: Between the Lines, 1992.
Omi, Michael, and Howard Winant. *Racial Formations in the United States: From the 1960s to the 1990s.* New York: Routledge, 1994.
Ortiz, Simon. *from Sand Creek.* 1981. Reprint, Tucson: University of Arizona Press, 2000.
Owens, Louis. *Mixed-Blood Messages.* Norman: University of Oklahoma Press, 1998.
Oxford English Dictionary Online. Oxford: Oxford University Press, 2017. www.oed.com. Accessed October 10, 2017.
Parikh, Crystal. *An Ethics of Betrayal: The Politics of Otherness in Emergent U.S. Literature and Culture.* New York: Fordham University Press, 2011.
Patel, Shaista, Ghaida Moussa, and Nishant Upadhyay, eds. "Complicities, Connections, and Struggles: Critical Transnational Feminist Analyses of Settler Colonialism." Special issue, *Feral Feminisms* 4 (2015): 5–19.
Pegues, Juliana Hu. "Rethinking Relations: Interracial Intimacies of Asian Men and Native Women in Alaskan Canneries." *Interventions: International Journal of Postcolonial Studies* 15.1 (2013): 55–66.
Phung, Malissa. "Asian-Indigenous Relationalities: Literary Gestures of Respect and Gratitude." *Canadian Literature* 227 (Winter 2015): 56–72.
Piatote, Beth Hege. *Domestic Subjects: Gender, Citizenship, and Law in Native American Literature.* New Haven, CT: Yale University Press, 2013.
Porto, Mauro. "Telenovelas and Representations of National Identity in Brazil." *Media, Culture, and Society* 3.1 (2011): 53–69.
Povinelli, Elizabeth. *Economies of Abandonment: Social Belonging and Endurance in Late Liberalism.* Durham, NC: Duke University Press, 2011.
Prashad, Vijay. *Everybody Was Kung Fu Fighting: Afro-Asian Connections and the Myth of Cultural Purity.* Boston: Beacon Press, 2002.
Pulido, Laura. *Black, Brown, Yellow, and Left: Radical Activism in Los Angeles.* Berkeley: University of California Press, 2006.
Quijano, Anibal. "Coloniality of Power, Eurocentrism, and Latin America." *Nepantla: Views from the South* 1.3 (2000): 533–580.
Radway, Janice. "What's in a Name?" *American Quarterly* 51.1 (1999): 1–32.
Reynaud, Anne-Marie. "Dealing with Difficult Emotions: Anger at the Truth and Reconciliation Commission of Canada." *Anthropologica* 56.2 (2012): 369–382.
Rifkin, Mark. *Beyond Settler Time: Temporal Sovereignty and Indigenous Self-Determination.* Durham, NC: Duke University Press, 2017.

———. *Settler Common Sense: Queerness and Everyday Colonialism in the American Renaissance*. Minneapolis: University of Minnesota Press, 2014.
Rivera Cusicanqui, Silvia. "Pachakuti: The Historical Horizons of Internal Colonialism." Published as "Aymara Past, Aymara Future" in *NACLA* 25.3 (1991): 18–23.
Roediger, David. "Making Solidarity Uneasy: Cautions on a Keyword from Black Lives Matter to the Past." *American Quarterly* 68.2 (June 2016): 223–248.
Rosaldo, Renato. *Culture and Truth: The Remaking of Social Analysis*. Boston: Beacon Press, 1993.
Roy, Patricia E. *A White Man's Province: British Columbia Politicians and Chinese and Japanese Immigrants, 1858–1914*. Vancouver, Canada: University of British Columbia Press, 1989.
Rymhs, Deena. *From the Iron House: Imprisonment in First Nations Writing*. Waterloo, Canada: Wilfrid Laurier University Press, 2008.
Sadowski-Smith, Claudia. *Border Fictions: Globalization, Empire, and Writing at the Boundaries of the United States*. Charlottesville: University of Virginia Press, 2008.
Sadowski-Smith, Claudia, and Claire Fox. "Theorizing the Hemisphere: Inter-Americas Work at the Intersections of American, Canadian, and Latin American Studies." *Comparative American Studies* 2.1 (2004): 5–38.
Saldaña-Portillo, María Josefina. *The Revolutionary Imagination in the Americas and the Age of Development*. Durham, NC: Duke University Press, 2003.
Saldívar, José David. *The Dialectics of Our America: Genealogy, Cultural Critique, and Literary History*. Durham, NC: Duke University Press, 1991.
Santa Ana, Jeffrey. *Racial Feelings: Asian America in a Capitalist Culture of Emotion*. Philadelphia: Temple University Press, 2015.
Saranillio, Dean Itsuji. "Why Asian Settler Colonialism Matters: A Thought Piece on Critiques, Debates, and Indigenous Difference." *Settler Colonial Studies* 3.3–4 (2013): 280–294.
Sarris, Greg. *Keeping Slug Woman Alive*. Berkeley: University of California Press, 1993.
———. *Mabel McKay: Weaving the Dream*. Berkeley: University of California Press, 1994.
Sayre, Gordon M. *The Indian Chief as Tragic Hero: Native Resistance and the Literatures of America, from Moctezuma to Tecumseh*. Chapel Hill: University of North Carolina Press, 2005.
Schacht, Miriam. "Movement Must Be Emulated by the People: Rootedness, Migration, and Indigenous Internationalism in Leslie Marmon Silko's *Almanac of the Dead*." *SAIL* 21.4 (2009): 53–70.
Schlund-Vials, Cathy. *Modeling Citizenship: Jewish and Asian American Writing*. Philadelphia: Temple University Press, 2010.
Sedgewick, Mitchell W. *Globalisation and Japanese Organisational Culture: An Ethnography of Japanese Corporations in France*. New York: Routledge, 2007.
Sexton, Jared. *Amalgamation Schemes: Antiblackness and the Critique of Multiracialism*. Minneapolis: University of Minnesota Press, 2008.
Shibata, Yuko, Hayashi R. Matsumoto, Rintaro Hayashi, and Shotaro Iida. *The Forgotten History of Japanese-Canadians*. Vol. 1. Vancouver, Canada: New Sun Books, 1966.
Shibusawa, Naoko. "Femininity, Race and Treachery: How 'Tokyo Rose' Became a Traitor to the United States after the Second World War." *Gender and History* 22.1 (April 2010): 169–188.

Shigematsu, Setsu, and Keith Camacho, eds. *Militarized Currents: Toward a Decolonized Future in Asian and the Pacific*. Minneapolis: University of Minnesota Press, 2010.

Shih, Shu-mei. "Comparative Racialization: An Introduction." Special issue, *PMLA* 123.5 (2008): 1347–1362.

Shohat, Ella, and Robert Stam. "Genealogies of Orientalism and Occidentalism: Sephardi Jews, Muslims, and the Americas." *Studies in American Jewish Literature* 35.1 (2016): 13–32.

Silko, Leslie Marmon. *Almanac of the Dead*. 1991. Reprint, New York: Penguin Books, 1992.

———. *Ceremony*. 1977. Reprint, New York: Penguin Books, 2006.

Silva, Noenoe K. *Aloha Betrayed: Native Hawaiian Resistance to American Colonialism* Durham, NC: Duke University Press, 2004.

Simon, Roger I. "Towards a Hopeful Practice of Worrying: The Problematics of Listening and the Educative Responsibilities of Canada's Truth and Reconciliation Commission." In *Reconciling Canada: Critical Perspectives on the Culture of Redress*, edited by Jennifer Henderson and Pauline Wakeham, 129–142. Toronto, Canada: University of Toronto Press, 2013.

Simpson, Audra. "Consent's Revenge." *Cultural Anthropology* 31.3 (2016): 326–333.

Smith, Andrea. *Native Americans and the Christian Right: The Gendered Politics of Unlikely Alliances*. Durham, NC: Duke University Press, 2008.

Smith, Linda Tuhiwai. *Decolonizing Methodologies: Research and Indigenous Peoples*. London: Zed Books, 1999.

Sokolowski, Jeanne. "Between Dangerous Extremes: Victimization, Ultranationalism, and Identity Performance in Gerald Vizenor's *Hiroshima Bugi: Atomu 57*." *American Quarterly* 62.3 (2010): 717–738.

Speed, Shannon. "Structures of Settler Capitalism in Abya Yala." *American Quarterly* 69.4 (2017): 783–790.

Stoler, Ann Laura. "Intimidations of Empire: Predicaments of the Tactile and Unseen." In *Haunted by Empire: Geographies of Intimacy in North American History*, edited by Ann Laura Stoler, 1–22. Durham, NC: Duke University Press, 2006.

Sugiman, Momoye, ed. *Japanese Canadian Redress: The Toronto Story*. Toronto, Canada: HpF Press, 2000.

Takaki, Ronald. *Iron Cages: Race and Culture in 19th Century America*. 1979. New York: Oxford University Press, 2000.

———. *Pau Hana: Plantation Life and Labor in Hawaii*. Honolulu: University of Hawai'i Press, 1984.

Takezawa, Yasuko I. *Breaking the Silence: Redress and Japanese American Ethnicity*. Ithaca, NY: Cornell University Press, 1995.

Teuton, Sean Kiccumah. *Red Land, Red Power: Grounding Knowledge in the American Indian Novel*. Durham, NC: Duke University Press, 2008.

Thobani, Sunera. *Exalted Subjects: Studies in the Making of Race and Nation in Canada*. Toronto, Canada: University of Toronto Press, 2007.

Thomas, David Hurst. *Skull Wars: Kennewick Man, Archaeology, and the Battle for Native American Identity*. New York: Basic Books, 2001.

Trask, Haunani-Kay. *From a Native Daughter: Colonialism and Sovereignty in Hawai'i*. Honolulu: University of Hawai'i Press, 1999.

———. "Settlers of Color and 'Immigrant' Hegemony: 'Locals' in Hawaiʻi." In *Asian Settler Colonialism: From Local Governance to the Habits of Everyday Life in Hawaiʻi*, edited by Candace Fujikane and Jonathan Y. Okamura, 45–65. Honolulu: University of Hawaiʻi Press, 2008.
Truth and Reconciliation Commission of Canada (TRC). "Honoring the Truth, Reconciling for the Future." Summary of the Final Report of the TRC, 2015. http://www.trc.ca/websites/trcinstitution/index.php?p=890.
Tsuchida, Nobuya. *American Justice: Japanese American Evacuation and Redress*. Minneapolis: Asian/Pacific American Learning Resource Center, University of Minnesota, 1988.
Tuck, Eve, and K. Wayne Yang. "Decolonization Is Not a Metaphor." *Decolonization: Indigeneity, Education, and Society* 1.1 (2012): 1–40.
Turner, Frederick Jackson. *The Frontier in American History*. New York: Henry Holt, 1920.
Vasconcelos, José. *The Cosmic Race/La raza cósmica*. Translated by Didier T. Jaén. 1925. Reprint, Baltimore: John Hopkins University Press, 1979.
Veracini, Lorenzo. *Settler Colonialism: A Theoretical Overview*. Basingstoke, UK: Palgrave, 2010.
Vizenor, Gerald R. *Griever: An American Monkey King in China*. Minneapolis: University of Minnesota Press, 1987.
———. *Hiroshima Bugi: Atomu 57*. Lincoln: University of Nebraska Press, 2003.
———. *Manifest Manners: Narratives on Postindian Survivance*. Lincoln: University of Nebraska Press, 1999.
Volpp, Leti. "American Mestizo: Filipinos and Anti-miscegenation Laws in California." *UC Davis Law Review* 33.4 (2000): 795–835.
Warrior, Robert. "Native American Scholarship and the Transnational Turn." *Cultural Studies Review* 15.2 (2009): 119–130.
Weaver, Jace. *That the People Might Live: Native American Literatures and Native American Community*. New York: Oxford University Press, 1997.
Williams, Maria *Shaa Tláa*. "Alaska and Its People: An Introduction." In *The Alaska Native Reader: History, Culture, Politics*, ed. Maria *Shaa Tláa* Williams. Durham, NC: Duke University Press, 2009.
Williams, Raymond. *Marxism and Literature*. Oxford: Oxford University Press, 1977.
Wolfe, Patrick. *Settler Colonialism and the Transformation of Anthropology: The Politics and Poetics of an Ethnographic Event*. London: Cassell, 1999.
Wong, Lily. *Transpacific Attachments: Sex Work, Media Networks, and Affective Histories of Chineseness*. New York: Columbia University Press, 2018.
Wong, Rita. "Decolonizasian: Reading Asian and First Nations Relations in Literature." *Canadian Literature* 199 (Winter 2008): 158–180.
Wong, Sau-ling Cynthia. "Autobiography as a Guided Chinatown Tour." In *Maxine Hong Kingston's* The Woman Warrior*: A Casebook*, edited by Sau-ling Cynthia Wong, 29–56. Oxford: Oxford University Press, 1999.
———. "Denationalization Reconsidered: Asian American Cultural Criticism at a Theoretical Crossroads." *Amerasia Journal* 21.1–2 (1995): 1–27.
Wright, Sharel. "Granddaughter Will Remember." *Ricepaper Magazine* 17.3–4 (2012): 52–56.

Yamashita, Karen Tei. *Through the Arc of the Rain Forest*. Minneapolis, MN: Coffee House Press, 1990.
Yang, Caroline H. "Indispensable Labor: The Worker as a Category of Critique in *China Men*." *Modern Fiction Studies* 56.1 (2010): 63–89.
Yoneyama, Lisa. *Cold War Ruins: Transpacific Critique of American Justice and Japanese War Crimes*. Durham, NC: Duke University Press, 2016.
Yoshizawa, Alejandro, dir. *All Our Father's Relations*. Canada: Right Relations Production, 2016. Film.

Index

"accumulation by dispossession," 116
adoption, 142, 143, 146, 151–152, 154, 155
affect, 158, 176n54; *Burning Vision* on, 91, 92;
   Canadian redress and reconciliation, 61, 64,
   66–71, 93–94; emotions in relation to, 16;
   ideology distinguished from, 16, 178n57;
   Obasan on, 77, 79; in relation to settler
   racial tense, 16–18
Ah Goong, 39–40, 41, 45–46
Ahmed, Sara, 16, 17, 62, 66
Alexie, Sherman, 33
"aliens," Asians as, 5, 10–11, 13, 41, 88,
   124–125, 158
Almanac of the Dead (Silko), 23, 96–97, 98,
   115, 116–126, 161–165, 202n64, 203n77,
   204n92
Altamirano-Jiménez, Isabel, 180n72
alternative historiographies, 29, 35, 36
Amadahy, Zanaib, 173n33
Anderson, Benedict, 29
anger: as managed by the state, 72, 158; as
   productive index of power, 92, 94, 122; in
   relation to shame, 141
anti-miscegenation laws, 14, 128, 134, 143–
   144, 146, 154, 208n59
anxiety: about mixed-blood background, 24,
   132, 143, 147, 149, 152, 154; of the settler
   state, 87, 145, 178n58
apologies. *See* public apologies (Canada)
Arapahoe people, 1–2, 159, 167n3
arrivant, ix, 10–11, 41, 152, 171n16

"Articulating a Silence" (Christian), 23,
   133–142
Asian Americans/immigrants/generations:
   as "alien," 5, 10–11, 13, 41, 88, 124–125,
   158; Bering Strait theory on, 13; black
   communities and, 8; in Brazil, 103–104;
   hemispheric perspective on, 3, 5, 14, 16, 18,
   19–20, 158–159; heroic tradition and (*see*
   heroic tradition); in Mexico, 99; *The New
   World in the Tropics* on, 96, 105; "perpetual
   foreigner" trope, 5, 14; *La raza cósmica* on,
   95, 101–103; "yellow peril" trope, 14, 123.
   See also historiographical tensions; *mestiza-
   je/mestiçagem* discourse; mixed-blood narratives; redress and reconciliation (Canada)
Asian settler colonialism, 9–10, 172nn27–28,
   175n47; in relation to "local" identification,
   32, 42, 186n63
assimilation: and Indian policies, 146, 147,
   150, 155, 205n4; liberal policies of, 3, 24;
   and *mestizaje/mestiçagem* discourse, 96,
   99–101, 103–105; and mixed-race discourse,
   130; in relation to the Native veteran tradition, 34
asymmetries: *Almanac of the Dead* on, 162;
   "Articulating a Silence" on, 133, 136; in
   Canadian redress and reconciliation, 63–70,
   159; historiographies on, 30; *Mabel McKay*
   on, 143, 152; of race and settlement, 3, 4, 5,
   6, 7, 10, 13, 19, 20, 27, 158, 160; *Through the
   Arc of the Rain Forest* on, 110–111

Atomic Bomb Dome (Japan), 48–49, 50, 53–54, 188n103
atomic bombing of Japan, 26, 28; *Burning Vision* on, 86, 87, 91, 93; *Hiroshima Bugi* on, 28, 47, 48, 49–52, 54–55
"attentive relational communication," 74, 81–85
"attentive silence," 78–79, 81, 84
autochthony, 5, 14, 37, 124

Bak Goong, 38, 43–44, 45
Bak Sook Goong, 38, 39, 41–42
Banks, Dennis, 52
Befu, Harumi, 201n45
Bering Strait theory, 13
Big Five Sugar Companies, 186n70
Bill C-31 (Canada), 128, 206n10
biopolitical tensions, 20, 127–156, 158. *See also* mixed-blood narratives
biopower, 168n8
black identity (communities), 32, 145, 146, 160, 163–164; Asian Americans and, 8; in Brazil, 95, 96, 104, 110, 115; military service of, 162; in relation to settler colonialism, 173n33; sexualization of, 144, 145, 199n30
black-white binary, 7, 8, 29, 171n15
Blauner, Robert, 7
blood-quantum measurements, 143, 146–147, 150, 154, 186n61
Bole Maru, 148
brasilidade, 198n27
Brazil, 3, 6, 7, 18, 19, 20, 22, 23, 95–96, 97, 98, 158; slavery in, 95, 104, 199n28; United States and Japan in (*see Through the Arc of the Rain Forest* [Yamashita]); Vargas-era *mestiçagem* in, 103–105
British colonialism, 6, 18, 19, 22, 104, 158
Brown, Wendy, 14–15
Buffalo Soldiers, 162
burden, settler colonial performance of, 63, 66, 67–68, 69, 70, 71
Burning Vision (Clements), 22, 61, 72, 86–94, 195n112
Byrd, Jodi, 5–6, 7, 9, 10, 41, 44, 47, 170n12, 172n23, 173n31

"cacophony of empire," 5, 7, 11, 44
Cahuilla people, 159
Calinescu, Matei, 33
Canada, 3, 5, 6, 7, 18, 20, 164; biopolitical tensions in, 20, 127–130, 131–132, 158 (*see also* "Articulating a Silence" [Christian]); British colonialism in, 19; legal/juridical tensions in (*see* legal/juridical tensions)

Canadian Multiculturalism Act, 65
Canadian Pacific Railroad, 128
Canadian Race Relations Act, 70, 71
Canadian Race Relations Foundation (CRRF), 59, 70–71
Canadian Uranium Mining, 86
Candomblé dance, 115
capitalism, 42–43, 45, 48, 52, 53, 130. *See also* global capital
Carroll, Al, 34–35
Cash, Johnny, 52, 55
Castellanos, M. Bianet, ix, 19
catharsis, settler, 45, 71–72
Central Pacific Railroad, 25
Ceremony (Silko), 125, 204n92
Chakrabarty, Dipesh, 30
Chang, Jason Oliver, 181n75
Cherokee people, 161–162
Cheung, King-Kok, 31, 43, 78, 84
Cheyenne people, 1–2, 159
Chin, Frank, 30–31, 184n35
China Men (Kingston), 18, 21–22, 27, 28, 36–46, 57–58, 161, 181n4
Chinese Head Tax, 134
Chinese immigrants: in Canada, 127–130 (*see also* "Articulating a Silence" [Christian]); enfranchisement of, 135; heroic tradition and, 30–33; in Mexico, 99, 102; restriction on women, 134; sex work and, 140–141; in the United States, 3, 26, 27, 30–33, 99, 102 (*see also China Men* [Kingston])
Chino (Chang), 181n75
Chow, Lily, 128, 134–135
Christian, Dorothy, 6, 132, 143, 150, 152, 154, 155–156; "Articulating a Silence," 23, 133–142
Chumash people, 159
civil progress narratives, 15, 21, 22, 60, 61, 63
Clements, Marie, 6, 63; *Burning Vision*, 22, 61, 72, 86–94, 195n112
Cold War, 121, 122, 203n80, 203n82
colonialism: Asian settler (*see* Asian settler colonialism); extractive, 19, 180n72; internal, 7–8, 19; neocolonialism, 19; racialization distinguished from, 9; settler (*see* settler colonialism)
colorblind discourse, 22, 130, 169n8
Cosmic Race, The (Vasconcelos), 95, 99–103
cosubstantiation, 11, 173n35, 194n83. *See also* relationality
Coulthard, Glen Sean, 45, 61–62, 80–81, 92, 94, 170n11, 176n52
counter-historiography, 29, 30, 57
Crazy Horse, 33, 183n21
critical ethnic studies, 4–5, 6, 7–11

crossings, Asian/Indigenous, 167n4
CRRF (Canadian Race Relations Foundation), 59, 70–71
cult of celebrity, 28, 48, 53
"culturalization of politics," 14–15
"culture of redress," 61
Cupeno people, 159
Curtis, Edward S., 49
Custer, George Armstrong, 40–41
Custer Died for Your Sins (Deloria), 172n24, 175n45

Day, Iyko, 7, 10–11, 31, 74, 76, 77–78, 131, 173n33
decolonization, 5, 155; *Almanac of the Dead* on, 96–97, 115, 116–117, 119–126; *Burning Vision* on, 91, 92
Deloria, Vine, Jr., 172n24, 175n45
"dialectic of remembering and forgetting," 184n34
"diasporic object," 55
Diaz, Porfirio, regime of, 99, 100
Dodge, Grenville M., 25
dominant historical narratives, 29
doubling, 77–78
Dream Dance, 148
Dreamers, 142, 148–149

"echoing world," 86
economic tensions, 20, 95–126, 158. *See also* global capital; *mestizaje/mestiçagem* discourse
economies of care, 117–119
"economy of affirmation and forgetting," 15, 26, 27, 112
"emotional transgressions," 63
emotions, 158; affect in relation to, 16; "Articulating a Silence" on, 139–141; *Burning Vision* on, 92; Canadian redress and reconciliation and, 61, 66–71; material work of, 175n52; mixed-blood narratives on, 129–130, 132
empire building, 3, 5, 12, 15, 26, 28, 29, 35
Ends of Empire (Kim), 121–122
Enlightenment, 125, 130
environmental devastation. *See Almanac of the Dead* (Silko); *Through the Arc of the Rain Forest* (Yamashita)
ephemeral crossings. *See* ghostly and ephemeral crossings
Estado Novo, 103, 198n24, 198n27
eugenics, 97, 146
extractive colonialism, 19, 180n72
EZLN (Zapatista Army of National Liberation), 204n89

Fabian, Johannes, 12
Fancydancing (Alexie), 33
Fanon, Frantz, 8, 80, 168n8
"felt theory," 176n52, 177n54
Ferguson, Roderick, 8, 79, 173n35, 193n76
Filipinos, 143, 144–146. *See also Mabel McKay* (Sarris)
foster care, 143, 155
Foucault, Michel, 79, 129, 168n8
Freud, Sigmund, 91
Freyre, Gilberto, 97, 98, 104–106, 109, 110, 111, 199nn28–31, 200nn35–36; *The Masters and the Slaves,* 95–96, 104, 105, 196n1, 200n38; *The New World in the Tropics,* 96, 104, 105
from Sand Creek (Ortiz), 1–2
frontier thesis, 38, 40, 181n1, 185n40
Fujikane, Candace, 9–10, 32, 42
future tense/futurity, 3, 12, 14, 128–129, 132, 158; in Canadian redress and reconciliation, 62, 64, 65, 66, 67, 68, 70, 71, 159; *China Men* on, 43; emotions and, 141; *Hiroshima Bugi* on, 48, 49, 51, 52; historiographies on, 33; *Mabel McKay* on, 149; mixed-race, 6, 131, 158; *Obasan* on, 75, 77; *La raza cósmica* on, 95; warrior tradition and, 34, 35

Garfield, Seth, 103, 198nn23–24
genocidal actions, 2, 26, 27, 130, 143, 147
Gercken, Becca, 33, 183n21
ghostly and ephemeral crossings: in *China Men,* 21–22, 28, 36, 37, 38, 43–45, 58; in *Hiroshima Bugi,* 21–22, 28, 48, 53, 54; theories of haunting on, 186n65
global capital, 6, 22–23, 95–126. *See also Almanac of the Dead* (Silko); capitalism
God Is Red (Deloria), 172n24
"going Native" trope, 37, 43, 74, 75, 147
"Golden Spike Photograph," 25, 26, 182n11
Gradual Civilization Act of 1857 (Canada), 135
Gramsci, Antonio, 4, 168n6
Grant, Agnes, 127
Grant, Howard, 155
Grant, Larry, 127–130, 132, 134, 154, 155, 205n1, 205n5
Great Bear Lake, 86
Great Mahele, 44
grief, 22, 63, 77–78, 79, 84–85, 94
Griever (Vizenor), 46–47
"grounded normativity," 45, 170n11
Guadalupe Hidalgo, Treaty of, 164

haksuba, 10, 173n31
Harper, Stephen, 59, 61, 63, 64, 65, 68–69

Hartman, Bunny, 143, 146
Harvey, David, 116
Hawai'i, 5, 9, 11, 28, 30, 31, 32, 172nn27–28, 175n47; Big Five Sugar Companies in, 186n70; *China Men* on, 36, 38–39, 41–42, 43–45, 57–58; sovereignty struggles in, 9, 14, 42
Hawaiian Land Distribution Act of 1848 (United States), 44
Hayes, Ira, 26, 52, 55
healing, 61, 63, 67, 69, 70, 71, 94; *Burning Vision* on, 86, 92–93; *Obasan* on, 73, 74, 80; "poetics of," 92
hegemonies, 4, 11, 168nn6–8. *See also* settler racial hegemonies
Helenius, Marja-Liisa, 119
hemispheric perspective, 3, 5, 14, 16, 18, 19–20, 158–159
Henderson, Jennifer, 60, 63, 86, 190n19, 194n93
heroic tradition, 6, 21, 27, 35, 184n37; *China Men* on, 36–37, 42–43, 45, 57–58; critical overview of, 30–33
heteropatriarchy, 27, 35
heterotopias, 79–80, 193n75
Hilario, Emilio, 143, 145, 146, 152
Hing, Hong Tim, 127
Hiroshima atomic bombing, 26, 28, 47, 48, 50, 51, 86, 87
Hiroshima Bugi (Vizenor), 21–22, 27, 28, 46–57, 58
historiographical tensions, 20, 21–22, 25–58, 158. *See also China Men* (Kingston)
historiographic metafiction, 29, 35–36, 183n33
"History 2," 30
Holland, Sharon P., 162
Homestead Act of 1862 (United States), 26
Hong, Grace Kyungwon, 8, 79, 173n35, 193n76
House of Commons Apology to Inuit, Métis, and First Nations Peoples for Residential Schools, 59
Howe, LeAnne, 173n31
Huhndorf, Shari, 204n94
Hutcheon, Linda, 36, 183n33

ideology versus affect, 16, 178n57
imperialism, 2, 7, 8, 11, 158, 160, 161; *Almanac of the Dead* on, 162, 164; code/grammar of, 14; *Hiroshima Bugi* on, 48, 49, 50, 51, 53; Japanese, 51, 102; U.S., 26, 28, 29, 35
India, 101, 200n35
Indian Act (Canada), 128, 134, 135, 155, 178n59, 205nn4–5

Indian Child Welfare Act of 1978 (United States), 146
"Indianness," 38–39, 45, 150, 155, 170n12, 174n38
Indian residential schools, 86, 87. *See also* public apologies (Canada): 2008 (Indian Residential Schools)
Indian Residential Schools Settlement Agreement (Canada), 59–60
indigenismo, 23, 98, 99, 100, 197n12
Indigenous lands, 5, 9, 20, 27, 164; in Brazil, 105; *China Men* on, 37; heroic tradition and, 35; mixed-race unions and, 129, 130; railroad encroachment on, 26, 32–33; *La raza cósmica* on, 101, 102–103; *Through the Arc of the Rain Forest* on, 111–114; uranium sourced from, 47, 86
Indigenous peoples: Bering Strait theory on, 13; self-determination struggles, 4, 5, 9, 37, 155; sovereignty struggles, 4, 5, 9, 14, 34, 37, 129, 132, 134, 151, 155; stripped of Indian status, 128–129, 135, 205n10; in the United States (*see* Native Americans); "vanishing Indian" trope, 5, 14, 37, 42, 43, 49, 76, 193n66
Indigenous studies, 5, 6, 7–11
individualism, 6, 15, 21, 27, 31, 37
"industry of apology," 62
internal colonial model, 7–8, 19
intersubstantiation, 11, 173n35, 194n83. *See also* relationality
"intimacies of four continents," 5, 177n54
Iracema, 109, 110, 111
Iron Cages (Takaki), 32–33
Itsuka (Kogawa), 73
Iwo Jima, Japan, 25, 26

Jacobs, Margaret D., 145, 146
Jaén, Didier T., 101, 197n14
Japan: *Almanac of the Dead* on, 121, 122, 125; Brazil and (*see Through the Arc of the Rain Forest* [Yamashita]); colonization of Korea by, 121; economic growth of, 201n44, 203n80; imperialism of, 51, 102; Pearl Harbor bombing by, 89; U.S. atomic bombing of (*see* atomic bombing of Japan); as U.S. "junior partner," 48, 53; U.S. occupation of, 26, 27, 28 (*see also Hiroshima Bugi* [Vizenor])
Japanese Brazilian/immigrants, 96, 103, 108, 110, 201n45
Japanese Canadians. *See* Nikkei internment
Juaneno people, 159

kami, 56, 57, 188n103
Kānaka Maoli peoples, 9, 18, 31, 42, 44
Kauanui, J. Kēhaulani, 9, 146–147
Keeping Slug Woman Alive (Sarris), 142
Kim, Claire Jean, 8
Kim, Jodi, 47, 49–50, 53, 121–122, 184n34, 203n80, 203n82
Kingston, Maxine Hong, 6, 29, 31, 185n45, 185n61, 186n63; *China Men,* 18, 21–22, 27, 28, 36–46, 57–58, 161, 181n4; *The Woman Warrior,* 33, 36, 184n35
Kipling, Rudyard, 68
Knight, Alan, 99, 196–197nn4–7
Kogawa, Joy, 6, 63, 92; *Itsuka,* 73; *Obasan,* 22, 61, 72, 73–85, 93–94
Korea, 121, 122, 123
Korean War, 121, 203n80
Koshy, Susan, 175n44, 200n40
Kumeyaay people, 159

Lai, Larissa, 86–87, 92
late liberalism, 14, 51
Latin América, 19, 20, 96, 132. *See also* global capital; *mestizaje/mestiçagem* discourse
Latinx communities, 160
Lawrence, Bonita, 128, 135, 173n33, 205n10
Lee, James Kyung-jin, 176n52
Lee, Julia H., 31
Lee, Rachel, 109
legal/juridical tensions, 20, 59–94, 158. *See also Burning Vision* (Clements); *Obasan* (Kogawa); public apologies (Canada)
Lesser, Jeffrey, 198n27, 201n45
liberal diaspora, 15
liberalism, 3–4, 19, 20, 21, 164; *Almanac of the Dead* on, 117–118, 119, 125; global capital and, 97, 98; late, 14, 51; mixed-race unions and, 129, 130; neoliberalism (*see* neoliberalism); settler racial tense and, 12, 13; social justice movement demands and, 15
Liberal Party (Canada), 64
Lightfoot, Sheryl, 66
Ling, Jinqi, 31, 184n37
"Little Boy" (atomic bomb), 47, 87
Lo, Marie, 73–74
Lowe, Lisa, 3, 5–6, 15, 18, 26, 112, 177n54
Luiseno people, 159

Mabel McKay (Sarris), 23, 142–154, 161
"Making Solidarity Uneasy" (Roediger), 170n11
Manifest Manners (Vizenor), 33–34
Marchi, Sergio, 64
Marx, Karl, 117

masculinity, 31, 32, 33, 40–41, 109, 111, 184n37
Masters and the Slaves, The (Freyre), 95–96, 104, 105, 196n1, 200n38
Mawani, Renisa, 129
Mbembe, Achilles, 168n8
McAllister, Kirsten Emiko, 85
McKay, Mabel, 142–143, 147–154
Medak-Saltzman, Danika, 43, 186n65
melancholy/melancholia, 63, 87, 91, 92, 93, 94, 158
meme, Indianness as, 5, 41, 170n12
memorialization, 27, 28, 33, 38, 46, 47–48, 50, 53, 57, 58
mestiçagem, 7, 20; defined, 95; settler logics of, 111–114; in Vargas-era Brazil, 103–105. *See also mestizaje/mestiçagem* discourse
mestizaje, 7, 20, 104, 116, 125; defined, 95; in revolutionary Mexico, 99–103. *See also mestizaje/mestiçagem* discourse
mestizaje/mestiçagem discourse, 23, 95–126, 130, 181n75; formation of, 95–97; settler racial teleologies of, 98–106. *See also Almanac of the Dead* (Silko)
mestizos, 101, 102, 106, 145–146
Métis people, 90, 91, 131, 132
Mexico, 3, 6, 7, 9, 18, 19, 20, 22, 23, 96, 97, 98, 125, 158; Philippines compared with, 145–146; revolutionary-era *mestizaje* in, 99–103
Miccosukee people, 159
Miki, Art, 59, 64, 194n91
Miki, Roy, 61, 85–86
Million, Dian, 69, 71, 176n52, 177n54
miscegenation, 104, 145–146. *See also* anti-miscegenation laws; mixed-blood narratives
mixed-blood narratives, 6, 22, 23–24, 127–156. *See also Mabel McKay* (Sarris)
Miyoshi, Masao, 107
"model minority" trope, 73, 120, 126
Mohanty, Satya, 141
Montague, Samuel S., 25
Moraga, Cherríe, 173n35
Moreton-Robinson, Aileen, 11, 194n83
Mulroney, Brian, 59, 61, 63, 64–65, 66–67, 68, 75, 88
multiculturalism, 6, 15, 21, 130, 132; *Burning Vision* on, 88; in Canada, 60, 61, 64, 65, 67; in the United States, 125
Musqueam nation, 127–130, 155
My Lai massacre (Vietnam), 1–2

NAJC (National Association of Japanese Canadians), 59, 64, 70
Nagasaki atomic bombing, 26, 28, 51, 86

Nandy, Ashis, 14
National Association of Japanese Canadians (NAJC), 59, 64, 70
Native Americans: historiographies of (see historiographical tensions); military service of, 3, 7, 26, 27, 28, 34–35; treaties between United States and, 175n45; warrior tradition in (see warrior tradition)
Native-Asian mixed-blood narratives. See mixed-blood narratives
neocolonialism, 19
neoliberalism, 23, 96, 98; *Almanac of the Dead* on, 117–118, 119, 124; mixed-race unions and, 130, 132; *Through the Arc of the Rainforest* on, 108
New World in the Tropics, The (Freyre), 96, 104, 105
Ngai, Sianne, 141, 196n118
Nguyen, Viet Thanh, 31, 168n7
Nikkei internment: in Canada, 22 (see also *Burning Vision* [Clements]; *Obasan* [Kogawa]; public apologies [Canada]); in the United States, 87
Nipp, Dora, 140
Nisei, 59
Northern Diegueño people, 159

Obasan (Kogawa), 22, 61, 72, 73–85, 93–94
O'Brien, Jean M., 9
Oikawa, Mona, 85, 195n112
Okamura, Jonathan, 9, 32
Omatsu, Maryka, 59, 193n69
Omi, Michael, 168n8
"Orientals," 95, 101, 105, 197n15
Ortiz, Simon, 1–2
Owens, Louis, 37–38

Pacific theater (World War II), 3, 26, 28
Parrish, Essie, 148, 151–152
past perfect tense, 13, 15, 33, 34, 54, 62, 75–76, 193n63
past tense, 5, 12, 13; *Burning Vision* on, 92; in Canadian redress and reconciliation, 60, 62, 64, 65, 66, 68, 70; *China Men* on, 36, 37, 38, 43; *Hiroshima Bugi* on, 48, 49, 51, 52, 54, 55, 56; historiographies on, 33–34, 36; *Mabel McKay* on, 149; *Obasan* on, 73, 74; *La raza cósmica* on, 95
paternalistic nationalism, 86–87, 88
Peace Memorial Museum (Japan), 48, 50
Pearl Harbor bombing, 89
Perez v. Sharp, 144, 208n57, 208n59
"perpetual foreigner" trope, 5, 14
Philippines, 68, 105, 145–146. See also Filipinos

Piatote, Beth, 135, 137
"playing Indian," 147, 149–150
"poetics of healing," 92
"poetics of relationality," 86, 92
polyphony in *China Men*, 43
Pomo tribe, 142. See also Mabel McKay (Sarris)
Porto, Mauro, 115
Portuguese colonialism, 6, 18, 22, 97, 100, 103, 104, 105, 110, 111, 115, 158
postmodern novel form, 106, 112, 114
Povinelli, Elizabeth, 11, 12–13, 14, 15, 17, 55, 62, 75, 178n57, 179n62, 194n83
present tense, 12, 14, 159; *Burning Vision* on, 92; in Canadian redress and reconciliation, 60, 64, 65, 66, 67; *China Men* on, 36, 43; *Hiroshima Bugi* on, 48, 49, 51, 52, 54
primitivism, 145, 147
progress narratives: in Canada, 22, 60, 62, 64, 69, 71, 74; *La raza cósmica* on, 102; in the United States, 26, 29, 30, 31, 32. See also civil progress narratives
public apologies (Canada), 59–72, 74, 75, 93, 158; 1988 (Nikkei internment), 22, 59, 61, 62, 63–71, 159, 195n112; 2008 (Indian Residential Schools), 22, 59–60, 61, 62, 63–72, 195n112; affect/emotions in, 61, 64, 66–71; *Burning Vision* on, 85, 86–87, 88–90, 195n112; monetary compensation and, 59; pseudoscientific language in, 68
Pulido, Laura, 204n93

race as private property, 6, 15, 21, 130
racialization, 2, 3, 5, 7, 11, 15, 19, 20, 157, 158, 160; *Almanac of the Dead* on, 119, 121, 125, 161, 162, 163, 164; "Articulating a Silence" on, 133; Canadian redress and reconciliation and, 63; *China Men* on, 37, 41; colonization distinguished from, 9; historiographies and, 30, 32; *Mabel McKay* on, 145, 147, 152; *Obasan* on, 73, 75, 79
racial mixing. See mestizaje/mestiçagem discourse; mixed-blood narratives
railroad building, 3, 25, 26, 31–33, 39–40, 128
Raza cósmica, La (Vasconcelos), 95, 99–103
Reconciling Canada (Henderson and Wakeham), 60
redress and reconciliation (Canada), 22, 59–94. See also *Burning Vision* (Clements); public apologies (Canada)
Refugee Act of 1980 (United States), 2
regret, settler performance of, 66–67
relationality, 11, 29, 159, 160, 173n35; *Mabel McKay* on, 147; *Obasan* on, 78; "poetics of,"

86, 92. *See also* cosubstantiation; intersubstantiation
resentment, 92, 94
Reynaud, Anne-Marie, 63, 94
Ricepaper Magazine, 133
Rifkin, Mark, 9, 14, 62, 176n52
Roediger, David, 170n11
Rosenthal, Joe, 25
Russell, Andrew J., 25
Rymhs, Deena, 66, 195n112

sadness, 63, 66
Sadowski-Smith, Claudia, 203n77
Saldaña-Portillo, María Josefina, 196n3, 197n12
Sand Creek massacre, 1–2
Sansei, 59
Santa Ana, Jeffrey, 176n52, 177n54
Saranillio, Dean, 9
Sarris, George, 143
Sarris, Greg, 6, 132; *Keeping Slug Woman Alive*, 142; *Mabel McKay*, 23, 142–154, 161
Sarris, Mary, 143
Sathu Dene Territory, 86
Schacht, Miriam, 202n64
Secwepemc-Syilx (Okanagan-Shuswap) Indian community, 133, 155
Sedgewick, Mitchell W., 201n44
self-determination, Indigenous, 4, 5, 9, 37, 155
Seminole people, 159
settler catharsis, 45, 71–72
settler colonialism, 1–18, 157, 160, 161; *Almanac of the Dead* on, 162, 164; Asian, 9–10, 172nn27–28, 175n47; British, 6, 18, 19, 22, 104, 158; Canadian, 60, 65–66; extractive colonialism compared with, 180n72; *Hiroshima Bugi* on, 47–48, 49, 50, 53, 55; Portuguese, 6, 18, 22, 97, 100, 103, 104, 105, 110, 111, 115, 158; Spanish, 6, 18, 22, 97, 100, 104, 158, 164; tensions of (*see* tensions); U.S., 27, 28, 29, 35
settler common sense, 35; *Almanac of the Dead* on, 163; Canadian redress and reconciliation and, 62–63; *China Men* on, 37, 43; defined, 9; *Mabel McKay* on, 147; *Through the Arc of the Rain Forest* on, 111, 112
settler grammars, 12, 13, 14, 157–158
settler racial hegemonies, 7, 11, 12, 22, 24, 157–158; defined, 4, 157; as a heuristic lens/barometer, 160–165; U.S., 27, 28, 29, 36
settler racial structures of feeling, 45, 69, 70, 74, 92, 93, 94, 160; defined, 62–63
settler racial teleologies, 98–106
settler racial tense, 7, 12–18, 157–158; in *Almanac of the Dead*, 163, 164; in *China Men*, 43, 45; conditional perfect future, 13; defined, 5, 12; durative present tense, 15, 51, 149; future anterior, 15; in *Hiroshima Bugi*, 48, 49, 50, 51; in *Mabel McKay*, 149; space and time of (*see* space; time); U.S., 29. *See also* future tense/futurity; past tense; present tense; social tense
"settler structures of feeling," 28, 37, 46, 58, 62, 176n52
Sexton, Jared, 131, 206n13
sex workers, 140–141
Seymour, Horatio, 32–33
shame: "Articulating a Silence" on, 133–134, 136–139, 140–141, 155; Canadian redress and reconciliation and, 62, 66; *Mabel McKay* on, 142, 143, 150–151, 152, 154; mixed-blood narratives on, 132
Shibusawa, Naoko, 90
Shih, Shu-mei, 8, 157, 171n22, 204n93
Shohat, Ella, 109
"Significance of the Frontier in American History, The" (Turner), 184n40
silence, 136–139, 141, 154. *See also* "attentive silence"
Silko, Leslie Marmon, 6; *Almanac of the Dead*, 23, 96–97, 98, 115, 116–126, 161–165, 202n64, 203n77, 204n92; *Ceremony*, 125, 204n92
Silva, Noenoe K., 183n31
Simpson, Leanne Betasamosake, 170n11
Sitting Bull, 76, 77, 78–79, 80, 81
"sixties scoop," 155
slavery, 95, 104, 161, 162, 163, 199n28
Smith, Linda Tuhiwai, 14, 181–182n5
social justice movements, 4–5, 14–15, 107, 116
social tense, 13, 15; affective production of, 16–18; in Canadian redress and reconciliation, 62, 65; *Obasan* on, 74, 75, 77
Sokolowski, Jeanne, 47, 49
solemnity in Canadian public apologies, 66, 68
sovereignty: Hawai'ian, 9, 14, 42; Indigenous, 4, 5, 9, 14, 34, 37, 129, 132, 134, 151, 155; temporal, 14
space, 158, 159; in *Almanac of the Dead*, 163, 164; in *Burning Vision*, 86, 91; in *China Men*, 37, 38, 41, 42–43, 45, 46; in *Hiroshima Bugi*, 48, 53, 55; in historiographies, 30; in *Mabel McKay*, 148; qualities and uses of, 12–15
Spanish colonialism, 6, 18, 22, 97, 100, 104, 158, 164
Speed, Shannon, 19

Spencerian Darwinism, 97
Stam, Robert, 109
stereotypes, 88, 120, 145
Stoler, Ann Laura, 177n54
structures of feeling, 16; settler, 62; settler racial, 45, 62, 63, 69, 70, 74, 92, 93, 94, 160
survivance, 33, 34, 35, 46, 47, 48, 53, 54, 57, 137, 155

Takaki, Ronald, 32–33, 40–41
telenovela form, 108, 114–115
temporal multiplicities, 14
temporal sovereignty, 14
tense. *See* settler racial tense
tensions, 16, 17, 19, 177n56, 178n58. *See also* biopolitical tensions; economic tensions; historiographical tensions; legal/juridical tensions
terra nullius paradigm, 65, 75
Teuton, Sean Kiccumah, 141
Therapeutic Nations (Million), 69
"third Asian invasion" discourse, 144
This Bridge Called My Back (Moraga), 173n35
Thobani, Sunera, 60, 61, 168n8, 205n4
Through the Arc of the Rain Forest (Yamashita), 23, 96, 98, 106–115, 126
time, 158, 159; in *Almanac of the Dead,* 163, 164; in *Burning Vision,* 86, 91; in *China Men,* 37, 38, 41, 42–43, 45, 46; in *Hiroshima Bugi,* 48, 49, 50, 53, 55; in historiographies, 30; in *Mabel McKay,* 148; qualities and uses of, 12–15
Tocabaga people, 159
Toguri, Iva ("Tokyo Rose"), 87, 89, 90
tolerance in Canadian public apologies, 66, 68, 70, 71, 159
transcontinental railroad, 3, 25, 26, 31, 39–40
transformative praxis, 80–81
"transitional justice," 62
transnational approach to American studies, 20, 179nn68–69
Trask, Haunani-Kay, 9, 32, 172n27, 175n47
TRC (Truth and Reconciliation Commission) of Canada, 60, 70, 71–72, 155
treaties, 14, 71, 128, 134, 175n45
Treaty of Guadalupe Hidalgo, 164
triangulations, 7, 8, 9, 10, 160, 171n22; Canadian redress and reconciliation and, 60; *China Men* on, 41; historiographies on, 32; *Obasan* on, 83
Truth and Reconciliation Commission (TRC) of Canada, 60, 70, 71–72, 155
Truth and Reconciliation Funding (Canada), 59

Tuck, Eve, 9, 165
Turner, Frederick Jackson, 38, 40, 41, 184n40

ugly alliances, 117–119
"ugly feelings," 141, 196n118
Under the Willow Tree (film), 140
Union Pacific Railroad, 25
United States, 3, 6, 7, 8, 18, 20, 23, 164; biopolitical tensions in, 20, 129, 130, 131, 132, 135, 158 (*see also* Mabel McKay [Sarris]); Brazil and (*see Through the Arc of the Rain Forest* [Yamashita]); British colonialism in, 19; historiographical tensions in (*see* historiographical tensions); Japan as a "junior partner" of, 48, 53; Japanese atomic bombing by (*see* atomic bombing of Japan); Japan occupied by, 26, 27, 28 (*see also Hiroshima Bugi* [Vizenor]); Korean War and, 121, 203n80; Latin América and, 19, 96; multiculturalism in, 125; Nikkei internment in, 87; Pearl Harbor bombing in, 89; Philippines colonized by, 105; Vietnam War and, 1–2, 162, 163, 175n45, 203n80; westward expansion by, 21, 26, 27, 31, 40
uranium mining, 47, 86

"vanishing Indian" trope, 5, 14, 37, 42, 43, 49, 76, 193n66
Vargas-era Brazil, 103–105
Vasconcelos, José, 95, 97, 98, 104, 105–106, 197n9, 197nn14–15, 197n17, 198nn20–21; *La raza cósmica,* 95, 99–103
Veracini, Lorenzo, 147
Vietnamese refugees, 2, 159
Vietnam War, 1–2, 162, 163, 175n45, 203n80
violence, 158, 159, 161, 163; *China Men* on, 40–41, 45–46; gendered, 137; *La raza cósmica* on, 103
Vizenor, Gerald, 6, 29, 36, 137; *Griever,* 46–47; *Hiroshima Bugi,* 21–22, 27, 28, 46–57, 58; *Manifest Manners,* 33–34
Volpp, Leti, 144, 145
voting rights, 135

Wakeham, Pauline, 60, 63, 86, 190n19, 194n93
warrior tradition, 6, 21, 27, 30; critical overview, 33–36; *Hiroshima Bugi* on, 47–48, 51–53, 54, 57
Weaver, Jace, 37
westward expansion, U.S., 21, 26, 27, 31, 40
"White Man's Burden, The" (Kipling), 68
white-nonwhite binary, 143, 152, 154
white supremacy/power, 26, 97, 100–101, 104, 128–129, 132, 145

"Why the Humanities Matter for Race Studies Today" (Koshy), 175n44
Williams, Raymond, 16–18, 74, 178n57, 179n67, 181n5
Williams, Rosalind, 136
Winant, Howard, 168n8
Wolfe, Patrick, 19, 70
Woman Warrior, The (Kingston), 33, 36, 184n35
"Women, Resistance, and Cultural/Community Activism" (panel), 155–156
Wong, Sau-ling, 20, 77, 91, 184n35

World War II, 26, 28, 46, 59
Wright, Mary, 151

Yamashita, Karen Tei, 6; *Through the Arc of the Rain Forest,* 23, 96, 98, 106–115, 126
Yang, K. Wayne, 9, 165
Yasukuni Jinja shrine (Japan), 48, 51–52
"yellow peril" trope, 14, 123

Zapatista Army of National Liberation (EZLN), 204n89

Quynh Nhu Le is an Assistant Professor of English at the University of South Florida.

www.ingramcontent.com/pod-product-compliance
Lightning Source LLC
Chambersburg PA
CBHW040747020526
44116CB00036B/2973